A FLORENTINE DIARY

SAVONAROLA
From the portrait by Fra Bartolomeo.

A FLORENTINE DIARY
FROM 1450 TO 1516
BY LUCA LANDUCCI
CONTINUED BY AN
ANONYMOUS WRITER
TILL 1542 WITH NOTES
BY IODOCO DEL
BADIA

TRANSLATED
FROM THE ITALIAN BY
ALICE DE ROSEN JERVIS

 BOOKS FOR LIBRARIES PRESS
FREEPORT, NEW YORK

LIBRARY
WAYNE STATE COLLEGE
WAYNE, NEBRASKA

First Published 1927
Reprinted 1971

INTERNATIONAL STANDARD BOOK NUMBER:
0-8369-5986-8

LIBRARY OF CONGRESS CATALOG CARD NUMBER:
75-169766

PRINTED IN THE UNITED STATES OF AMERICA
BY
NEW WORLD BOOK MANUFACTURING CO., INC.
HALLANDALE, FLORIDA 33009

TRANSLATOR'S PREFACE

ALTHOUGH Del Badia's ample and learned notes are sufficient for an Italian, it seemed to me that many allusions might be puzzling to an English reader, especially to one who did not know Florence well; therefore I have added short notes on city-gates, churches and other buildings which now no longer exist; on some of the festivals and customs; on those streets which have changed their nomenclature since Landucci's day; and also on the old money.

His old-fashioned spelling of names and places has been retained (amongst other peculiarities the Florentine was in the habit of replacing an *l* by an *r*); also the old calendar; and the old Florentine method of reckoning the hours of the day (see notes to 12 January, 1465, and to 27 April, 1468). As for the changes in the Government, they were so frequent and so complex, that it is necessary to have recourse to a consecutive history in order to understand them.

A. DE R. J.

Florence 1926.

The books to which I am indebted are as follows:

Storia della Repubblica di Firenze (2 vols.), Gino Capponi, Firenze, 1875; Pianta geometrica della città di Firenze, F. Fantozzi (out of print), Firenze, 1843; Notizie storici sulle Chiese di Firenze (10 vols.), G. Richa, Firenze, 1758; Studi storici sul centro di Firenze, Carocci ed altri, Firenze, 1889; Firenze scomparsa: ricordi storici e artistici, Carocci (out of print), Firenze, 1897; Firenze vecchia, G. Conti (out of print), Firenze, 1899; Storia della moneta della Repubblica florentina, Orsini (out of print), Firenze, Viviani, 1760; Vite de' più eccellenti Pittori, Scultori, e Architetti, G. Vasari, Firenze, Le Monnier, 1852.

PREFACE

IN searching for and collecting notices and reminiscences of the buildings in the city of Florence and old Florentine customs, the Diary of Luca Landucci can certainly not be neglected by anyone who has lately seen modern scholars discover and bring to light curious, unknown and interesting notices, only made use of at times by past generations. No sooner had I advanced some way in reading this book, than I perceived that I had in my hands not a confused mixture, from which one could extract and prize a few individual recollections, but a true and exact chronicle, most varied and minute. Varied, indeed, inasmuch as the writer, whilst giving us notices of many domestic facts, of political events, of fêtes, of those men of his day who excelled in any art, of any extraordinary phenomena, and of the magnificent buildings which were then being erected, represents to us vividly the public and private life of the second half of the fifteenth century, and of the first and most splendid years of the sixteenth century. Most minute also, because the facts, especially the political ones are generally noted day by day, and not all at once as, often to the detriment of lucidity, they are registered by historians. I found, in fact, a book which, when confronted with others of the same kind and of the same date, much resembles the so-called *Storie* of Giovanni Cambi, for the unsuitable publication of which I ask myself whether the Carmelite friar, Father Ildefonso di San Luigi, has been pardoned even in the other world. Landucci is much pleasanter reading, inasmuch as he does not, like Cambi, intermingle the narration of facts with the registration of the names of the *Gonfalieri* and *Priori* who were appointed every half-year; a series of magistrates which one can reconstruct more authentically from so many sources. With the recollection of having read in Macchiavelli that, "if there is anything which pleases and instructs us in history, it is that which is described in detail," I set about publishing this Diary, being persuaded that even in our day the sentence of the Florentine secretary on the earnest words pronounced by Niccolò Tommaseo in the *Archivo Storico Italiano*, holds good, as to the necessity of publishing, with proper care, the records of past ages which still remain unedited, and the historical documents buried in public and private collections in Italy.

That the work of Landucci is worthy of esteem is proved by the fact that it was held in account in the past also; as is indisputable when we see that the well-known Diary of Agostino Lapini, for almost all the first half of the sixteenth century, is nothing but a remodelling of Landucci; Vincenzio Borghini made an extract of it which was included in the *Naniana* of Venice; in the *Spogli* of the Senator Carlo Strozzi, a well-known Florentine scholar, many fragments are quoted; Giovambatista Casotti made no little use of it in his *Memorie istoriche della miracolosa immagine di M.V. dell' Impruneta*, which he dedicated to the Grand Duke Cosimo III. in 1712. And in the same work it is attested how greatly this Diary was prized by scholars when we read that it *was going round being copied*, which means, in my opinion, that copies of it were in great request. A considerable part of it is also transcribed in a codex of last century, belonging to the Florentine Archives of State, in which are collected many records of Florentine history taken from writers who for the most part lived in the sixteenth century. A copy was possessed by Domenico Manni, and he often quotes from it in his pamphlets. Pietro Fanfani, who had good taste in publishing ancient writings, printed, under the title of *Savonaroliana*, almost all that part of the book in which the vicissitudes of the celebrated Dominican are narrated; and was also desirous of publishing the description of the magnificent fêtes held in Florence at the time of the visit of Pope Leo X.

I have been unable to discover the fate of the codexes of this Diary, which, according to Casotti, must have been several in number, a fact that is confirmed by Moreni in his *Bibliografia Toscana*; the autograph one is still preserved in the *Biblioteca communale* of Siena, and is written on a parchment which originally consisted of eighty-eight numbered pages. In the autograph, however, the complete diary no longer exists, as page 17 and the pages from 32 to 72 are wanting; the pages of this codex have lately been renumbered, and reach the number 89, whilst in reality there are 90, as by an error two pages were numbered 61; and the pages from 75 onwards are blank.

In spite of all my researches, there was no way of filling up the gaps in the autograph but by making use of a codex in the *Maruccelliana* at Florence; a copy badly written, but sufficiently exact, which dates from the beginning of the seventeenth century.

As the documents and writings relating to the political history of the Italian States up till the fall of the Florentine Republic are so very numerous, I considered it unnecessary to make any notes on those parts of the Diary which concern this history; especially as the writer describes these events at sufficient length, as for instance when he discusses the conspiracy of the Pazzi and its results, the acts of Lorenzo de' Medici, of Carlo VIII., of Alessandro VI., and of Valentino, the details of the war with Pisa, and so on. For this part, as I say, I have limited myself to giving a few explanations which may serve to elucidate the text, especially for those who do not possess detailed knowledge of Florentine history four centuries ago. Where I have made a point of giving ample notes is in the case of those records relative to matters concerning the city of Florence and its customs: and in this I have preferably had recourse to documents in the archives, to contemporary writers edited or unedited, and to monographs published at various times on special subjects.

It now remains to say something about the author, of whom no one, so far as I am aware, has given any details. We find many particulars relating to the life of himself and his family in the Diary; others we obtain from the declarations for the *Catasti* and the *Decime* (taxes), which confirm me in the belief that he was son of an Antonio, son of Luca di Landuccio, a Florentine citizen, described in the *gonfalone* (the division under one banner) of the *Chiavi*[1] of the quarter of S. Giovanni, inhabiting the parish of S. Pier Maggiore. This Antonio, a native of the manor of Dicomano, was not without fortune, especially if we take into account the possessions of his mother Felice. In 1469 he was seventy-five years of age, and Agnola his wife

[1] *Chiave* (key): the city was formerly divided into *Sesti* (sixths), and the arms of the *Sesto* of Porta San Piero were yellow *keys*, on a field red above and white below. [Trans.]

seventy-two; they had two sons: our Luca, and Gostanzo, six years younger than Luca: that Gostanzo, enthusiastic for Barbary-horses, who went to procure them in the Levant, and who, after having won twenty races, came in 1485 to the miserable end described in these pages. Of Luca his father says, in this declaration for the *Catasto* of 1469, that he had an apothecary's shop, set up with the dowry of his wife Salvestra, whom he married when he was hardly seventeen [1]: that this shop was "more of an expense than a profit," and that he was "in a hopeless state of debt," and that the said Luca "was in bed with a very serious fever," and that, if he died, "he (the father) would be undone if he had to repay the dowry," which was 828 florins in the State funds. (This is all according to the declaration, in which it was generally endeavoured to evoke the pity of the official deputed to assess the taxes.) Antonio finishes the lament with these words: "He did it against my will" (probably not the marriage, but the purchase of the shop), "and ill will come of it." Luca certainly does not complain of his wife, who had twelve children; he even calls her "a dear companion, and unequalled for virtue," and adds that during the forty-eight years that they lived together she never once made him angry. In 1514, when he remained a widower, he had seven children living; four of these were sons, Benedetto, Antonio, Filippo and Battista: the first probably followed his father's calling, and attended to the household business, seeing that whenever the master's presence was necessary at Dicomano, where he possessed hereditary property, part of which was increasing, he always sent Benedetto, whether it was a question of arranging quarters for soldiers passing through, or of repairing the damages caused by violent storms. Antonio studied medicine, and in 1503 his father sent him to study at Bologna in order to become a doctor; where he evidently took his degree, because in 1506 he was back in Florence with the title of *maestro*, and was present with the doctors and scholars of the university at the dissection of the corpse of a criminal. It seems that Benedetto was the only one who continued the family, having had a son called Luca, who

[1] This is curious; as Luca Landucci himself, in his Diary, says that he was fourteen years old in 1450, and that he married in 1466, which would make him *thirty* at the time of his marriage. [Trans.]

in his turn had two sons, Antonio and Benedetto, the latter leaving a son called Vincenzio, who died in 1649.

That Luca was a kind-hearted and mild man, although living at a time when party hatred and the continual spectacle of tortures and executions hardened the hearts of the best men, one sees on every page. Through strong religious feeling and love of liberty, he was one of the ardent followers of Savonarola; but the misfortunes of his neighbours always grieved him, even when the sufferers were not of his party. Thus, when the Medici were expelled in 1494, he pities the young cardinal whom he sees kneeling in terror at one of the windows of his palace, with his hands raised to heaven in supplication: and he considers him a good lad. Thus he forgives the man who wounds his son Benedetto; and weeps over the corpse of Lorenzo Tornabuoni, one of the five condemned to death in 1497 for the plot of Del Nero. He followed Savonarola with great faith, frequenting his sermons and taking part in the processions; he was much edified by these things, and rejoiced that some of his sons were among "The blessed and virtuous troop" of the Friar. The excommunication of 1497, however, if it did not destroy his faith, kept him, as he himself confesses, like so many others, from attending the sermons, "because he did not wish to run the danger of going to hear him, since he was excommunicated." On which words the following are a comment: "the wicked have been more powerful than the good," as we read farther on; and the pleasure with which, some years after, he repeats, on each occasion when facts give him the opportunity, that "the saying of the Friar had been verified," or that such and such a one "had come to grief in consequence of having gone against the Friar," etc.

This Diary, which Landucci must have written in his shop at the *Canto de' Tornaquinci*,[1] one of the central and most-frequented parts of the city, near the houses of the Tornabuoni and the Strozzi, was not put together from the vague and uncertain chatter of the customers; but that which the author had not witnessed himself he derived from reliable sources, for there is no doubt that he had relations with men who took part in the Government, the holders of different offices, and persons on the staff of the

[1] The corner where the two streets of the *Vigna Nuova* and the *Spada* join the *Tornabuoni*.

embassies; and, by his own showing, he was on friendly terms with members of the Priors' household.

Besides being correct in his dates and in his narrative of the facts, it is worthy of mention that he is never too violent in representing them; for when things happen according to his wishes, he takes pleasure in it, and thanks God; and when events turn, or appear to turn, against the free and popular Government (which was his ideal), he notes it also, observing that this has happened on account of men's sins, and is a punishment sent by God, to whose will he bows with resignation. But after the deposition of the *Gonfaloniere* Soderini and the return of the Medici he is more sparing in these moderate comments, either because the many changes which he has seen have made him indifferent, or from fear of harm coming to him, supposing his words were to reach the ears of the new rulers. It may even have been because of the exhortations of his sons, who possibly were not against the Medici; it happening frequently in every age that the younger generation fights in a different political camp to that of their parents. In his case, besides, we can imagine that the vicinity and probably frequent intercourse with the Tornabuoni, all for the Medici, had made him well-disposed towards them. Another fact worthy of notice is that in 1512 Benedetto, together with other citizens, accompanied the viceroy Raimondo di Cardona, who wished to ascend to the cupola of the *Duomo*: and neither these Medici recently restored, nor those who acted for them, would have had persons about them who were against them or even of doubtful fidelity.

I cannot decide with precision when the autograph was begun; but I believe it was towards the end of the year 1500 that Landucci decided to leave to posterity this book, in which he would record certain of the principal facts that he remembered or that he had noted down, and would continue to write, following these, all that happened day by day. We must not argue from the fact of seeing his wife's death, which took place in 1514, recorded in the first pages, that the whole Diary was written during the last year of Luca's life; because this record was evidently inserted long after that of the marriage and of the outfit and expenses.

Notwithstanding his great desire of being cognizant of the daily occurrences in the city, and also of those outside it, when they were of special importance, the writer nevertheless had no ambition to take an active part in public life. In a republican Government, the mechanism of which was changed so many times during his life, and under which so many citizens held office in turn, he is not known to have filled any official position; and perhaps did not even wish that his name should be written on the tickets for the election-bags. Only in 1512 he was balloted for in the large election which then took place, but it was through the work of his friends, and considerably against his own will, merely "so as to act like the *Signori*." He guarded the interests of his calling, and contributed to reanimate the Guild of Apothecaries, which was nearly extinct. Having almost reached the age of eighty, his hand could no longer continue the parchment where he had noted down with so much care all that had happened for more than half a century, but his will was not arrested. Although Luca's writing stops at the end of the year 1515, the record is continued by another hand, perhaps by that of one of his sons, whom he had begged that this work, begun by him should not be broken off during his lifetime, and should even be continued after his death. And this was done; and a cross which one sees on the margin in the middle of the account of the campaign against Urbino, made by Lorenzo de' Medici, was doubtless placed there by the pious continuator to record the death of Luca, who, as we read in the register of deaths in the city, was buried in S. Maria Novella on 2 June, 1516. After this date the records become scantier and shorter, and stop altogether in 1542: but notwithstanding this, I decided to publish this continuation also; partly because it did not appear to me entirely without interest, and partly because to do otherwise would have seemed to me contrary to the wish of the good Landucci.

IODOCO DEL BADIA.

December 1882.

LIST OF ILLUSTRATIONS

SAVONAROLA . . . . *Frontispiece*	
THE EXECUTION OF SAVONAROLA AND HIS COMPANIONS . . . . . . *facing page*	17
FLORENCE: THE OLD MARKET-PLACE, NOW DEMOLISHED . . . . . . ,,	32
AT PISA (PIAZZA DEL DUOMO) . . . ,,	81
PIERO DE' MEDICI . . . . . ,,	96
A RELIGIOUS PROCESSION OF THE XVTH CENTURY ,,	161
FLORENCE: THE OLD BRIDGE AND COVERED WAY ,,	176
INTERIOR OF THE CHURCH OF SANTA CROCE . ,,	225
VIEW OF FLORENCE AND THE ARNO . . ,,	240
A SEA-FIGHT BETWEEN GALLEYS . . . ,,	288

A FLORENTINE DIARY

FROM 1450 TO 1516

I record that on the 15th October, 1450, I, Luca, son of Antonio, son of Luca Landucci, a Florentine citizen, of about fourteen years of age, went to learn book-keeping from a master called Calandra; and, praise God! I succeeded.

And on the 1st January, 1452, I entered the shop of the apothecary Francesco, at the sign of the *Scala*, in the *Mercato Vecchio*.[1]

And on the 1st February, 1453, my father's mother died, and was buried in San Piero Maggiore.[2]

And on the 3rd November, 1454, my father Antonio received his mother's inheritance, of which we possess a document giving the details; he inherited all her property both in Florence and in the country; amongst the rest a house which was left as a legacy to her and Antonio for their lives. Messer Otto Niccolini arranged a compromise, by which the monks of Castello,[3] who had the reversion, were to pay Antonio twenty-three *lire* a year for the rest of his life, taking back the said house, and they paid this sum as long as Antonio lived.

[1] The Old Market, now demolished, and replaced by *Piazza Vittorio-Emanuele*. [Trans.]

[2] In the Piazza of the same name. This was a parochial church dating from the fifth century. In very ancient times the mystic function here took place of the nuptials between the new archbishop of the city and the abbess of the Convent of *San Piero*. In 1783 the church was partly demolished, and partly turned into private dwellings. A street goes under the central arch of the façade, whilst there are shops in the other arches. [Trans.]

[3] The old name of the monastery in Borgo Pinti, which belonged to the Cistercian monks till 1628, when they were transferred to San Frediano, the Carmelite nuns from there coming here in their stead, and remaining till the Government of United Italy took it over for schools, and the few nuns remaining were sent elsewhere. They had called it after their abbess, Santa M. Maddalena de' Pazzi, who had died at S. Frediano in 1607, and whose body was brought here in 1628, and buried under the high altar. [Trans.]

In March 1458 a tax was made, called *Catasto*,[1] the decree being passed in the *Sala del Papa*.[2]

At this time the lantern of the cupola of *Santa Maria del Fiore* was begun; and the palace of Cosimo de' Medici[3]; and the churches of San Lorenzo and Santo Spirito, and the Badia on the way to Fiesole[4]; also many houses near the walls in the neighbourhood of San Barnabà and Sant' Ambrogio, and in several other parts.

And at this same time the following noble and valiant men were living: Archbishop Antonino,[5] who had been a monk in the monastery of *San Marco*, and always continued to wear the habit of the Domenican Order, a man who may be called *Beato* (holy); Messer Bartolomeo de' Lapacci,[6] a bishop and preacher excelling all others in our day; Messer Paolo,[7] a doctor, philosopher and astrologer, of holy life; Cosimo, son of Giovanni de' Medici, who was called the great merchant, as he had places of business in every part of the town; and to compare anyone to Cosimo de' Medici was as much as to say that no richer or more prosperous person existed; Donatello, the sculptor, who made the tomb of Messer Leonardo d' Arezzo in Santa Croce; and Desidero the sculptor, who made the tomb of Messer Carlo d' Arezzo, also in Santa Croce. Later came

---

[1] A tax imposed according to the estimate of a person's possessions. This date must be when the collection was begun, for the decree for the renewal of the *Catasto* (first imposed in 1427) was passed on 11th January, 1457-8 (Boninsegni, *Storie della Città di Firenze*, p. 118).

[2] In 1418 the Republic added some magnificent rooms to the convent of S. Maria Novella, to lodge Pope Martin V., and later also the great hall for the sessions of the Council. These rooms were used to lodge royal personages and for other needs of the Commune.

[3] In *Via Larga* (now Via Cavour), called *Pal: Riccardi*, this family having bought it from the Medici, and greatly enlarged it.

[4] The abbey at San Domenico. [Trans.]

[5] Canonised later, and inscribed amongst the saints by Clement VII. The testimony of this contemporary writer is a fresh proof of the great estimation in which the Florentines held their archbishop in his lifetime.

[6] On account of his merits made Bishop of Cortona, and later of Corone in Magna Grecia. He died in 1466. In the library of the convent of S. Maria Novella of Florence, where he had taken orders, many volumes written by his hand are still preserved (Lapini Frosino, *Vita di S. Antonino*; Firenze, Sermartelli, 1569; Ughelli, *Italia Sacra*, Venetiis, MDCCXVII., vol. i., p. 627).

[7] This is the famous Paolo dal Pozzo Toscanelli, a Florentine.

Rossellino,[1] a very small man, but great in sculpture; he made the tomb of the cardinal in San Miniato, which is in the chapel on the left; Maestro Antonio,[2] an organist, who surpassed everyone in his day; Maestro Andreino[3] degl' Impiccati, a painter; Maestro Domenico da Vinegia (Venice), also a painter, was beginning to be spoken of; Maestro Antonio and his brother Piero, called the Pollaiuolo, goldsmiths, sculptors and painters; Maestro Mariano, who taught book-keeping, and also my master Calandra, who taught the same subject, and was a very kind and courteous man.

And on the 4th September, 1462, I left Francesco, son of Francesco, the apothecary, at the sign of the Sun, who gave me, the sixth year, the salary of fifty florins, and I joined company with Spinello, son of Lorenzo, the hope of gaining more causing me to give up the gain which was sure. And we opened an apothecary's shop in the *Mercato Vecchio* (Old Market), at the sign of the King, which had formerly been the shop of a second-hand dealer, and had a very low roof. We raised the roof, and spent a fortune although I was unwilling to outlay so much. All was done without stint, one cupboard alone costing 50 gold florins. Seeing that the costs were so great, and that the said Spinelli had no money to produce, being very badly off, and considering besides that I had already spent 200 gold florins of my own, whilst he had not yet contributed a penny, although we had agreed to go shares, I thought of withdrawing from the enterprise as soon as possible. And on the 27th July, 1463, we agreed to separate, I telling him that I would leave him everything in the shop as it stood, without considering the cost, but that I must have my share of the profits, namely, 50 gold florins, for the time I had been with him, and he must repay me the money which I had put into it. And no agents were required. He replied that it should be so; but that I must give him a few months' time; and to this I agreed, as he gave me sufficient sureties, amounting to 200 gold florins, paid by his brother Lorenzo and Maestro Lorenzo, son of Maestro

[1] Antonio Gamberelli, called il Rossellino, made the monument for the Cardinal Jacobo of the house of Portugal, who is buried in San Miniato-al-Monte.

[2] Antonio Squarcialupi, whose monument can be seen in the Duomo of Florence.

[3] Andrea del Castagno.

Leonardo. I left there on the 10th December, 1463, and began chaffering for the shop of San Pulinari; but we could not come to terms over it; I therefore repaired to Giovanni da Bruscoli, who was opening the shop of the *Agnus-Dei*,[1] and who gave me 36 florins a year, so that I was able to buy the shop of the Tornaquinci, on the 1st September, 1466.

1465. 10th April. A young woman, who was the daughter of Zanobi Gherucci, was tried, for having killed, and then thrown into a well, the little girl of Bernardo della Zecca, a goldsmith, for the sake of stealing a pearl necklace and certain silver ornaments that the child wore round her neck. She was taken away in the executioner's cart, and was beheaded.

17th April. There passed through Florence a son[2] of Don Ferante, King of Naples, on his way to Milan to fetch the daughter of the Duke of Milan to be wedded to his brother. This lad was twelve or thirteen years old; he was made much of, and was lodged at Santa Maria Novella. And afterwards he returned through Florence with the bride, accompanied by many signori[3] and dukes, with a large troop of horse; and besides other things, there were so many damsels and matrons in his train that it was magnificent.

And at this time a man was found coining false money, and he was beheaded.

1st December. There was an election in the *Palagio*,[4] and Niccolo Soderini became *Gonfaloniere*.[5] He reduced the tax on wine to 14 *soldi*,[6] for which the people called down blessings on his head.

12th January.[7] During the night, the Arno began to

---

[1] The shop with the sign of the *Agnus-Dei*.

[2] Federigo d' Aragona; and his brother, the bridegroom, was Alfonso, Duke of Calabria.

[3] The lords of towns and districts. [Trans.]

[4] The *Palagio de' Signori* was the name of the *Palazzo Vecchio* at that time, and "the *Palagio*" will be understood to have this signification all through this Diary. [Trans.]

[5] The *Gonfaloniere* was the highest official during the time of the Republic.

[6] On the *soma* = two barrels.

[7] It will be noted that the date of the year is not changed in January. The Florentines began their year on 25 March, and used the term "*in the year of the Incarnation.*" This dating is used throughout the Diary. [Trans.]

be in flood, although there had not been a drop of rain; but the snow had melted suddenly, so that the river entered the town and flooded it as far as the *Canto a Monteloro*,[1] and benches from the church of Santa Croce floated across to that point.

And the water went into the *Piazza del Grano*,[2] reaching more than half-way up the door of the apothecary's shop, and past the *Palagio del Podestà*.[3] The river overflowed its banks opposite Messer Bongianni's houses,[4] and filled the *Prato* and the Via della Scala. Many mules and horses were drowned in their stables, and all the wine-casks went floating about, mostly towards the Arno. This flood had come suddenly.

1466. 24th May. A Saturday and the eve of the *Spirito Santo*, I was wedded to a daughter of Domenico, son of Domenico Pagni, whose name was Salvestra. She had a dowry of 400 florins, in the state funds,[5] praise God!

5th July. A Sunday evening, I gave her the ring, the contract being made before Ser Giovanni, son of Francesco di Neri. (Should be 6*th* July. [Trans.])

27th July. A Sunday evening, I took my wife to *Casa Domenico*. She had as bridal outfit the following:

A pale blue sack-garment, with narrow sleeves, embroidered with pearls.
A purple gown, with sleeves of *brocatello*.[6]
A white under-gown.
Twenty-four kerchiefs of hand-woven linen.
Six linen towels.
Twenty-four *benducci da lato*.[7]

[1] The *Canto a Monteloro*; the point where the Via de' Pilastri and that of Cafaggiolo (now degli Alfani) meet the Borgo Pinti. [Trans.]
[2] The point where the Via de' Neri, Via de' Leoni, and Via della Ninna meet. [Trans.]
[3] The *Bargello*, now National Museum.
[4] The houses of Bongianni Gianfigliazzi on the Lungarno near the Ponte a Santa Trinità; and the *Prato* was the meadowland all along by Ognissanti. [Trans.]
[5] *Monte* or *Monte redivisbile* (redeemable) was the debt made by the State for a certain large sum, which was divided into small equal shares, under the obligation to repay them at a fixed interest within a certain time. The creditors were given bonds, called *lnoghi di monte*, which could be bought and resold by others.
[6] A thin brocade. [Trans.]
[7] Strips of stuff fastened to the shoulder to be used as a handkerchief. [Trans.]

Eight shifts, woven in lozenge-pattern; new.
Twelve coifs.
A girdle of white silk webbing, with silver threads.
Three caps of various kinds.
A green reticule, with silver ornaments.
A pincushion, with pearls.

They were estimated by two dealers at the value of thirty-eight florins *di suggello*.[1]

	lire	
For fine cotton material, for the robe	5	8
For twisted gold fringe, for the robe	1	15
For making little rings (or eyes)	2	0
For blue silk and a piece of leather		7
For linen material, for the gown		18
For making the gown, to Lorenzo, tailor	5	12
For bits of enamel, to put between the pearls of the necklace	2	3
For little hooks, for the gown	1	2
For gold ribbon, for the gown	1	13
For the lining for the gown		15
For linen material, for the gown	1	13
For cotton, for the gown		2
For red cotton material, for the gown		9
For a small gold badge	2	0
For silk cords, for the gown		10
For tress (of silk, silver, or gold), for the robe	1	10
For a *balascio*,[2] for the pendant	1	5
For blue silk, for the robe		6
For blue selvages, for the tassels of the robe.		7
For ermine, for trimming the gown	8	0
For the fringe, for the gown	2	16
For the fringe of the robe	4	4
For silk cords, for the gown		2
For ribbon to hem the robe		4
For seven twisted gold dangles, for the collar	1	12

And I will record my own expenses (for the marriage-gift): *lire*

Silk webbing for a girdle, with gold and silver ornaments, in all . . . . .[3]

[1] Sealed florins: that is, weighed, tested, and then sealed up in cardboard-boxes or purses. [Trans.]
[2] A kind of ruby of a pale red. [Trans.]
[3] This space is blank in original.

		lire	
For an ounce of pearls, for snoods, 6 gold *fiorini*		27	6
A little jewelled brooch, 3 gold *fiorini*		16	16
A couple of little knives, 2 gold *fiorini*		11	4
A pearl band for the forehead, 10 gold *fiorini* and 5 *soldi*		45	5
A pearl necklace, 120 *fiorini*		40	4
For 6 *denari* (half-ounces) of pearls, 1 *fiorino* 10 *soldi*		6	2
For ornaments (or finishings) for the snoods		1	15
For 6 *denari* (half-ounces) of pearls, 1 *fiorino* 15 *soldi*		6	7
For serge, for the robe [1]		17	15
For fine longcloth, for the robe			12
For 1 ounce of pearls, for the robe, 5 *fiorini* 15 *soldi*		26	0
For 1 ounce of spun gold, for the robe		5	2
For a ribbon to twist in the hair		2	14
For 6 *denari* of pearls		3	8
For a piece of ribbon		1	0
For some silk, for the robe			6
For cloth, for the lining of the robe		1	4
For some ornaments, (or finishings) for the robe			9
For silk material, for the collar		1	12
For silver and silk, for the robe			15
For crimson silk material, for the gown,[2] 26 gold *fiorini* 6 *soldi*		151	10
For a clasp, for the collar of the robe		4	17
For brokerage to Tommaso di Currado		12	14
For a diamond, 2 gold *fiorini* and 2 *grossi* [3]		11	15
For a sapphire, 2 gold *fiorini* and a half		13	19
For a ruby, 1 gold *fiorino* and a half		8	8
For a broken ring, loss		1	3
To Lorenzo, tailor		1	0
For setting the stones in the pendant			14

My above-mentioned wife and dear companion, who had not her equal for kindness and virtue, died after living with me for forty-eight years, and never once having given me cause for anger. She had twelve children; and at her death left me four boys and three girls, one of

[1] The *giornea* was a luxurious dress worn without a girdle, and with long wide sleeves. [Trans.]

[2] The *cotta* was also a luxurious gown, often trimmed with fur, probably worn over the *giornea* or over the *gamurra*. [Trans.]

[3] A *grosso*, or *grossone*, was a coin equal to 20 *quattrini*, and about a third of a Tuscan *lira*. [Trans.]

the latter a nun at Foligno, and the two others at home.
God be praised!

In my time there have been the following popes, though
I do not know the day of their election [1]:

Papa Ugenio, who left Florence about 1440, when I was
about four years old.

Pope Niccolaio succeeded him. In Ugenio's time Felice
was also elected Pope . . . by a Council . . . and there
were . . . (Hiatus in MSS.)

Pope Calisto succeeded Niccolaio.

Pope Pio, a Sienese.

Pope Pagolo.

1st September. I bought the apothecary's shop at the
Canto de' Tornaquinci [2]; and took over the keys on
the 4th.

On this day a *parlamento* (assembly) was held in the
Piazza, and there was a great commotion in the city;
the shops were closed several times, for fear that they
might be looted. Niccolò Soderini, Messer Dietisalvi,[3]
and Messer Luca Pitti were exiled, for having been the
leaders in the plot against Piero, son of Cosimo de' Medici,
when it was attempted to murder him in his way from
Careggi.[4] And after the failure of the plot, many citizens
connected with it were exiled, about twenty-seven of
them being restricted within certain boundaries and
made ineligible for office, according to the sentences inscribed on a document inserted in this book; except Messer
Luca Pitti, who made an alliance with Giovanni Tornabuoni, giving him his daughter as wife, and in consequence
he was reprieved from exile, and they remained friends
and at peace.

23rd November. I took my wife to my own house.

---

[1] The popes mentioned by Landucci are as follows: Eugene IV.,
a Venetian, of the family of Condulmier, elected 1431. Nicholas V.,
who was Tommaso Parentuccelli of Sarzana, elected 1447, and this
Felix is the anti-pope Amedeo of Savoy. Calixtus III. is Alfonso
Borgia, a Spaniard, elected 1455. The fourth is the Sienese Eneo
Silvio Piccolomini, elected 1458, who took the name of Pius II. The
last is Paul II., a Venetian, of the family Barbo, elected 1464.

[2] The *Canto de' Tornaquinci* was the point where the streets of
the *Vigna Nuova* and the *Spada* end in the *Via Tornabuoni*.

[3] Dietisalvi Neroni.

[4] They had laid in wait for Piero on his return from Careggi, but
he had notice of the danger, and took another road. [Trans.]

1467. 12th May. I returned to Casa Domenico, my father-in-law's.

1468. 27th April. At about 15 in the morning (11 a.m.) [1] we had the news that peace was concluded.[2] It was celebrated with bonfires, and the shops were closed.

15th July. A tax was decreed, called the *Ventina*,[3] but it was not kept up long. Later on, in 1469, a renewal of the *Catasto* was decreed instead.

17th September. Eight men were taken in the hangman's cart to be hung, because they had intended to give over Castiglioni di Marradi.[4]

1470. 15th April. Fifteen men were brought from Prato, who had intended to give over the place, and they were hung.[5]

1471. 26th May. I bought some of the first sugar that came here from Madeira; which island had been subdued a few years before by the King of Portugal, and sugar had begun to be grown there; and I had some of the first.

27th May. A Monday, the gilt copper ball was put up on the lantern of the cupola of *Santa Maria del Fiore*.[6]

30th May. They placed the cross on the said ball, and the canons and many other people went up and sang the *Te Deum* there.

---

[1] All through this Diary *Florentine time* is used. They then began to count *from eight o'clock p.m.*; that is, the present eight o'clock was called 24; and the present nine o'clock was called one o'clock, ten o'clock was two o'clock, etc. The idea was to count the fresh day from the hour of the sun going down on the last one. [Trans.]

[2] Alamanno *Rinuccini* (*Ricordi*, etc. Firenze, 1840), says that the news of the universal peace amongst all the powers of Italy, pronounced by the Pope two days previously, reached Florence at 13 *ore* (9 a.m.) on the 27th April.

[3] A tax of the twentieth part.

[4] This rebellion was raised by the *Signori* of Forli and Faenza.

[5] This was the plot of Bernardo Nardi.

[6] Some writers place this fact in 1472, and others in 1474, some mistake the year and not the month; but Landucci states the truth, which is confirmed by the following two extracts taken from the Archives of the *Opera di Santa Maria del Fiore*. On the 28th May, 1471, 2 *lire 8 soldi given to Marchione, servant of the Opera* (Administrative Office), *to buy bread and wine for the workmen when they put up the ball*. And on the 1st June 3 *lire paid to the trumpeters of the Palagio ; taken by Matteo di Madonna Andreagia, to be given them for their trouble when they played on the lantern when the cross was put up* (*Quaderno di Cassa, ad an*).

28th July. We had the news that Pope Pagolo was dead; he died on the 26th, Friday night, a little before dawn.

9th August. Sisto IV. was elected Pope. He was from Savona; a Franciscan monk, and general of the Order; then he had been made cardinal by Pope Pagolo, and now Pope. He was elected on Friday, the eve of San Lorenzo, and was crowned on San Sisto's day.

23rd September. Six ambassadors left Florence to visit the said Pope; namely: Lorenzo de' Medici, Messer Domenico Martegli, Messer Agnolo della Stufa, Messer Bongianni Gianfigliazzi, Piero Minerbetti and Donato Acciaiuolo; and the said Pope made Piero Minerbetti a knight and he returned to Florence with this title.

22nd October. It was voted in the Palagio that sealed florins should no longer be used in trade,[1] but florins as large as *grossi*, at 5 *lire* 11 *soldi*, the florin of *grossi*, at 20 *quattrini* the *grosso*; and they were fixed at 20 per cent. higher. It was also voted that the property of the (Guelf) party should be sold.

1472. 27th April. We heard that Volterra had suddenly revolted; and troops were sent there.

6th May. The Bishop of Volterra came as ambassador, but settled nothing. And on the 7th two mortars were loaded to go there. And on the 10th the Count of Urbino [2] went there with men-at-arms; and by the 19th he took all their castles; and on the 24th he took many prisoners and captured their bastion. And on the 1st June their ambassadors arrived here to demand terms, and almost came to an agreement, but everything was upset when they returned there. And so far two mortars had been used. And on the 8th June, the attacking party beheaded one of the Bartolini; and on the 9th they used another mortar.

[1] This decree is published by *Vettori* in his treatise on the gold florin. The *fiorini larghi* were called so because they were enlarged in circumference. It was decreed that they should be increased in weight by one old *denaro*, that is, by the 240th part; and they were also to be larger and flatter (*fiorini larghi di grossi* is only another name for *fiorini larghi*). They were worth more than the old *fiorini di suggello*; but their value on the market was continually fluctuating, and gradually increasing; in 1469, they were worth 5 *lire* 6 *soldi*; in 1485, 5 *lire* 4 *soldi*; in 1493, 6 *lire* 11 *soldi*; in 1500, 7 *lire*, and in 1531, 7 *lire*, 10 *soldi*. The *scudo d' oro* (a crown) was not coined till 1530. [Trans. from *Orsini*.]

[2] Federigo da Montefeltro.

18th June. A knight came to us with the olive-branch, and an agreement was made, guaranteeing their property and persons. There was much rejoicing. But when the attacking-party entered, one of their constables, a Venetian, began to cry: "Sack it, sack it!" and our men began plundering, and it was impossible to make them observe the agreement. The count had this Venetian hung and also a Sienese. Nevertheless the unfortunate people fared badly. The count came to Florence on the 27th June, 1472; he was given the Patriarch's house, a banner, two basins, two silver ewers, 180 *lire*, and a helmet. He went away on the 1st July, 1473.

1473. 2nd June. A bell was hung in *Santa Maria del Fiore*, the largest of all, recast.

5th July. A lazzerino of the *Mangano* [1] was condemned to death, and was beheaded. He had committed the crime of violating a girl of about twelve years old in such a way that she died; and then he had buried her body outside the *Porta alla Giusticia*.[2] And later it was discovered, as the dogs raked it up. Sentences were issued against him, but he could not be found. When captured some years after, he confessed having committed the outrage.

18th July. We heard that our archbishop, who was one of the Neroni of Florence, had died at Rome; and the archbishopric was given to the Cardinal of San Sisti, called Brother Piero.[3]

11th December. A poor woman in Camaldoli,[4] who had several grown-up daughters, was praying to the crucifix in their house, when they saw it break into a sweat, and speaking of it in the neighbourhood, people began to go and pray to it. When the Carmelite friars heard of it, they went and fetched it reverently and placed

---

[1] This may mean a worker at the Mangano (cloth-press).

[2] This gate was not far from the *Torre della Zecca Vecchia*, and was so called because criminals passed under it on the way to execution. [Trans.]

[3] Piero Riario, nephew of the Pope.

[4] A portion of the city near the gate of *San Frediano*, which received its name from an old monastery of the *Camaldolensi*. It is the abode of the roughest and poorest of the people, and the name was extended to a district near San Lorenzo (the Camaldoli of San Frediano, and the Camaldoli of San Lorenzo), the appellation now signifying "rough people." [Trans.]

it in a tabernacle in the *Cappella della Croce*,[1] and it was worshipped there.

1474. 25th September. We received a letter written by Matteo Palmieri, captain of Volterra, which I saw and read; it related the following marvel, namely, that in these days there had been born in Volterra a boy (that is, a monster) which had the head of a bull, and three teeth, with a lump of skin on the head like a horn, and the top of the head was open like a pomegranate, with fiery rays coming out. Its arms were all hairy, and its feet were like a lion's with lion's claws. Its body was of the nature of that of a female of the human race, but its legs down to the feet were those of a bull like the head. And it lived about three hours. The mother died the fourth day. The midwives and the other women present half died of fright. And this was shown to the said Matteo as a terrible thing. And the said Matteo, captain of Volterra, wrote here to Florence with his own hand; and I copied the said letter, in the actual words, neither omitting nor adding anything. And because the said Matteo was my father's intimate friend and my godfather, the letter itself came into my hands, although it was directed to other citizens.

1475. 1st April. A lad of about twenty-three, a peasant from the neighbourhood of the Sieci, was arrested, who on Easter night had shut himself up in *Santa Maria del Fiore*, and hidden under the altar of Our Lady towards the Chapter-house; the next morning he robbed the Madonna of certain silver ornaments on her arms and legs and eyes, and behaved in a disgusting way to show his contempt. And imagine how utterly worthless this crazy fellow was, when he had only been liberated by the captain on Holy Thursday after having been imprisoned for theft. On Saturday he was hung from the Campanile. I have mentioned him rather than others, because having been let out of prison on Thursday, the very next Sunday he committed this outrage.

7th May. I, Luca Landucci, went to Rome for the Jubilee, and took with me my mother-in-law; and we travelled for fifteen days going and coming.

1476. 29th December. We heard that the Duke of

---

[1] This is doubtless the crucifix known as *La Providenza*, and concerning which a certain G. F. B. published the *Notizie* (Florence, 1852).

Milan [1] had been stabbed and killed by one of his citizens called Giovanni Andrea,[2] who was moved to commit the crime by certain unjust acts of the duke. He was put to death by the populace, out of zeal for the common good. There were several conspirators; and the first who reached the duke was this Giovanni Andrea, who feigned to offer him a letter with one hand whilst he stabbed him with the other. It happened as with Scevola the Roman, when they took life for life. Such men are rarely found. And I believe that they carry out their crimes by divine permission. This was on the day of *Santo Stefano*, in church, during the mass. And when they tried to flee, they could not, because of the crowd of people, and mostly the women who hindered them by spreading out their gowns [3] in such a way that the barons of the duke, and chiefly a certain Ghezzo who stood next to him, caught and slew the said Giovanni Andrea. And three others were taken and hung. Some people said that these three who were caught were quartered by four horses.

15th January. We heard that the Duke of Burgundy [4] had been killed by the Swiss in the war made on Switzerland; and his men suffered such a defeat [5] that it was never known what became of the duke's body, and it was never found; so that some were of opinion that he was not dead, but had been carried off, and would one day appear again. This Duke of Burgundy was considered to be a most cruel man, it being a common report that he in the West and the Grand Turk in the East delighted in men's blood, and that they caused people to be slaughtered in a barbarous fashion. The Lord sometimes frees the world of such men. The death of this duke was astonishing, because he had so many soldiers that he could not be defeated by the enemy in an ordinary way, as their numbers were as nothing to his. But when he refused to make a treaty with them, they became desperate, and having communicated, they went into battle carrying a banner painted with an Annunciation, and blessed at the church of the *Nunziata* in Florence. And it being thus, the few conquered the many, as it pleased the Lord, by a

---

[1] Galeazzo Sforza. [Trans.]   [2] Lampugnano.
[3] The women used to sit on the floor during these long ceremonies. [Trans.]
[4] Charles the Bold.   [5] The Battle of Nancy. [Trans.]

miracle of the *Nunziata* at Florence. And, as is known, they brought this very banner, with which they had conquered, to the church of the *Nunziata* in Florence, and I saw it at the *Servi*,[1] with many other gifts.

1477. 7th June. The duty on wine was raised, so that where 14 *soldi* used to be paid, it was now 20; but a promise was given that it would not last for more than five years.

And at this time the cupola of the *Servi* was finished (i.e. of the SS. Annunziata).

15th August. Four of the city gates in Florence were closed; the first was *Porta San Miniato*, the second was the *Porta alla Giustizia*,[2] the third *Porta Pinti*,[3] and the fourth the *Porticciuola della Mulina* [4] (of the Mill).

15th January. Pope Sisto nominated several cardinals; one he nominated for the emperor. And he ordered that the feast of San Francesco should be observed like the other feasts which are enjoined.

1478. 25th March. The Holy Father gave a plenary indulgence in *Santa Maria del Fiore* for one day, from vespers on the 24th March till the next vespers, on the 25th March, which people availed themselves of with great devotion. The cause of this was the preaching of Brother Antonio da Vergiegli in *Santa Maria del Fiore* during Lent, which bore good fruit.

On this same 25th March, a law was determined upon, at the *Palagio*, which forbade anyone who had killed a man to return to Florence.[5]

---

[1] *SS. Annunziana*; This church was founded in 1262, by the *Sette Beati fiorentini*, who called themselves *Servi di Maria*. [Trans.]

[2] See note to 15th July, 1473.

[3] The *Porta a Pinti*, demolished with the walls in 1866, was at the end of the *Borgo Pinti*, and was a very picturesque gate, with a group of old cypresses. [Trans.]

[4] The *Porticciuola della Mulina* was near the Prato, down by the river, leading to the *Mulina* (Mill) of the *Vagaloggia*. It was sometimes called *Porticciuola del Prato*. The three last gates were taken down when the walls were demolished. [Trans.]

[5] This provision is of the 16th March, 1478, Old Style, and perhaps the 25th is the day on which it was published. It was made to limit the concession of safe-conducts, and the causes which led to it may be read in the exordium which I have pleasure in publishing as a document which describes the way of thinking at that time.

"The high and magnificent *Signori* having in mind how grave is the sin of homicide, by which man, a creature made and created in the image of God, is destroyed; and seeking the reasons why it is

26th April. At about 15 in the forenoon (11 a.m.) in *Santa Maria del Fiore*, whilst high mass was being celebrated and the Host elevated, Giuliano, son of Piero, son of Cosimo de' Medici, and Francesco Nori were killed, near the choir of the said church towards the door which goes to the *Servi* [1]; and Lorenzo de' Medici was wounded in the neck, and fled into the sacristy and escaped. They were killed in consequence of a certain conspiracy made by Messer Jacopo de' Pazzi and Franceschino de' Pazzi and Guglielmo de' Pazzi, the which Guglielmo was the brother-in-law of Lorenzo de' Medici, his wife being a sister of theirs, called Bianca. And the sons of Messer Piero de' Pazzi were also there, that is, Andrea and Renato and Niccolò; and of the house of Salviati, there were Francesco, Bishop of Pisa, and Jacopo Salviati, who was son-in-law to Filippo Tornabuoni, and another Jacopo also a Salviati, and Jacopo, son of Messer Poggio, Bracciolini and Bernardo Bandini of the house of Baroncegli, and Amerigo Corsi, and many others. The con-

so very frequent under our jurisdiction; find among other things, that it is encouraged by the facility of pardon and proper severity not being used in punishing such a detestable and abominable excess, he who commits the homicide being allowed to be continually in the presence of those who have suffered from the offence and of those who desire to live virtuously; none of whom can regard such manslayers without great indignation and perturbation of mind. And although the laws of the Florentine people bitterly avenge and punish such crimes, and give security against them; notwithstanding, whatever may be the reason, either too great humanity (which in reality one ought rather to call cruelty), or else undisciplined charity, such entirely right and just decrees are not properly observed. And the high *Signori* and discreet chief citizens wish to remedy these things which are so contrary to honest living and against the divine laws, by making the fear of punishment deter men from committing them, when they are deprived of all hope of pardon, and by adjuring the magistrates not only not to overlook such things, but to enforce the law with severity, hoping firmly that this provision may have a good effect" (State Archives of Florence, *Consigli maggiori Provv. Reg. ad annum*).

The term "*Signori e Collegi*" used in the decrees meant as follows: the *Signori* were the eight *Priori* and the *Gonfaloniere della Giustizia*, and the *Collegi* were the sixteen *Gonfalonieri delle Compagnie* and the twelve men (three from each quarter) formerly called the twelve *Buonuomini*, who were summoned by the *Signori* to take council on almost every occasion. [Trans.]

[1] Landucci always uses this expression to indicate the second door in the left-hand aisle, opposite the *Via dei Servi*, that is, *on the north*. [Trans.]

spirators brought Cardinal di San Giorgio[1] here, who was a young man; he entered Florence on the day above-mentioned, and they all came together in *Santa Maria del Fiore*, and, as I have said, at the elevation of the Host seized their swords, and it is said that Francesco de' Pazzi struck Giuliano, and Bandini the other. And having killed Giuliano they wanted to kill Lorenzo, but did not succeed, as he fled into the sacristy. Meantime the Bishop de' Salviati, with Jacopo, son of Messer Poggio, and two of his relatives who were both called Jacopo, went to the *Palagio*, with several priests, feigning to desire to speak to the *Signoria*, and they spoke to the *Gonfaloniere*, and became somewhat confused. The *Gonfaloniere* perceived the treachery, and he and his companions shut themselves up here and there, and ordered the doors to be closed, and the bell rung for a *parlamento*. And what with the rumour which came from *Santa Maria del Fiore* of Giuliano's death and the bell ringing at the *Palagio*, the city was immediately in arms. And Lorenzo de' Medici was taken to his house. Meantime Messer Jacopo de' Pazzi rushed on horseback to the Piazza de' Signori, crying "*Popolo e libertà!*" (The People and Liberty!), wishing to take the *Palagio*, but the bishop not having succeeded in getting possession of it, Messer Jacopo was not able to enter. He then went towards his own house, and was advised to take to flight; and he fled by the *Porta alla Croce*, together with many men-at-arms and with Andrea de' Pazzi. Meantime all the city was up in arms, in the Piazza and at Lorenzo de' Medici's house. And numbers of men on the side of the conspirators were killed in the Piazza; amongst others a priest of the bishop's was killed there, his body being quartered and the head cut off, and then the head was stuck on the top of a lance, and carried about Florence the whole day, and one quarter of his body was carried on a spit all through the city, with the cry of: "Death to the traitors!" That same evening the cardinal was taken to the *Palagio*, barely escaping with his life, all his companions being captured without exception.

And the bishop remained in the *Palagio* with all the rest. And that evening they hung Jacopo, son of Messer Poggio, from the windows of the *Palagio de' Signori*, and likewise the Bishop of Pisa, and Franceschino de' Pazzi,

[1] Raffaello Riario.

THE EXECUTION OF SAVONAROLA AND HIS COMPANIONS
From the XVIth-century original in the Museum of S. Marco.

naked; and about twenty men besides, some at the *Palagio de' Signori*, and others at the *Palagio del Podestà* and at the *Casa del Capitano*, all at the windows.

The next day (the 27th) they hung Jacopo Salviati, son-in-law of Filippo Tornabuoni, and the other Jacopo, also at the windows, and many others of the households of the cardinal and of the bishop. And the day after that (the 28th April, 1478), Messer Jacopo de' Pazzi was captured at Belforte. And that evening of the 28th, about 23 in the evening (7 p.m.), Messer Jacopo de' Pazzi and Renato de' Pazzi were hung at the windows of the *Palagio de' Signori*, above the *ringhiera* [1]; and so many of their men with them, that during these three days the number of those killed amounted to more than seventy. The cardinal remained a prisoner in the Palagio, and no harm was done him, except that he was made to write to the Holy Father, with his own hand, all that had happened. And the same day the prisoners in the *Stinche* [2] managed to break open the prison, and all escaped—with the exception of one unfortunate man who was captured and hung.

29th April. There was a little rest and quiet, without more bloodshed, but people were still bewildered with terror.

30th April (Ascension-day). The obsequies of Giuliano de' Medici took place in San Lorenzo.

[1] The *ringhiera* was the platform consisting in three steps and a railing, which used to be round the *Palagio* (Palazzo Vecchio) on the front and on the north. It was used for haranguing the people, and was only demolished in 1812, when the present steps and platform replaced it. [Trans.]

[2] The *Stinche* were the old prisons, which formed a large rectangular mass between the Via del Diluvio (now Via del Fosso), the Via del Palagio (now Via Ghibellina), the Via del Mercatino, and the Via de' Lavatoi. The exterior walls were extremely high, and windowless. The name was derived from that of a fortress which had rebelled against Florence at the beginning of the fifteenth century, and which the Florentines retook, bringing the prisoners back as a trophy. Originally intended for traitors and rebels, these prisons were used afterwards for various purposes, even for madmen; whilst later on debtors and bankrupts were confined there, and others with life-sentences. In 1835, under the Grand-duke Leopold, it was decreed that they should be sold, and shops and houses were built on the area; also the large hall, called *Filamonica*, and a riding-school, afterwards replaced by the *Pagliani* theatre, now called the *Verdi*. [Trans.]

1st May. The new *Signoria* entered into office. That evening Andrea de' Pazzi and Brigliaino [1] were captured. And also, the same evening, returning from Pisa, Messer Piero Vespucci was captured and taken to the *Palagio*, as it was said that he had aided the escape of a man concerned in the plot.

3rd May. At about 18 in the afternoon (2 p.m.), a priest [2] was captured in the *Badia* of Florence, who was a chancellor (secretary) of Messer Jacopo de' Pazzi, and another at the same time, from Volterra [3]; they had remained hidden there from the day of the murder till now. And that evening Brigliaino and one of the cardinal's chancellors were hung at the windows of the *Palagio*, and when the ropes were cut, they fell down on the platform. The soldiers quarrelled over robbing the dead bodies of doublets and hose.

4th May. The above-mentioned priest and the man of Volterra who had been captured in the *Badia*, were hung at the *Palagio del Podestà*; and Giovanbattista, Count of Montesecco,[4] was beheaded, under the Loggia of the *Podestà*, for the same cause.

5th May. The horses and mules of Messer Jacopo and others were sold by auction.

9th May. Ambassadors came to Florence from the Pope; and finally, after a few days, they were sent away again, without our having consented to give up the cardinal, whom they had wished to take back with them. And at this time many armed men were placed in the Piazza, and a patrol of *birri* (sergeants) paraded the city day and night, and the city-guards all night. No one went out after one o'clock (9 p.m.), whatever class he belonged to; not a sound was heard in the city at night; and no one carried arms at any time.

15th May. The body of Messer Jacopo was disinterred in

[1] Giovanni di Domenico, called Brigliaino, a hanger-on of the house of Pazzi, and a worthless man.
[2] Stefano di Ser Niccolò of Bagnone, a priest in San Procolo at Florence.
[3] Antonio di Gherardo Maffei of Volterra, scribe of the *Camera Apostolica*, or notary of the *Ruota* (a society of Doctors of Law).
[4] The Count di Montesecco, one of the first soldiers of his time, had a less ignominious death, perhaps out of regard for his rank. He was implicated in the plot by association with the Count Girolamo Riario, nephew of the Pope.

Santa Croce, and buried near the city wall, between the Porta alla Croce and the Porta alla Giusticia, inside.

17th May. At about 20 in the evening (4 p.m.), some boys disinterred it a second time, and dragged it through Florence by the piece of rope that was still round its neck; and when they came to the door of his house, they tied the rope to the door-bell, saying: "Knock at the door!" and they made great sport all through the town. And when they grew tired and did not know what more to do with it, they went to the Ponte al Rubiconte and threw it into the river.[1] And they sang a song with certain rhymes, amongst others this line: "Messer Jacopo is floating away down the Arno." And it was considered an extraordinary thing, first because children are usually afraid of dead bodies, and secondly because the stench was so bad that it was impossible to go near it; one may imagine what it was like, from the 27th April till the 17th May! And they must have had to touch it with their hands to throw it into the Arno. And as it floated down the river, always keeping above the surface, the bridges were crowded with people to watch it pass. And another day, down towards Brozzi, the boys pulled it out of the water again, and hung it on a willow, and then they beat it, and threw it back into the Arno. And it is said that it was seen to pass under the bridges of Pisa, always above the surface.

10th May. They sent Andrea de' Pazzi and two of his younger brothers into a new prison, in the vault of a tower at Volterra.

20th May. Guglielmo de' Pazzi gave his word to keep within fixed boundaries; and he was sent to his own estate and there limited to a distance of from five to twenty miles from Florence. And Messer Piero Vespucci was imprisoned in the *Stinche* for life, because he had aided in the flight of a certain Napoleone Francese, who was proscribed for having been concerned in the conspiracy of Messer Jacopo narrated above.[2]

[1] History says that the magistrates had the body thrown into the Arno, to put a stop to the boys' treatment of it. [Trans.]
[2] It is probable that Vespucci was led to assist the flight of Francese not so much from friendship and humane feeling, as from hatred for Giuliano de' Medici, victim of the plot; the latter being the favoured lover of Piero Vespucci's daughter-in-law, the beautiful Simonetta Catani, wife of Marco Vespucci, the continual and avowed object of Giuliano's love-poems.

1st June. The clothes and household effects of the said Pazzi and others were sold by auction, under the roof of the *Zecca* (Mint), and they filled the place from end to end, for their possessors had been very rich.

5th June. The cardinal was set free.

7th June. He was accompanied by the "Eight";[1] and many citizens from the Palagio to the Nunziata; and he was in dread of being killed by the populace. That same day the Pope excommunicated us.

12th June. The cardinal left Florence.

13th June. It was voted in Council to put on many new taxes, *Sesti* and *Decime*[2]; and 50 thousand florins on the priests.

2nd July. An ambassador came to Florence from the King of France.

5th July. The feast of San Giovanni was kept, not having been kept on the actual day, and perambulating shows went about, and there was a procession; the *palio*[3] was also run, and there were *girandole*[4] and *spiritegli*[4] and *giganti*[4] and many fine things, as if it had been the real day.

[1] These were the *Otto di Guardia e Balia*, at this time at the height of their power. [Trans.]

[2] The "Seventy," in the lifetime of Lorenzo, fearing the rigorous equality sought for by the *Catasto*, changed it to a form of subtle progressive taxation, which they called the *Decima scalata*. This *apparently* favoured the lower classes; there were certain cases in which the lower classes paid only a twentieth of their income, and the upper classes paid a *Sesto* (the sixth part). The Medici, however, were extremely clever in favouring their friends by *sgravi* (remissions), and oppressing their enemies by *aggravi* (increases) or demands for old debts. The citizens had to make a full declaration of their family, possessions and means, as for the *Catasto*. A man who had twelve children was exempt, only having to pay the registration fee, so as to be eligible for office. [Trans.]

[3] The *palio* was actually the prize for which the races so called were run, and consisted of a costly piece of drapery of velvet or silk, which was displayed at the winning-post. The famous *palio* of San Giovanni is mentioned by several historians as having taken place in the thirteenth century; the race was run from the Porta alla Croce to the Porta al Prato; and the prize was originally of scarlet velvet, and later of scarlet silk. [Trans.]

[4] The *edifizi* (shows mounted on carts) were platforms on wheels, upon which figures were placed, representing scriptural, mythological or other subjects, and sometimes short scenes were enacted. At the present time, on the day of San Giovanni, the band plays in the evening, mounted on a similar platform on wheels. [Trans.] *Girandole* were platforms covered with rockets, and wheels of fire, which took the form of ships, houses, etc. *Spiritegli* were people

10th July. Another ambassador came from the King of France; he was going to the Pope, and was lodged in the house of Giovanni Tornabuoni.

And at this time the horsemen of the Duke of Milan came by the Pisan road, and passed near Poggibonizi, and the troops of the king continued to approach.

13th July. The King of Naples sent a herald to Florence, with the proclamation displayed, stamped with the arms of the king, and he went to the *Signoria* to declare war, being deputed to tell us that the king and the Holy Father were ready to oblige us in every way, if we sent away Lorenzo de' Medici: to which the citizens would not agree; and so war began.

19th July. The Sienese invaded our territory and took booty and prisoners, and on the 22nd they captured Calciano.

23rd July. They captured Rincine and destroyed it, and took away men and women of all classes; and our soldiers were worse than they, pillaging and working great havoc all through Valdelsa, so that everyone left their homes and felt safe nowhere but in Florence. Each day there was some incursion or other, and the enemy overran Panzano, pillaging and burning.

27th July. Our men made an incursion into the territory of the Sienese, and pillaged and burnt the mills and captured on various occasions more than 100 horses. At this time the enemy's camp was before the Castellina, and ours was on the *Poggio Imperiale* [1]; and then our troops moved to Imola. The Marchese di Ferrara [2] was appointed *Capitano* [3] of the Florentines, being given 50 thousand florins a year during the war, and when there was no war 30 thousand florins, and he had to maintain 1500 horse at his own cost.

on stilts, who amidst the dense crowd appeared to be walking in the air, over the heads of the rest, like spirits. *Giganti* were men with their feet bound to high stilts, who wore masks and were dressed up to appear like giants; they supported themselves on poles made to resemble walking-sticks (Vasari, *Lives of the Painters*). [Trans.]

[1] This is the Poggio Imperiale near Poggibonsi, not to be confused with the other near Florence.

[2] Ercole I. (d'Este), Duke of Ferrara and of Modena, *Capitano* of the League of the Florentines, the Duke of Milan, and the Venetians, in the war which followed the plot of the Pazzi.

[3] The *Capitano generale della Guerra* was elected for the duration of the war; he had to be a stranger, and a *Signore*; his position corresponded to that of a field-marshal.

31st July. Our men took much booty in the neighbourhood of Volterra. He who seeks evil, finds it. It was not very intelligent of them (the Sienese) to let themselves be drawn into making war in their own territory, for they will suffer two-thirds of the damage, and we the rest; whilst the King of Naples and the Pope, who brought it about, will get off easily.

1st August. The enemy took Lamole, and captured more than 100 persons, and also continued to bombard the Castellina. The rule for our Italian soldiers seems to be this: "You pillage there, and we will pillage here; there is no need for us to approach too close to one another." They often let a fort be bombarded for several days, without attempting to succour it. We require to be taught by the northern soldiers how to make war.

10th August. The French ambassador and the Florentine ambassador [1] returned from Rome, without having arrived at anything satisfactory.

15th August. The French ambassador left; and at this time we lost the Castellina. And Messer Niccolò Vitellozzi [2] was going about sacking certain forts of Città di Castello, and burning men, women, and children, with every sort of cruelty. After that, Messer Lorenzo of Città di Castello [3] burnt some of our fortresses in the district of Arezzo, and committed atrocities, burning people. They were both cruel men. Such generally come to a bad end. Godly people, as we read in Holy Scripture, never come to a bad end.

18th August. We lost the Castellina (as above said); the inhabitants escaped.

19th August. A peasant was tried and hung, and was taken down as dead and placed on a bier; but having reached the *Tempio*,[4] he recovered consciousness, not being dead. He was taken to (the hospital of) *Santa Maria Nuova*, where he died after a few days. All Florence saw him.

And on the same day the enemy encamped before Radda and Panzano.

20th August. They bombarded the said castles all day.

[1] Guidantonio Vespucci.
[2] Or rather, Vitelli, ally of the Florentines and of Lorenzo de' Medici.
[3] Lorenzo Giustini, who held that city for the Pope.
[4] The Oratory of the Company of *Santa Maria del Tempio*, which consoled those condemned to death, and buried their bodies. It was beyond the *Porta alla Giustizia*, near the *Porta alla Croce*, outside the walls.

21st August. A commissary came to us from Venice, who hired for us 3 thousand soldiers, to be paid by the Venetians.

22nd August. The enemy made an incursion as far as Ponte a Grassina, carrying off a smith and many others.

24th August. The people about Rovezzano took fright, and the alarm was sounded and they fled into Florence with all their possessions, by the *Porta alla Croce*, so that it really seemed as if the territory were lost. Such a terror was never seen, everyone being utterly dismayed. They did not consider themselves safe even in Florence, and suffered much discomfort and misery.

And on the same day we lost Radda, which was sacked and burnt.

25th August. Three men were hung, who were caught outside the *Porta Sa' Niccolò*, having gone about pillaging in the guise of the enemy; and it was they who had struck such terror into the hearts of the people outside *Porta alla Croce*, and caused them to desert their homes. These men were Florentines.

27th August. We lost Meletuzzo and San Polo, the constable there having been guilty of treachery.

And on the same day, Pretone and his brother the constable of Radda, and Jacopo Vecchietti who was a commissary there, were arrested, and they were imprisoned in the *Stinche*, as it was said that they had been guilty of treachery. A man of San Polo was also taken, and was put to the rack.

2nd September. We heard that a conspiracy had been discovered at Venice, and that several persons had been beheaded or imprisoned.

7th September (Monday). Our *Capitano*, the Marchese di Ferrara, came to Florence, arriving at about 22 in the evening (6 p.m.), with a great company of crossbowmen on horseback, and musketeers, and we escorted him into the city with great honour, lodging him in the same house which he had before. He had about 50 mules laden with baggage, and remained in Florence till Saturday, the 12th, when he took his bâton and went into camp.

14th September. Brolio was taken by assault. And on the same day a man died of plague, in the *Casa del Capitano*,[1]

---

[1] The house of the *Capitano del Popolo*, which was behind the Palazzo Vecchio.

in prison, to which he had been condemned for life; and another man who was sick of the plague was taken out of prison and carried to the hospital of *La Scala*,[1] where all those sick of the plague were carried. At this time the plague had increased so much, that 40 or more were sick at the hospital, and 7 or 8 died every day, and some days even 11; besides others in the district who did not go to the hospital.

25th September. Cacchiano was lost and was given over to the flames.

And on the same day, mortars were sent to Casoli di Volterra, and our camp was set up before it; but our troops never went to succour those who were losing.

29th September. We regained Castelnuovo. At this time there were between 60 and 70 sick of the plague in the hospital and district together, and it was spreading to the camp also.

On this same day the enemy's camp was moved to the *Monte a Sansovino*. They were beginning to go a little further away.

5th October. Our forces began to besiege Casoli.

6th October. Six Sienese were arrested here, one of them being the *Podestà* of Castelnuovo, which had been regained.

And at this time there were about 100 sick of the plague, at the hospital of La Scala, and in many houses in Florence; amongst others a man was found dead upon one of the benches in Santa Maria Novella.

11th October. A boy was found sick of the plague at the gate of the hospital of San Pagolo,[2] and no one could be found to carry him to the hospital of La Scala.

At this time the enemy were bombarding the Monte a Sansovino.[3]

---

[1] The hospital of the Scala was in the street of that name, at the corner of the Via Polverosa (now Via degli Oricellari), and where the convent of San Martino was afterwards built.

[2] On the Piazza Nuova di Santa Maria Novella, under the *Loggie*. This building, diminished in size, remained a hospital for many years. Lately, however, it has been changed into an educational institution for poor girls. [Trans.]

[3] The Republican Government, at this time, made many solicitations to the Florentine commissaries and to the Duke of Ferrara, urging that they should proceed more boldly against the enemy. An innumerable quantity of letters exist on this head, in the correspondence of the *Dieci di Balìa* (the Magistracy of the Ten). The Florentine commissaries also were insistent with the *Capitano*; but he, whether (as some thought) on account of being related to

14th October. A sick woman was on her way to La Scala, the attendants helping and supporting her by the arms, but when she got as far as the hospital of the Porcellana,[1] she fell dead; so that one may say that the plague is exceedingly serious.

20th October. A truce was made with the enemy for eight days, two days' notice to be given. Intelligent men did not approve of it.

31st October. Notice was given, and the enemy pressed hard on the Monte a Sansovino. And there was a plot in our camp; and the *Capitano* hung one of the chief men under him.

1st November. The "Eight," who were in office, and their notary, were deposed, for having burnt certain books.

And on the same day, the Monte a Sansovino was lost; the garrison capitulating on condition that their persons and property should be respected. And everyone said that if the truce had not been made, the enemy would have had to break up their camp, as they were so short of provisions that they could not have held out more than three days. Our forces never chose to make a sortie. Hence came the evil; and everyone marvelled that the enemy were not completely victorious after this, for they won much glory.

14th November. A father and son from Pistoia were arrested for treason. They were scourged.

15th November. Messer Piero Vespucci was taken out of the *Stinche* and sent to the *Podestà*; and the same day they put him back in the *Stinche*, for some good end.

3rd December. The traitor from Pistoia, called Piero Baldinotti,[2] was taken in the executioner's cart and hung, and the son was imprisoned for life in the *Stinche*.

And at this time our soldiers went into quarters in the Pisan territory and elsewhere, and also the *Capitano*.

7th December. Messer Tommaso Soderini went as ambassador to Venice.

24th December. A peasant of the neighbourhood,

the King of Naples, whose daughter he had married, or for some other reason, never really did what might have been expected of a man whose valour was so renowned; hence the enemy gained this victory and many others during the war.

[1] This hospital was in the Via della Scala, at the corner of the Via della Porcellana.

[2] He had wished to deliver Pistoia from the yoke of the Florentines, and give it to the King of Naples.

belonging to the Popoleschi, was found dead in his house, having hung himself with a towel.

And during these days the Arno was very high and overflowed its banks opposite Messer Bongianni's houses. It caused great damage.

And the plague was also causing much mortality; it pleased God to chastise us.

And at this Christmas-time, what with terror of the war, the plague, and the papal excommunication, the citizens were in sorry plight. They lived in dread, and no one had any heart to work. The poor creatures could not procure silk or wool, or only very little, so that all classes suffered.

10th January. Four French ambassadors arrived at Florence, two of whom were going to the Pope and two to the King of Naples. They declared to the *Signoria* here, that they were going to make peace in Italy amongst Christians, and to settle all differences, giving judgment according to reason, and protested that their king would proceed against anyone who hindered peace; if the Pope were the one to be obdurate, he would be summoned to a Council; and when peace had been made, all the powers would undertake a crusade against the Unbelievers. They left on the 16th January.

17th January. A certain hermit came here to preach, and threatened many ills. He had been at Volterra, serving at a leper hospital. He was a lad of twenty-four, barefoot, with a wallet on his back; and he declared that St. John and the Angel Raphael had appeared to him. And one morning he went up on to the *ringhiera* of the *Signori* to preach, but the "Eight" sent him away. And each day some incident happened.

And at this time, a son of the Duke of Milan,[1] who was confined within certain boundaries in the territory of Pisa, fled from there, and went to Genoa to the Signor Roberto,[2] and joined him.

27th January. My brother Gostanzo returned from the Levant.

4th February. Chianti was pillaged.

And now the plague had lessened considerably. God be praised!

---

[1] This was Ludovico Sforza, called *Il Moro*, uncle to the reigning duke, and at that moment exiled.

[2] Roberto da Sanseverino.

8th February. Four galleys reached the Port of Pisa, two from the West and two from Barbary, which had joined forces. They came in great terror, for fear of the fleet of the king and the Genoese. It was considered a great piece of news.

9th March. A man who was said to be a Venetian was hung in the *Mercato Nuovo*, for having stolen some florins off a money-changer's table the evening before, in broad daylight; and he had been caught and taken to the rector,[1] and was condemned to be hung.

At this time Signor Roberto made an incursion into the Pisan district with many men, and came as far as the Port of Pisa and set it on fire, but did not do it much harm; and then he advanced into the *Val di Calci*, and burnt the mills and took much booty, after which he retired beyond the Serchio. And in this direction the Duke of Calabria[2] penetrated as far as the *Poggio Imperiale*, with the design of capturing it, but he did not succeed.

And meanwhile our troops advanced as far as Siena, and pillaged the country, and took a certain fort called Selvoli and held it for some time, that is to say, till the 4th April.

And the plague was making now great ravages, having increased again.

And we were continually raising fresh bands of infantry; and the Venetians sent us a number of soldiers, that were all despatched to the Pisan territory.

And the *Capitano* now went into the Pisan territory, awaiting Count Carlo[3] and a large body of cavalry.

1479. 12th April. There was a skirmish outside Pisa between our *Capitano* and Signor Roberto, and a good number were slain. And it was said that our *Capitano* had no wish to vanquish the enemy, and therefore did not do his duty; this was the unanimous opinion of the people.

18th April. The plague had increased to such an extent that I went away to my villa at Dicomano with all my family; leaving my apprentices to attend to the shop.

At this time Count Carlo came to Florence, and was appointed a *Capitano*, and two separate camps were formed, he going into the Perugian territory and defeating the papal troops, which departed utterly routed. And

[1] The rector of the *Arte del Cambio* (Money-changers' Guild).
[2] Alfonso d'Aragona, son of Ferdinando, King of Naples.
[3] Count Carlo da Montone, son of the famous Braccio, sent by the Venetians to aid the Florentines.

after this the ducal forces[1] could have been broken up; but through the fault of our *Capitano*, the Duke of Ferrara, and through the dissensions amongst the citizens, no action was taken, or else the enemy would certainly have been conquered. The Duke of Calabria pitched his camp before Colle. People continually deceive us, and we cannot be victorious, as God punishes us for our sins.

8th November. At midnight the alarm was rung in the Mugello, and everyone was overwhelmed with terror, wanting to rush to Florence. But the enemy came to Piancandoli, and did not enter the Mugello.

15th November. The Duke of Calabria took *Colle di Valdelsa*. He had besieged it for about seven months before he was able to take it; the mortars had been fired against it 1024 times, so that the greater part of the walls was destroyed. And now the enemy went into quarters.

24th November. A herald came with the olive-branch to announce that peace was already being negotiated.

6th December. Lorenzo de' Medici left Florence and went to the king at Naples.

8th December. Sarzana was lost.

23rd December. Bernardo Bandini de' Baroncegli was captured at Constantinople, the Grand Turk having given him up. He had fled from Florence when Giuliano de' Medici was murdered, believing that his life would be safe at Constantinople.

News arrived that the Duke of Calabria had taken possession of Siena, but it was not true. However, to all intents and purposes, he was master of the place, for the Sienese were helpless, having let him come in with all his troops, and he did what he chose.

28th December. Bernardo Bandini was hung at the windows of the *Palagio del Capitano*, he being the one who was said to have slain Giuliano de' Medici in the Conspiracy of the Pazzi. Certain arrangements had been made with the sultan that he should be given up.[2]

[1] The forces of the Duke of Calabria.
[2] Some important letters written to Lorenzo Carducci, Florentine consul at Constantinople, on the arrest of Bandini made by order of the sultan, and the instructions given to an Antonio de' Medici sent to thank the sultan himself, and to take over the prisoner exist in the Florentine Archives of State, and form part of a collection of Oriental documents which will shortly be brought to light by the *Reale Soprindenza* of the Tuscan Archives.

20th January. It seemed doubtful whether the peace would come to anything. And the plague was also making great ravages.

13th March. Lorenzo de' Medici arrived in Livorno, on his return from Naples. It was considered a marvel that he should have returned, as everyone had doubted the king allowing him to resume his post, and a still greater marvel that he should have been able to arrange everything so diplomatically. God help him![1]

15th March. He arrived in Florence at 21 in the afternoon (5 p.m.).

16th March. The ratification of peace arrived in the night, about 7 (3 a.m.). There were great rejoicings, with bonfires and ringing of bells.

22nd March. The city gates, which had been shut shortly before, were re-opened.

1480. 25th March. Peace was proclaimed, and the image of Our Lady of *Santa Maria Impruneta* was brought to Florence for the fête.

29th March (Ash Wednesday). The Pope sent an *aggravatoria*[2] forbidding anyone to communicate; but as it was not made public, almost everyone communicated, and was troubled in conscience after it became known.

9th April. Two ambassadors were sent to the Pope and to Naples: Messer Antonio Ridolfi and Piero di Lutozzi.[3]

28th April. Messer Piero Vespucci[4] was liberated from prison, and left Florence, and went to the Duke of Calabria at Siena and stopped there.

At this time it was noised abroad that the Pope had made a league with the Venetians, the Sienese, and the Duke of Urbino.[5] It was not true.

---

[1] Lorenzo de' Medici had gone on his own initiative, seeing that the war could no longer be borne, and not wishing to lose the favour and authority that he had acquired in Florence, especially after the Conspiracy of the Pazzi. The Florentines feared lest harm should come to him, and remembered the case of Jacopo Piccinino, who in 1465 unwarily put himself into the hands of the same king, and lost his life. Lorenzo, however, must have felt his ground carefully before moving, and when he returned after having concluded peace, he became more popular and powerful than ever.

[2] A kind of excommunication. [Trans.]

[3] Nasi.

[4] The Duke of Calabria, and his father King Ferdinand, had made urgent solicitations in favour of Vespucci.

[5] Federigo di Montefeltro.

7th May. Ten *Sesti* and one *Decima* were voted; and a *Sgravo* (decrease) of 3 thousand florins was made and an *Aggravo* (increase) of a thousand florins.[1]

At this time the Duke of Calabria was sent a sum of 30 thousand florins, on several occasions. It may be imagined what need there was for these taxes of *Sesti* and *Decime*. We Florentines have the wise custom of giving money in payment to everyone who does us an injury, and who destroys and pillages our territory. And this is not a solitary instance; it will always be the same; anyone who wants money from the Florentines has only to do them an injury.

27th May. The wife of Giovanni de' Pazzi, and one of the Giugni, and many others, were arrested, who wished to liberate the Pazzi at Volterra.

2nd June. Signor Roberto entered Florence.

3rd June. Messer Piero Vespucci was permitted to return to Florence, and was restituted in all his rights, according to the wish of the duke.[2]

At this time the price of grain fell to 15 *soldi* the bushel, and the like low prices.

20th June. The Duke of Calabria confined within limits 18 knights and citizens of Siena. He also kept his soldiers in the city, so that he was master of the situation. And the Sienese did not consider it at all just that he should act in this way, but he chose to do so. He had the idea of acting in the same way with regard to us; but please God, by a great miracle, it happened that on the 6th August the Turkish army came to Otranto and began to besiege it; so it was necessary to leave our neighbourhood, at the king's command, and return to defend the kingdom. The Turks were encamped in three places, being at Rodi (Rhodes), and with the Hungarians, besides at Otranto.

18th August. A cardinal,[3] one of the king's sons, arrived in Florence, on his way from Hungary to Rome.

---

[1] A *Sgravo* means that some taxes were lowered or remitted; whilst on others there was an increase (*Aggravo*). See note to 13th June, 1478. [Trans.]

[2] He, however, preferred leaving Tuscany, and went to offer his services to the Sforza in Milan, and was appointed Ducal Councillor by Ludovico il Moro. Sent to exercise his authority at the city of Alessandria, he met with a tragic end, being killed in 1485 in a popular rising.

[3] Giovanni d'Aragona.

2nd September. Two silk-mercers' shops in Porta Santa Maria, near *Vacchereccia* [1] were burnt down; and the other night the whole *Canto di Vacchereccia* as far as the *Chiassolino del Buco* was burnt down.[2] And the fire rushed across to the opposite side of the street and burnt down all the other corner of the *Vacchereccia*, destroying about 20 shops of the silk-mercers and money-changers. There was great loss, many having all their property consumed.

And at this time there was much talk about the loss of Otranto, and Leccio was feared for.

27th September. A certain hermit came to the house of Lorenzo de' Medici at the *Poggio a Caiano*; and the servants declared that he intended to murder Lorenzo, so they took him and sent him to the *Bargello*, and he was put to the rack.

15th October. This hermit died at *Santa Maria Novella*, having been tortured in various ways. It was said that they skinned the soles of his feet, and then burnt them by holding them in the fire till the fat dripped off them; after which they set him upright and made him walk across the great hall; and these things caused his death. Opinions were divided as to whether he were guilty or innocent.

4th November. Twelve ambassadors were appointed to go to the Pope; and they set out on the 15th November.

5th December. The Cardinal of Mantua [3] passed through Florence, on his way from Mantua to Rome.

11th January. Two more ambassadors were appointed to go to Rome: Messer Guido Antonio Vespucci and Pierfilippo Pandolfini.

12th January. Antonio Pucci being *Gonfaloniere*, carried through the vote for a *balzello* (a special tax) of 39,000 florins; and had it levied, making it arbitrary.

6th February. There was an earthquake at about half-past 4 (12.30 at night), but not a very severe one.

1481. 31st March. The fortresses of Colle, Poggibonizi, Monte a Sansovino, and Poggio Imperiale were restituted

---

[1] The street still so called, between *Via Por San Maria* and the Piazza, named after the tower of the *Vacca*, belonging to the old *Casa del Foraboschi*, and forming the lower portion of the present tower of the *Palazzo Vecchio*. [Trans.]

[2] The first little alley leading from the *Vacchereccia* to the *Via Lambertesca*, when you came from *Via Por San Maria*; it took its name from an old inn. [Trans.]

[3] Francesco Gonzaga.

to us, together with other places, except the Castellina, Montedomenici, Piancaldoli, and Sarzana.

The plague was now decreasing.

13th April. The Pope sent us an Indulgence, to be obtained by attending six churches: Santa Maria del Fiore, the Nunziata dei Servi, Santa Croce, Santa Maria Novella, Santo Spirito, and Sa' Jacopo in Campo Corbolini.[1] And it began on this day and lasted till Easter. Everyone who wished to obtain it had to visit these six churches on three mornings, confessing and doing penance; and had to lend aid, at the said churches, to the forces sent against the Turks.

28th May. We heard that the Turkish sultan was dead; but nevertheless the Christians did not yet make a move.

2nd June. One of the Frescobaldi, and one of the Baldovinetti, and one of the Balducci, were arrested; and on the 6th June they were hung from the windows of the Bargello, or rather, of the *Casa del Capitano*, having confessed that they had intended to murder Lorenzo de' Medici.

8th June. The *Porta a Faenza* [2] was closed, because the plague was very bad outside this gate, and was in three or four houses in Florence.

4th August. Twelve men were appointed, and given powers to act for the whole people of Florence. The first thing they did was to decree that whoever owed the commune anything should pay three florins interest on each florin lent.

22nd August. We apothecaries arranged that we should not keep our shops open on holidays till 22 in the evening (6 p.m.), as had hitherto been the custom, but that four shops in the whole city (to be chosen by lot) should remain open all day.[3]

---

[1] This church, which was founded in the year 1000, is preceded by a little peristyle closed by wooden gates, as the church is no longer in use. On the capitals of the columns are the arms of the Alberti. In 1206 it passed into the possession of the Knights of Jerusalem, and a good many of their tombs are in the interior. It stands in the *Via Faenza*, and must not be confounded with either of the two other churches of the same name: San Jacopo tra Fosse, and San Jacopo in Borgo San Jacopo. [Trans.]

[2] This gate, which was on the *Prato*, was demolished when the Fortezza di Basso was built, or rather, it was built into the keep of the fort. [Trans.]

[3] With regard to this custom, I am pleased to add that, on the 15th October, 1547, a decree was published by the *Otto di Guardia e di*

FLORENCE: THE OLD MARKET-PLACE, NOW DEMOLISHED

This day it snowed in the mountains of Pistoia.

10th September. Lorenzo de' Medici married one of his daughters to Jacopo Salviati.

18th September. We heard that Otranto had been regained. There were rejoicings, bonfires, etc.

2nd October. Signor Gostanzo di Pesaro[1] arrived in Florence, with a fine troop of men-at-arms, and several squadrons of crossbowmen on horseback, being on his way to Milan.

8th October. My brother Gostanzo won the *Palio* at Santa Liperata, and this was the first that he had won with his horse called "*il Draghetto*" (the Little Dragon). He had brought two horses from Barbary: one called "*il Pelligrino*" (the Pilgrim) he sold to the Count of Urbino, getting 100 ducats for it.

The prisoners of the *Stinche* escaped. They opened the doors with the keys given them by one of the warders, called Domenico di Cristofano. They got out at about 7 in the night (3 a.m.), the warder also escaping.

30th November. The tax called the *Scala*[2] was collected.

26th December. My brother Gostanzo won the *Palio* of Prato with his horse *Draghetto*.

4th March. The authorities considered that this new tax of the *Scala* was not a suitable one for the city; therefore they had recourse to the *Sesto* again, and doubled it, with advantage, as it seemed to those who understood the business. But certainly some people who were already in sorry plight were completely ruined by the *Sesto*.

At this time the Venetians declared war upon the Duke of Ferrara, and we much feared lest we should be drawn into it.

14th March. A chancellor of Count Girolamo was hung at the windows of the *Bargello*. He had been captured by

Balìa (the Eight), on the observance of the fêtes, forbidding any work to be done on these days, and the shops to keep open, with certain exceptions, amongst which is the following: "And four apothecaries' shops, to be drawn by lot among the *Arte* (Guild), may remain open all day; the others may sell from 21 in the evening onwards" (5 p.m.).

[1] A Florentine captain, to whom the bâton of *Capitano generale* was given two days later.

[2] Probably the *Decima scalata*; see note to 13th June, 1478.

one of the Altoviti,[1] who was a proscribed rebel, and in order to be pardoned, found out this man, and caught him between Piombino and Pisa; and he won his pardon.

19th March. A horseman of Signor Roberto was arrested on the *Ponte a Valiano*, who was carrying letters to Signor Roberto's son; which letters shed some light upon an intended conspiracy; and in consequence of this, Antonio Pucci and other citizens left for the Pisan territory, and in a few days got a number of soldiers together.

1482. 25th March. Madonna Lucrezia, wife of Piero, son of Cosimo de' Medici, and mother of Lorenzo, died on the day of the Annunciation. And at this time the Pope sent us an Indulgence at *Santa Maria del Fiore*.

5th April. The Pazzi, who were imprisoned at Volterra, had their rights restituted, and were liberated and sent out of Italy; two of the younger ones had been liberated two months earlier, on account of illness, or else they would have died.

This year there were severe earthquakes at Rodi (Rhodes) which ruined the church and killed many people, mostly in a church where 40 *Cavalieri Fieri* (Knights of Rhodes) met their death. The precise day is not known to me, but it was during this year.

20th April. There was a quarrel at Rome between the Orsini and the Colonnesi; and the city was thrown into confusion as usual. Everyone has to suffer for the disputes of these great men.

At this time the cupola of Santo Spirito was finished; and in fact sermons were preached beneath it.

28th April. The Duke of Urbino came to Florence, lodging in the house of Giovanni Tornabuoni, and he was

---

[1] This must have been the famous Cola Montano, a Bolognese; not a chancellor, but maintained by Count Girolamo Riario, and the Pope, and the King of Naples, and all the enemies of Florence, during the war following the Conspiracy of the Pazzi. That he was taken by one of the Altoviti is not mentioned elsewhere. Brought to Florence, he was put in the prison of the *Bargello* or Captain of the *Piazza dei Signori*; where he wrote with his own hand a *Confessione*, which is preserved in the State Archives of Florence, amongst the *Carte Strozziane*, still unedited, but well worth publishing, as important contributions to the history of that time. The order of the *Signori e Collegi* to the *Otto di Custodia e Balìa*, of the 12th March, and another of the *Otto* (the Eight) to the *Bargello*, of the 13th, for the execution of Montano, still exist in the said archives amongst the papers of these magistrates.

received with honour. And on the 29th he left for Milan, to take up his post as *Capitano generale*, stopping at Ferrara where Signor Roberto was. There they besieged a fort called Ficheruolo till the 1st June.[1]

And in these days the Duke of Calabria on the other hand was besieging Ostia, near Rome; and on the 10th June it was said that he had taken it, but this was not true. He sacked Corneto,[2] however. The Sienese now recalled some of their exiles.

12th June. Signor Gostanzo came to Florence, on his return from Ferrara.

At this time there was much talk of the worship of an image of Our Lady at Bibbona, or rather in a tabernacle about a bowshot from Bibbona. It is, namely, a Virgin seated and holding the dead Christ in her arms, after He has been taken down from the Cross; which is called by some a *Pietà*. This worship began on the 5th April, when it was transfigured: that is, it changed from blue to red, and from red to black and divers colours. And this is said to have happened many times between then and now, and a number of sick persons have been cured, and a number of miracles been performed, and quarrels reconciled; so that all the world is running there. Nothing else is talked of at this moment; I have spoken to many who tell me that they themselves have seen it transfigured, so that one must perforce believe it.

20th June. We heard that Messer Niccolò Vitegli had taken *Città di Castello* for us, and we sent a mortar there. War had broken out in several parts.

2nd July. We took Ficheruolo.[3]

4th July. We heard that all the forts of Città di Castello had now been taken, and the whole place.

11th July. Antonio Belandi of Siena was restricted to certain boundaries near Monte Alcino.

[1] This is not correct; see note to 2nd July.

[2] These are all facts relating to the war which had lately broken out between the Venetians and the Pope on the one hand, and the Florentines, Milan, and Naples on the other. Federigo, Duke of Urbino, was *Capitano generale*, and Commander of the League against Venice, and Roberto di Sanseverino was in the service of the latter.

[3] The text appears to say that the Florentines or the League besieged and took this place; but it really was exactly the contrary. Ficheruolo belonged to the Duke of Ferrara, with whom the Florentines were allied, and now fell into the hands of the Venetians.

25th July. We heard that the papal troops had defeated the Duke of Calabria, and had taken 300 men-at-arms and 19 leaders; and it was a fact.

27th August. Many people here saw fiery flames in the air above Florence, towards the west, at about one o'clock (9 p.m.); and they were also seen at Dicomano and elsewhere.

10th September. The Count of Urbino died at Bologna.

14th September. Roberto *il Magnifico*[1] died at Rome; he who had been so famous for his victory over the Duke of Calabria near Rome, when he took 300 men-at-arms. These two great captains died within a few days of each other, just when they imagined that they were at the height of their glory. What errors are made by the world! Men incur so many perils in order to slay and kill others, and to obtain a short-lived fame on this earth, not considering what it means to kill a man, and how soon they themselves will have to die and render an account.

24th December. The Cardinal of Mantua, papal legate, came to Florence on his way to Ferrara. He was received with all due honour.

5th January. The Duke of Calabria came to Florence, leaving again on the 8th for Ferrara, and taking 800 horsemen with him; amongst his force were many Turks.[2] He was received with great honour.

6th February. Some of the Turks whom the duke was sending back, passed through. As 400 of them had deserted to the Venetians, he thought it best to send back the remainder; and we raised a Christian brigade for him here in Florence.

12th February. Lorenzo de' Medici left Florence, going as ambassador to Ferrara, in very fine array.[3]

8th March. Lorenzo de' Medici returned from Ferrara, where he had been honourably received as a man of merit.

1483. 1st April. At Siena, four men were thrown out of the windows of the *Palazzo de' Signori*, and six more were hung, who belonged to the *Monte de' Nove*[4]; and many citizens fled into Florentine territory.

[1] Roberto Malatesta, a captain sent by the Venetians to aid the Pope.
[2] Taken into his pay after the recapture of Otranto.
[3] To the diet which was held there, to treat of negotiations with regard to the war.
[4] A certain political party at Siena.

6th April. The Turkish ambassador came to Florence.[1]

7th April. The Sienese beheaded three of their citizens, one being Antonio Belandi, and another one of the knights made by the Duke of Calabria. Thus, in the opposition of parties, are treated those ambitious men who are not contented with the state of life to which God has called them.

23rd April. There was an eclipse of the moon. And it happened that three people fell dead on this day: a boy about twelve years old, whom I myself saw lying dead in the church of San Simone, a notary called Ser Bonacorso, and a girl. It was considered in Florence to have been an extraordinary day, the moon having had a powerful influence.

30th May. Our Lady of Impruneta was brought into the city, for the sake of obtaining fine weather, as it had rained for more than a month. And it immediately became fine.

14th June. A league was made with the Sienese for twenty-five years, and our fortresses were restored to us. At this time there died at Faenza a Brother of the Order of the *Servi di Maria*,[2] who had performed many miracles; the bells having rung of their own accord when anyone died, and sick persons being healed. People went to him from all the country round. I spoke to a trustworthy man, who said that he had witnessed these facts. Miracles were constantly happening; sometimes down by the river and sometimes up in the mountains; and sometimes he was seen speaking with a woman, who was the Virgin. I mention this to show that people were in the mood to expect great things from God.

21st June. In a tabernacle in Orto Sa' Michele there was placed the figure of San Tommaso beside Jesus, and the

---

[1] This was a certain Ismail, sent by Bajazet II. after the death of Maometto II. to invite the Republic to resume commercial relations with the Turkish Empire. A curious record of the statement made by this ambassador to the *Signori*, and of the reply given him by the *Gonfaloniere*, can be read in the above-mentioned Oriental documents, 7th April, 1482.

[2] From the *Historie di Faenza* by Giulio Cesare Tonduzzi, and the *Annali dell' Ordine de' Serviti* by Arcangelo Giani, we find that this was the *Beato Jacopo Filippo Bertoni*, who died on the 25th May, 1483. These writers also testify to the prodigies referred to by Landucci, which so moved the *Faentini* that they wished honours to be conferred upon Misserino Bertoni dalla Cella di Monte Chiaro, father of the defunct, by a public decree.

Jesus in bronze, which is the most beautiful thing imaginable, and the finest head of the Saviour that has as yet been made; it is by Andrea del Verrocchio.

At this time the Duke of Calabria and Signor Roberto left Ferrara and went into Lombardy, where much damage was being done on all sides, and Signor Gostanzo was poisoned there.

5th August. The exiled Sienese came against their city, as far as the fortress of Sitorno, but were unable to do anything. The citizens took many prisoners from the fortress and carried them into Siena.

In these days the Florentines destroyed a fortress in the upper valley of the Arno, called Monte Domenici, because it had rebelled.

During this August of 1483, the Duke of Calabria captured many fortresses in Lombardy from the Venetians,[1] and crushed the Venetian troops in such a manner that they could not hold out any longer. This occurred because the Church had excommunicated all those who gave aid to the Venetians, which prevented them having soldiers from beyond the Alps. And the fleet of the King of Naples came into the port of Ancona, and that of the Venetians set out to find it. But on the 5th September, the king's fleet sailed away without waiting for their opponents. Great things had been expected if they had encountered each other.

7th September. Ambassadors came to Florence from the King of France, on their way to Rome to arrange peace in Italy; and whilst they were here they received the news that their king had died on the 30th May, 1483. And on the 13th September one of these ambassadors died at Santa Maria Novella, and the others set out for Rome.

During these days, for fear of hunger and of the war going on in Lombardy, many families left it, and there passed through Florence on their way into Roman territory 50 to 100 at a time, till they amounted to several thousands. Many also went to Romagna and elsewhere. It was said that there were more than 30 thousand persons altogether. It was a most pitiful sight to see these poor people pass, with a wretched little donkey, and their miserable household possessions: saucepans, frying-pans,

---

[1] From the 12th December, 1482, the Pope had made peace with the League, and then associated himself with it in the war against Venice.

etc. One wept to see them barefoot and ragged; and it is the cursed wars which have caused all this. No one went by without receiving some little help from us.

8th October. Certain stone seats which had been made round the *Mercato Vecchio* a short while before were taken away again.

23rd October. A cardinal-legate came to Florence, who was going to the King of France as ambassador, to confirm to him his father's crown. And this cardinal chanced to be the very man whom the last King of France [1] had kept for many years in prison, in a cage.

10th November. Three Florentine ambassadors left Florence, being sent to the King of France; they were Messer Gentile, Bishop of Arezzo, and Antonio Canigiani, and Lorenzo, son of Piero de' Medici.

1st January. The new *Signoria* [2] entered into office, and were stricter than the last. They sent for the citizens and required everyone to pay his debts; and they imprisoned them in the *Bargello* and the *Stinche*. Many were afflicted and worn out by so many wars.

In addition to other hardships, corn was at 50 *soldi* a bushel, beans at 46 *soldi* a bushel, white bread at 1 *soldo* 8 *denari* a pound, and flour rose to 3 *lire* a bushel.

On this 1st March our ambassadors returned from France, and Antonio Canigiani had been knighted by the French king. We did him honour, sending an escort to meet him.

The price of crushed beans now increased to 4 *lire* a bushel, peas to 5 *lire*, corn to 59 *soldi*, and everything dearer; and a little later corn rose to 3 *lire* 8 *soldi* a bushel.

1484. 6th April. Seven shiploads of grain arrived at Pisa, comprising 7 thousand *moggia* [3]; 3 thousand *moggia* were brought here, and 4 thousand went to Ferrara and Lombardy, where there was great scarcity.

9th April. Three more shiploads of grain arrived at Livorno; but it still cost 50 *soldi* a bushel, and the commune sold it at 42 *soldi*.

---

[1] Louis XI. The name of the cardinal was Jean Balue, whom Louis XI. had persuaded Pope Paul II. to make a cardinal; and later, for political reasons, he had imprisoned him in an iron cage, from which he was liberated in 1481 through the intercession of Pope Sixtus IV. [Trans.]

[2] Alamanno Rinuccino in his *Ricordi Storici* also speaks ill of this *Signoria*.

[3] A Tuscan *moggio* was generally 8 *staia* (bushels). [Trans.]

14th June. The plague broke out again; and this morning one of the Brogietti buried three children at once, two girls and a boy, all having died of plague.

19th June. Corn cost 9 *soldi* 33 *denari* a bushel.

In this July a worship of an image of the Virgin Mary [1] at Prato began; people rushing there from all the country round. It worked miracles like that of Bibbona, so that building was begun and great expense incurred.

9th August. We received news of the Peace.[2] There were bonfires and great rejoicings.

14th August. At 6 in the night (2 a.m.) we heard that Pope Sisto was dead. He died on the 13th, at 14 in the forenoon (10 a.m.). On the 20th the bells were tolled for his death.

At this time as many men as possible were being hired to send to Sarzana and Pietrasanta.

30th August. We heard that the new Pope was chosen, and the bells were rung at 4 (midday) on Monday. He had been a Genoese cardinal, Messer Giovanni de' Zeboni,[3] Cardinal of Molfetta; and he took the name of Innocent VIII.

8th September. The Peace was published in Florence, and there were rejoicings.

23rd October. The State arrested a son of Filippo Tornabuoni, called Alessandro, and he was confined within certain boundaries in Sicily. It was said to be because he had designs against Lorenzo de' Medici, who was his relative; this may not have been the case, but I only repeat what was said.[4]

At this time Pietrasanta was besieged very closely.

---

[1] This is the Madonna called *delle Carceri*, which is worshipped at Prato, where there was soon built a very elegant temple after the design of Giuliano da San Gallo. Ferdinando Baldanzi wrote a fine description of it, which can be read in the *Calendario Pratense* of 1847. A church was also built at Bibbona in the Volterrano, in honour of the other image mentioned on the 12th June, 1482. Savonarola alludes to the prodigies worked by these two images in the second of his *Poesie tratte dall' autografo*, in which he says:

> " O anima cecata
> Tu senti mille segni
> A Prato e a Bibbona."

[2] The peace between the Venetians and the *Lega Santissima* (Most Holy League).

[3] Innocent VIII. was of the house of Cibo (then also called Zibo), a name which our chronicler has mangled.

[4] Other chronicles say that he confessed himself guilty of ordinary crimes, but not political ones.

There were many of our commissaries there, with a fine troop of men.

The wax tapers and the *palii* were now removed from San Giovanni, and the order was given that they should no longer be placed there.[1] The church was thoroughly cleaned, and remained perfectly simple without these decorations; up till this time all the offerings of tapers and *palii* used to be placed here, so that nothing of the church itself could be seen.

6th November. Antonio Pucci, a commissary of Pietrasanta, was brought back dead to Florence.

7th November. We captured Pietrasanta, which capitulated to Lorenzo de' Medici, and on the 11th we took the fortress. Piero, son of Filippo Tornabuoni, was made warden, and Jacopo Acciauoli commissary; Bartolomeo Tedaldi being put in command of the walls. The news reached here at 14 at night (10 p.m.), and the next day the shops remained closed, and there were great rejoicings and bonfires. And the same day Messer Bongianni Gianfigliazzi, another commissary there, was brought back to Florence dead.

13th January. The Genoese fleet came to Livorno, and approached the towers, but did nothing. It left again on the 1st February.

1485. 10th April. Two long and thick oak beams, of great weight, were hoisted up to the top of the tower of the *Palagio de' Signori*, to support the big bell and adjust it better.

18th April. A herald came to Florence.

23rd April. Corn was sold at 16 *soldi* a bushel.

17th July. The Florentines made the Count of Pitigliano [2] *Capitano*, and gave him the bâton. And the Sienese made the Signore da Farnese their *Capitano*.

[1] On the day of San Giovanni (24th June) the magistrates stood on the *ringhiera* of the Palagio, to receive the deputations sent by tributary towns, the *palii* being hung round the *ringhiera* in order: from Pisa, Arezzo, Pistoia, Volterra, Cortona, Lusignano, Castiglione, Aretino, etc. The tapers were brought on splendid painted cars. The *Marzocco* was crowned four days before and four days after, and during this time there was an indemnity for debtors, etc. The tapers and *palii* were all put in San Giovanni, the *palii* being hung on iron rings, and remaining there for one year, when they were removed to make place for the fresh ones. The old ones were used for decoration on public fêtes, or for altar-cloths, or were sold by auction. [Trans.]
[2] Niccola Orsini.

And up till now my brother Gostanzo had gained 20 *palii* with his Barbary horse *Draghetto*, that is, 20 races from the 8th October, 1481, to the 25th June, 1485; the first was Santa Liperata, the next Sant' Anna, and San Vittorio several. Once when he won San Vittorio he sold the *palio* to the Aretini for 40 gold florins, and then he went to Arezzo and won it back again. And when he went to race at Siena, there was a tie between his horse and one belonging to Lorenzo de' Medici, called *La Lucciola* (Firefly), that of Gostanzo being in reality one head's length in advance of the other. And the people who were present declared that he had won, and told him to go to the magistrate, and they would bear witness. Gostanzo, however, refused to do this, out of respect for Lorenzo, and as it happened, Lorenzo was proclaimed the winner. Another year, also at Siena, a meaner trick was played him: namely, when Gostanzo's horse was a bowshot in advance, and reached the winning-post, he dismounted and got up on the *palio*; then another horse came up, and they said that Gostanzo's horse had not passed the winning-post, and that the other one had passed it. Therefore the prize was given to the other. A very great injustice, that a rider who had not won the *palio* should receive it! It was most unfortunate, as my brother had such a good horse. He rushed about so much after this Barbary horse that in the end it proved his death. He died on the 12th September, 1485.

1st December. At Rome they burnt the houses of the Orsini at Monte Giordano, and there was great excitement. The Duke of Calabria went to the help of the Orsini, because they were at war with the Pope; and the consequence was war in Rome.

11th December. There came a certain hot wind from the south, as if it were July, and all the walls of the houses dripped inside, all over Florence, even in the living-rooms, although they had been quite dry.

And in these days of February and March, soldiers were continually being hired, to send to the Duke (of Calabria), who was fighting against the papal forces; so that everyone in Florence who had taken part against the Church was excommunicated. All intelligent people wondered that anyone should go against the Church, especially as it had nothing to do with us. However, this mistaken conduct was the result of our sins and of our not fearing God.

1486. 9th May. Here in the Piazza de' Tornaquinci, by the house of the Tornabuoni, it happened that a bear of an extraordinary size, bred up in this city, being tormented by some children, seized a little girl of about six years old, a daughter of Giovacchino Berardi, by the throat, and it was with great difficulty that several men freed her, covered with blood and with her throat badly torn. But, thank God! she did not die.

10th May. We heard that the Duke of Calabria had had an encounter with Signor Roberto, and had a great battle, many men being slain. The duke had the advantage.

10th July. The Duke of Calabria was pressing the papal forces hard, and we were contributing to the cost of all this.

On this same day happened the death of Antonio, son of Guido, a singer who made improvisations, an extremely clever man. I mention him because he surpassed everyone else in this art.

1487. 28th March. The following case happened: A man was hung on the gallows here in Florence, and was taken down for dead, but was later found not to be so. He was carried to Santa Maria Nuova (hospital), and remained there till the 11th April. And those in charge at Santa Maria Nuova finding him of a bad nature, and hearing him talk of taking vengeance, etc., the "Eight" decided to have him hung a second time, and their sentence was carried out.

15th April,. The Genoese were defeated by the Florentines at Serrazana, and there were many killed. Our troops captured the fort and all their artillery, and succoured Serezzanello, and sent two prisoners here, Messer Luigi del Fiesco and a nephew of his.[1]

22nd June. Sarzana was captured at 12 in the morning (8 a.m.). We had the news of it here at 20 in the evening (4 p.m.).

30th September. The relics of San Girolamo, that is to say, a jaw-bone and a bone of the arm, were taken from the altar of the Cross at *Santa Maria del Fiore*,[2] and were set in silver and gold, very richly, at a great cost; and then a fine procession was made, and they were replaced in the said chapel with much reverence. This was done at the cost of the estimable Messer Jacopo Manegli, one of the

---

[1] Orlandino son of Obietto, brother of Luigi.
[2] Sanseverino.

canons of the said church. It was reported that he had spent 500 gold florins on the setting; and besides this he had endowed a chapel. And every year these beautiful relics were devoutly carried in procession.

9th November. Two Venetian ambassadors passed through here on their way to Rome.

11th November. Certain animals arrived here, which were supposed to have been sent by the sultan; afterwards we heard, however, that they came from some good friends of Florence, who hoped to be duly rewarded. The animals were as follows: A very tall giraffe, beautiful and graceful; her picture can be seen painted in many parts of Florence, as she lived here for many years. Also a large lion, a goat, and some very strange wethers.

12th November. There was an attendant who looked after the lions, and with whom they were quite tame, so that he could go into their cages and touch them, especially one of them; and just lately, a boy of about fourteen, son of one of the Giuntini, a Florentine citizen, wished to enter the lions' cage with this tamer. But after he had been inside a little while, this lion threw himself upon him, seizing him by the back of his head; and it was only with difficulty, by shouting at the beast, that the tamer got him away. But the lion had so torn and mauled the boy, that he died in a few days.

18th November. The aforesaid ambassador of the sultan presented to the *Signoria* the giraffe, lion, and other beasts; and he sat in the midst of the *Signoria*, on the *ringhiera*, he speaking and they thanking him by means of an interpreter. A great crowd had collected in the Piazza that morning to see this. The *ringhiera* was decorated with *spalliere*[1] and carpets, and all the principal citizens had taken their places upon it. This ambassador remained here several months, and was maintained at our cost and presented with many gifts.

25th November. The Turkish ambassador presented Lorenzo de' Medici with certain perfumes in beautiful Moorish vessels, and flasks full of balsam, and a magnificent large tent, striped in the Moorish fashion.

12th March. One Fra Bernardino,[2] of the Franciscan

---

[1] *Spalliere* were pieces of linen or wool, painted or embroidered, to hang on the wall behind seats. [Trans.]
[2] The *Beato* Bernadino da Feltre.

Order, having been elected preacher for Lent in *Santa Maria del Fiore*, preached very enthusiastically over and over again, persuading the people to make a *Monte di Pietà*, and to send away the Jews. As a consequence the boys got incensed against the Jews, and a number of them went to the house of a Jew called Manullino, who was a moneylender at the *Vacca*,[1] wanting to assassinate him and to pillage his premises. The "Eight," however, promptly sent their men to stop the mischief and published proclamations threatening offenders with the gallows. Thus the commotion was soon ended. The next morning, the 13th, the "Eight" sent to Fra Bernardino forbidding him to continue preaching, and despatched him to the *Osservanza di San Miniato*.[2] But even that did not satisfy them, and the morning after, Friday the 14th, the "Eight" sent their men again, some of them actually going in person, and commanded him to leave the neighbourhood entirely. This seemed a bad prognostic to those who were desirous to live a Christian life, as he was considered a saint. And it was not long before misfortunes happened to some of these "Eight": one of them broke his neck by falling from his horse, another this thing, and another that. Amongst the rest, that one who had gone in person to drive Fra Bernardino away from the *Osservanza* died mad in hospital. Thus the matter ended ill. God save us!

1488. 16th April. We heard that Count Girolamo, *Signore* of Imola, had been stabbed to death, in the city of Forlì, by some men of the place; and it proved to be true.

A number of soldiers and militia were sent from here to Piancaldoli, men of the Romagnuoli and of the Mugello; so that by the 29th we took it. The commandant of the fortress, who was from Imola, capitulated; and he was given 4 thousand florins and a house, and the right of bearing arms for life, here in Florence, where he remained.

1st May. We heard that the Duke of Milan had entered Forlì, and had had several men put to death.

1st June. We heard that the *Signore* of Faenza had been

---

[1] The *Vacca* was that piece of street which began between the houses of the archbishop's palace and the Ghetto, and led to the Piazza degli Orlandini. There was a money-changer's office in this spot in the fourteenth century also, and it belonged to a Christian.

[2] See note to 21st July, 1489.

stabbed to death, with the consent of the wife of Messer Giovanni Bentivogli, who was the mother-in-law of the said *Signore* of Faenza. This was confirmed.

5th June. We heard that Messer Giovanni Bentivogli had been arrested by the men of Faenza, at the instance of the Florentines, and there were cries of "Marzocco" through the city; and all this was true.

12th June. Messer Giovanni Bentivogli was liberated by the Florentines. Lorenzo de' Medici went into Mugello, where Messer Giovanni had been brought, and having conferred with him courteously, sent him back to Bologna with an escort and his mind set at rest.[1]

17th June. The Bolognese, out of spite, being ungrateful, made certain *marzocchi* of straw, and certain coats of arms of our citizens, and burnt them on the Piazza of Bologna in disdain.

24th June. The Day of San Giovanni. Whilst mass was being said, a Bolognese was arrested who was cutting off the tassels of the men's belts and stealing them; and within an hour, not having any regard for the sanctity of such a saint, they hung the thief at the windows of the *Palagio del Capitano*. And his body remained there till the evening, when the attendants went and took it down. At this hour a strong wind arose, and there was such a tempest of rain and hail as the like was never seen. The awnings [2] which are placed in the *Piazza di San Giovanni* were torn into thousands of pieces, and became worthless rags, so that it was necessary to have entirely new ones. This was thought to be a wonderful and marvellous thing, which had happened on account of the homicide. It was terrible in the eyes of wise and prudent men, because it seemed to have been done by the people out of rage, as he was a Bolognese, and these *marzocchi* had been burnt at Bologna a few days before. They were in rather too great a fury; they might have waited till another day. And it was impossible for the *palio* to be run that evening.

30th July. Madonna Clarice, wife of Lorenzo de Medici, died.

[1] This was not exactly the case, for Bentivoglio always bore a grudge against Lorenzo de' Medici afterwards. [Trans.]
[2] These awnings were fastened to iron rings in the wall of the baptistery, and stretched down all round. They were blue, with gold lilies upon them. [Trans.]

12th September. The Palagio de' Signori was struck by a thunderbolt at about 14 in the morning (10 a.m.); it struck the lion and pursued its way downwards. There were two strangers at the top, just next to the bells, when it happened, a chancellor of the Pitigliani and another. The former fell unconscious, as if dead, and the other was little better; however, they did not die after all. Neither was there a great deal of injury done to the Palagio. It seemed wonderful that this should have happened to two strangers, when there were hundreds of Florentines in the Palagio. People went to look at the tower and the bells afterwards.

15th January. The daughter [1] of the Duke of Calabria passed through Florence, on her way to wed the Duke of Milan,[2] with a large escort of horsemen, and many *Signori* and matrons and damsels in her train; a very great and noble company. A magnificent escort was sent to meet her, at incalculable cost.

10th March. We heard that the Pope had made six cardinals, who were as follows: two French, one Milanese, two of his nephews, and one Florentine, son of Lorenzo de' Medici.[3] Thank God! It is a great honour to our city in general, and in particular to his father and his house.

1489. 13th April. We heard that a monster had been born at Venice; its mouth was split up to the nose, and one eye was by the nose and the other behind the ear; the face was cracked all over, as if it had been hacked with a knife, and on the forehead was a horn. It lived three or four days only; for they cut off the horn, and it died directly. They say that the lower parts of its body were very strange, and it had an animal's tail. And another was born at Padua, on Good Friday, that had two heads, and two hands on each arm. This one also lived two or three days; one of the heads died first, and when it was cut off, the other did not live much longer. Besides the above cases, a woman of sixty gave birth to three children at once. All these strange things happened in Venetia within a few days of each other. The letter described the facts exactly as I have set them down, and was sent to the bank of Tanai de' Nerli. I copied it, and the facts are true. Such signs signify great trouble in the city where they take place.

[1] Isabella d'Aragona.   [2] Giangaleazzo Sforza.
[3] Giovanni de' Medici, who later became Pope Leo X.

10th July. They began to bring gravel to make the foundations of the *Palagio* of Filippo Strozzi, on the side of the *Canto de' Tornaquinci*, which was begun first on this side.

16th July. They began to dig the foundations on this side, and took about 10 *braccia*[1] off the Piazza.[2]

6th August. They began to fill in the foundations, at 10 in the morning (6 a.m.), here and there; and Filippo Strozzi was the first who began to throw down the gravel and chalk, on this side, together with certain medals.

20th August. They finished filling in the foundations on this side, in the *Piazza de' Tornaquinci*. And all this time they were demolishing the houses, a great number of overseers and workmen being employed, so that all the streets round were filled with heaps of stones and rubbish, and with mules and donkeys who were carrying away the rubbish and bringing gravel; making it difficult for anyone to pass along. We shopkeepers were continually annoyed by the dust and the crowds of people who collected to look on, and those who could not pass by with their beasts of burden.

21st July.[3] They began to build the walls upon the aforesaid foundations.

And at this time all the following buildings were erected: The *Osservanza di San Miniato de' Frati di San Francesco*[4]; the sacristy of *Santo Spirito*; the house of Giulio Gondi[5]; and the church of the *Frati di Sant'*

[1] A *braccio* was about 23 inches, so 10 *braccia* was about 19 feet.

[2] The *Piazza de' Tornaquinci*; the Strozzi had permission from the Republic and from the *conserteria* (assembly) of this family to occupy a portion of it. These records relating to the building of the palace are much more copious than those written by its founder and published in the appendix to the *Vita di Filippo Strozzi* (Firenzi, 1851). To show their exactitude they can be compared with those left us by Tribaldo de' Rossi in his *Ricordanze*.

[3] This date is written in the MS. seemingly in mistake for *August*.

[4] The monastery (lately built near San Miniato) of the *Osservanza*, a Franciscan Order, who already had one at Fiesole. [Trans.]

[5] In our days we have just seen this palace completed on its southern side, thanks to the care of its owner. In finishing this work the remains of the house opposite in Via de' Gondi were demolished; this used to be the *Casa della Dogana*, and in still older times the *Casa delle Prestanze*, that Giuliano Gondi bought from the *Arte della Lana* (Guild of Wool) to use in his building, and in it Leonardo da Vinci lived as a boy, a fact which I was the first to prove in July 1872.

Agostino,[1] outside the *Porta a San Gallo*. And Lorenzo de' Medici began a palace at the *Poggio a Caiano*, on his property, where so much has been beautifully ordered, the *Cascine*, etc. Princely things! At Sarrezana a fortress was built; and many other houses were erected in Florence: in the street which goes to Santa Caterina, and towards the *Porta a Pinti*, and the *Via Nuova de' Servi*, at Cestello,[2] and from the *Porta a Faenza*[3] towards San Barnaba, and towards Sant' Ambrogio, and elsewhere. Men were crazy about building at this time, so that there was a scarcity of master-builders and of materials.[4]

1490. 18th May. On the Palagio degli Strozzi they now placed the first cornice, below the *bozzi* (rough projecting stones), at the *Canto de' Tornaquinci*, always beginning at this corner before the others.

2nd June. They set up the crane for raising the stones, always at the *Canto*.

11th June. They placed the first *bozzo* (rough block of stone) on the said *palagio*.

27th June. I, Luca Landucci, opened my new shop, here opposite the said *palagio* of the Strozzi, and I chose the sign of the *Stelle* (Stars). The old shop at the other corner, which I left, belongs to the Rucellai, whilst this one belongs to the Popoleschi.

21st September. In *Santa Maria del Fiore* a stone half as big as a mule's pack fell from one of the round windows high up under the cupola, towards the sacristy where the priests robe themselves; it fell just at the side of the choir. It happened at the hour when the priests robe themselves

---

[1] *Chiesa di Sant' Agostino*. In the siege of 1529 it was demolished, together with the convent which was united to it. They occupied almost the same area as the *parterre* and oratory of the *Madonna delle Tosse*. The monks were moved into the city, where they were given the church of *S. Jacopo tra' Fossi*.

[2] *Cestello* was at that time the name of the present convent of *S. Maria Maddalena* in Borgo Pinti, which belonged to the Cistercians. In 1628 they exchanged it for that of the nuns of *S. Maria degli Angeli* of Borgo S. Frediano, still called *S. Maria Maddalena de' Pazzi*.

[3] See note to 8th June, 1481.

[4] In May 1489 the *Signoria*, desirous of providing for the beauty of the city, and for the wants and convenience of those who might wish to inhabit it, granted an exemption for forty years from any tax for those new houses which should be built within five years "in places where there was no house or any beginning of one." In March 1494 this term was prolonged to the end of the year 1497.

to say vespers, but although the church was already full of people, it hurt no one, which was a marvellous thing. God was pleased to be gracious.

19th October. The bronze dragon was placed on the Palazzo Strozzi.[1]

22nd December. The chapel, that is, the *Capella Maggiore*, of *Santa Maria Novella* was opened. Domenico del Grillandaio had painted it, at the order of Giovanni Tornabuoni. And the choir of carved wood was also made round the chapel. The painting alone cost 1000 gold florins.

10th January. The Arno froze entirely, so that *"palla"*[2] was played upon it, and bonfires were made; the cold was great.

17th January. This night there began, and continued until the 18th, a certain fine rain, which froze whilst it fell, and made icicles upon the trees. There was such a quantity of it, that the weight bowed the trees down to the ground and broke the branches. Note, by the way, that this was on the hills. For about half a mile near the river it did no injury. It began at Fiesole, and extended to the Mugello; and at San Godenzo and Dicomano it did much harm. On my land at Dicomano it tore from the roots several chestnut-trees and oak-trees, and broke nearly all the branches of the olive-trees and every other kind of wood, so that at one of my farms the branches alone made twenty piles of wood; and some of the broken limbs of the chestnuts were more than two feet thick, such as was never seen before. Those who chanced to be in the woods, thought the world was coming to an end, when they heard everything cracking, and the deafening noise overhead. There was such a heap of grass that it weighed several pounds; and the stubble of the corn in the fields looked like organ-pipes. The stacks appeared to be roofed with glass, and it was too dangerous for anyone to walk in the country. The farms were ruined for many years, the fruit-trees not bearing fruit, the olives remaining like suckers, and the oak-trees being all spoilt. It was incredible, but true.

[1] To understand and correct where necessary these notices, it will perhaps be a help to refer to the above-mentioned *Tribaldo de' Rossi*: "20th October, 1490, I record that at the palace which Filippo Strozzi is having built, the builders put up the *campanella* at the corner which is opposite the Loggia de' Tornaquinci, that is to say— the *campanella del Serpente*. . . ."

[2] Here equivalent probably to a kind of tennis.

The Arno rose very high, and ruined the mill of the Ponte a Rubiconte, next to Santa Maria delle Grazie, and a porter was drowned there. This mill was a spinning-mill. The river overflowed its banks in several places.

1491. 1st May. The coinage was changed: that is, silver coins began to be used; and it was decided that the *grossone* should be worth 16 *quattrini* and a half, like the old silver ones. All the taxes were to be paid in silver, which meant a little increase to the people, as a quarter more had to be paid, when there was need, on the contrary, to relieve them. This increase was made by divine permission, on account of our sins; because the poor are generally worse than the rich and great. Praise be to God!

This same day they began a causeway between the Loggia de' Signori and the Palagio, so high that one could walk on a level from the door of the Palagio into the Loggia; with steps leading towards San Piero Scheraggio [1] and towards the Piazza, so that neither horses nor any other animals could pass there any longer. It was also rather inconvenient for people, having to go up and down again. Some persons liked this causeway, and others not; I myself did not care for it much.

15th May. That Filippo who was building the abovementioned palace died; and he did not see it carried up even as far as the lanterns. He only saw it carried up to the *campanelle*.[2] One sees how vain are the hopes of transitory things! It appears as if we were master of them, but in reality it is the other way about; they are master of us.

[1] This church was one of the oldest in Florence; it was in the form of a basilica, its interior somewhat resembling San Miniato al Monte. Many political meetings were held in it. The Florentines hung the "Caroccio" of Fiesole on the marble façade (afterwards copied in marble, but destroyed with the rest of the church); and tradition says that the ancient marble pulpit or ambone was also from Fiesole. This pulpit, when the church was suppressed, was given to the little church of San Leonardo in Arcetri, which was connected with San Piero Scheraggio, and it can still be seen there. The north wing of San Piero was demolished first, to widen the street between it and the Palazzo Vecchio (this street is named after the Capella delle Ninne), and the south wing was also closed, the central aisle being still used for service till the year 1560 when the church, chapter-house and loggia were all demolished to make place for the Uffizi. [Trans.]

[2] *Campanelle* are the large iron rings on the walls of the palaces to which horses and other beasts of burden were attached, and which often had sockets above, intended for flags, those at the corners being specially ornamented. [Trans.]

This palace will last almost eternally: has not this palace mastered him then? And how many others! We are not masters, but only dispensers, in so far as it pleases the goodness of God. All lies in God's hands, and happens as is meet for His universe. Therefore I pray that God may pardon Filippo Strozzi his sins.

7th September. They finished making the arch of the gate of this palace, on this side, *tra' Ferravecchi*.[1]

5th January. The Spaniards quartered here in Florence made great rejoicings and lighted bonfires, because they heard that their king had conquered the whole of Granada, and had driven out all the Moors who were there. This was not only a beneficial and glorious thing for Spain, but also a beneficial and glorious thing for us and for all Christians, and for the Holy Church. Good and faithful people considered it a great acquisition for the faith of Christ, and the first step towards winning the Levant and Jerusalem from the Unbelievers.

10th March. Lorenzo's son, the cardinal, received the hat from the Pope.[2] It was given him at the Badìa on the way to Fiesole (i.e. at San Domenico), and many citizens went out to meet him when he came into Florence to visit the *Signoria*; and the next day he went to hear mass in *Santa Maria del Fiore*. And on this day the *Signoria* presented him with 30 loads of gifts carried by porters, being silver plate, and basins, and ewers, and dishes, and all the silver utensils that can possibly be used by a great lord. According to what was said, they were estimated at more than 20 thousand florins, although that seems impossible to me; but it was public report, and therefore I set it down. It was certainly a rich and magnificent gift. Praise be to God!

12th March. The said cardinal went to Rome, to visit the Pope.

1492. 1st April. The front of the Palagio degli Strozzi was begun.

5th April. At about 3 at night (11 p.m.) the lantern of the cupola of *Santa Maria del Fiore* was struck by a thunderbolt and it was split almost in half; that is, one of

---

[1] The *Via tra' Ferravecchi* was the old name of the street now called *Via Strozzi*. [Trans.]

[2] When he had been made cardinal in 1488 he had not received the insignia, being only thirteen years old.

the marble niches and many other pieces of marble on the side towards the door leading to the *Servi*,[1] were taken off in a miraculous way; none of us had ever in our lives seen lightning have such an effect before. If it had happened at the time when the sermon was being preached (for a sermon is preached every morning now, with 15 thousand people listening), it must of necessity have killed hundreds of persons. But the Lord did not permit it. This marble niche fell and struck the roof of the church between the two doors which lead to the *Servi*, and broke the roof and the vaulting in five places, finally fixing itself in the brick floor of the church. And many bricks and much other material from the vaulting fell also, reaching as far as the benches placed for the sermon, where many people would have been sitting. Some material fell in the choir as well, but not very much. Many pieces of marble fell outside the building, beyond the door leading to the *Servi*; one piece falling on the stepping-stones in the street, and after having split the stone, burying itself underground; another piece was hurled across the street, and struck the roof of the house opposite the said door, where it split the roof and many beams and vaultings, and finally buried itself in the ground under the cellar. Although the house was full of people, no one was injured. A man called Luca Ranieri lived there. You may imagine that they nearly died of amazement and terror at the fearful noise; for besides that which fell into the cellar, many pieces fell on the roofs all round. The gallery on the cupola was also injured.[2]

And observe that this great niche fell inside the church, and made a large hole in the pavement; but did not spoil anything, not even the worth of a *grosso*. It was considered a great marvel, and significative of some extraordinary event, especially as it had happened suddenly, when the weather was calm, and the sky without a cloud.

8th April. Lorenzo de' Medici died on his estate at Careggi; and it was said that when he heard the news of the effects of the thunderbolt, being so ill, he asked where

[1] See note to 26th April, 1478.
[2] In the Maruccellian Code we read on the margin this note: "The following fact happened in the year . . . that the same church was struck by lightning, with a similar effect, and a block of marble was detached and remained resting on certain beams, which would have killed many if it had fallen; and Messer Vincenzio, the sculptor, was there."

it had fallen, and on which side; and when he was told, he said: "Alas! I shall die, because it fell towards my house." This may not have been so, but it was commonly reported.

And they brought him to Florence the same night, at 5 in the morning (1 a.m.), and put him in the monastery at *San Marco*; and he remained there the whole of the next day, which was a Monday. And on the 10th April, Tuesday, he was buried at San Lorenzo at about 20 in the evening (4 p.m.). Well may we consider what a transitory thing is human life! This man, in the eyes of the world, was the most illustrious, the richest, the most stately, and the most renowned among men. Everyone declared that he ruled Italy; and in very truth he was possessed of great wisdom, and all his undertakings prospered. He had succeeded in doing what no citizen had been able to do for a long time: namely, in getting his son appointed cardinal; which was not only an honour for his house, but for the whole city. In spite of all this, however, he could not live one hour longer when the end came. Then, O man, man, what hast thou to be proud of? True humility is the fit human attribute, and each time that we grow proud, and esteem ourselves above others, failing to recognise that every spiritual, corporal and temporal good comes from God, we exceed the proper limits of humanity. Everything that exceeds its limits is evil, and those things which should be good, turn to ill. The desirable quality for man is true gentleness and humility, and always to esteem God. Man is naught, if not what God has made him; to whom be praise from all creatures, as is His due. May He pardon me my sins! And may He pardon the sins of the dead man, as I trust He may pardon me and all human beings!

20th May. A Sunday; the Cardinal de' Medici returned to Florence.

26th July. A Thursday; Pope Innocent VIII. died; and on Sunday, the 29th, the bells were tolled for his death.

6th August. There was a furious storm, the air seeming for some time to be full of bursting fireworks, so incessant was the thunder and lightning. When the storm was over, about eight different places were counted which bore visible traces of having been struck. One was the Campanile of Santa Croce; another the Porta di San Gallo; another the Porta al Prato; another the Porta a Pinti, etc. But it did not cause much damage, and no one was killed.

11th August. At 23 in the evening (7 p.m.) we heard that the new Pope had been chosen. He was a cardinal, and the vice-chancellor; a Spaniard by birth. He called himself Pope Alessandro VI.

12th August. We received confirmation of this news at about the *Nona* (11.30 a.m.), and the bells were rung for his election.

17th November. We sent ambassadors to Rome to visit the Pope. They were Piero son of Lorenzo de' Medici, the Bishop of Arezzo, Pier Filippo Pandolfini, Francesco Valori, and Tommaso Minerbetti. They went in fine array, especially Piero de' Medici.

20th December. This Tommaso Minerbetti returned, having been knighted by the Pope.

1493. 17th August. It happened that a certain unbeliever, to spite the Christians, but mostly out of folly, went about Florence disfiguring the images of Our Lady, and amongst others, that which is on the pilaster of Orto San Michele, outside. He scratched the eyes of the Child, and of San Nofri (Onophrius), and threw mud in the face of Our Lady.[1] On this account, the boys began to throw stones at him, and they were joined by grown men, who in their fury stoned him to death with great stones, and then dragged his body about with much vituperation.

20th September. We heard that the Pope had made some new cardinals.

20th January. The Day of San Bastiano (St. Sebastian); there was the severest snowstorm in Florence that the oldest people living could remember. And amongst other extraordinary things, it was accompanied by such a violent wind that for the whole day it was impossible to open the shops, or the doors and windows. It lasted from the *Ave Maria* one morning till the *Ave Maria* the next morning,

---

[1] This statue of the Virgin is by Mina da Fiesole, who made it for the Doctors and Apothecaries' Guild, whose arms were the Virgin and Child in an archway. After this act of desecration it was removed to the interior of the church for a time, and then placed outside again, when it obtained the reputation of working so many miracles that great crowds used to gather in front of it, till it was taken back into the interior of the church in the time of Cosimo I. Now, in the year 1926, it has once more been placed outside, in a niche on the south side. Formerly it used to stand in the niche now occupied by the copy of Donatello's San Giorgio, and therefore next to the group of Four Saints, one of whom is Saint Onophrius. [Trans.]

twenty-four hours, without ceasing for a minute, and without the wind abating, so that there was not the slightest crack or a hole, however small, that did not let a heap of snow into the house. In fact there was not a house so hermetically sealed as not to become so full of snow that it took several days to clear it out. All along the streets one saw heaps of snow, so that in many places neither men nor beasts could pass. There was such a quantity that it took a long time to melt away, as sometimes when boys make a snow-lion. In fact, these mountains lasted a week. It is difficult to believe without having seen it. And the same thing happened in my villa at Dicomano. I sent Benedetto to clear the house, and he found as much snow inside as if it had been roofless; and this was after a week. So it was everywhere alike.

29th January. We heard that the King of Naples was dead. Some said that he had died of despondency, because he was continually hearing that the King of France was on his way.

10th March. A man threw himself from the windows of the *Casa del Capitano*, to escape from prison, and was killed.

1494. 26th April. Lorenzo and Giovanni, sons of Piero Francesco de' Medici, were detained in the Palagio; and it was said that some wished them to be put to death, but the reason was not given. On the 29th they were liberated; and on the 14th May they went away, being restricted within certain boundaries.[1]

4th May. Four French ambassadors entered Florence.

[1] Florentine historians give as the motive of such provisions a dissension between these Medici and Piero, but disagree as to its causes. Contemporary writers, however, point to their too close adherence to the King of France. I hoped to throw some light upon this matter from the documents, but a deliberation of the *Signori* and *Collegi* of the 29th April, 1494, by which they are condemned for life to remain a mile outside the city, only has these words: *justis causis, ut dixerunt moti, et ad Statum multum pertinentibus*, etc. And another, of the 9th November, which permits them to return, begins thus: *Attenta humanitate et bonis moribus Laurentii et Ioannis Pier Francisci de Medicis et qualiter, contra justiciam et omne debitum, et ad instantiam tirannorum, fuerunt relegati*, etc. They actually left the city on the 14th May, as Landucci says, that is, fifteen days after the deliberation, as it had been decreed; and on the day following, the proof of their presence beyond the boundary fixed was produced, they having gone to inhabit the villa of Castello (*Libro di deliberazioni ad annum* of the *Signori e Collegi*, in the State Archives of Florence).

They were lodged in the house which formerly belonged to Messer Jacopo de' Pazzi.

5th May. They went to the *Signoria*, and having set forth the matters entrusted to them, received a reply. On the 7th they left, and went to Rome.[1]

19th May. Our Lady of *Santa Maria Impruneta* was brought into the city, in hopes that the rain might cease: and our prayers were granted.[2]

10th June. The Arno overflowed its banks, and many cornfields were inundated, much damage being caused both above and below Florence. It was the worst flood within anyone's recollection, and began in the evening. The corn, which was almost ripe, suffered greatly.

10th July. The French ambassadors returned from Rome; one of them remaining in Florence.

In these days the fleet of the King of Naples came to the Port of Pisa, and besieged Spezia and Porto Venere.

22nd July. We sent ambassadors to Venice; they were: Pagoloantonio Soderini [3] and Giovan Battista Ridolfi.

5th August. Piero de' Medici went to meet the Duke of Calabria, in the neighbourhood of Arezzo, to visit him, as one visits a great gentleman, a lord. The French ambassadors who were in Florence, having asked for their safeconduct, and not receiving it at once, when they knew of this journey of Piero's began to suspect us of not being friendly to their king; at least this was said in the city, and it was said that the king threatened the Florentines. It was difficult to persuade them that we were faithful friends, and that their suspicions were without foundation. All this, however, I only heard by report.

In these days the fleet of the King of France arrived at Genoa, and there was much talk of an encounter.

11th September. The fleet of the King of Naples was defeated at Rapallo by that of the King of France and the Genoese; not in an encounter, but the Neapolitan fleet rashly landed 3 thousand soldiers, thinking to take Rapallo; and in the end they were cut off by the Genoese and the

---

[1] During their sojourn in Florence they were served with the silver plate of the *Signoria*; and to do them honour, the musicians of the *Signoria* were sent to play before them.

[2] It was decreed on the 13th of the same month that this image should be brought, and on the 14th some of the *Collegi* were chosen and charged with making suitable arrangements.

[3] He was recalled on the 9th November.

king, and could not return to their ships. They fled towards the mountains, and were all killed or taken prisoner; the fleet of the King of Naples being disarmed and destroyed.

21st September. We heard that the King of France had entered Genoa, and that the Genoese were preparing to receive him with great honour, having decorated the whole city, and even taken down the gates and laid them on the ground, to show more splendour and to ensure the king's safety. But it was not true that the king was going there, although they expected him and had made all these preparations. It was said that he felt distrustful of the citizens.

4th October. More ambassadors from the King of France came to Florence, and going to the *Signoria*, could not obtain a decisive answer but only a vague one; so that on the 9th they both left Florence in indignation, and returned to the king without a safe-conduct. It was then said that the king swore to let his soldiers pillage Florence; and everyone thought that it had been a piece of folly and rashness not to give the safe-conduct readily.

23rd October. We heard that the Duke of Calabria was dead, having died a natural death at Naples, possibly from despondency. It was extraordinary that father and son should have died within such a short interval, just when their country was in so much danger. Truly the fullness of time had come, and the hand of God struck. These things make us lay aside our pride, and take refuge in faith, when we consider that it will be the same for us all. *Messer Francesco* (Ah, you Frenchmen!), what is the use of subjugating other countries? May God pardon us our sins!

26th October. Piero de' Medici left here to go on the way to Pisa, to meet the King of France; and when he reached the king, he caused the keys of Serezzano and of Pietrasanta to be given him, and also made him promises of money. The king wishing to know whether in truth he had been given this commission, sent Lorenzo, son of Giovanni Tornabuoni, who had gone with Piero de' Medici, back to Florence, to get it confirmed by the *Signoria*; but they refused to confirm it. Lorenzo, in some consternation, did not return to the French camp, and Piero was rather at fault. He acted like a young fellow, and perhaps with good results, since we remained friends with the king, thank God!

29th October. The French took Fiovizzano by assault and sacked it.

4th November. A proclamation was published by the *Signoria*, obliging everyone to give lodging to the French; and assuring them that nothing would be touched or taken away.[1] Most people were not pleased, because the *Signoria* showed more fear than was needful; they might have waited till any trouble began, although it was unpleasant for us. But God never removed His hand from off our head, because He heard the tears, and sighs, and prayers of His servants, who walk in truth, and who pray to Him all the day long that He should be merciful to the good and upright of heart, and to those who love the honour and glory of God above all things, praising Him in adversity as in prosperity, and desire nothing but to fulfil His will.

5th November. Certain messengers of the King of France arrived and went about Florence marking the houses which they preferred. They came indoors and entered all the rooms, marking one for such and such a lord, and another for such and such a baron.

And observe that there were not hundreds but thousands of the French, so that the whole city was occupied in every corner; for those houses that were not marked were occupied in a moment when the men-at-arms and the infantry arrived, going into every street, and saying: *Apri qua!* (Open there!) and not caring whether the owners were rich or poor. They gave it to be understood that they meant to pay: but there were not many who paid. And when they did pay a certain amount, *they paid for the horns and ate the ox* (Italian proverb): "They didn't pay anything like what they cost." Few of us had sent away our womenkind, except the young girls, who were sent to convents and to relatives where no soldiers were quartered; but the French were really very well-behaved, for there was not a single one who said an unsuitable word to a woman. In their hearts they felt a secret dread, and kept asking how many men Florence could dispose of; and they were told that at the sound of a bell the city would have 100 thousand men from within and without at her command. The truth was this: that they had come with the

[1] I find that on the 11th November the *Signori e Collegi* decreed: *Quod nullus audeat resistere aperire et reservare domum suam quin gentes Regis Francorum possint capere lodiamenta et habere recepium. Significando cuilibet persone quod nulli erit facta aliqua iniuria.*

idea of sacking Florence, as their king had promised them; but they could not see the game begun, much less won. And all this was the doing of the Almighty.

On this same day, five ambassadors were chosen to go to the King of France, who was at Pisa. They were as follows: First, Fra Girolamo, a preacher of the Order of San Domenico, dwelling at San Marco, a native of Ferrara; whom we believe to be a prophet, and he does not deny it in his sermons, but always says *da parte del Signore* (I have it from the Lord . . .), and he preaches on important subjects. The second, Tanai de' Nerli; the third, Pandolfo Rucellai; the fourth, Giovanni Cavalcanti; and the fifth, Piero Soderini; all Florentine citizens. And they left the next day.

On the same day a number of French arrived, who were the vanguard of the king, and lodged in the houses assigned to them, which were marked with chalk.

This evening at about 2 o'clock (10 p.m.) a few strokes of the bell were heard from the *Palagio*; and immediately the Piazza was full of men, it being thought that a *parlamento* was going to be summoned, for everyone was excited and distrustful, continually expecting great events.

8th November. Piero de' Medici returned to Florence, coming from the King of France, who was at Pisa; and when he reached his house, he threw out *confetti* (sweetmeats), and gave a lot of wine to the people, to make himself popular; declaring that he had settled everything satisfactorily with the king, and appearing to be in the best of humours.

This same day, the *Signori* published a proclamation that as long as the king should stay in Florence there would be no tax on firewood or on any kind of food; and only the half of the usual tax on wine; also that anyone might sell and provide meals.[1]

9th November (Sunday). About 20 in the afternoon (4 p.m.), when it was ringing for vespers,[2] Piero son of

[1] This proclamation is really of the 6th November, and the exemptions and diminutions of the tax conceded by it are a little different from those quoted here: the duration of these was from the 9th to the 20th, and on the latter date they were prorogued for the whole month. This was done "in order that there should be abundance of victuals in the city both for its inhabitants and the foreigners, and to help the poor people."

[2] Vespers was at five o'clock in November. [Trans.]

Lorenzo de' Medici wished to go to the *Signoria* in the
Palagio, taking his armed men with him. The *Signoria*
not allowing this, he did not choose to go alone, and turned
back.[1] Now men began to collect in the Piazza, and in the
Palagio were heard cries of *Popolo e Libertà!* (The People
and Liberty!), whilst the bell was rung for a *parlamento*,
and men appeared at the windows with the same cry.
Immediately the *Gonfaloniere del Bue*[2] came into the
Piazza, and behind him Francesco Valori and other citizens
on horseback, all crying *Popolo e Libertà!* These were the
first to arrive; but before an hour had passed, the Piazza
was filled with all the *Gonfaloni* and all the citizens, troops
of armed men crying loudly, *Popolo e Libertà!* Although
the people did not very well understand what all this
tumult was about, nevertheless not many citizens went to
Piero de' Medici's house. The Tornabuoni and some other
citizens went there armed, with many men under their
command, and coming into the street before his door,
cried, *Palle!* Piero then mounted his horse, to come into
the Piazza with his men, starting several times, and then
stopping again. I think that he perceived how few citizens
were with him, and also he must have been told that the
Piazza was full of armed men. Meanwhile the cardinal,
his brother, left his house, accompanied by many soldiers
and by those citizens who were there, and came down the
Corso as far as *Orto San Michele*, crying *Popolo e Libertà!*
like the rest; declaring that he separated himself from
Piero. The only consequence was that the Piazza turned
against him, menacing him with the points of their weapons,
shouting at him as a traitor, and not choosing to accept
him. He turned back, not without danger. And now a
proclamation was issued, at the *Canto della Macina*[3] and in
the *Via de' Martegli*[4] next to the *Chiassolino* (little alley),
ordering every foreigner to lay down his arms, and forbidding anyone on pain of death to aid or abet Piero de'
Medici. In consequence of this, many abandoned Piero and

[1] In the book already quoted of the *Deliberazioni dei Signori e Collegi*, the second entry of this date is the order that Piero must appear within an hour of the notification.
[2] The "Banner of the Bull" was that of the Borgias.
[3] The *Canto della Macina* is where Via Ginori meets Via Guelfa. [Trans.]
[4] The *Via de' Martegli* is the Via Martelli, between the Piazza del Duomo and Via Cavour. [Trans.]

laid down their arms. They dropped off on all sides, so that few remained with him. Therefore Piero left his house and went towards the *Porta a San Gallo*, which he had caused to be kept open for him by his brother Giuliano with many soldiers and by friends outside. Signor Pagolo Orsini was waiting outside with horses and armed men in readiness to enter, but it did not seem the right moment, and when Piero arrived they decided it would be best to go away, taking Giuliano with them. The poor young cardinal remained in his house, and I saw him at a window kneeling with joined hands, praying Heaven to have mercy. I was much touched when I saw him, considering him to be a good lad and of upright character. It was said that when he had seen Piero ride away, he disguised himself as a monk and took his departure also. Another proclamation was published in the Piazza, announcing that whoever slew Piero de' Medici should have 2 thousand ducats and whoever slew the cardinal should have a thousand. And after this many soldiers left the Piazza with Jacopo de' Nerli, and going to the house of Ser Giovanni son of Ser Bartolomeo,[1] pillaged it. And then the crowd rose, with the cry of *Antonio di Bernardo*,[1] and pillaged his house also, and pillaged the *Bargello*. The number of soldiers and of the people going about robbing increased every moment; and this all happened before 24 in the evening (8 p.m.), less than four hours from when the disturbance began. Then the *Signoria* published a proclamation forbidding any more houses to be pillaged, on pain of death; and the *Gonfaloni* went about the city all night to guard it, crying *Popolo e Libertà*, carrying lighted torches, so that no more harm was done, except that a certain serving-man of the *Bargello* who cried *Palle*, was killed in the Piazza. And now Girolamo son of Marabotto Tornabuoni, and Pierantonio Carnesecchi, and others of that party, turned and cried *Popolo e Libertà* like the rest. When they were about to enter the Piazza, however, weapons were pointed against them, and they were only saved by their cuirasses, and had to escape as best they might. In fact, Girolamo Tornabuoni had his cuirass torn off in Orto Sa' Michele, but when he begged for mercy, his life was spared. And Giovan Francesco Tornabuoni was severely wounded in the throat, and returned home. When the disturbance began, some of the

---
[1] See note to 10th November.

French who were quartered in Florence armed themselves and joined Piero's party, crying *Francia*. I believe that it was pointed out to them that the matter was between citizens only, and that if they were to do anything against the *Palagio*, they would put themselves in the wrong; therefore they acted accordingly, returning to their lodgings and then going about the city unarmed.[1]

10th November (Monday). The citizens again came armed into the Piazza, and sent to recruit more men. Antonio di Bernardo, Ser Giovanni son of Ser Bartolomeo, Ser Simone da Staggia, Ser Ceccone son of Ser Barone, Ser Lorenzo of the Dogana, Lorenzo son of Giovanni Tornabuoni, and Piero Tornabuoni, were fetched from their houses and made prisoner. The *Signoria* published a proclamation commanding anyone who either had, or knew of anyone who had, property belonging to Piero de' Medici or to the cardinal his brother, or to Ser Giovanni, Ser Simone, Ser Bernardo, and Ser Lorenzo of the Dogana,[2] to declare it, on pain of death. And a second proclamation was published, which had been decided upon by the council composed of all the *veduti e seduti*[3] There were an immense number of citizens present. And this morning they pillaged the cardinal's house, which was in Sant'

[1] The confusion of this day must have been great, and something of it appears even in our Luca when he was writing about the various events which happened hour after hour, as he notes some which do not seem to belong to the same date. For instance, with regard to the prices placed upon the heads of the Medici, I find some contradiction in the documents, because the *Signoria*, on the 20th, in two distinct councils, first banished Piero and declared him a rebel, and afterwards offered 2000 florins reward to anyone who delivered him alive into their hands, 1000 to anyone who captured Ser Piero son of Francesco da Bibbiena, his chancellor, and 500 for the capture of Bernardo brother of Ser Piero, another chancellor. He also forgets the order given to liberate the prisoners of the *Stinche*, and the appointment of Francesco Pepi and Braccio Martelli as ambassadors to the King of France.

[2] The documents give the names and positions of these keen supporters of the house of Medici as follows: Antonio son of Bernardo son of Miniato Dini, purveyor of the *Monte Comune*; Ser Giovanni son of Ser Bartolomeo of Pratovecchio, notary of *Riformagioni* (a magistracy whose office it was to keep a register of the decrees, etc.); Ser Simone Grazzini of Staggia, notary of the *Tratte* (election ballot); and Ser Lorenzo son of Antonio Tucci, alias of the *Dogana* (Customs).

[3] Those citizens who had filled one of the higher offices, and those who had been next in order to those elected. [Trans.]

Antonio [1] di Firenze, sending their men to claim the last things that still remained.

11th November (Tuesday). A man arrived in the Piazza, having entered the city by the *Porta alla Croce*, and said that he had passed men-at-arms and infantry on the road to Florence, belonging to Piero de' Medici. Cries of *Popolo e Libertà* immediately resounded everywhere, and in less than half an hour the whole city was in arms, men of all classes rushing to the Piazza with incredible haste, and with deafening cries of *Popolo e Libertà*. I verily believe that if the whole world had come against them, such a union could not have been broken; it being permitted by the Lord that the people should make such a demonstration, during this danger from the French, who had come to Florence with the evil intent of sacking it. But when they saw of what sort the people were, their heart failed them. As soon as the truth was known, that no armed men were approaching, a proclamation was made ordering all to lay aside their weapons, and this was about the dinner-hour. The *Gonfaloni*, however, remained on guard day and night, with a good number of men; and horsemen and foot-soldiers belonging to the King of France were continually entering. The *Signoria* had had the Porta di San Friano [2] opened. This evening the King of France remained at Empoli; and more than 6 thousand men came before the king, and as many with him, and another 6 thousand behind him. And at this time the taxes were lightened and many pardons granted.[3]

12th November (Wednesday). Lorenzo son of Piero Francesco de' Medici returned, and dined at his own house of the Gora, and the same evening he went to meet the king, who was stopping at Legniaia, in the house of Piero Capponi. And on this same day the *Bargello* was made

---

[1] *Sant' Antonio di Vienna* was in the Via Faenza, and was founded in the year 1358. There was a beautiful church and a large convent, with three large cloisters and extensive gardens. The canons were called *Frati del Fuoco*, and *Frati del T.* that being their arms. The church and convent were both destroyed when the *Fortezza di Basso* was built; but the canons built a new church near.

[2] The Gate of San Frediano, towards Empoli. [Trans.]

[3] I here add, that the office of the *Otto di Pratica* (the Eight Councillors), the *Consiglio del Settanta* (Council of the Seventy), and that of the *Hundred*, all institutions of the Medici and of their adherents, were done away with and annulled.

prisoner in the church of the *Servi*.¹ Also more French entered the city than any other day, and they filled every house, even the poorest, including all Camaldoli.

13th November (Thursday). We heard that the Pisans had risen and taken possession of the city; and pulling down a certain marble *marzocco*, had dragged it all over Pisa, and then thrown it into the Arno, crying, "*Libertà!*" We also heard that Piero and his brothers were at Bologna; and such a crowd of French and Swiss were coming into Florence, that there was great confusion and alarm and suspicion amongst all classes. You may think what it was to have all this crowd in our houses, and everything left as usual, with the women about, and to have to serve them with whatever they needed, at the greatest inconvenience.

14th November (Friday). Lorenzo son of Francesco de' Medici and his brother, and several other exiled citizens, returned to Florence, because the sentences were remitted of all those who had been exiled from 1434 onwards. Observe that Lorenzo de' Medici and his brother were also reinstated in their rights. And every house in the city was full.

15th November (Saturday). Numbers of French were still coming in; and preparations were made to receive the king with great honour.²

16th November (Sunday). Many decorations were made for the king's arrival in the house of Piero de' Medici, and principally at the entrance of the palace. Two large columns were erected outside, one on each side of the gate, with ornamentation representing the arms of France, etc., too intricate to describe. It truly was a triumph; everything was done so well and on such a grand scale. I will not even begin to tell you how the interior was ordered. And *spiritegli*³ and giants and triumphal cars went about the town, and stages on wheels for the miracle-play of the *Nunziata*, whilst there were innumerable embellishments

---

¹ His name was Piero Antonio dall' Aquila. The day before, a reward had been promised to anyone who would give information as to where he was hidden; and on the 14th the Priors decreed *quod dono tradatur* to the Signor Giovanni da Maddaloni, *oratore* (representative) of the King of France, who would receive him in the king's name.

² Already on the 11th the *Signoria* had ordered that all the citizens, on the king's arrival, should go towards the *Porta San Frediano*, in as fine array as they could muster, to do him honour.

³ See note to 5th July, 1478.

F

and the arms of France all over Florence. Above the gate of the *Palagio de' Signori* were the said arms, very large and magnificently blazoned.

17th November. The King of France entered Florence at 22 in the evening (6 p.m.) by the Porta a San Friano, and passed through the Piazza (de' Signori), proceeding so slowly that it was already 24 (8 p.m.) before he reached Santa Maria del Fiore. He dismounted at the steps, and walked up to the High Altar, there being so many torches that they made a double row from the door to the altar, leaving a way clear in the middle, along which he went with his barons and all his suite, amidst such tumultuous shouting of *Viva Francia* as was never heard. Only think that all Florence was there, either in the church or outside. Everyone shouted, great and small, old and young, and all from their hearts, without flattery. When he was seen on foot he seemed to the people somewhat less imposing, for he was in fact a very small man. Nevertheless there was no one who did not feel favourably disposed towards him. Therefore it should have been easy to make him understand that our hearts are innocent of guile, and that we are truly devoted to him; so that he ought to feel moved towards us in uncommon measure, and to trust us absolutely. This is really the case, and he will see in the future what the faith of the Florentines signifies. Upon coming out of church, he remounted his horse and rode on to the palace of Piero de' Medici, amidst continued cries of *Viva Francia*. Never was such joy seen before, or so much honour done to anyone, with heartfelt sincerity, as we were in hopes that he would bring us peace and rest. In the end it proved not to be so, as he took Pisa from us and gave it to the Pisans, which he had no right to do, seeing that he could not give what was not his.[1]

18th November (Tuesday). The said king went to hear mass in Sa' Lorenzo, and I was at the same mass, and saw him quite close.

19th November. He again heard mass in Sa' Lorenzo;

[1] On the same day the *Signoria* itself decreed that as long as the king remained in Florence each householder should keep a light burning every night in a window looking on to the street, from eight o'clock in the evening till one o'clock in the morning. And there was also a debate whether the keys of the *Porte a San Frediano*, *San Gallo*, and *San Piero Gattolino* (now *Porta Romana*) should be given to him.

and then went for a ride through Florence, going to see the lions.[1] And it was his wish that some of the prisoners in the *Palagio del Capitano* should be liberated, those namely who were detained for political reasons; amongst them a Ser Lorenzo, and an Andrea, and others; and this desire of his to benefit the prisoners on the occasion of his passing through the town was granted.

20th November (Thursday). There were murmurs all over the city to the effect that the king wished to reinstate Piero de' Medici, and the ruling citizens seemed much vexed about this matter.

21st November (Friday). About 21 in the evening (5 p.m.) the *Signori* called a council of the most worthy men in the city, and explained to them how the king had said one thing and now wished another, and how he demanded the reinstatement of Piero de' Medici, and asked them what answer they advised to be given him. And they all replied to the effect that Piero's return could not be consented to upon any condition whatever, even if the king wished it; and that the king should be told that everything else but this would be granted him. They declared, moreover, that if it were necessary to take up arms, they should go against the king and everyone who differed from them saying, "If the king has 20 thousand men, we can call up 50 thousand of our own in the city"; showing no fear of the king, and also showing that a great hatred had arisen between the citizens and this Piero de' Medici; why this was, the Lord alone knows. At this time, as it pleased God, there was a little disturbance in the *Piazza de' Signori*, all the people being suspicious, and excited at the least noise, and always on the look-out for some danger. They really lived in dread and a sort of dismay, mostly caused by having their houses full of the French. And it was continually being repeated that the king had promised his soldiers Florence should be sacked. Therefore, as soon as there was this little disturbance in the Piazza, everyone hastened home, and all the shops were closed, one sending his silk goods and another his woollen goods away to his

[1] According to ancient custom, the Republic kept some lions in cages. These cages were behind the *Palazzo del Capitano*, now incorporated in the *Palazzo Vecchio*, whence the piece of street between the *Piazza di S. Firenze* and the *Logge del Grano* is still called *Via de' Leoni*. This custom was discontinued towards the end of the seventeenth century.

house or to some place of security. This suspicion was tacit, not a word being said; but many of the French, no less dismayed than we were, suspecting they knew not what, took up arms, and seized the *Porta a San Friano* and the bridges, so as to be able to escape. Possibly it had been so arranged among themselves beforehand, in case it should be needful. The result was that the *Signoria* and the council who had held the aforesaid consultation, when they heard that all the shops were being closed, felt still more acutely the danger of Piero's return; and the *Signori* urged the most worthy men of the council to go to the king and point out to him the danger of the city, begging him not to demand this thing, as it could only entail evil, etc. Hence the king, seeing the opposition of the citizens, and also realising his own danger, replied: "I am not here to cause disturbances, but to bring peace; and if I thought of this thing, it was only in the idea of pleasing the people and everyone. I wish for nothing but the general good, and no more need be said about Piero's return." Then the citizens made this offer to the king: "Whatever you may be pleased to ask from us freely, we shall be ready to bring to your aid." Thereupon the king asked that the city of Florence should lend him 120 thousand florins, 50 thousand to be paid at once, and 70 thousand before the end of July; and besides this, that for the duration of the war they should lend him 12 thousand a year. After the end of the war, our city should be left entirely free; and whether he died, or whether he conquered or not, it should still be left free. He only demanded the forts of Pisa and a few others that he had taken, Sarzana, etc., so that he should be able to return in safety to his country. He did not receive a reply immediately. Everyone said that a little time was needed, on account of the money.

22nd November (Saturday). The city was in great dread of being pillaged, and it was considered a bad sign that the king did not wish to sign the agreement. The French seemed to be becoming more and more masters of the place; they did not allow the citizens to go about armed, day or night, but took away their weapons, and kept striking and stabbing them. No one ventured to speak or to go out after the *Ave Maria* (at 5 o'clock); and the French went about robbing in the night, their guards parading the city. Everyone was so discouraged and intimidated, that when they saw anyone carrying stones or gravel they went crazy and struck out.

23rd November (Sunday). The king rode out with a great troop of horsemen, and came to the *Croce di San Giovanni*; and when he was near the steps of *Santa Maria del Fiore*, he turned back and went towards the *Servi*; but having gone a few paces, he turned round again, and again went to the *Croce di San Giovanni*,[1] going at the back of *San Giovanni*, through that narrow *Chiassolino*,[2] and coming under the *Volta di San Giovanni, d' Cialdonai*[2]; and those who saw him laughed,[3] and said slighting things of him, causing his reputation to suffer. Then he went through the *Mercato Vecchio*, and on as far as *San Felice in Piazza*, to see the *festa* of San Felice, which they were having on his account; but when he reached the door he would not enter; and they repeated everything several times, but he did not enter once.[4] Many people said that he was afraid, and did not wish to be shut in, and this proved to us that he was more afraid than we were; and woe to him if a disturbance had begun, although there would also have been great danger for us. But the Lord has always helped us, on account of the prayers of His servants and of the number of holy monks and nuns in the city, who are in truth on their way to God. At this time two Venetian ambassadors to the king arrived, and there were also the Genoese ambassadors, who came, it was said, to demand Serezzana and other things from him.

[1] The column with a small cross at the top of it, which was put up to commemorate the miracle of San Zenobi, in the year 341, as stated in the inscription. It was broken down by the flood of 1333 and set up again, which accounts for the inscription not being so old. [Trans.]

[2] This *Chiassolino* (alley) and the *Volta da' Cialdonai* were demolished when the Piazza was enlarged. [Trans.]

[3] The autographic MS. has a gap from page 17 till the 1st December, 1494; therefore I have supplied the missing pages from the MS. copy at the Marucelliana Library (Jodico del Badia).

[4] I copy this fragment from the *Storie* of Jacopo Nardi, who disagrees from what Landucci says here: "His Majesty the King, having rested a few days, was entertained by the representation of some solemn and beautiful *feste*, like that very singular one of the *Virgine Annunziata*, which is represented with ingenious and marvellous skill in the Church of *San Felice in Piazza*, and which pleased and delighted him so much, that having seen it once publicly, he wished to see it again incognito and privately." Our author also mentions this *edificio* (representation) of the Annunciation on 16th November, 1494. In Vasari's Life of Brunelleschi this is finely described.

24th November (Monday). There was much whispering amongst the people, who said suspiciously: "This king doesn't know what he wishes; he has not yet signed the agreement." And many declared that some of his counsellors were endeavouring to hinder it, as there was a certain Signore di Bre,[1] lodging in the house of Giovanni Tornabuoni, who said that he had promised some people to get Piero reinstated, and to persuade the king to ask for this, but perhaps it was not true. This was, as I say, the opinion of many of the citizens, and therefore they were in great dread; still more so when it was said that the king was going this morning to dine in the *Palagio* with the *Signoria*, and that he had caused all the armed men to be removed from the *Palagio*, and he was going there with many armed men, so that everyone suspected him of evil designs. There was no one who did not take pains this morning to fill his house with bread and with weapons and with stones, and to strengthen his house as much as possible, everyone being of the mind and intention to die fighting, and to slay anyone if needful, in the manner of the Sicilian Vespers. And fear was so widespread[2] that when at the dinner hour people began to say *Serra, serra!* (Shut everything!), it came about that the whole of Florence locked itself in, one fleeing here and another there, without any fresh cause or disturbance, the consequence being that many of the French rushed to the *Porta a San Friano* and took possession of the *Ponte alla Carraia*. And in *Borgo Ognissanti* and in *Via Palazzuolo*, and in *Borgo San Friano*, so many stones were thrown from the windows that they were not able to get to the gates; and when they asked the reason of it, no one knew. Therefore the king did not go to dine in the *Palagio*; and, by divine permission, the French became so uneasy that it caused them to change their evil intentions towards us who only had good ones. Anyone can see that God does not abandon Florence, but we are not sufficiently grateful. At this time we heard that the French troops which had been in Romagna were passing by in the neighbourhood of Dicomano.

[1] Some Florentine historians call him di Bles, and it was Philippe de Bresse, afterwards Duke of Savoy.

[2] The greatest confusion seems to have been caused by the Swiss, who were quartered near the Porta al Prato inside and out, and who tried to force their way through *Borgo Ognissanti*, in order to approach the king's quarters.

25th November (Tuesday). There was nothing new, except that the French were so alarmed that they stood on guard night and day. They took the citizens' arms from them, and robbed anyone whom they encountered at night; so that some of those bold Florentines who had had the idea of slaying the French when they met them at night, were themselves slain or wounded. If the French had stayed longer they (these rash Florentines) would have gone the right way to work to bring about trouble. It is always the case that certain thoughtless men endanger cities, not considering what it means to kindle the spark; it may happen that a man of no account arouses the anger of a king by some piece of folly, without the city being to blame.

26th November (Wednesday). The king went together with the *Signoria* to hear mass at *Santa Maria del Fiore*, and here he swore to observe the articles which had been drawn up, and which were as follows: that we should lend him 120 thousand florins, giving him 50 thousand florins now, and the rest before the end of July 1495; and that he should leave and give back to us the forts of Pisa and all the others; and leave our territory free and unmolested; and that Piero de' Medici should be confined to boundaries 100 miles away from Florence; and that the price of 2000 florins placed upon his head should be taken off, and also off his brothers'. All this he swore to observe, on the altar of *Santa Maria del Fiore*, before Christ Jesus, on the word of a king.[1]

27th November (Thursday). The king went out to see certain tents which had been set up on the *Prato d'Ognissanti*, and which had been presented to him by the Duke of Ferrara; there being one for the king himself that was really magnificent, with a sitting-room, a bedroom, and a chapel, and many other things besides. He was to have left this morning, but did not do so; the joy-bells were rung and bonfires were made. This morning more of the troops from Romagna reached Dicomano, and were quartered there, about 20 horses being put into my place

---

[1] These articles had been signed the preceding day in the palace of the Medici, where the king was quartered. The Marquis Gino Capponi published them in the *Archivio Storico Italiano*, I Serie, vol. i., pp. 348–75. There are twenty-seven articles, and the last twelve regard entirely the persons and interests of the Medici.

even. I left my young son Benedetto there, and they nearly slew him several times, although he paid them proper respect, as I had impressed upon him. It was at a great cost to us. They were quartered everywhere, in the *Val di Sieve*, as far as the *Ponte a Sieve* and the *Sieci*, and then they went on along the upper valley of the Arno.[1]

28th November (Friday). The king left Florence after having dined, and went for the night to the *Certosa*, and all his men went before or after him, so that few remained here. It was said that Fra Girolamo of Ferrara, our famous preacher, had gone to the king and declared that he was not doing the will of God in stopping, and that he ought to leave. It was even said that he went a second time, when he saw that the king did not leave, and declared again that he was not following God's will, and that whatever evil should befall others would return on his head. It was thought that this was the cause of his leaving more speedily, because at that time the said Fra Girolamo was held to be a prophet and a man of holy life, both in Florence and throughout Italy. At the same time there came to Florence the captain of the French troops in Romagna, whose name was Begnì,[2] and he told the king rather dictatorially that he ought to leave on every account, as the weather was favourable, and he declared that it would be ill to delay the advance. And in fact the king did leave, for he put more faith in this *seigneur* than in all the rest, and deservedly, as he was an extremely intelligent and worthy man, according to what was said; and this was in reality the strongest reason which induced him to leave.[3]

29th November (Saturday). The rest of the king's troops

[1] The king having proclaimed that all those who were with him should pay, on leaving, for everything that they had had, the *Signoria*, with a proclamation on this date, ordered the Florentines to be lenient in their demands, and requested anybody who thought himself overcharged to have recourse to them, threatening to cut off the hand of anyone who should offend the French. The following day they imposed the punishment of six blows of the lash upon anyone who should molest or strike the French.

[2] Robert Stuart, Comte de Beaumont le Roger, Seigneur of Aubigny-sur-Nerre.

[3] On this day the *Signori* designated Guglielmo d'Antonio Pazzi, Braccio di Domenico Martelli, Niccolò Antinori, and Lorenzo di Pier Francesco de' Medici to go the following morning and accompany the king as far as Siena. Afterwards they substituted Francesco de' Rossi for the Medici.

which were in Romagna went past here, coming from San
Godenzo to Dicomano and to the Ponte a Sieve, and then
going along the upper valley of the Arno, doing much
damage. At Corella they slew about eleven men, and took
others prisoners and placed ransoms upon them; ruining
all the country like a flame of fire. The wall of my house
at Dicomano was broken, and also all the locks, whilst
my farm was entered forcibly, and suffered not a little,
the wine and corn being consumed, and any household goods
to which they took a fancy being carried off. Those whom
they slew at Corella were certain old men who had come to
receive them, but there was a misunderstanding. It
is true that at first certain young men had come out and
tried to force them back, but these old men caused the
others to desist; these brutes of Frenchmen, however,
struck them on the head and left them lying dead in the
fields; and they committed cruelties on all sides.

30th November. Nothing else was spoken of but these cruelties.

1st December (Monday). These things continued. The rest of the troops from Romagna were passing along the *Val di Sieve*.

2nd December (Tuesday). A *parlamento* was held in the *Piazza de' Signori* at about 22 in the evening (6 p.m.), and all the *Gonfaloni* came into the Piazza, each with his respective citizens behind him unarmed. But there were a number of armed men placed at all the ways leading into the Piazza; and many articles and statutes were read out, which formed several folios. Before beginning the reading it was asked whether two-thirds of the citizens were present; and the bystanders said that it was so. Then the reading began, and it was declared in the said articles that all the laws from 1434 onwards were annulled, and that the *Settanta*, the *Dieci*, and the *Otto di Balìa* were also abolished, and that the government must be carried on by the Council of the People and the Commune, and that the balloting-bags must be closed and the names drawn by lot, as was usual in communes; and that an election should take place as soon as possible. For the present, twenty of the noblest and ablest men should be appointed who would do the work of the *Signoria* and the other offices, together with the *Signori* and *Collegi*, until the election should be arranged. And the citizens must be content with the result of the ballot. And the said twenty men should choose ten among them, who should attend to the war with Pisa and to other necessary things.[1]

3rd December (Wednesday). These twenty men were appointed, and they appointed the *Dieci della guerra* (Ten for war) and other offices.

4th December (Thursday). An embassy from the Duke of Milan came to Florence.[2]

5th December (Friday). The "Eight" began to arrest certain citizens and send them to the *Podestà*, that he should proceed against them.

6th December (Saturday). Fra Girolamo preached, and ordered that alms should be given for the *Poveri Vergognosi*[3] in four churches: *Santa Maria del Fiore, Santa Maria Novella, Santa Croce,* and *Santo Spirito*; which were collected on the following day, Sunday. And so much was given that it was impossible to estimate it: gold and silver, woollen and linen materials, silks and pearls and other things; everyone contributed so largely out of love and charity.

7th December (Sunday). The said offering was made. And he preached again in *Santa Maria del Fiore*, and ordered that a procession should be made, in order to thank God for the benefits received.

8th December (Monday). The procession was made, and

---

[1] Many of the things decreed in this assembly are merely a confirmation of the orders given by the *Signoria* in November, and to which it was wished to give a ceremonious sanction. The offices entirely abolished were the *Consiglio del Cento* (Council of the Hundred, appointed under Lorenzo after 1480); the *Settanta* (the Seventy, also instituted under Lorenzo; both these acted as if they had full powers, without summoning an assembly); the *Dodici Procuratori* (chosen from the Seventy every six months, who looked after internal affairs); the *Otto di Pratica* (also chosen from the Seventy every six months, who were ministers of foreign affairs), and the *Accoppiatori* (these ten officials were only appointed during the time of the elections, and had gradually usurped more and more power under Lorenzo). The rest were only reformed.

[2] To congratulate the Florentines upon their recovered liberty.

[3] The Company of *Buonuomini*, who care for the *Poveri Vergognosi*, was formed before 1521, and used to care for the wants of the prisoners in the *Stinche* and the *Bargello*. They met in the old church of *San Martino*, to which offerings were brought, and they later extended their administrations to other honourable poor in the city. In the church of San Martino the twelve *Buonuomini* are painted in twelve frescoed lunettes. [Trans.]

more offerings were given for the *Poveri Vergognosi*, without stint. It was a marvellous procession, of such a number of men and women of high estate, and carried out with perfect obedience to the *Frate*, who had ordered that no woman should stand upon the stone seats along the walls, but that they should stay inside their houses with the door open, if they wished. Not a single woman was seen standing on the stone seats or elsewhere. Such devotion was shown as perhaps will never happen again. The alms given were not less than on the previous day. I did not hear the exact amount, but it must have been thousands of florins.

9th December (Tuesday). It was proclaimed that Piero de' Medici was to be confined within boundaries 100 miles outside the Florentine territory.[1]

10th December (Wednesday). Money was continually being found hidden in the *Dogana* (city customs), underneath coals and heaps of nails, etc., to which the abovementioned citizens who were imprisoned confessed by degrees. It was said that the king had reached Viterbo, and that the Pope had consented to give him a safe-conduct.

11th December (Thursday). A sum of money arrived in Florence from Pistoia, which had been hidden in the convent of the Jesuits by Salvalaglio. They kept on torturing Antonio di Bernardo and Ser Giovanni son of Ser Bartolomeo, and they confessed these things.

12th December (Friday). Antonio di Bernardo di Miniato was hung, in the morning before dawn, at the windows of the *Casa del Capitano*; and he remained hanging there till 24 in the evening (8 p.m.). During these days the French in the district of Cortona had taken some silk belonging to the Florentines, which was coming from the Levant, and was worth 40 thousand florins, and were not willing to return it. They returned it in the end, however, though it cost a lot of trouble.

13th December (Saturday). We heard that the king was having the houses in Rome marked with chalk for the quarters of his soldiers.

14th December (Sunday). It was said that the king was

---

[1] On the 2nd of this month the *Signoria*, in order to carry out the articles stipulated upon with the French king, absolved Piero from his condemnation as a rebel, and on the same day they consigned him to boundaries 100 miles from Florence. These decrees were published on the 9th.

in Viterbo, and that his men were doing brutal things as they did here.

14th December (Sunday). We heard how those Frenchmen who were marking the houses in Rome had been driven away, and many had been killed; the Romans wishing to defend themselves and not accept the Frenchmen in their city.

This same day we heard that the Pope and the cardinals had entered the castle of *Sant' Angelo*, and that the Duke of Calabria had arrived there with a large force, so that it was judged that it would fare badly with the French. It was also said that the king had sent a proclamation to Pisa, to the effect that the Pisans should submit to the Florentines; otherwise the Florentines would make such war upon them that they would be entirely destroyed, at the expense of the said King of France; that is to say that the money which he was to receive would be used instead for the cost of such an expedition; which was not true, but there was always a great deal of talk.[1]

The same day Fra Girolamo did his utmost in the pulpit to persuade Florence to adopt a good form of government; he preached in *Santa Maria del Fiore* every day, and to-day, which was a Sunday, he wished that there should be no women, but only men; he wished that only the *Gonfaloniere* and one of the *Signori* should remain in the *Palagio*, and that all the offices of Florence should be there; and he preached much about State matters, and that we ought to love and fear God, and love the common weal; and no one must set himself up proudly above the rest. He always favoured the people and he insisted that no one ought to be put to death, but there must be other forms of punishment; and he continued to preach in this manner every morning. Many forms were drawn up, and there was much controversy among the citizens, so that every day it was expected that the bell would be rung for a *parlamento*.

[1] There must have been some truth in it, as we read in the *Memoriale* of Portoveneri, where there are so many notices of the rebellion and war of Pisa, that on the 4th December there reached this city a herald from the king with the articles which the latter had agreed to with the Florentines, in which it is said: "Everything must be given back that formerly belonged to the Florentines. And this day the said messenger of the King has gone to Sarzana and to Pietrasanta and to Fivizzano and to Bagnone and to Castel-Nuovo and all Luligiana, to consign it to the Florentines." This was agreed to in the treaty.

15th December (Monday). Nothing new here. From Pisa we heard that they were holding out, and making raids on all sides, pillaging and doing as much damage as they could.

16th December (Tuesday). Nothing but the sermons of the said *Frate*.

19th December (Friday). Many schemes of government were taken to the *Palagio*. Each *Gonfaloniere* made a scheme, as the *Frate* had proposed.

21st December (Sunday). He preached again; and still he did not wish any women to come; he went on discoursing about State matters, and great fear was felt lest the citizens should not agree. *Chi la volava lesso e chi arrosto* (One wished it boiled and another roast): i.e. everyone had a different opinion, one agreed with the *Frate*, and another was against him; and if it had not been for him there would have been bloodshed.

This evening it was permitted by the Lord, about 2 at night (10 p.m.), in the *Via tra' Ferravecchi*,[1] near the *Volta della Luna*,[1] that my son Benedetto was stabbed in the face, across the cheek, by no means slightly; and we cannot think by whom. We believe it must have been a mistake, as he has never offended anyone or suspected anyone of having a grudge against him: it happened in punishment of our other sins. I freely pardon the aggressor, as I hope that the Lord may pardon me, and I pray God to pardon him and not send him to hell for this.

22nd December (Monday). It was said that the king was still at Viterbo; everyone went on talking of the French, of Rome, and Pisa, and how Rome would not give a safe-conduct. The Duke of Calabria had arrived there, to resist the French.

This day many things were voted in the *Palagio*: Anyone who slew a man could not return to Florence; and a law as follows against the unmentionable vice: the first time, the offender to be punished with the *gogna*,[2] the second

[1] *Via fra' Ferravecchi* = the present *Via Strozzi*; and the *Volta della Luna* was on the north side of it, between *Via Vecchietta* and *Piazza Vittorio-Emanuele*. [Trans.]

[2] *Alla gogna* was when a prisoner was exposed on the outer wall of the prison of the *Bargello*, with his hands bound behind him to one of the iron rings, bare-headed, with his hat at his feet to receive *soldi*, and a placard on his breast upon which his crime was written. He had to remain there an hour, during which time the old bell of the prison was rung. [Trans.]

time, to be fastened to a pillar, and the third time, to be burnt; and many other laws, all recommended by the *Frate*.

25th December (Christmas Day). Nothing was talked of but the French; how they had reached Rome and were outside the walls, and how they were investing it, having taken San Paolo, and made bridges of wood.

28th December (Sunday). Fra Girolamo preached, and again wished no women to be present. There was a great crowd; it was judged that there were always 13 to 14 thousand people at his sermons. Everyone felt very distrustful, fearing some trouble in the beginning of this new government.

29th December. The new *Signori* were drawn by lot, which is a fresh way of choosing them. The First *Gonfaloniere* is one of the Corbizi, this news being received joyfully, seeming to promise a popular and more impartial government.

30th December (Tuesday). Ambassadors were chosen to go to Pisa: Piero Capponi and Francesco Valori, together with the French one; and they were to take letters from the king with them, saying that Pisa should be given back to us.[1] They were, in fact, playing us such tricks that the people thought that the king was making fools of us, which was considered a bad prospect, as indeed it was.

31st December (Wednesday). We heard that certain of the king's ships which were bringing him a quantity of victuals had gone down, which was a misfortune for him.

1st January. The new *Signoria* entered into office, and it was a great joy to see the whole Piazza filled with citizens, quite different from other times, as a new thing, thanking God who had given this impartial government to Florence, and delivered us from subjection. And all this had been done at the instigation of the *Frate*.

2nd January (Friday). Two ambassadors were sent to

---

[1] On the 13th November the *Signoria* had elected Capponi, together with two other citizens, as *Proveditori* for the guardianship and care of the city of Pisa. On the 24th December the *Dieci di Libertà e Balìa* deputed Capponi and Valori "General Commissioners with full authority in every place outside Florence"; and the same day they ordered that forty gold florins should be paid to them, as "elected commissaries to go with the ambassador of the Most Christian King, to Pisa." According to Portoveneri, they were not allowed to enter the city.

Milan, Messer Luca Corsini and Giovanni Cavalcanti. They went in fine array.[1]

3rd January (Saturday). The ambassadors returned from Pisa, without having concluded anything; and we were in much fear about the place. It was said also that Piero de' Medici had gone to the King of France to complain of having been banished, because he had kept his word; and that the king had been gracious to him; and that the said Piero made threats, especially against a certain Girolamo Martegli, who was deputed to find Piero's hidden property.[2]

On the same day the sentence was passed that Ser Giovanni son of Ser Bartolomeo should be sent to Volterra into the vault of a fortress; and Ser Zanobi, who had been notary to the "Eight," was fined 500 florins, and confined in Florence; and Ser Ceccone was confined in the *Stinche*, together with others who had been captured.

4th January (Sunday). We heard that the King of France had entered Rome by agreement,[3] but, nevertheless, they did not give up the *Castel Sant' Agnolo* to him. It was said that he had pillaged the Orsini.

6th January (Tuesday). The Epiphany. The "Eight," in searching for money, found in *San Marco* 1200 florins belonging to Ser Giovanni. Some gave the blame to Fra Girolamo; but in preaching he exonerated himself, saying that he had not known anything of this money, nor had he been applied to with regard to it.

7th January (Wednesday). The men who were nominated to grant remission of debts met in the archbishop's palace and began their work. They were so fine and magnanimous that a man who owed thousands of florins paid only one or two florins. Their mercy was without measure. They imitated the Lord, who does likewise.

8th January (Thursday). It was said that the King of France wished to have the *Castel Sant' Agnolo* and the Pope

---

[1] To congratulate Ludovico Sforza, called *Il Moro*, on his becoming Duke of Milan.

[2] Martelli was one of the three citizens deputed by the Republic, on the 10th December, *pro computo Comunis bonorum heredum Laurentii, qui una cum tribus ex creditoribus dictorum heredum, propterea deputandorum, habeant auctoritatum cognoscendi et judicandi etc.*

[3] *Giuseppe Molini*, p. 22 of vol. i. of the *Documenti di Storia Italiana*, publishes the agreement made on the 15th of this month between the Pope and the King.

and the cardinals, and the brother of the Turk,[1] who were in the said *castello*, delivered over to him.

9th January (Friday). We heard that the king had caused the French to give up certain silks belonging to Florence, which they had taken, and that they were in the hands of the Florentines in Rome; and that he was treating the Florentine nation well. And every day there passed horses with loads of French clothes (probably uniforms), which went to the French camp at Rome.

11th January (Sunday). Fra Girolamo preached, and spoke much concerning the reforms in the city; and exculpated himself from various accusations, saying that there were devils who disturbed the life of the commune; and that they wrote forged letters, which made it appear as if the *Frate* had given Piero de' Medici hopes of returning, in order to make the people turn against him. But nevertheless all this was untrue; he was entirely for the people and the common weal. He was calumniated by these foxes; but the truth would always prevail. It is the fact that he always encouraged this community of feeling amongst the people.

12th January (Monday). Soldiers were mustered for Pisa and sent there, and we hoped to win it back shortly.

13th January (Tuesday). The mortars were fetched from Arezzo and sent to Pisa, and many *spingarde*,[2] and a quantity of powder. All this time it was endeavoured to keep peace, amongst the discords of the citizens.

17th January (Saturday). Fra Girolamo preached; and concerned himself much about this peace and union of the citizens; and many of them began to grow angry with him, saying, *Questo Fratuccio ci fa capitare male* (This wretched monk will bring us ill-luck).

18th January (Sunday). A loan of 100 thousand florins was demanded,[3] to be subscribed to by all the citizens; and

---

[1] This was Zim or Gemme, son of the great Maometto and brother of the reigning Bajazet II., with whom he was disputing the Empire, and therefore he had taken refuge with the Pope.

[2] *Spingarda*; a small old-fashioned piece of ordnance.

[3] This loan was demanded, after having been approved by the *Consiglio del Popolo* on the 12th January, and by the *Consiglio del Comune* on the 13th, judging that "for the preservation of liberty and to defend ourselves from the insidious attacks made upon it, it is necessary to have a provision of money." The citizens were to be entered as creditors in a book which was called "the Loan of MCCCCLXXXXV., so that it may always be known who felt affection for their city, and that others might follow their example," etc.

At Pisa (Piazza del Duomo)

the people were so much dismayed, that almost every one stopped working, and gave way to discontent. Every one said, "This thing cannot be; the poor who live by their labour will die of hunger, and will be obliged to apply for the alms of San Martino."[1]

20th January. Many Florentines arrived here, about 400, driven out from Pisa by the Pisans, and having left their wives and children and their shops, after being very ill-treated.[2] There was much talk of their outrageous behaviour (the Pisans').

21st January. Our commissioners left for Pisa, and took with them many courageous young men fully determined to punish the Pisans. We hired many soldiers also, and large bodies of infantry went from the neigbhourhood of Pistoia and all the country round, without pay. Everyone was ready to go there, thinking that the whole district would be sacked. No one thought much of their power of resistance; but we were mistaken, as will be seen later, for they were very persistent and united in their defence.

22nd January. An ambassador came to us from the emperor, who was going on to Rome to the King of France.

23rd January. We continued sending men to Pisa.

25th January. Fra Girolamo preached, and asked leave of absence, saying he had to go to Lucca. The people were much displeased.

27th January. The *Consiglio Maggiore* (Great Council) met and appointed a council of 80 men, who with the *Signoria* would have to choose the ambassadors, reply to letters, and do much other business.[3]

28th January. We heard that our troops had captured

---

[1] See note to 6th December, 1494.

[2] Of this bad treatment there is testimony even in the Pisan documents. A letter of the 27th January, 1494 (1495, New Style), refers to an apothecary who "on his departure was nearly dead," and "his wife was insulted and frightened, ... and threatened with being carried off" (*Archivo di Stato di Pisa Lettere agli Anziani*, i. 29).

[3] On the 23rd December a provision was made which established that by the 15th January these 80 citizens must be appointed. "It is seen to be necessary, for matters that may happen any day, that the *Signoria* or other magistrates should have a certain number of citizens with whom they may confer and whose opinion they can ask, and so that the magistrates should not have to call up one more than another on their authority."

many forts from the Pisans and were making raids all over the country.¹

31st January. The "Eighty" wanted to carry through certain things, but they did not succeed.

1st February. They did not carry through anything, because they said that the only thing they wished to carry through was a tax on property.

2nd February. We heard that the King of France had been defeated at Terracina, on entering the Kingdom (of Naples), and that there were hundreds slain.

4th February. The tax on property was passed by the "Eighty."

5th February. The tax on property, that is to say, the *Decima*, was passed by the *Consiglio Maggiore*; but with the provision that it could not be imposed more than once a year, or less frequently.²

5th February. The French Cardinal Sammalò,³ who had just been made cardinal by the Pope, entered Florence. He had come here with the King of France as a bishop; and now he was returning to France. He had many horsemen with him. He was lodged in Santa Maria Novella in the papal apartments. All this time it was said that the King of France was in a bad situation, and there was cause for fear.

6th February. Costly presents were sent to him (i.e. to the cardinal).

8th February. The *Signoria* went to visit him, and later, after having dined, sent eight⁴ of the chief citizens to hear

¹ See Ammirato and Portoveneri.
² It was called *Decima* because the tenth of the value on all land and house property had to be paid. See note 5th February, 1495.
³ Guillaume Briçonnet, Bishop of Saint-Malo. From the 25th January, the Pisan ambassadors had written that the *Reverandissimo* of Saint-Malo, a man, they said, "of great intellect and authority," was going to be sent to Florence by the King of France, not on his way to France, but to remain in Tuscany or the neighbourhood, in order to preserve peace during the stay of the king in the kingdom of Naples; and in case of his going to Pisa begged the *Signori* to receive him and his suite with honour, "going to meet him outside, and with as many men" as was possible. He had left Rome the morning of the 27th January (*Lettere*, quoted, i. 38).
⁴ Ammirato and the documents published in vol. i. of the *Négotiations diplomatiques de la France avec la Toscane* give five, and their names are as follows: Guidantonio Vespucci, Tanai de' Nerli, Guglielmo de' Pazzi, Francesco Valori, and Lorenzo de' Medici, who had changed his family name, taking that of Popolani.

what he desired. And he asked for the money which had been promised to the king, and the loan of 40 thousand florins besides.

9th February. The *Signori* burnt all the tickets of the ballot-bags, because they said that the names had been chosen according to the wishes of a few powerful citizens.

11th February. There were negotiations with the cardinal concerning giving Pisa over to us, and he wanted 70 thousand florins.

17th February. The Cardinal Sa' Malò left here, and went to Pisa in order to give it over to us. And some of our citizens went with him, amongst others Francesco Valori and Pagolantonio Soderini.

19th February. It was proclaimed that during the whole month of March the papers should be distributed (on which were to be filled in all particulars) for the tax of the *Decima* about to be imposed upon property.

19th February. We heard that the king had been defeated.

20th February. We heard that he had taken Gaeta.

22nd February. We received the news that the King of France had taken Capua, and was near Naples. It was thought that he would capture it quickly.

24th February. The Cardinal di Sa' Malò returned from Pisa without giving it over to us. And it was said that we should have to take it by assault. It was also said that the king had a hand in it, for he held both the new and the old citadels.

25th February. We heard that the King of France had taken Naples, and how he had entered it on the 21st without a blow. The King of Naples took refuge in the *Castello dell' Uovo*. This news was proclaimed here with great rejoicing, with drums and fifes, and the shops were shut. There were many bonfires and lights [1] on the towers, and other manifestations, to commemorate such a conquest.[2]

26th February. A great procession was made, and the cardinal joined in it, and it took place three days running.

27th February. The Cardinal Sa' Malò left here, who

---

[1] These *panegli* were pieces of stuff swimming in oil or dipped in grease, and placed in flat round tins..

[2] This is confirmed by a decree of the *Signori* on this date, which besides commanding the shops to be shut, also orders processions to be made on three successive mornings.

had come to deliver Pisa over to us, and had not done so; but he carried away with him 22 thousand florins, and returned to the king at Naples.

2nd March (Monday). Our troops made a raid into the Pisan territory, and destroyed their mills, and took many prisoners and much cattle.

4th March. There were very grateful letters from the King of France, telling us how pleased he was that we had celebrated the conquest of Naples.

5th March. Four ambassadors were chosen to go to the King of France and Naples, who were: Messer Guido Antonio, Pagolo Antonio Soderini, the Bishop de' Pazzi, and Lorenzo son of Piero Francesco de' Medici.[1]

6th March. There was much argument as to why the king did not give Pisa over to us, seeing that we were such friends of his country and also that he had promised it us on the capture of Naples.

10th March. Piero Capponi went to our camp at Pisa and took money to the soldiers.

13th March. It was said that the king was about to return north.

16th March. There was a debate how to keep peace amongst the citizens, and about doing away with the authority of six votes[2]; and this was carried through by the *Signori* and *Collegi*.

12th March. It was carried through the "Eighty" also.

[1] Landucci is not correct in the names of these ambassadors. In the work already quoted, *Négotiations*, etc., we read the instructions given to them and their names, but instead of Soderini and Pazzi are Bernardo Rucellai and Lorenzo Morelli. Ammirato, however, gives Soderini instead of Morelli; the truth is that the latter was appointed to replace the former, who was prevented from leaving on account of illness.

[2] The original provision (see *Reg. di Provv. ad an.*) is entitled *Lex pacis et appelationis sex fabarum Provosio*, and contains the arrangements for the peace, as the Diary says; which consist in an indulgence, or amnesty as we should now say, within certain limits, for anyone who had favoured the Government in power till the 9th November. There is also an article which ordains that anyone eligible for office who for some reason of State has been condemned by the *Signori* or the *Otto di Balia* or *di Guardia* to death, confinement, banishment, or imprisonment, or to a fine above 300 (large) florins, can and may appeal to the Great Council," and be absolved by them with certain ceremonies. And it is this, I think, that was meant by *doing away with the authority of six* fave, i.e. the six votes with which the *Signori* or the *Otto* could condemn.

19th March. It was carried through the Great Council. And the petition declares that all political offences would be cancelled from the day of Piero de' Medici being driven out, except where fraud was involved; and that the *Signoria* should not be able to imprison without the consent of the Great Council.

22nd March. We heard that the king had taken the *Castello dell' Uovo*.

1495. 26th March. Large bodies of soldiers were mustered to send to Pisa.

1st April. Fra Girolamo preached, and said and testified that the Virgin Mary had revealed to him, that after going through much trouble, the city of Florence was to be the most glorious, the richest, and the most powerful that ever existed; and he promised this absolutely. All these things he spoke as a prophet, and the greater part of the people believed him, especially quiet people without political or party passions.

2nd April. It was said that a league had been made between the Venetians, the Duke of Milan, the Emperor, the Pope, the King of Spain, and the Genoese; and we should be given till the end of April to decide whether we would join it.

5th April. We heard that the King of France had acquired the whole kingdom of Naples; and that the King of Naples had fled into Ischia, having lost hope.

7th April. We heard that the king intended to return here.

8th April. Fra Girolamo preached in the *Palagio*, confirming everything that he had said before.

9th April. We heard that the King of France had sent to demand that all the part of Florence beyond the Arno should be assigned him for quarters; and it was said that he would give Pisa back to us.

13th April. We heard that our soldiers had made a raid into the Pisan territory as far as San Piero in Grado, taking much cattle.

17th April. We heard that the Pisans had made a raid on our territory, in the district of Pescia.

21st April. We heard that the Pisans were encamped before Librafatta and pressing it hard.

22nd April. Our troops set out to search for them, but they raised their camp and did not wait. Our troops captured their artillery.

25th April. We heard that there had been an encounter,

and many killed and taken prisoner on both sides. A certain leader of ours, whose name was Francesco Roverso, had penetrated as far as the gates of Pisa, and had been captured.

26th April. There was much talk in the city to the effect that some of the citizens had deceived us, and that we should not get Pisa back after all, as they were plotting various things with the king; but this may not be true. Certain leaders were summoned, so as to try and learn the truth; and there was much confusion and disagreement.

28th April. It was said that the King of France was returning here; and although he might appear to be friendly, and had heard that we rejoiced at his conquest, nevertheless everyone waited in fear lest we should be suddenly plundered. No one trusted in his friendship.

3rd May. Fra Girolamo preached, and tried to reassure the people, declaring that things would not turn out ill.

9th May. About 400 French came to Pisa, sent by the king to our help.[1]

11th May. It was carried through that the *Dieci del Consiglio* (Council of Ten) should be chosen.[2]

16th May. Two sons of Giovanni dell' Antella were arrested; and they were put to the rack, and confessed to a plot that they were making to bring Piero de' Medici back to Florence. A brother of theirs, who was commissary in Romagna, was also sent for.

17th May. We heard that the men of Librafatta had routed the Pisans.

18th May. Dell' Antella (the commissary) was arrested.

20th May. We heard that Librafatta was lost, as we had failed to send succour.

21st May. It was voted that a *balzello*[3] should be imposed; which meant ruin for the city, and caused great dissatisfaction amongst the citizens.

23rd May. We heard that the King of France had left Naples and was coming here.[4]

[1] The Florentine historians believed that these soldiers were sent by the king to reinforce the garrison of Pisa, but instead they were sent to help the Pisans and fought for them with the approval of the king (*Portoveneri*, work above quoted).

[2] This means that from now onwards the *Dieci di Libertà e Pace* should be elected by the Great Council.

[3] A special loan.

[4] In the discussions of the 16th and the 19th May, the *Signoria* had deputed various citizens to provide for everything that was necessary when the king came into Florentine territory.

24th May. Some people wanted to attack Fra Girolamo, in the Via del Cocomero, after he had preached.

28th May. One of the Albizi was sent as a courier to the king, because it was understood that the ambassadors did not really go; but perhaps this was not the case.

29th May. We sent three more ambassadors to the king, to discover the truth.[1]

31st May. The Council and many *Richiesti* [2] met, and there were great discussions concerning the coming of the king. And amongst the rest, it was insisted that the king should be asked two things: the first, to respect our liberty; the second, not to try and force Piero de' Medici upon us.

1st June. We heard that the king had entered Rome, on his way here.

2nd June. Pandolfo Rucellai, who was already an old man, became a monk at *San Marco*.

3rd June. The Gonfaloni assembled in the churches and held many discussions concerning this coming of the king. And it was again proposed that he should be asked four things: first, to leave us our liberty, secondly to understand that we did not choose to have Piero de' Medici return, as had already been said; thirdly, that he should give us back all that belonged to us; fourthly, to ask him whether he came as a friend or an enemy; and everyone agreed to this.

4th June. The city was in great uncertainty, and the houses were provided with stores of provisions and arms.

5th June. The tabernacle of Our Lady of *Santa Maria Impruneta* was sent for, and great honour was paid to it.[3] Fra Girolamo ordered that the result of these offerings should be given to the poor. And he ordered two tables to be put in *San Felice in Piazza*, and two in *Santa Maria del Fiore*, where a great number of florins and *grossi* were

---

[1] They were Domenico Bonsi, Giuliano Salviati, and Andrea de' Pazzi. *Ammirato* makes a mistake when he puts Pandolfo Rucellai in the place of the last: it is true that the commission was given to him, but he refused it, as he was about to become a Dominican friar.

[2] *Richiesti*; the name of one of the councils which only lasted one session. A majority of more than half could pass a vote, and when this was not achieved, the matter was referred to another council or to the three highest offices. [Trans.]

[3] The idea of bringing this tabernacle into Florence had been discussed by the *Signoria* on the 28th May, in order that the Florentines should have grace in the midst of the troubles which were afflicting them. Two days later, the 5th June was fixed as the date for bringing the tabernacle to Florence.

collected as alms. It was in fact an immense contribution, and was arranged by the said *Frate*, who was obeyed even by those who did not believe in him. In *Santa Maria del Fiore* he made the women stand on one side and the men on the other, so that there were no men mixed up with the women; and the procession was so well arranged and so devout, that there never was another like it.

7th June. The twenty men who had been elected to the government of the city retired, and left the Great and Universal Council to rule; and to everyone who wishes to live quietly and without excitement this appears to be the most worthy government that Florence has ever had. Nevertheless all the chief citizens were careful to provide themselves with arms and have enough men in their houses, as if a *parlamento* were imminent; but it was not so. They did it because they were afraid of being pillaged. Everyone fortified his house. The country districts were deserted for Florence, especially those where the king would have to pass. And yet Fra Girolamo preached every day and assured everybody that they need have no fear, that God would help us.

11th June. Lorenzo son of Pier Francesco de' Medici, who was ambassador to the king, returned.

12th June. Bernardo Rucellai, who was also ambassador to the king, returned. And all this time the city was providing itself with arms, and placing wood at each corner, so as to be able to barricade the streets. Everyone felt the greatest distrust and ill-will, because it was thought that the king did not wish us well, as we were continually losing our castles. The news came that Palaia was lost, and Montetopoli.

13th June. We heard that the king had reached Siena with all his army.

14th June. His army reached Poggibonizi, and did every kind of damage. Everyone prayed God that it would not come to Florence, and our prayers were heard.

15th June. Fra Girolamo went to meet the king at Poggibonizi, and waited for him there.

16th June. The king came to Poggibonizi, and his vanguard went to Empoli, where they sacked the whole town, and took prisoners, and worked havoc.

17th June. Fra Girolamo spoke to the king at Poggibonizi. And it was said that this was the cause of his not coming to Florence; that the *Frate* had begged his favour for the city, and said that it was God's will that he should treat it well, it being entirely his friend. So he really was of great assistance to Florence, and the king listened to him. At this time the *Frate* was held in such esteem and the people were so devoted to him, that there were many men and women who, if he had said, *Entrate nel fuoco* (Go into the fire), would have actually obeyed him. He was considered by many to be a prophet, and he himself claimed to be one.

18th June. We heard that they had burnt Montetopoli, and sacked Gambassi and Castel Fiorentino, and committed many depredations, as the French and all soldiers are in the habit of doing.

19th June. Towards Settimo some Florentines assaulted certain French ambassadors who were leaving Florence, so that they began to drive the people away in all this plain as far as Peretola, which was caused by certain wicked and thoughtless men of ours, who did not reflect how wrong it was to put us into danger, for the sake of stealing a few trifles.

20th June. Fra Girolamo returned from the king, and on the 21st he preached, saying that he had spoken to the king, who had made fair promises, and that he had declared that if he were not to keep these promises, it would go ill with him; God would take his office from him, so that he would no longer be God's minister, and he would also lose the dearest thing that he possessed. And the preacher called upon the whole congregation of 13 or 14 thousand people to witness that so it would be, infallibly. He also said that he had revealed to the king some secrets concerning his own affairs.

22nd June. The king left (Poggibonizi) and went towards Pisa.

23rd June. We heard that the king's vanguard had been slightly worsted by the League at the *Salto della Cervia*. Also that the Lucchesi had called many soldiers of the League into their city, not choosing to receive the king. Also that our troops have defeated the enemy at Montepulciano,[1] and taken prisoner a Messer Giovanni Savello, a Sienese leader.

24th June. The king entered Lucca, being received after

---

[1] The men of Montepulciano, supported by the Sienese, had rebelled against Florence since the 27th March, crying *"Libertà e Lupà."*

all. They had changed their minds. And it was said that the king did not choose to give Pisa back to us, and that the Pisans had offered it to the king's son. It must have been so, for he left in the end without having given it back to us, although he had sworn it upon God's altar.

25th June. The king left Lucca and went towards Serezzana. Our ambassadors who had gone to the king returned without any decision as to Pisa; so that there were great discussions, and our idea was to win it back by force without fail. The enemies of the *Frate* said: "There, you see how you can trust the *Frate*, who declared that he held Pisa in the hollow of his hand."

26th June. The *Signoria* was elected for the first time by voting, according to the new reforms, as is done for the other offices, and no longer by the "Twenty" as before; they having retired, as already said. The *Gonfaloniere* was Lorenzo Lenzi; and all the people seemed content with this manner of election. Everyone agreed that this present manner responded more nearly to the true Florentine idea than ever before.

27th June. We heard that an agreement had been made with Montepulciano.

29th June. We heard that the king was in possession of Pietrasanta and Serezzana, and all that neighbourhood. What a pitiable state of things for them!

30th June. We heard that the king had sacked a fortress near Pontremoli.

1st July. We heard that the king was unable to advance, on account of the soldiers of Lombardy, and of the Bolognese territory and all those parts, swarming round; most of them without pay. It was feared that it would fare ill with the king.

2nd July. We heard that our troops had captured 50 men of Casina; amongst them a son of the Pisan commander, de' Malvezzi.

3rd July. We heard that the King of France was beyond Pontremoli, in a district where his army was dying of hunger. They were hard pressed, and had suffered some small defeats from the League.

6th July. The Florentines sent ambassadors to the king: Messer Guido Antonio and Neri Capponi.[1]

---

[1] On the 23rd June the king had written to the Florentines that he would receive their ambassadors as soon as he arrived at Asti,

8th July. We heard that on the 6th July a battle had broken out between the King of France and the League at Parmigiano, on the Taro, at 16 in the day (noon); it lasted till night, and there were 3 thousand dead counting both sides. Many famous and important men were amongst those killed, and many others were taken prisoner and put to ransom. The French lost the greater part of their baggage and artillery. The Count of Pitigliano deserted from the French and went over to the League. And amongst those killed on the side of the League were: Signor Ridolfo da Gonzaga, Signor Anton Maria, Signor Carario, Count Bernardo dal Monte, and Messer Giovanni, *Capitano generale* of the Marchese di Mantua. Signor Rinuccio da Farnese was wounded and taken prisoner.

9th July. Piero de' Medici's household effects and clothes were sold by auction; this work took several days, in Orto Sa' Michele.

11th July. We heard that the King of Naples had regained his city, and that many French had been killed. There was also the news that the King of France was leaving Italy, and that the League seconded him and let him go; because there were some members of the League who were not loyal to it. If all of them had been in agreement, none of the French would have returned to France, not even the king.

14th July. We heard that there was a short truce, and that the French had been able to cross a certain river. And by good fortune for the French, as it pleased God, this river became flooded, because there had been heavy rains, and our troops not being able to cross it, could not pursue the French, who took to their heels.

15th July. We heard that the French had reached Asti, and many said that it was by a miracle. And it was said that the king swore that he would return and conquer Milan, and that he was very bitter against the Venetians and those of the League.

18th July. We heard that the Genoese had captured the king's fleet, taking many vessels and prisoners, so that the French expedition was shamed and ruined, and Florence and the two mentioned here were precisely those which were sent. In the registers of the *Deliberazioni de' Signori e Collegi* of the year 1495 one reads a copy of the articles drawn up by the king and these ambassadors at Turin, on the 16th August, and ratified by the *Signori* on the 8th September.

could say that all the king's misfortunes came from having broken the oath that he had made on the altar of *Santa Maria del Fiore* to give Pisa back to us when he conquered Naples; and that being a man of little understanding, he never knew his friends. He saw plainly that we were the only ones who did not join the League against him, which made us the enemies of all the rest of Italy, for his sake. Moreover, we had spent a fortune to secure his friendship. However, according to what this *Frate* says (whom we consider a prophet), worse things are in store for him; and the office of being God's minister and purging Italy of her sins will be given to another.

On the same day the first row of windows of the Palagio degli Strozzi was finished. And at the *Dogana* the foundations for the Great Hall[1] were being made; and the *Frate* encouraged this work. The above-said hall was built on his advice. All this time we kept on sending soldiers to Pisa.

29th July. We heard that the Sienese were in arms and slaying each other, on account of wishing to reinstate a certain *Monte di Nove* which they had. Some were for it and some against.

31st July. We heard that our troops had taken the *Ponte di Sacco* and pillaged it. Here we did nothing else but send reinforcements to Pisa.

1st August. We heard that the Sienese had imprisoned many citizens, and set up the *Monte de' Nove* again.

On the same day, our soldiers at the *Ponte di Sacco* had captured about 70 Frenchmen[2] who were fighting for the Pisans in this castle. And our men, behaving like barbarians instead of Italians, having learnt from the French, and hating them for many reasons, took pleasure in slaughtering and butchering them all without pity, because you can find Italians who are wicked and cruel.

3rd August. Several fortresses belonging to the Pisans capitulated upon certain terms: Lari, and others.

[1] This *Sala Grande* was to be used for the meetings of the Great Council. It was designed by Simone del Pollaiolo, a friend of the *Frate*; and various marble and bronze busts which had been in the palace of the Medici were destined to adorn it. Cosimo I. afterwards caused this hall to be heightened and decorated, and it is now called the *Salone del Cinquecento*. Part of the Palazzo Vecchio, on the north side, was used as the custom-house, and was therefore known as the *Dogana*.

[2] These were some of those who had been sent by the king in May, and who the Florentines believed had sold themselves to the Pisans against their master's will.

4th August. We heard that the emperor had published a proclamation that no subject of his should enter the service of the Venetians or of the duke,[1] and that he intended to summon the Pope to a council; and if he would not go there he would have to come to Florence. He did not summon him, however.

6th August. Our commissaries Francesco Valori and Pagolantonio Soderini left for the camp in the district of Pisa, which was now at *Ponte ad Era*, taking large sums of money with them, about 20 thousand florins, for the soldiers.

9th August (Sunday). During vespers the cupola was struck by a thunderbolt. It did not do much harm, but terrified those who were in the choir, because some bits of plaster fell there; not much, however.

11th August. All these days they were selling by auction in Orto Sa' Michele Piero de' Medici's household effects; there were velvet counterpanes embroidered in gold, and paintings and pictures, and all kinds of beautiful things; showing what fortune may do in this transitory life, or rather divine permission, to the end that man may recognise that all comes from God, who gives and takes away, and that he may not become proud and set up at being rich and powerful; on the contrary, the more a man has received from God, the humbler he ought to be, appearing more ungrateful to God than others; for the greatest sin is ingratitude.

12th August. The vaulting of the roof of the Great Hall was finished, that part which covered the court of the *Casa del Capitano*.[2]

During these days it was said that the Duke of Milan did not allow letters to pass which came from the King of France.

13th August. It was voted in the Great Council that

[1] Of Milan.

[2] The *Capitano del Popolo*, in early times, lived in a house at the back of the Palazzo Vecchio, in a block of buildings which was entirely separate from the latter, till it was enlarged. After the Medici came into power, the *Gonfaloniere* was the head of the government, and the *Podestà* and the *Capitano del Popolo* were subordinate; the *Podestà* becoming only a judge, and the *Capitano* hardly more than the head of the soldiers of the *Palagio* and executor of the orders of justice, being reduced to the condition of a *Bargello*. He moved from the house by the Via de' Leoni to the palace formerly called the *Palagio del Podestà*, and later the *Bargello*, in the year 1539. [Trans.]

anyone who spoke about calling a *parlamento* should lose his life and his possessions. At this time Palaia was hard pressed.

14th August. Palaia capitulated on condition that the persons and property of the garrison should be safe, and they paid 400 florins.

18th August. Our camp went to Cascina, and took the *Badìa* of *San Severino*,[1] but did not enter it, going on instead to Vico Pisano, where the next day they gave battle to the enemy, and lost many men. They fought on and off for several days, and more than 20 men were killed.

29th August. The camp at Vico was raised.

31st August. We said every day: "The king must have sent letters for Pisa to be handed over to us, but they are not allowed to pass." It was nothing of the sort, however.

1st September. My brother-in-law, Piero, returned from camp, wounded by a shot in the heel. It was serious.

4th September. Our camp moved nearer to Pisa.

5th September. The French, who were in the (new) citadel at Pisa, having asked for the old citadel also, it was given them. And it was suspected that the Pisans received aid from the League.

7th September. We heard that our camp in the suburb of San Marco at Pisa had captured the fort of Stainpace.

8th September. We received letters patent from the King of France directing that Pisa should be given over to us; but they were worth nothing, because the Pisans were supported by the League, principally by the Venetians.

10th September. Two of the *Dieci*, two of the *Otto*, and two of the *Collegi* went to our camp at Pisa, to force Pisa to give in.

14th September. We heard that our soldiers had taken the bastion of the Pisans and some prisoners, but the French commandant [2] began to fire the spingards [3] at us, killing some of our men. Vitegli [4] was wounded. Thus the French

[1] Means *San Savino*.
[2] This commandant, to whom the king had entrusted the fortress of Pisa, was Robert de Balzac, an old friend of Louis XI., councillor and chamberlain of the king, Seneschal of Anjou and of Gascony, Baron of Entraques and of St. Amand. Comines, in his *Mèmoires*, calls him "a man of great worth, a servant of the Duke of Orleans." To me, his biassed and insubordinate conduct appears to show that he was a man of bad character.
[3] *Spingard*; see note to 13th January, 1494.
[4] Paolo Vitelli.

did not keep their promise of rendering the fortress to us, according to the king's letter.

16th September. Monseigneur de Lille,[1] a Frenchman, who was here in Florence, went to Pisa to endeavour to make them give up the citadel, as those French who held it would not yield. He travelled in a litter, because he was ill, but it was all of no use.

18th September. We heard that Fracasso[2] had entered Pisa with a few men, and believed that he was sent by the League.

20th September. Alfonsina, the wife of Piero de' Medici, fled from here and went to join her husband at Siena.

23rd September. There was a proclamation that if a son of Bernardo de' Medici[3] did not appear before the "Eight" he would be declared a rebel, because he had taken her to Siena.

25th September. There was a proclamation that whoever should kill Piero de' Medici should have 4 thousand ducats and the right to bear arms for life; and he could obtain the pardon of any one rebel whom he chose. And if he who killed Piero were himself a rebel, he should be pardoned, and have 2 thousand gold ducats, and the right of bearing arms for life, like the others.[4]

2nd October. The vaulting of the Great Hall of the *Dogana*[5] was finished; it will be magnificent.

3rd October. There began to be suspicions about certain meetings which were held in the *Agnoli*,[6] concerning an Assembly. And Don Guido and certain other *Frati* of the *Agnoli* were arrested. It was said that they had a hand in this plot. I did not hear whether it was true.

4th October. Our camp was moved to Cascina.

[1] Jean Dumas, Seigneur de Lille, councillor, chamberlain and house-steward to the king.

[2] *Il Fracasso*; Gaspero son of Roberto da San Severino, a captain of men-at-arms.

[3] This was Averardo son of Bernadetto de' Medici.

[4] The sentences were renewed in consequence of Piero having made efforts to re-enter Florence.

[5] See note to 18th July, 1495.

[6] This church and convent was in the Borgo de' Pinti (being one of the three called by that name in Florence); it was occupied alternately by monks and nuns. The monks there at this time were of the Cistercian Order. It was suppressed on the Union of Italy, and the building is now used for schools. It is now called Santa Maria-Maddalena de' Pazzi. [Trans.]

5th October. Monsignore di Lilla returned, and said that he had protested with the castellan, telling him that if he did not surrender the citadel to us, he was a rebel to the king. The said *monsignore* died.

6th October. Near Campi the plague was discovered in one house, and in the house of Antonio di Bono an apprentice and a serving-girl died; in the house of Andrea di Bono there were some persons sick of the plague; also in the house of Jacopo son of Piero di Berardi, and in another in the Via della Scala and in several places. People were dying of it.

15th October. Was the funeral of Monsignore di Lilla; a grand ceremony. He was buried at the *Servi*. There were 250 torch-bearers, and a discourse was held over his body in the Piazza di Sa' Lorenzo.

On the same day, it was voted that if the slayer of Piero de' Medici should be killed, his heir should have the 4 thousand florins.

17th October. One of the Ricasoli, who was plotting with Piero de' Medici to give him Ricasoli, was declared a rebel.

18th October. Fra Girolamo preached, and still besought us to hold firm to this Government and the Great Council.

27th October. A messenger came, who brought us the news that the King of France was sending a *signore* who would cause Pisa to be given over to us. This latter, however, deceived the king; he got 100 ducats from the *Signoria*, and did nothing at all.

29th October. The crane which drew up the stones at the *Palazzo Strozzi* fell, one of the ropes over the Loggia having broken. It fell towards Santa Trinità, breaking in the middle where it was joined, but no one was hurt.

3rd November. An ambassador came from the King of France, whose name was Lancio in Pugno, and he came to give Pisa over to us. He went there, and was taken prisoner by the Pisans, but was liberated later. We were continually being ensnared like this. The plague was now causing some mortality.

14th November. We heard that Piero de' Medici was in the Perugian district with a considerable force.

All this time Piero's effects were being sold by auction.

PIERO DE' MEDICI
From the miniature by Homeri (1488).

24th November. A certain bridge which had been made not long before, between the *Palagio de' Signori* and the *Loggia de' Signori*, which was on a level with the gate of the *Loggia di Palagio*, was taken down again.¹

26th November. Three decrees were passed in the *Palagio*: first, a reward for anyone who slew Giuliano de' Medici; secondly, to sell the property of the *Torre*; thirdly, the reform of letting the lots be drawn without declaring the name.²

3rd December. We heard that Piero de' Medici was nearly captured at Cortona. He had to flee.

4th December. We heard that Ramazzotto, a friend of the house of Medici, was falling upon people on the road to Cavrenno, and carrying off loaded mules; and later, that the other day the *Podestà* of Firenzuola had captured some of the thieves. Men were recruited in the Mugello to go in aid of Firenzuola.

7th December. It was voted in the *Palagio* to impose a tax of 50 thousand florins on the priests, and 30 thousand on the effects of Piero de' Medici.³

8th December. We heard that the King of Naples had recaptured the *Castello Nuovo*, and thus he was gradually reconquering everything.

9th December. A David which had been in Piero de'

¹ A decision of the *Signoria* on the 22nd November runs thus: *Quod pavimentum saxis politis stratum ante portam Dominorum, paucis ante annis confectum, dictum el Rialto, removiatur et remaneat ut prius erat ad maiorem Palatii pulcritudinem, ne conspectus Palatii a lateribus deformatus videatur; et lapides illi dentur Operariis novae Salae ad Salam conficiendam.*

² The substance of these provisions is more clearly as follows:

By the first, a reward of 2000 large gold florins and other privileges was promised to whoever should slay Giuliano; by the second, the *Ufficiali di Torre* were ordered to sell forty-eight shops on the *Ponte Vecchio* and twenty in the *Mercato Vecchio*; by the third, it was ordered that the names of citizens who were to occupy certain offices should be placed in bags, and then drawn by lot, instead of their election going *a mano*, as it was called (that is, by show of hands), in the Great Council, as had hitherto been the custom.

³ The provision entitled *Officialium Presbiterorum Ordinatio* is of the following day. Five citizens were to be elected from the Great Council, with the authority to "claim from those not paying the ordinary taxes the sum of at least 50,000 florins." The *Signoria*, on the 30th January following, ordered the *Officiali delle Grazie dei Contadini* to cede to them, for their residence, part of the quarters which they occupied in the archbishop's palace.

Medici's house was brought into the Palagio de' Signori, and set up in the centre of the court there.[1]

10th December. We heard that the King of France had burnt the houses of the French castellan who was at Pisa, on account of his not having obeyed the king and given up to us the citadel which he held.

11th December. We heard that the Pope had sent to command Fra Girolamo not to preach; and he obeyed for some days.

12th December. Commissaries were sent to all the passes to watch over them.

The same day the news reached us that the Tiber had risen so high at Rome that the water was up to the first story on the Banks, and was several *braccia* above the mark of former years. Many cattle perished, and also men, especially those who were imprisoned in the vaults of towers, and others besides.

And I heard the following incredible thing, namely, that a woman had appeared to a shepherd in the Kingdom of Naples, and had said to him, "Give me one of these sheep," and when he gave it, she said: "Cut it in half." And when it was cut in half, there came out of it a quantity of serpents and vipers and scorpions and other horrible animals. And then she said to him: "Close it up again, and join it well, and it will come back to life." And when this was done, she said to him: "Go and tell the Pope that there will be a great plague; that everyone must do penance and fast next Saturday, and not eat meat for three days."

There was also another ludicrous thing, which I will record, as it is spoken of everywhere, namely, that the murdered duke appeared in the street at Milan, and gave a letter to a man, saying: "Carry this to the Signore Ludovico." And when it was carried (to the ducal court), the chancellor could not open it. But as soon as the Signore Ludovico took it in his hand, it opened; and as he read it, he bent his head and stood for a moment lost in

---

[1] On the 9th October, the *Signori* ordered that the two bronze statues, the David and the Judith, standing, the former in the court of Piero's palace, and the latter in the garden of the same, should be handed over to the artisans of the *Palagio*, to be erected in whatever part of the building seemed most suitable. This consignment was made six days later. Landucci's authority, supported by these documents, serves to correct what *Moise* says about it in his *Illustrazione del Palazzo dei Signori*, pp. 74, 75.

wonder. And when the messenger asked for a reply, the Signore Ludovico said: "It has been given," and the messenger immediately disappeared. This gave rise to much talk: of plague, famine, and most of all, wars; which certainly did follow.

14th December. An ambassador came to us from the King of France.[1] We hoped for Pisa; and he only came to Pistoia and not to Florence, saying he intended to go to Pisa. Our citizens went to visit him at Pistoia, but it did not help.

15th December. The beams for the roof of the *Sala di Dogana* (the new Great Hall) were hoisted up.

21st December. The bronze Judith, which had been in the house of Piero de' Medici, was placed on the *ringhiera* of the *Palagio de' Signori*, by the side of the door.[2]

26th December. The rest of the electors' schedules were burnt at the *Palagio*.[3]

1st January. We were expecting (the capitulation of Pisa) on account of the arrival of this ambassador; but quite the contrary happened, because the next day the castellan gave the forts to the Pisans; and all the French who were there went away to Lucca.[4]

[1] Monsignore de Gemel.
[2] The Judith by Donatello. The words *Exemplum salutis publicae cives posuere MCCCCXCV.*, which one reads round the pedestal, were placed there, I believe, to record the vanquished power of Piero de' Medici, and not the remote fact of the Duke of Athens having been driven away, as stated by Moise. In 1504, being taken away from the *ringhiera* of the *Palazzo* when Michelangelo's David was placed there, it was put into a niche in the Court of the *Palazzo*; and in 1560 it was moved to the *Loggia dei Signori*, where it stood till moved to the steps of the *Palazzo* in 1919 near the Marzocco, where it now stands.
[3] This was done in order to carry out the decree of the 26th November, which reformed and extended the manner of putting the schedules with the names of those eligible for office into the balloting-bags, as I quoted in the note 2, page 97, and which prescribed, amongst other things, that after the schedules had been put in, the schedules of those bags which would not have to be drawn from were to be burnt. On the 30th December the *Signori* ordered the chancellor of the ballot to bring them *omnes registros scrutineorum preteritorum ut illos comburant*.
[4] This fact was a great joy to the Pisans, as was natural, who hastened to announce it without delay, by means of ambassadors, to the Duke of Milan, the Commune of Genoa, the Pope, the *Signore* of Piombino, Siena, and others; "the material and actual possession of the new citadel, with all the towers and forts," considered by them as the real acquisition of their much-desired liberty, was taken on the 1st January following, "at 6 o'clock" (*Lettere degli Anziani di Pisa*.)

Hence one can see plainly that the king was mocking us, and did not choose to give us the place back. And everyone was angry; and where they ought to have blamed the king, they turned their hatred against the *Frate*, going round San Marco at night shouting and calling out unseemly things: "*Questo porco di questo frataccio si vuole arderlo in casa,*" etc. (This wretched pig of a monk, we will burn the house over his head.) And there were some who wanted to set fire to the gate of the convent.

4th January. We sent messengers riding in furious haste to France, to complain of having been tricked. But nothing ever helped.

9th January. Two peasants were taken on the executioner's cart to be hung; having meant to give over Montecatini to Piero de' Medici. And on the same day a proclamation was made forbidding people to argue about the government, or the king, or the monks, and also to wear masks; on the penalty of 25 florins or to be stretched on the rack ten times.

17th January. Our messengers returned from France; one of them having broken his thigh. They said that the king had assured them that the affairs of Pisa, Sarzana, and Pietrasanta should be put into the hands of St. Malo, and that everything should be given back to us, as he bore us good will. Nothing further happened, however.

19th January. Letters came from the King of Naples demanding help, or otherwise he would do things that Italy would regret.

At this time there was a great question whether we ought to join the League or not. Some said that the (French) king would return here, and some that he would not do so, because his son was already dead; and there were many disputes and differences of opinion.

26th January. The Sienese exiles left Florence and set out for Siena,[1] going there with the Florentine force, consisting of a large body of men, with our *Capitano generale*, the Count of Urbino, and all our leaders. The Perugians also came, with a number of soldiers, and brought the rest of the exiles with them, wishing to restore them to their own city, the total force amounting in a day or two to about 8 thousand persons. But these citizens had to leave Siena, and went to Colle.

---

[1] Malavolti in his *Storia* also says that they were unable to enter Siena, and that "after a bloody encounter" they turned back.

29th January. A Maestro Ludivico, a doctor of medicine, and others, were declared rebels, for having wished to give over Bucine to Piero de' Medici.

7th February. Some boys took away a girl's veil-holder in the Via de' Martegli, and her people made a great disturbance about it. This happened because Fra Girolamo had encouraged the boys to oppose the wearing of unsuitable ornaments by women, and to reprove gamblers, so that when anyone said, "Here come the boys of the *Frate!*" every gambler fled, however bold he might be, and the women went about modestly dressed. The boys were held in such respect that everyone avoided evil, and most of all the abominable vice. Such a thing was never spoken of by young or old during this holy time; but it did not last long. The wicked were stronger than the good. God be praised that I saw this short period of holiness. I pray Him that He may give us back that holy and pure life. And in order to realise what a blessed time it was, you have only to consider the things that were then done.

16th February. The Carnival. Fra Girolamo had preached a few days before that the boys, instead of committing follies, such as throwing stones [1] and making huts of twigs, should collect alms for the *poveri vergognosi*; and as it pleased the divine grace, such a change took place that instead of senseless games, they began to collect alms several days beforehand; and instead of barriers [2] in the streets, there were crucifixes at each corner, in the hands of holy innocents. On this last day of Carnival, after vespers, these troops of boys assembled in the four quarters of Florence, each quarter having its special banner. The first was a crucifix; the second was an image of Our Lady, and so on; and with them went the drummers and pipers, the mace-bearers and serving-men of the *Palagio*, the boys singing praises to Heaven, and crying: "*Vivo Cristo e la Vergine*

[1] *Jacopo Nardi* wrote in his *Istorie*: "Amongst other things the following appeared very noteworthy, namely, that at this time was voluntarily discontinued that stupid and brutal game of stone-throwing, which in Carnival-time was so inveterate from its antiquity, that even severe and terrifying proclamations of the magistrates had never been able to repress it, much less root it out." However, this was only a suspension, seeing that this barbarous custom was still in vigour even in the second half of the sixteenth century.

[2] Formerly the young men and boys used to bar the streets with poles, and let no one pass without payment, especially women. They used the huts in their rough fights.

Maria nostra regina!" (Christ and the Virgin Mary our queen!), all with olive-branches in their hands, so that good and thoughtful people were moved to tears, saying: "Truly this change is the work of God. These lads are those who will enjoy the good things which the *Frate* promised." And we seemed to see the crowds of Jerusalem who preceded and followed Christ on Palm Sunday, saying: *Blessed art thou who comest in the name of the Lord.* And one may well repeat the words of Scripture : *Infanzium e lattenzium perfecisti lalde.* And observe that there were said to be 6 thousand boys or more, all of them between five or six and sixteen years of age. All the four troops united at the *Servi*, in the portico (i.e. under the colonnade of the *Innocenti*—the Foundling Hospital), and in the *Piazza* (of *SS. Annunziata*); and then they all went into the church of the *Nunziata*, and after that to *San Marco*. Then they took the way of all processions; they crossed the *Ponte a Santa Trinità* (and went round over the *Ponte Vecchio*) into the *Piazza (della Signoria)*, and so to *Santa Maria del Fiore*, the church being crowded with men and women, divided, the women on one side and the men on the other; and there the offering was made, with such devotion and tears of holy emotion as was never seen. It was estimated that there were several hundred florins. Many gold florins were put into their collecting-bowls, but the greater part consisted in *grossi* (copper coins) and silver. Some women gave their veil-holders, some their silver spoons, kerchiefs, towels, and many other things. All was given without grudging. It seemed as if everyone wished to make an offering to Christ and His Mother. I have written these things which are true, and which I saw with my own eyes, and felt with so much emotion; and some of my sons were amongst those blessed and pure-minded troops of boys.

17th February. This was the first day of Lent, and an immense number of boys came to hear Fra Girolamo's sermon in *Santa Maria del Fiore*. Certain steps were erected along the walls, opposite the chancel, for these boys, behind the women; and there were also many boys amongst the women; and all those who stood on the steps sang sweet praises to God before the sermon began. And then the clergy came into the chancel and sang Litanies and the children responded. It was so beautiful that everyone wept, and mostly healthy-minded men, saying: "This is a thing of the Lord's." And this went on each morning of Lent, before the *Frate* came. And note this wonder: not a boy could be kept in bed in the morning, but all ran to church before their mothers.

25th February. The *Signoria* moved into their new hall, which was now ceiled, but not yet paved, nor were the benches made. The door from the *Palagio* into the hall was broken through and roughly made, but not yet finished off in any way.[1] In this hall were placed two marble epitaphs. One was in the vulgar tongue, and in verse, and the other in Latin. The first consisted in a stanza of eight lines, meaning: "Whoever wishes to have a *parlamento*, wishes to take the government away from the people." The Latin one said: "This Council is from God, and ill will befall anyone who tries to go against it."

26th February. The tax of the *Decima* was voted.

27th February. The boys were encouraged by the *Frate* to take away the baskets of *berlingozzi*,[2] and the gambling-tables, and many vain things used by women, so that no sooner did the gamblers hear that the boys of the *Frate* were coming than they fled, nor was there a single woman who dared go out not modestly dressed.

28th February. We heard that the French castellan had given Sarzana and Serzanello to the Genoese.[3] Who would not rebel against the King of France? Truly one may say that the Florentines have been the most faithful and obedient servants in the world, but he does not appear to have recognised it.

29th February. The said boys went about everywhere, along the walls of the city and to the taverns, etc., wherever they saw gatherings of people; this they did in each quarter, and if anyone had rebelled against them, he would have been in danger of his life, whoever he was. At this time the plague was increasing.[4]

---

[1] Three days before the *Signori* had given leave to Pollaiuolo to break through the wall, so as to go from the *Palagio* into the new hall.

[2] *Berlingozzi* were cakes made of sweet dough and raisins, sold especially in Lent.

[3] *Portoveneri* says that Sarzana, bought by the Bank of San Giorgio, was given over on the 26th of the same month; and laughs at the Florentines, who had paid many thousand ducats "to have it," and they had been treated in the same way as about Pisa.

[4] By a decree of the 3rd March, the Republic, in order to obviate the dangers which might arise from the contagion of the plague, "which is much feared for the coming summer, as it has already

8th March. Fra Girolamo, during his sermon, made the congregation cry *Viva Cristo!* and other pious words, causing great excitement. On every week-day there were 14 thousand or 15 thousand persons present, who for the most part thought him a prophet.

14th March. Certain laws were made against notaries, decreeing that anyone who wished to practise as a notary could not hold office in the government.[1]

22nd March. There was a hailstorm, and snow fell till it reached the depth of half a *braccio*. Fruit and flowers were destroyed.

1496. 27th March (Palm Sunday). Fra Girolamo caused a procession to be made by all the boys, with a wreath of olive on their head and a branch of olive in their hand, each carrying a red cross, about a span high or more. There were said to be 5 thousand boys, and also a great number of girls, dressed in white like the boys, with the cross and the olive-branch in their hands, and the olive-wreath on their heads. Following them came all the city officials and the heads of the guilds; and after these the rest of the men, and then the women. I do not believe that there was a single man or woman who did not go to make this offering on the altar of *Santa Maria del Fiore*, the proceeds of which were to set up the *Monte della Pietà*. Very large sums were given. At the head of this procession there was a tabernacle with a painted Christ upon the ass, as He rode through the streets of Jerusalem on Palm Sunday; and over it the umbrella was carried, whilst all cried: *Viva Cristo ch'è 'l nostro Re!* (Christ our King!), through the whole city.

28th March. It was said that the King of France intended coming.[2] And the Venetians hired many soldiers.

appeared in some places," ordered that the Great Council should elect four citizens, whose office should last till the end of October. They were to have full powers to endeavour to remedy and keep away the plague, and to assist the poor who became victims of it.

[1] This provision, besides obliging the notaries "to choose one of two employments, it not seeming just that a notary should have a government-office at the same time as practising as a notary," also prohibits substitution in the government offices, and considers other provisions for the regulation and disinterested fulfilment of the same.

[2] "It is considered almost certain that the King of France will make a (second) expedition into Italy." Thus wrote an *oratore* (representative) of the Pisans at Milan to the *Signoria* of Pisa. (*Lettere agli Anziani*).

4th April. A bombard, of a new kind, was taken to the *Porta alla Giustizia* to be tried, and they ruined a house in the *Cappanaccia*.

7th April. We heard that it had rained blood over two gates of Siena, and that a woman had appeared at Viterbo who had declared that the True Prophet was at Florence. I merely record this to show what foolish things are said.[1]

10th April. Our camp was assaulted at night by the Pisans, and they captured more than 100 horses, and slew two men-at-arms, after having put out their eyes. They did not capture the castle of Buti, however.[2]

12th April. Signore Piero took some Pisans prisoner, and imitating their behaviour, put out their eyes.

14th April. We heard that the men of Faenza had chased away from the city all those who were for the Venetians, and slain a messenger of theirs.

17th April. Fra Girolamo preached at Prato in the church of San Marco, and there were so many people from Florence and the country round that there was an immense crowd. He declared that they would be blessed in the end, after all their tribulations.

24th April. We heard that the Pisans had increased their army, and that our men had been worsted, and that they were now harassing us.

26th April. The Council met in the Great Hall to elect the *Signoria*; and the *Frati* of *San Marco* said Mass there. It was Fra Domenico who said the Mass, and he gave a short sermon after it. During the meeting some men were discovered trying to give out voting-schedules secretly, and the "Eight" ordered them to be arrested. Amongst the rest was a Giovanni da Tignano; and they sent him to the *Podestà*, who sentenced him to be stretched on the rack four times. They also arrested Filippo Corbizi and Giovanni Benizi and others, and many were detained in the *Palagio*. There were some, however, who could not be discovered; and the Council sat till 22 in the evening (6 p.m.)

---

[1] *Allegretti*, in his *Diari Sanese* (in *Rev. Ital. Script.*), registers this fact which terrified many people in that city. He also looked upon it as does our author, concluding with these words: "*tamen*, sensible people do not believe it."

[2] "8th April: we have the news that our men have routed the enemy, and that there are 50 of the enemy killed, 25 taken prisoner, and 220 horses and some mules, and that Messer Francesco Secco is wounded" (*Lettere degli Anziani di Pisa*).

before the business was finished. The *Signori* ordered that guards should be placed in the city all night.

28th April. Filippo Corbizi and Giovanni Benizi and Giovanni da Tignano were imprisoned in the *Stinche* for life, on account of the above business. Besides this more than twenty-five citizens were deprived of the right of voting.

2nd May. The Florentines sent the King of France two lions in wooden cages on the back of two mules; but nothing was ever of any use with him.[1]

3rd May. We received a letter from the King of France saying that he had forbidden the Venetians, Lombards and Genoese to trade in his territory, and that he had sent to protest with the Genoese and Lucchesi concerning Serezzana and Pietrasanta which ought to be given up to their rightful owners. But this was not in earnest.

4th May. We heard that the King of Naples had recaptured everything in his kingdom except Gaeta, and that many French were slain. During all this time it never ceased raining, and the downpour had lasted about eleven months, there never being a whole week without rain.

8th May (Sunday). In the afternoon the big bell of the *Palagio* rang, to summon the Great Council; and it was the first time that it had rung for such a council. Those imprisoned in the *Stinche* and those deprived of their right of voting appealed to this Great Council, and their case was tried, but not carried through. They must still have patience.[2]

11th May. The paving of the Great Hall of the Council was finished.

14th May. There was a return of the plague in several districts of Florence.

16th May. We heard that our troops had routed the

[1] On the 9th of the same month, the Priors *deliberaverunt et preceperunt Romulo Bernardi Antonii de Monte Catino, famulo eorum Camere armorum, quatenus vadat simul duobus leonibus, mictendis per dictos Dominos ad Cristianissimum Regem Francorum, et dictos leones in itinere gubernet donec ad curiam dicti Regis perveniat; et eos postea presentet oratoribus Florentinis penes dictum Regem existentibus, ut executioni mandent in predictis quod habent in mandatis. Et casu quo dictus Romulus in huiusmodi itinere deficeret, tunc in eum locum famuli dicte Camere, et pro eius remuneratione, succedat Bernardus eiusdem Romuli filius.*

[2] This appeal and its rejection are registered in the book of *Deliberazioni dei Signori e Collegi, ad an.*

Pisans and captured 40 men-at-arms. We lost only one man.¹

18th May. There was such a great flood that it washed away the young corn in the fields, even down in these plains; and here at Rovizzano it broke two walls on the roadside.

20th May. We heard that the Duke of Milan had declared himself an enemy of the Florentines.²

22nd May. A Hebrew girl, of about twenty years of age, was baptised; she had fled from her mother, Madonna Perla, a Hebrew. The same day a French ambassador arrived, a bishop,³ and he was given a lodging at the *Canto de' Pazzi*.⁴

24th May. The said bishop, the ambassador, went to the *Signoria* in the *Palagio*, and declared that he was our friend, and that he had recognised what true friends the Florentines were to France; he undertook to compensate us for our wrongs, and to give back to us what was ours, with more besides. We had a great many fine words from him, but no facts followed. France was always very

¹ Pietro Popoleschi, one of the commissaries, wrote from Bientina to the *Dieci di Balìa* the same day, at noon: "This morning our men encountered the enemy near Vico, who defeated them rancorously, and between Cecina and here have taken prisoner about thirty men-at-arms, most of them cavalry; and our enemy Gianetto da Palaia has been taken prisoner by us. The *Illustrissimo Monsignore* Francesco Secco was seriously wounded in the arm by an arquebus, after having borne himself valiantly." Perhaps Landucci exaggerates when he puts the Florentines' loss at only one man; whilst *Portoveneri*, in order to detract from the merit of the Florentines, says that they were many in number and confronted by only a few Venetians; although they were victorious, "the artillery of the Pisans slew about six men-at-arms and leaders of the Florentines, amongst whom was one Messer Francesco Secco, an exile from Mantua and formerly a Florentine leader." One can compare the documents with the chroniclers, and see that Secco died the same day from his wound. But it is impossible to make *Ammirato's* account agree with the others, as he states that this leader died a month earlier.

² The Florentines of those times must have been very short-sighted. I have already observed how continually they were tricked by the French, and yet went on placing their hopes in them; and now comes the case of the Duke of Milan, whom they only perceive is their enemy in the middle of May, whilst *Portoveneri* says that on the 4th April he sent soldiers in aid of Pisa.

³ Philippe Hébert d'Aussonvilliers, Archbishop of Aix, who was received with great honour, and given costly presents, as is shown by the books of the *Dieci*.

⁴ The corner where the present *Via Proconsole* meets the *Corso*. [Trans.]

ungrateful to us; but the Florentines, like fools, allowed themselves to be tricked continually. The said ambassador went to visit Fra Girolamo at *San Marco*, and there was an end of it. Matters remained the same with regard to Pisa.

28th May. A certain complaint began to be prevalent here, which was called "French boils," and looked like smallpox; it went on increasing, and no cure could be found for it.[1]

30th May. The sons of Bartolomeo Pucci went to the *Arte della Lana* (Wool-merchants' Guild), and breaking into the prison, liberated their father.[2]

31st May. They were sent to the *Bargello*.

6th June. There was such a great flood that the river Rifredi[3] became higher than ever before, and much damage was done. This year the price of corn did not rise above 34 *soldi* a bushel.

10th June. We heard that the Pope was sending his son with men-at-arms towards Siena, and that Piero de' Medici was with them.[4]

12th June. We heard that many *stradiots* (Greek soldiers) sent by the Venetians had arrived at Pisa; and, in my opinion, it is this that is the root of the trouble with the Pisans; they are supported by others who are able to bear the cost.

17th June. We heard that the Pisan cavalry had made a raid into the territory of Bibbona and taken much booty.

23rd June. The Pisans made a raid into Valdinievole, and burnt Borgo a Buggiano.[5]

24th June. The *festa* was not celebrated, except for having the procession and making the offerings at San Giovanni.[6]

[1] Perhaps this complaint only began then in Florence, but it had already been in Italy, according to several writers, since 1492.

[2] Bartolomeo Pucci had gone bankrupt, and was in prison on that account (Litta, *Famiglie celebri*).

[3] A small river between Florence and Prato.

[4] The son of the Pope was the Duke of Candia. These reports (as to the papal forces coming to the aid of Pisa) were current at the time, as proved by a letter written from Rome on the 8th by Ricciardo Becchi, and arriving precisely on the 10th at the office of the *Dieci di Libertà e Balìa*.

[5] This place was stormed "with difficulty and with much loss on both sides" (*Lettere degli Anziani di Pisa*).

[6] Perhaps Landucci means that the *palio* was not run; for there exists a proclamation of the *Signori* as to lights on the towers, and they also gave permission to three conjurers to draw teeth, juggle, and, in short, ply their trade, on that day; which shows that there must have been a numerous concourse, even that year, of country people at least.

25th June. Elections were begun to be made with gold balls, like at Venice.¹ At this time the plague was in about twenty houses.

5th July. The Pisans made an incursion into the territory of Volterra; our troops surrounded and defeated them, taking 60 horses and killing 20 men. It was a great rout for the Pisans.

8th July. An embassy came to us from the Sienese, who have now made a league with us for two years. At this time the complaint called "French boils" began to increase, so that the city was full of it; almost all the sufferers being grown-up men and women.

16th July. One of our leaders, whose name was Signore Rinuccio da Farnese, collected a force of 400 men and went to our camp at Pisa.²

23rd July. A forced loan from the priests, of 50 thousand florins,³ was voted by the Great Council; and it was also voted to reduce the salaries of the offices in the city by half, and of those outside by a third, for one year.

24th July. We heard that the Pisan troops had advanced as far as Bientina. Everybody wondered that they should have dared to do this. It was all caused by the secret aid of the Venetians.

28th July. Our troops made a glacis near Cascina, ready for a battle, but the Pisans would not accept it.

29th July. We heard that our troops had made such a successful incursion, that they had captured the castle

---

¹ By a decree of the 22nd June it was ordered that in the Great Hall of the Council there should be placed certain vases of copper or brass, or other material, narrow at the mouth, and so high that a man could not see inside; in which were to be "copper balls, some yellow or gilt, and some silvered or otherwise whitened." At an election, the councillors on entering the room had to draw out a ball; if this was a yellow one, they had to go through *al segreto*, to nominate their candidate for the office in question.

² Not finding at this time any Farnese in the pay of Florence, I believe that Landucci meant the Count Rinuccio da Marciana, who certainly was in Florence two days before this, as we see from the permission given by the *Signori* to the *Suonatori del Commune* (Town Musicians) to go and play in his honour (*Libro di Deliberazioni de' Signori, ad an.*).

³ It was in fact decreed that day that the Council should elect five citizens who, together with two friars, should impose this tax upon the clergy and such pious establishments as were not subject to the ordinary taxes. Their office was in the archbishop's palace as before.

of Fivizzano and the *Marchese*.¹ How the fortunes of war vary! Now up and now down, so that the Pisans in their fear have retired into strongholds.

31st July. We heard that the French who were in certain fortresses in the Kingdom of Naples had offered the King of Naples to capitulate on conditions, and he agreed to spare their lives and send them back to Provence.

2nd August. The *Monte della Pietà* was opened for the first time, in the house of Francesco Nori.²

4th August. It was voted that the taxes and the rate on salt should be paid in silver; and according to some, it was a sad day for the poor people.³ Tommaso Antinori was *Gonfaloniere*. At this time the plague was almost at an end.

8th August. Our commissary at Firenzuola, one of the Canignani, was killed. People said it was because he had had one of the murderers' brothers beheaded.

10th August. The bushel of corn cost more than 40 *soldi*; there had been a bad harvest everywhere.

15th August. Fra Girolamo preached in *Santa Maria del Fiore*, and on account of the great crowd, one of the wooden stands for the boys, towards the door of San Giovanni, broke, but no one was hurt. It was considered a miracle. You must know that there were four stands: two against the walls facing the chancel; the other two, one above by the men, and the other below by the women, in

¹ Fivizzano belonged at this time to Gabriello Malaspina. It was Tommaso, Marchese di Villafranca (also a Malaspina), who was taken prisoner. The *Dieci* paid twenty-five gold florins to those who captured him and brought him to Florence.

² As far back as the 28th December, the Republic had ordered that eight directors of the *Monte della Carità* should be elected, to enter into office on the 1st January, 1496, who were to look after and consider the arrangement of the said *Monte*. In the same decree many orders were made against the Jews, who for sixty years had alienated people by their usury; we read in the preamble, for instance, that in fifty years 100 florins became 49,792,556 florins, 7 *grossi*, and 7 *danari*. By another provision, of the 21st April, the capital of the *Monte* is established, and the rules for working it.

³ If this decree was burdensome, the motive which caused it to be made was a good one; for the money that was gained by the increase of these taxes was destined for the officers of *Abbondanza*, created by the same decree, in order that they should provide, as far as was possible, that during this scarcity, "both in the city and in the country, corn should keep at such a price that everyone who had need of it could buy it easily."

the body of the church. The number of boys had so increased that it had been necessary to make these stands. And observe that there was such a feeling of grace in this church, and such sweet consolation in hearing these boys sing, now above, now below, now from the side, all in turn, quite modestly and low, as if to themselves; it seemed impossible that it was done by boys. I write this because I was present, and saw and heard it many times, and felt much spiritual comfort. Truly the church was full of angels.

19th August. There came to Florence an ambassador from the Emperor Maximilian, and on the 29th he went to the *Signoria* at the *Palagio*, and protested that we must bind the Pisans to keep the peace, and must join the League, leaving the King of France, whom he declared was not of the royal blood.[1]

22nd August. There was a storm here above Quinto and as far as Fiesole and Montereggi, which tore many walnut-trees and other fruit-trees from their roots, and blew down the olive-trees; there was so much hail that it spoilt our harvest of grapes and olives and everything.

24th August. The said ambassador of the emperor left.

2nd September. A letter from the Duke of Milan was read in the *Palagio*, which said that the *Frate* was writing to the King of France to come, and he could not put up with it any longer. And the French ambassador went to the *Signoria* and told them that the *Frate* was the one who was ruining Florence. He had so many enemies, poor man![2]

5th September. The vaulting of the little cupola of the sacristy of Santo Spirito was finished.

9th September. We heard that our troops had defeated the Pisans, and that there were 80 men killed.[3]

[1] Instead of only one, there were two ambassadors: Gualterius de Stadio, a castellan, and Ludovicus Brunus, a doctor. The *Gonfaloniere* replied briefly to their oration, and took time to consult. The messengers were received again two days later, and then the chancellor, Bartolomeo Scala, replied in a fine speech, saying that on such a proposition Florence must send ambassadors to the emperor. These were elected, being the Bishop Cosimo de' Pazzi and Francesco Pepi, jurisconsult. On the 30th August they were ordered by the *Signori* to leave Florence within three days; their instructions, however, were not given them till 7th September.

[2] Further details concerning this can be found in the documents relating to Savonarola, published by Professor Isidoro del Lungo in the *Archivio Storico Italiano*, Nuova Serie, vol. xviii.

[3] Ammirato says that these encounters took place in the district of Bientina.

19th September. We heard that the King of France had had a son. At this time there was not a week without rain, like the year before, so that in many places the corn had not yet been reaped; for neither the corn, nor grapes, nor figs ripened; everything was behindhand.

24th September. We heard that the Pisans had captured 30 of our mules laden with sugar and leather.

26th September. We heard that Piero Capponi had been killed in the camp by an arquebus. On the 27th his funeral was held in Florence.[1]

2nd October (Saturday). The price of corn was 50 *soldi* or more.

13th October. We heard that the King of Naples was dead, and that Don Federigo had become king, and had compelled the French army to retire.

14th October. We heard that the emperor was leaving Genoa and coming to Pisa.

16th October. There was a proclamation ordering anyone that knew who had thrown an unknown girl of about twenty-two years of age into a tomb at Santa Maria Novella, after having murdered her and tied her up in two sacks, to give notice; but the murderer was never discovered.

24th October. We heard that the emperor had reached Pisa,[2] and that he had sent letters here, wishing us to join the League; otherwise he would come against us, and would attack Livorno and all our territory, and put everyone to the sword.

30th October. We sent for the tabernacle of Nostra Donna di Santa Maria Impruneta. And when it reached

---

[1] The *Anziani di Pisa* write as follows: "The enemy yesterday began to besiege Soiana, which is on our side . . . and there was a cruel battle, lasting more than four hours, and in which many men were killed, amongst others Piero Capponi, commissary-general of the enemy's camp, who was killed by an arquebus; and to-night our troops went to succour them, and *tandem* the siege has been raised. The whole of the enemy's camp has retired" (i. 135).

[2] "The night between Friday and Saturday, 22nd, at six o'clock in the night (2 a.m.), His Cæsarean Majesty arrived here, accompanied by Count di Caiazzo and all the representatives of the Most Holy League, and other lords and barons; and we gave them quarters in the house which formerly belonged to the Medici, on the Arno. We received them with as much honour as possible, with salutes from the mortars, fires, torches, bells, and shouts of joy" (*Lettere degli Anziani*, i. 150).

Florence, news came from Livorno that twelve ships of corn had arrived there, but it was in reality the fleet of the King of France, and the Livornese went out and routed the camp of the emperor and the Pisans, and slew about 40 men, and captured their artillery. It was the work of God, in return for our devout worship of Our Lady. This news reached us at the very moment in which she arrived in Florence. Besides, it happened that when there was a debate as to whether she should be sent for, that on that very day the ships sailed from Marseilles; and as she was moved, they reached the harbour of Livorno. It was considered, therefore, that the Virgin Mary really wished to aid Florence, and that this was a proof. There could be no doubt that the miracle had happened expressly.[1] At this time the price of corn was 58 *soldi*, and some of the best sorts 3 *lire* a bushel.

10th November. The small cupola of the sacristy of Santo Spirito gave way when the supports of the vaulting were removed.

17th November. We heard that the fleet of the Venetians and the Genoese had gone down in the harbour of Livorno, and that many men were drowned. The people of Livorno won much treasure. And there was amongst the fleet a certain ship of corn which they had captured from us, and we now regained. There was also a vessel prepared for the emperor, with all his personal belongings and silver plate on board (he had not gone on shore long when the mishap occurred), which was there at Livorno to help the Pisans to besiege it. They consequently raised their camp, and the emperor lost his ship, having almost lost his life too. It can easily be seen that such a sign is a miracle, showing God's aid to the Florentines; for he immediately went off and abandoned his enterprise, after having come all the way from Germany to take possession of Pisa, which the Pisans had offered to him. And now in one day this conflagration was extinguished. This miracle could bear comparison with any of those in the Old Testament. Nevertheless there were some ungrateful Florentines who would not recognise it as such, although the large proportion of good and wise men, who are conscious of God's grace and the marvels that He works, recognised it fully and gave Him due praise.

---

[1] This tabernacle was ordered to be brought by a decree of the *Signori e Collegi* on the 26th October.

21st November. He went away shamed, and God, still desiring to impress upon him the injustice of his enterprise, caused that when he was passing through Lucca and demanded provisions, the Lucchesi set a price upon the head of anyone who should give him anything; so that I believe he doubted more than once whether he would ever be able to reach Germany again.

27th November. We heard that the emperor had reached Lombardy, and was marching as fast as possible.

30th November. The fleet of the King of France, with certain galleys from Brittany, came to Livorno, and these Bretons landed and raided the Pisan territory, doing great damage. During these days the price of corn was 3 *lire* a bushel, and kept so.

5th December. A case of plague was discovered, after there had not been one for some months.[1] At this time the complaint of French boils had spread all through Florence and the country round, and also to every city in Italy, and it lasted a long time. Anyone who tried to doctor them suffered severe pains in all his joints, and in the end they returned; so it was no use doing anything. Not many people died of this complaint, but they suffered much pain and annoyance.

12th December. We sent our army to Cascina.

15th December. We heard that our troops had taken Tremoleto, and had pillaged it and put all the inhabitants to the sword.[2] The cause of this was that when the terms of capitulation were being discussed, as to giving hostages, etc., our forces approached the gates, and some fool (one of those who do so much injury to those who wish to live in peace) threw a huge block of stone from the walls, and it fell on the head of a French constable, whose name was Pitetto, killing him on the spot. When the French in our camp saw this, they made the rest of our men recede, saying: "It is for us to avenge him!" and they forced their way in, and slew everyone, pillaging the whole place.

---

[1] The plague not ceasing, and the office of the citizens summoned to make the necessary provisions against it having closed, the Republic, on the 23rd November, ordered the creation of two other officials for six months, with the same authority as the first had had.

[2] The Pisan documents also record "the great slaughter of Ceuli, Santa Luce, and Tremoleto, and the loss of Colognole, Terricciuola Santa Regulo," and of other castles on the hills (*Lettere degli Anziani*, i. 173 t).

In such a case, our men ought not to have allowed these barbarians, who seem to enjoy weltering in human blood, to act in such a way.

17th December. The price of corn was lowered 5 *soldi*, and all this time a number of mules were being sent to Livorno to fetch it.

21st December. We heard that our troops had taken Soiano by assault, and hung and slain several men, and the soldiers had even robbed women and children, leaving them nothing but their shifts.

23rd December. We heard from our ambassadors in France that they could not make the king understand that we were his friends. And it being discovered how the citizens in power here were acting, there was great excitement amongst the "Eighty," who declared that justice ought to be done and the sinners punished; but that was all.

3rd January. We heard that two small ships belonging to certain merchants had arrived at Livorno.

5th January. It was voted to levy a tax of 200 thousand florins, and that it should be collected by 20 men.[1]

11th January. Monsignore Begnì reached Florence from Naples, with about 50 horsemen. He was suffering from the French boils, and came in a litter. He lodged in the house of Messer Jacopo de' Pazzi, and was honourably received and presented with gifts.

20th January. It was voted that the taxes and the rate on salt should be paid in silver for another two months.[2] It was also voted that young men of 24 years and upwards [3] should be called to the Council if necessary. At this time the price of corn was 3 *lire* 10 *soldi* a bushel.

23rd January. Signore Begnì left Florence and went back to France, the whole Kingdom of Naples having been

---

[1] These men were to be chosen as quickly as possible by the Great Council, amongst the citizens eligible for office, and of at least forty years of age. The distribution was to be made within sixty days, for which time their office lasted.

[2] There is a prorogation of two years, and not two months, in the decree of the 4th August, conditions having grown much worse, especially because of the siege of Livorno, etc. Besides this, the number of the officials of the *Abbondanza* was increased by five.

[3] *Ammirato* gives many details about this resolution, passed in order always to have the number of a thousand in the Council; for which it was necessary to have 2200 citizens *netti di specchio* (with a clean slate), that is, who were not inscribed amongst the debtors of the commune.

lost; not without shame for the King of France, who never sent any aid. He had conquered this great kingdom in a few days, and he lost it again as quickly.

25th January. The price of corn was 3 *lire* 14 *soldi* a bushel. And at this time a woman died in the crowd in the *Piazza del Grano* (the Corn Market), where bread and corn of the commune was being sold. And we heard that a poor peasant, who had come into Florence to beg for bread, having left three small children starving at home, finding them dying on his return, and not being able to succour them, took a rope and hung himself.

28th January (Saturday). The price of corn was lowered by 12 or 15 *soldi* a bushel, and the most ordinary kind was sold at 54 *soldi* a bushel.

3rd February. A preacher belonging to the *Frati Minori*, who was preaching in San Lorenzo, was sent away.

6th February. Several women were suffocated in the crowd in the *Piazza del Grano*, and some of them were brought out half-dead, which may seem incredible, but it is true, because I saw it myself.

10th February. Another woman and a man were suffocated in the *Piazza del Grano* whilst bread was being given out by the commune.

11th February (Saturday). The price of the best corn was 4 *lire*.

19th February. The *Piazza del Grano* was looted.

20th February. We heard that the French king's fleet, which was at Livorno, had captured two small merchant vessels bringing corn to the harbour of Piombino, and had taken them to Livorno. This was an advantage to us.[1]

28th February. The price of corn remained unchanged.

10th March. The tax of the *Ventina* (the twentieth part) was collected.

12th March. We heard that three shiploads of corn had arrived in the harbour of Pisa for us.

13th March. We heard that the Pope had bought back Ostia from the French.

15th March. We had a *Pardon* in *Santa Maria del Fiore*.

19th March. More than one child was found dead of hunger in Florence.

[1] The "two ships laden with corn, captured near Piombino by the five French boats," belonged to the Pisans (*Lettere degli Anziani di Pisa*).

20th March. The mother-in-law of Piero de' Medici was condemned to banishment, and she left the city the same day.[1]

21st March. There was suspicion of a plot of Piero de' Medici, who it was said wanted to enter Firenzuola, and to give flour and corn to the people, making them cry *Palle*; but all this was not true.

24th March (*Venerdì Santo* = Good Friday). A friar[2] preached in Santo Spirito, who spoke against Fra Girolamo, and all through Lent he had been saying that the *Frate* was deceiving us and that he was not a prophet. He said childish things, and there continued to be greater crowds than ever to listen to Fra Girolamo. There were continually 15 thousand people at his sermon every week-day.

1497. 27th March. During all this time, men, women, and children were falling down exhausted from hunger, and some died of it, and many died at the hospital who had grown weak from starvation.

2nd April. A horrible thing happened outside the *Porta di San Piero Gattolino*[3] at a tallow-chandler's. The house caught fire and was burnt down, with all the people in it, four women and girls and three boys, one of them a big lad, making seven people. No one escaped except the father, who chanced to be at Arezzo just then.

4th April. Many women swooned in the *Piazza del Grano*, and two of them died.

5th April. There came a certain nun from Ponte a Rignano who had some repute for holiness, and she began to speak against Fra Girolamo. She was not allowed to continue long, however.[4]

8th April. The price of corn went up to 4 *lire* 10 *soldi*.

12th April. The price of corn went up to 5 *lire*; and I sold a small quantity that I had over, at 4 *lire* 13 *soldi*. I call myself on that account ungrateful.

[1] She was the Contessa Caterina da San Severino, whom the *Otto di Guardia e Balia* had ordered, on the 17th March, *pro bono reipublice*, to leave the city and territory of Florence. The "Twenty" commanded two citizens to accompany her as far as Siena (*Libro di Partiti e Deliberazioni di detti Ufficiali, ad an*).

[2] This must have been that Fra Leonardo mentioned further on, on 18th June, 1497. [3] Now *Porta Romana*.

[4] Savonarola told her to attend to her spinning and the business of a nun (Burlamacchi, *Vita di Fra Girolamo*). In the *Storia fiorentina* MS. di *Piero Parenti* we read that her name was Suora Maddalena, and she belonged to the convent of *Santa Maria a Casignano*.

14th April. We heard that a ship had arrived at Livorno with 2500 *moggia* (1 *moggio* = 8 bushels) of corn.

16th April. We heard that our troops had captured the bastion of *Ponte a Stagno* from the Pisans.

18th April. There was a commotion in Florence, which arose in the Piazza de' Signori and in the Piazza del Grano. Some poor women went to the door of the *Palagio* begging for bread, and all over the city ran the cry of *Serra, serra!* (Close everything!); so that everyone took in their wares (from the outside shelves), and some shut up their shops.

19th April (Wednesday). The price of corn went down 8 *soldi* a bushel.

21st April. Those marble columns in the passage from the *Palagio* into the Great Hall, towards the *Mercatantia*, were finished.[1]

25th April. We heard that Piero de' Medici was at Siena with a large body of soldiers, so that we set guards at night.

27th April. We heard that he was at Staggia.

28th April. We heard that he was at Castellina; and then again that he was at Certosa. In fact, before 24 hours had passed he was at Fonte di San Gaggio, with 2000 men on foot and on horseback. Therefore, towards the dinner-hour, the *Gonfalonieri* and all the chief citizens armed themselves and went to the *Porta di San Piero Gattolino*. And at about 21 in the evening (5 p.m.) he turned back and went away, seeing that he had no supporters in Florence. It was considered a most foolish thing for him to have put himself in such danger, for if we had wished, we could have captured him; if the alarm-bell had been rung outside, he would have been surrounded. As it was, he returned to Siena, not without fear.[2]

1st May. We heard that Giuliano de' Medici was mustering men in the neighbourhood of Bruscoli.

4th May (the Ascension). Fra Girolamo preached in *Santa Maria del Fiore*, and certain unscrupulous enemies of his played him a villainous trick. The night before, out of spite, they had forced their way into the church, breaking

---

[1] As far back as the 9th December, 1495, the *Signoria* had ordered the controllers of the property of the Medici to consign to the purveyor of works at the *Palagio* the columns of Piero de' Medici's Chapel, *ut illa deputent in Palatio*, etc. The *Mercatanzia* was opposite the north side of the *Palagio*.

[2] The *Anziani di Pisa* wrote on the same day: "the enterprise of Piero de' Medici turned to smoke."

open the door next to the belfry, and entering the pulpit, had covered it with dirt, which had to be scraped off before he could begin preaching. This morning, too, when he had got about two-thirds of the way through his sermon, there was a certain noise in the neighbourhood of the choir, like someone knocking a stick in a box. We believed that it was done on purpose by these same men. There was a commotion immediately, everyone crying: "Jesu!" because the people were excited, and on the look-out for these bad men to cause a disturbance. Soon after the people had calmed down again, there was another cry of "Jesu!" on account of a disturbance near the pulpit, where stood some men secretly armed, in defence of the *Frate*. They now caught sight of some whom they suspected, and approaching the pulpit, a man of the name of Lando Sassolino struck another called Bartolomeo Giugni with the flat of his sword. By chance the latter was one of the "Eight," therefore the said Lando was condemned as a rebel by the "Eight" if he did not appear before them. But he did appear, and there was a great scandal.

5th May. The *Signori* made a decision that no order of *Frati* could preach without their permission, and they had all the stools, and benches, and the stands for the boys removed from *Santa Maria del Fiore*.[1] This was done from a grudge which they had against the poor *Frate*, who had said beforehand: "I know that you do not wish me to preach, but do not forbid me, or it will go ill with you," and he would not obey them. All thoughtful people, expecting serious disturbances, and believing him a true prophet who announced great things (which were confirmed by facts), said that it ought to be written everywhere that there was a *Frate* in Florence who preached the renovation of the

[1] The *Signoria*, by a decree of the 3rd May, considering that the summer was approaching, and that the assembling of many people caused danger from the plague, because of this and other motives, prohibited all sermons in future during this *priorato*, except for the following day, which was the Ascension. They also ordered that within five days all stools, benches, etc., placed in the churches for those who attended the sermons should be removed. These decisions, therefore, were not taken in consequence of the disorders which happened during the sermon on Ascension Day. The debate is published in vol. ii. of the *Storia di Girolamo Savonarola e dei suoi tempi*, a valuable work of Professor *Pasquale Villari*, which may be consulted with profit by the readers of this Diary who wish to verify the facts here related concerning the *Frate*.

Church, and that he said: "Write this also: that I have it from God." At this time the *Signori* and the "Eight" gave themselves over to gambling and indulged in every sort of vice, opening the *Frascato*,[1] taverns, etc.

6th May. The price of corn was lowered 20 *soldi*; it returned to 3 *lire*.

8th May. Fra Girolamo wrote an epistle, and had it published, which exhorted people to stand firm in the faith, declaring that wicked and infuriated men had pronounced their own condemnation, by being so villanous as to violate the temple of God.

11th May. The *Signoria*, Piero degli Alberti being *Gonfaloniere*, had the balls which were the arms of the Medici destroyed and chiselled away on the palace of the Medici, in Sa' Lorenzo, and elsewhere.[2]

12th May. It was voted in Council that for certain high offices the elections should be made as formerly; and for the lesser offices, six should be drawn by lot, and the names which came out should be put in again and drawn for again.[3]

13th May. The price of corn rose again to 4 *lire* 15 *soldi*.

18th May. At this time many people died of fever in the city and at the hospitals, this fever making them rave and lose consciousness, and when that happened they died in two or three days. At Santa Maria Nuova twelve died every day. An order was given that the poor should

---

[1] *Frascato* was the name given in very early times to a place near the *Piazza de' Succhiellinai*, not far from the *Mercato Vecchio*. It is now incorporated in the *Ghetto*. There was an ancient and celebrated tavern there, a brothel, and men went there to gamble. It is this place that *Franco Sacchetti* alludes to in his Tale 187. In the edition of these Tales, Florence, 1857, this word is explained as follows: *Pergola di frasche davanti all' osterie di campagna* (An arbour of green boughs before country inns). And townspeople have used this misnomer!

[2] The decree is of the 8th and orders that wherever the Commune of Florence has jurisdiction, the arms of Lorenzo de' Medici and his sons and heirs shall be destroyed; and that in place of these (wherever it can conveniently be done) shall be placed the arms of the Florentine people, i.e. the red cross in a white field; all this at the expense of officials of the rebels and of the controllers of their heirs, as was decided in another decree of the 13th.

[3] This decree, which reforms the mode of election, contains other orders on this subject, besides that of the six electors. They were to be observed till the end of December 1498, unless other dispositions were made later.

be sheltered in the Pope's stables, and each of them given a loaf of bread every evening.¹

24th May. It was said that the Pope had sent a summons to Fra Girolamo.

25th May (the *Corpus Christi*). A number of children walked in the procession, carrying little red crosses in their hands; and because it was the order of Fra Girolamo that they should carry these red crosses, everybody hated poor Fra Girolamo, the young men even more than the old ones. You will always find that anyone who hates the things that are in their nature good, and does not see or recognise truth in another, errs and sins. But this morning the following villany and profanation took place: When the said procession was crossing the *Ponte di Santa Trinità*, some lads stood to watch it beside the chapel which is on the bridge to the right hand going towards Santo Spirito.² Seeing the boys with these crosses, they said: "Here come the boys of Fra Girolamo!" And one of them approaching, snatched a little cross from one of the boys, and broke it and threw it into the river, as if he were a heathen; and all this was only out of hate for the *Frate*. This lad avenged himself on Christ. Intelligent and judicious men thought this a shocking thing. Fools mock at good and evil alike.

27th May (Saturday). The price of corn was 4 *lire* 10 *soldi* a bushel, and that of the commune was given at 52 *soldi* or at 3 *lire* a bushel, but it was very difficult to obtain it. At this time we were deprived of the word of God. No sermons were allowed to be preached in any church. Certain most infamous epistles were now pub-

¹ The decree of the *Signoria* ordered that there should be consigned *illis de Sancto Martino, videlicet Societatis de Vergognosi, Stabula quae nuncupantur* of the Pope, *posita in* Via della Scala, *ut in eis hospitentur pauperi et mendicantes existentes in civitate Florentie, non habentes domicilium vel hospicium in quo possint hospitari*. They were also consigned for the same object *omnia loca et mansiones hospitalium peregrinantium existentia in civitate Florentie*. The following day, this business of receiving the poor was entrusted to the *Collegi*, i.e. to the *Gonfalonieri* of the companies and to the twelve *Buonuomini*, to whom the officials of *Abbondanza* were to give every day six bushels of corn, *ut possint eosdem pauperes in aliqua parte alere*.

² Perhaps that oratory of San Michele alluded to by Manni in vol. vii. of the *Sigilli*, and which was destroyed with the bridge in the flood of 1557.

lished against Fra Girolamo, from the hand of a *Frate* of Santo Spirito.

31st May. The price of corn was 5 *lire* a bushel, and I sold it at 4 *lire* 16 *soldi*; I could have had more than 5 *lire* if I had wished, although I had very little to sell.

1st June. Many people died of fever after being ill only a few days, some in eight days and some in ten; and there was one man who died in four days. It was said that during these last days of the waning moon there were 120 cases at the hospitals and in the city together. It was also said that there was a touch of plague at the hospital. Ten or twelve cases went there each day, and 24 have died just lately at Santa Maria Nuova. At the same time there was another trouble, the spiritual discouragement and physical weakness, which caused the poor to be indifferent as to dying; and numbers of them did die, in fact. Everyone said: "This is an honest plague."

10th June. There was fresh corn in the market, and the price dropped a little.

11th June. The *palio* of Santo Barnabà [1] was run, which had not been run for years in Florence, on account of the prophet's sermons. This *Signoria* decided to allow it to take place, and no longer pay attention to the warnings of the *Frate*, saying: "Let us cheer up the people a little; are we all to become monks?" And still they deprived us of the word of God.

13th June. There died in one day about 100, between the hospitals and the city, whilst the moon was at its full (*nella quintadecima*).

16th June. A little bell fell down in *Santa Maria del Fiore*, one of those which are rung at the elevation of the Host, and it struck a certain Dino on the head and nearly killed him. Several pieces of bone were taken out of his skull.

18th June. An excommunication came from the Pope excommunicating Fra Girolamo, which was published this morning in Santo Spirito, in Santa Maria Novella, in Santa

[1] The *palio* of San Barnaba was instituted to commemorate the victory of the Florentine militia at Campaldino on this saint's day in the year 1289. The *palio* won by the victorious horse was of scarlet silk, and cost twenty gold florins. The horses started from the *Ponte sul Mugnone* (called on this account Ponte alle Mosse), and ran through the city, to the Piazza di Sant' Apollinare (now part of Piazza San Firenze). [Trans.]

Croce, in the Badìa, and at the Servi. I heard it read and proclaimed in Santo Spirito, in the chancel, between two lighted tapers, and amidst a number of friars. It was read and proclaimed by Fra Leonardo, their preacher, and the adversary of Fra Girolamo. It declared that the said *Frate* had not obeyed a certain Brief which had been sent as far back as the November of 1496, summoning him on his vow of obedience to go to the Pope; and if he did not choose to obey the excommunication, no one was to give him aid or support, and no one must go and hear him, nor go to any place where he was, on pain of excommunication.[1]

19th June. We heard that a son of the Pope had been murdered and thrown into the Tiber.[2]

20th June. Fra Girolamo published an epistle in protest against the excommunication, by which he justified himself, in some people's opinion.[3]

23rd June. A boy fell from the big bell of the *Palagio* on to the gallery, and died in a few days.

24th June (Saturday). The price of corn at the corn market was 3 *lire*.

28th June. It was said that there were 60 deaths a day from fever.

30th June. Plague broke out in several houses in the city, and in eight houses in the *Borgo di Ricorboli*.

1st July. Domenico Bartoli was *Gonfaloniere*.

2nd July. Many were dying of fever and plague, and one day there were 25 deaths at *Santa Maria Nuova*.

3rd July. More houses infested with plague were dis-

---

[1] It has been repeatedly printed that this excommunication, i.e. the Brief of the 12th or 13th May, was published in *Santa Maria del Fiore* on the 22nd June. I believe, however, that we must keep to the date given by Landucci, which is the same as we read in the before-mentioned *Storia* of *Parenti*. In fact, it must have been read on a feast-day, and the 18th June fell on a Sunday. *Parenti* also agrees with our author in his indication of the five churches in which it was proclaimed, only putting *San Francesco del Monte* in the place of *Santa Croce*, as does also *Nardi*. There were necessarily several copies of the Brief, so as to send one to each of the convents mentioned; and consequently that published by *Villari* and addressed to the *Serviti* is as authentic as that edited by Professor *Del Lungo* and addressed to the monks at the *Badìa*.

[2] The Duke of Candia, ordered to be murdered by Valentino.

[3] Placing the 18th as the date of the excommunication, this letter was really written as a defence, and not in anticipation, as some have thought, naturally not finding any other way of making it agree with the supposed publication of the excommunication on the 22nd.

covered here, making everyone think of fleeing from it. At this time the price of fowls was 3 *lire* a couple, and of capons 7 or 8 *lire* a couple; there were so many sick persons.

8th July. The officials of the *Abbondanza*[1] fixed the price of corn at the corn market at 35 *soldi*.

9th July. Plague broke out in *San Marco*, and many of the *Frati* left it and went away to the villas of their fathers and relatives and friends. Fra Girolamo remained at *San Marco*, with only a few *Frati*. At this time there were about 34 houses with plague in Florence, and there was also a good deal of fever.

11th July. We heard that the *Signore* of Mantua had gone to Venice, and the Venetians wanted to behead him: or rather, he suspected it; and he let himself down from his window by tying linen sheets together and fled back to Mantua. This was on account of its being said that he had been appointed a captain of the King of France.

12th July (Wednesday). The price of fresh corn of good quality was 45 *soldi*.

16th July. There was plague in about 30 houses in Florence, and there were also many deaths from fever. And it is to be noticed that all those who died were heads of families, from 20 to 50 years of age, not children. It seemed as if the prophecy of the *Frate* were to be realised as to the renovation of the Church and the world.

20th July. Many poor people fell down in the streets from exhaustion, and all day long they were picked up by those appointed to the work, and carried in litters to the hospital, where they died.

23rd July. A priest who was officiating in *Santa Maria Maggiore* was arrested by the "Eight," and he confessed to having secretly declared that Fra Girolamo and Fra Domenico and all the *Frati* at *San Marco* were Sodomites, on account of a grudge that he had against them. This morning he was sent by the "Eight" to proclaim the good repute of the *Frati*; and he mounted a pulpit placed on the steps of *Santa Maria del Fiore*, in the *Piazza di San*

[1] The business of these "Officers of Abundance" was to regulate the supply, examine the quality, and settle the price, of the corn; in times of scarcity they sent to distant countries to procure it, and made arrangements for distributing it at a moderate cost to the poor. The rich merchants would send large quantities to be disposed of as these officers might direct. [Trans.]

Giovanni, against the *Campanile*, and in the presence of all the people said that he had told lies and publicly confessed his error. Nevertheless the "Eight" sent him to the *Stinche*, where he was confined in a cage.

29th July. There was an eclipse of the sun, and many people were dying of plague and fever, which caused the city to empty itself of its inhabitants, everyone who could, going into the country.

5th August. One of the Dell' Antelli was arrested; and when flogged he confessed to a certain plot with Piero de' Medici, and accused many,[1] who were sent for and detained in the *Palagio* and the *Bargello*, and put to the rack. Amongst these were Lorenzo Tornabuoni, Gianozzo Pucci, Bernardo Del Nero, Niccolò Ridolfi, and others who fled, Piero, son of Filippo Tornabuoni and Butte de' Medici[2] being among the latter.

6th August. Signore Rinuccio and other leaders were sent for, and soldiers were hired in the Piazza.

10th August. There was much talk in the city as to what would be done with them (these prisoners); some said they were not guilty, and some said they were.

13th August. It was said that the Tornabuoni had despatched an *estafette* to the King of France, to beg that he should request the liberation of Lorenzo.

15th August. The following case happened: At the church of San Pagolo, in the churchyard outside it, the gravediggers were burying someone, and one of them dropped his keys into the grave, and went down into it to get them; but there was such a stench that he died there before they could draw him up again.

16th August. The price of corn went down to 3 *lire*.

17th August. The *Pratica* (Court) met and sat in the *Palagio* from the morning till midnight. There were more than 180 men. And the five prisoners were condemned by word of mouth to be put to death and their property to be confiscated according to law. The five men condemned were Bernardo Del Nero, Niccolò Ridolfi, Giovanni Canbi, Gianozzo Pucci, and Lorenzo Tornabuoni, for whom all Florence was sorry. Everyone marvelled that such a thing could be done; it was difficult to realise it. They were put

---

[1] The confession of this Dell' Antella, whose name was Lamberto, was published by *Villari* amongst the documents of his *Storia*.
[2] Andrea de' Medici, called *il Butta*.

to death the same night,[1] and I could not refrain from weeping when I saw that young Lorenzo carried past the Canto d' Tornaquinci on a bier, shortly before dawn.

And although they had asked for an appeal, and were told by the lawyers, principally by Messer Guido Antonio Vespucci, that it could be made, it was not granted them; which seemed too cruel to such men as they were. However, everything happens in accordance with God's will. May all be to His glory!

And a proclamation was published ordering anyone who had property belonging to these five men to declare it.

24th August. A good many were banished to certain boundaries: Tinca Martegli and Jacopo, son of Messer Bongianni, Tomasino Corbinegli, Lionardo Bartolini, and Francesco Dini.

17th September. The boys went to the *Signoria* to ask that Fra Girolamo might preach, and that the stands might be replaced in *Santa Maria del Fiore*.

1st October. A *Frate* of the Carmelites, from that church of the *Virgine Maria* which is at the corner of the city walls near the *Porta di San Friano*, preached; and he confirmed much of the doctrine of Fra Girolamo, saying: "God has told me that he is a holy man and that his doctrine is true, and whoever has resisted him and spoken ill of the divine work, whether they are *Signori*, or monks, or great *Maestri*, their tongues shall be torn out and thrown to the dogs," and more follies. He was sent for to the archbishop's palace, and was forbidden to preach.

5th October. There came to Florence a son [2] of Messer Giovanni Bentivogli, in the pay of the Florentines, with 100 armed men. He was in fine array and went to Pisa.

16th October (Monday). They exiled many citizens to certain boundaries for the same fault. Then Filippo dell' Antella and Sforzo Bettini were taken out of prison and assigned certain boundaries in our territory. And besides this, those who had been cited to appear and had not done so, were also confined to certain boundaries; that is to say, Messer Piero Alamanni, Messer Tommaso Minerbetti, Messer Luigi Tornabuoni, and Piero his brother.

[1] They were put to death on the night of the 21st, the day on which their appeal had been rejected and a second Court had been held.

[2] Alessandro; and we find that precisely on this day the *Suonatori* (Musicians) of the *Signoria* had permission to go and play in his honour (*Deliberazioni de' Signori e Collegi, ad an*).

18th October. Many heads of households and worthy citizens kept dying of fever, but no women or children.

19th October. At this time the plague was discovered in several houses, so that the citizens stayed in their villas.

28th October. In the *Mercato Nuovo*, on one of the stone seats against the wall, next to the tables of the money-changers, there was a man of about 50 years of age sitting with his face in his hand, as if he wished to sleep; and whilst he sat there he passed from this life, without any of those standing by noticing it. He did not make a single movement. Presently seeing his pallor and touching him, they found that he was dead. And so he sat there dead for hours with his face on his hand, and no one went near him, thinking that he had died of the plague, which struck down so many.

1st November. The truce with the Pisans [1] and all Tuscany ended, and we kept hiring soldiers continually, because it was said that the Venetians were sending men to Pisa [2]; and we were always in suspense, expecting the king (of France), who was supposed to be going to pass through.

3rd November. We heard that a thunderbolt had fallen upon the Castello Sant' Agnolo at Rome last Sunday, the 29th October, at 14 in the morning (10 a.m.). Great mischief was done: the thunderbolt struck the angel and threw it to the ground, and then it fell among the munitions and set them on fire, so that the tower burst, and wood and stones, crossbows and armour were hurled to the other side of the Tiber; men were killed also. It was a frightful thing.

6th November. The Pisans came to make an agreement; but nothing was concluded.

7th November. The plague began at Dicomano.

9th November. The Studio [3] returned to Florence from

---

[1] The truce made between Spain and France, in which the Pisans were included, being considered as adherents of Spain. Hostilities, however, did not begin at once: in fact the *Anziani di Pisa* wrote on the 12th November: "The enemy waits, and we also."

[2] "The *Illma Signoria* of Venice has sent here the Magco M. Marco Martanengo, with 600 horsemen well-arrayed, and with him he sends 200 *stradiotti*, Greeks and Albanians" (*Archivio pisano, Lettere degli Anziani, ad an.,* c. 218 t).

[3] This was opened in the year 1348, the moment that the plague was over, and obtained from Pope Clement VI. the privilege of conferring degrees; but it never became one of the large universities, partly because the expense seemed too great to many of the

Prato where it had been holding its meetings; there were about 40 readers.

13th November. Cavalry sent by the Venetians arrived at Pisa; and here we went on hiring soldiers, expecting war to break out.[1]

15th November. One morning at dawn a dead girl was found under the portico of the Spedale di San Pagolo here at Florence; she was discovered by those who looked after those sick of the plague, and they judged that she had not died of the plague but had been strangled. When the "Eight" heard of it, they published a proclamation, declaring that anyone who knew about it and concealed his knowledge would be put to death.

18th November. The price of corn went down, returning to 50 *soldi*; and the *abbondanza* put it at 40 *soldi*.

19th November. The "Eight" made a proclamation against Fra Mariano da Ghignazzano and others who were his companions, forbidding them to enter Florentine territory on pain of death; because he was accused of having had a hand in plotting for Piero de' Medici to return to Florence.[2]

26th November. We heard that the Pisans had raided our territory as far as Bibbona, driving away cattle.

29th November. The crucifix was taken off the altar at *Santa Maria del Fiore*, and put down below, where the canons sit; and on the High Altar was placed instead a

citizens, and partly because art appealed more than science to this mobile city. Boccaccio commented here on Dante. It flourished mostly in 1421. Niccolò da Uzzano left the greater part of his fortune to found a college in connection with it; but jealousy prevented his behest being carried out. The street in which stood the house intended for this purpose took the name of *Sapienza*; and the house was bought by Savonarola for San Marco to use for schools. [Trans.] The *Studio* had removed to Prato in consequence of the rebellion of Pisa. *Parenti*, who was one of the directors, wrote that it was now (in 1497) taking refuge in Florence, "the plague being at Prato, and the Pistolese and the *Aretini* quarrelling as to which of them should have it."

[1] Here begins the gap in the autograph MS., and I, Jodsco del Badia, have supplied that which follows from the MS. of the Maruccelliana at Florence.

[2] The debate of the "Eight" on the 17th calls him Magister Marianus de Ghinazano, a monk of the church of San Gallo fuori delle mura, belonging to the Order of Sant' Agostino. By his companions are not to be understood the monks of the same Order, only one of whom we find condemned, but his accomplices in this plot, amongst whom was also a lay brother of the *Certosa*.

carved wooden tabernacle for the Host, not yet gilt, but beautiful to see.

2nd December. There came to Florence a cardinal, son of the Duke of Ferrara, on his way to Rome to visit the Pope, who had lately made him cardinal. He was a boy of about 22 years old. We did him honour, many citizens going to meet him.[1]

14th December. We heard that our troops had made a raid as far as Pisa,[2] and taken much booty in the Val di Calci.

16th December. Cegino was beheaded in the court of the *Capitano*, for the same crime of having plotted for the Medici.[3]

6th January. The *Signoria* of Florence went to the offering at *San Marco*, and kissed Fra Girolamo's hand at the altar; to the great surprise of thoughtful men, not only his adversaries but also among his friends. It was the Epiphany.[4] At this time the cold was very severe, and the Arno froze.

11th February. Fra Girolamo began to preach in *Santa Maria del Fiore*, and the stands (for the boys) were made as

---

[1] This cardinal was Ippolito d'Este.

[2] A letter written by the *Anziani di Pisa* gives many details as to this raid; amongst other things, that the Pisans made a sortie and recovered part of the booty, of which there had been a great quantity.

[3] As far back as the 14th November, the "Eight" had condemned Francesco d'Agostino Ciegia and Luca Speranzini to death, as partisans of Piero de' Medici. In the *Archivio di Stato di Firenze* is found a book of this Agostino Ciegia, formerly belonging to the library of the Senator Carlo Strozzi; and it is entitled *Libretto sagreto*, and signed *A piccola*. On the first page one reads: "I record to-day, this 14th March (1495), that I have begun this secret book concerning the disturbances and changes of government which have taken place in our city, and chiefly on the 9th November last." And he narrates the driving away of the Medici, and continues as follows: "and when Piero was gone, I had to hide myself because I was his adherent, and Sunday night I remained in the house of Francesco Guardi, and afterwards on Monday, Tuesday, and Wednesday, in the house of Silamo the barber in *Via di San Gallo*, and on Thursday I went before the *Signoria*, as I was ordered to appear on pain of death. I was detained for ten days, and all that time was in great dread; but I was liberated through God's mercy and the King of France."

[4] This date was that of the chief feast, the dedication of the church, and the *Signoria*, in accordance with old custom, went to the offering. I was much surprised to see that this act was fulfilled that year also, without regard to the excommunication of the *Frate*.

before.[1] Many people went there, and it was much talked of, on account of his excommunication; and many did not go, for fear of being excommunicated, saying : *giusta vel ingiusta, temenda est.* I was one of those who did not go. We did not hear much of the plague now; it was in one or two houses, but not more.

15th February. Fra Girolamo preached in *San Marco*, only wishing for the attendance of priests and monks, and he told them of their defects, according to what was reported to me by one of them.

During these days the war with Pisa was less active, on account of the hard winter.

17th February. Fra Girolamo preached in *Santa Maria del Fiore*, and fewer people went. At this time the cold was intense, there having been frost for more than two months, so that it was feared the grain would be destroyed and the harvest spoilt in the colder districts.

24th February (Saturday). Fra Girolamo preached in *Santa Maria del Fiore*, continuing to show that he took no heed of the excommunication; and observe that all the said sermons have been written down and published by a young notary, whose name is Ser Lorenzo Vivioli, who has achieved a superhuman feat, as we may say, having written down things that this *Frate* never said in the pulpit, and epistles and other things written and spoken during many years. You could not find anything more marvellous in the world, and no other miracle can be required in this work than the fact of the very least word and act being inscribed exactly, without a single iota wanting, which may well seem impossible, but it was done by divine permission, as is thought by righteous men.

27th February (the Carnival). There was made on the *Piazza de' Signori* a pile of vain things, nude statues and playing-boards, heretical books, Morganti,[2] mirrors, and many other vain things, of great value, estimated at thousands of florins. The procession of boys was made as the year before; they collected in four quarters, with crosses

---

[1] Savonarola's friends had ordered the stands and benches to be replaced in great haste during the last days of January, for they felt sure that he would preach on Candlemas Day.

[2] *Il Morgante maggiore* was a heroic poem by Luigi Pulci, well known, but now little read. The subject was treated jestingly, and its style pleased Lorenzo de' Medici and his companions ; the most sacred things were scoffed at, under a veil of delicate irony. [Trans.]

and olive-branches in their hands, each quarter arranged in order with tabernacles in front, and went in the afternoon to burn this pile. Although some lukewarm people gave trouble, throwing dead cats and other dirt upon it, the boys nevertheless set it on fire and burnt everything, for there was plenty of small brushwood. And it is to be observed that the pile was not made by children; there was a rectangular woodwork measuring more than 12 *braccia* [1] each way, which had taken the carpenters several days to make, with many workmen, so that it was necessary for many armed men to keep guard the night before, as certain lukewarm persons, specially certain young men called *Compagnacci* wanted to destroy it. The *Frate* was held in such veneration by those who had faith in him, that this morning, although it was Carnival, Fra Girolamo said mass in *San Marco*, and gave the Sacrament with his hands to all his friars, and afterwards to several thousand men and women; and then he came on to a pulpit outside the door of the church with the Host, and showing it to the people, blessed them, with many prayers: *Fac salvum populum tuum Domine*, etc. There was a great crowd, who had come in the expectation of seeing signs; the lukewarm laughed and mocked, saying: "He is excommunicated, and he gives the Communion to others." And certainly it seemed a mistake to me, although I had faith in him; but I never wished to endanger myself by going to hear him, since he was excommunicated.

28th February (the first day of Lent). He preached, and said that the wicked had their hide full, having indulged in every sort of evil, especially at night, when certain suppers were given by the *Compagnacci*, all lukewarm persons who considered that they took a more broad-minded view, not being so hard upon sin, and condoning the life of an epicure.

1st March. Fra Girolamo preached in *Santa Maria del Fiore*, and took his leave, saying that a ban had come from the Pope [2]; and this being so, he took leave and would only preach in *San Marco*. One of his friars preached in *Santa Maria del Fiore* in the evening; and after this the number

---

[1] A *braccio* was about 23 inches. [Trans.]
[2] The Pope sent a Brief to the canons of the *Duomo*, ordering them to forbid Savonarola to preach in that church (*Villari*, op. cit., vol. ii., p. 90).

of people at *San Marco* kept increasing; and it was said that he had written to the Pope, admonishing him to amend his ways, or else ill would come of it, and heavy punishment might be expected, and that quickly.

11th March. Continuing to preach in *San Marco*, he declared to the city that there would be a tyrant, and he already saw many signs of it.

14th March. Councils were held to consider how they could act with regard to this *Frate*, and it ended with many citizens making harangues: one wished to forbid him to preach, and another not; and there was a serious controversy, influenced by reasons of State; none the less he continued to preach, and the Pope threatened to put the city under an interdict. It seemed extraordinary that the Pope could not silence him, and still more so that he stood firm and did not cease preaching.

17th March. The *Signoria* sent five citizens to Fra Girolamo in the evening, begging him not to preach for a few days; and he replied that he must first ask Him who sent him to preach; nevertheless, during his next sermon in *San Marco*, he took leave of the congregation, with threats against whoever was the cause of this.[1]

18th March. Fra Domenico da Pescia preached in *San Marco*, and one of the *Frati* of *San Marco* preached at *Santa Maria del Fiore* in the evening.

21st March. We heard that the Pope was so incensed with the Florentines that nothing would appease him. Many merchants received letters which made them fear lest their places of business in Rome should be sacked. Besides this there were letters saying that Fra Mariano da Ghignazzano was fanning the flame to the best of his ability, having preached one sermon amongst others, in Rome, in which he called Fra Girolamo a drunkard; and he became so enraged during his sermon, at which several cardinals were present, that he said that if it were not for his respect for the Pope, he would use still coarser language, and he actually dared to make unseemly gestures in the pulpit (according to what was said by those who came from Rome). This shows what envy can do! And observe, it appeared to be envy, because before he was excommunicated they were still more inimical and accused him

[1] That day the Court had assembled again, seeing that nothing was concluded on the 14th.

falsely. Thus it appeared as if it were only envy, but may be not.

24th March. We heard that the Duke of Milan had come to Genoa, bringing with him 200 citizens, having fled on account of the distrust that he felt.

1498. 25th March. Certain writings were found at the door of *Santa Croce* and of *Orto San Michele*, which said: *Popolo, e' non è il Frate la tua malattia, ma sono certi pinzocheroni* (People, it is not the *Frate* who is your undoing, but certain bigots); and Francesco Valori and Pagoloantonio Soderini were named, it being said: *Andate a casa loro con fuoco* (Go and set fire to their houses). Note that at this time spiritual things were mocked at; and there were some scoffers in the city who behaved in an unscrupulous way, taking candle-ends and pretending to go about searching, saying: *Io cerco della chiavicina ch' ha perduto el Frate* (I am looking for the little key that the *Frate* has lost); one of them seizing hold of people and making them kneel down before a lighted lantern, saying: *Adora el vero lume* (Adore the true light), and another lighting up the *finestre impannate* [1] (windows), and other contemptuous things. This was because the *Frate* had used the word *la chiavina*, and had said that the renovation of the Church would be *el vero lume*, and it was done by young men of little intelligence.

26th March. Some said that the interdict for Florence had arrived, and that the fact was concealed from us, but this was not true; and all the while the *Frate* was making processions inside the monastery of *San Marco*, walking at their head with a cross in his hands, and all those partaking in them repeating prayers with tearful devotion, some of the citizens having come in, unknown to others.

27th March. Fra Domenico da Pescia, also a friar of *San Marco*, during his sermon invited a preacher who preached at *Santa Croce* to pass through the fire for the truth, when he spoke against Fra Girolamo; and several citizens went to *Santa Croce* as ambassadors.[2]

---

[1] Linen material stretched across the window-frames instead of glass, and soaked in turpentine to make it transparent. These frames opened either upwards or sidewards. [Trans.]

[2] There is much confusion in both the ancient and modern writers in declaring who gave the challenge, and Professor Villari, pointing out the discordance, thinks that we must conclude that the first to do so was the preacher of *Santa Croce*, Fra Francesco da Puglia;

28th March. Fra Domenico preached in *San Marco*, saying that he was willing to pass through the fire; and he said besides that many of his companions would do the same; then turning to the women, he declared that some of them would do this also; and such was the spiritual impetus that many stood up, saying: "*Io sono di quelle*" (I for one am ready).

On this same day the preacher at *Santa Croce* declared that he was willing to pass through the fire, accepting the invitation, and saying: "I believe that I shall burn, but I am content to do so for the sake of liberating this people; if *he* does not burn, then you may believe that he is a true prophet."

29th March. Several friars from *San Marco* went to the *Palagio*, and also several from *Santa Croce*, bringing the decisions to which they had come and the conditions as to how they would make the test; and it was settled that Fra Rondinegli should enter for the Franciscans and Fra Mariano Ughi for *San Marco*.[1]

1st April. Fra Mariano Ughi, of *San Marco*, who had undertaken to enter the fire, preached in *Santa Maria del Fiore*; and this evening he reaffirmed his desire, kneeling in the pulpit before the crucifix, promising absolutely to enter the fire for the truth, and begging that whoever it concerned should proceed with the work. And these things he declared publicly in the pulpit.

2nd April. Fra Girolamo formed a procession within the monastery of *San Marco* with all his friars and many citizens: they came out of the cloisters, went all round the Piazza, and then returned to the church, Fra Girolamo carrying the crucifix and singing psalms.

Landucci makes Fra Domenico give the challenge. It appears to me, after consulting the books and documents, that there were two challenges: first the Franciscan challenged Savonarola, but without result, because the Dominican paid no heed to the provocation. Then Fra Domenico, on his side, not able to bear the attacks of the Pugliese, formulated the doctrine of his master in six conclusions, and invited the adversary to enter the fire to prove them. The latter, however, fenced, saying that his dispute was with Savonarola, and he would enter the fire with *him*. Both sides had gone so far that they could not recede without a scandal, to avoid which it was agreed that Fra Giuliano Rondinelli, another Franciscan, should make the test with Fra Domenico.

[1] Concerning this fact of the trial by fire we may read amongst the documents published by Villari three debates of the *Signoria*.

6th April. Fra Girolamo began to preach in *San Marco*, and declared that he was prepared to let his *Frati* pass through the fire for the truth that he preached; and not only some of his *Frati*, but all were ready to do so by acclamation, and several thousand secular men and women and children; in fact, in the middle of his sermon all the congregation rose to their feet with a cry, offering their life for this truth.

7th April. There was arranged in the *Piazza de' Signori* a scaffold 50 *braccia*[1] long, and 10 *braccia* wide, and 4 *braccia* high; and its foundation was of certain wooden beams, on the four sides of which was made a wall of unbaked bricks, half a *braccio* high, with gravel and rubbish in the middle, and everything covered, in fact, so that the fire could not touch the beams underneath; all along the edges of the said platform were laid big logs of wood, to the height of $2\frac{1}{2}$ *braccia*, the length being 40 *braccia* on each side, 4 *braccia* being left at each end; whilst in the middle a space was left of 2 *braccia* in width, along which the *Frati* would have to pass. Outside and inside of these logs of wood was piled a quantity of brushwood and boughs, so that the passage remaining was only one *braccio* in width; and, besides this, all the wood was soaked with oil, spirit and resin, to make it burn better. The date having been fixed, the *Frati* of San Marco and of San Francesco, who were to pass through the fire, as they had agreed and signed to do, were to present themselves at 17 in the afternoon of the said day (1 p.m.); it having been resolved that Fra Domenico of Pescia should enter for those of *San Marco*, and Fra Giuliano de' Rondinegli of the Osservanza for the Franciscans. At the time fixed, the Franciscans arrived, and went into the Loggia de' Signori, which had been divided by a boarding in the middle, and they stood silently at the end towards San Piero Scheraggio. Then came the Dominicans, with much pomp, a number of *Frati*, about 250, walking two and two, followed by Fra Domenico carrying a crucifix, and then Fra Girolamo carrying the Host; whilst behind them was an immense crowd with torches and tapers, devoutly singing psalms. Having entered the Loggia and prepared an altar, they sang a mass; and the people awaited the great spectacle. After a wait of several hours, everybody began to wonder.

[1] See note to 27th February, 1497.

The reason of the delay was some argument between the *Frati*, the Franciscans wishing Fra Domenico to strip himself of all his outer garments, as they declared he was bewitched; this he was ready to do, but then they made another condition, namely, that he should not carry the Host through the fire with him, which showed that they were desirous to avoid the test. This controversy lasted till the evening, the *Frati* going backwards and forwards to the *Palagio* all the time; and when the dispute ended in the Franciscans leaving, the Dominicans soon followed them, causing great perturbance amongst the people, who almost lost faith in the prophet. The fact was much discussed, especially by those who were against the *Frate*, who felt greatly encouraged. The *Compagnacci* began to fume, saying infamous things, and scoffing at all those who believed in the *Frate's* work, calling them *Piagnoni*[1] (psalm-singers) and hypocrites and other opprobrious names; so that not one of the *Frate's* friends was able to speak.

8th April (Palm Sunday). The following sort of thing began to happen: In *Santa Maria del Fiore*, when vespers were about to begin, and quite a large congregation of men and women was sitting down ready for the sermon, the priests delayed beginning vespers, some said because there was not going to be a sermon, and perhaps on account of these *Compagnacci*, who began to strike the backs of the seats where the women were sitting, using rough language, and saying: *Andate con Dio, piagnonacci* (Go away, go away, you whining old psalm-singers), so that many stood up, and there was a great tumult in the church, anyone who could find the door being lucky. If some of the other men protested, they (the *Compagnacci*) tried to strike at them arrogantly and begin a dispute; and having used their weapons against some of the partisans of the *Frate*, fleeing towards the Via del Cocomero,[2] some were struck and wounded, so that in a few hours the whole city was in arms. The adversaries of the *Frate*, especially the *Compagnia de' Compagnacci*, rushing towards the convent, cried: *A' Frati, a' Frati, a San Marco!* and all the people and the children joined them and ran along with stones,

[1] *Piagnoni* was the name given to Savonarola's followers, who were *Popolani* and averse to the Medicean faction, called *Palleschi*.
[2] Now Via Ricasole.

making it impossible for many men and women who were
in *San Marco* to come out. I chanced to be there; and if
I had not managed to get out through the cloister, and go
away towards the *Porta di San Gallo*, I might have been
killed. Everyone was arming himself, in fact; and a proclamation from the *Palagio* offered 1000 ducats to anyone
who should capture Fra Girolamo and deliver him up to
the authorities. All Florence was in commotion, and
none of the *Frate's* adherents dared to speak, or else they
would have been killed. Before 22 in the evening (6 p.m.),
some of the *Gonfaloni* came armed into the Piazza, and
crying *Popolo!* nearly all of them being *Compagnacci*,
and beginning to shout: *A casa Francesco Valori!* (To
Francesco Vallori's house!); *a sacco!* (sack it!), they ran
there and set fire to the door, and pillaged everything.
Meanwhile Francesco Valori came out of *San Marco*
secretly, into the garden at the back and along by the
walls, where he was seized by two wretched men and
taken to his house. Later in the evening he was fetched by
the mace-bearers of the *Signori*, who promised that his
life should be spared, and led him away to the *Palagio*.
On the way, however, when they were near *San Procolo*,[1]
at the *Canto* where is the tabernacle to the *Vergine Maria*,
a man came up behind him and struck him on the head
with a bill-hook two or three times, so that he died on the
spot. And when they pillaged his house, they had wounded
his wife so that she died, and they also wounded the children
and their nurses, robbing everything.

They also pillaged Andrea Cambini's house,[2] and a house
in Via Larga[3] belonging to a poor man who threw some
tiles out of the windows. Meanwhile there was fighting
round *San Marco*, where the crowd increased all the

[1] The church of San Procolo was built before the year 1000. It is
still standing, although closed, at the corner of the streets Giraldi
and Pandolfini, which last runs into Via Proconsole. It is a small
and low church, which fact has probably saved it from being turned
into a factory. It contains the tombs of the illustrious family of the
Valori. The shrine at the opposite corner still exists also, but
entirely repainted. Francesco Valori was killed by the relatives
of some of those five whom he had so sternly and hastily condemned
to death (Lorenzo Tornabuoni and old Bernardo del Nero, and the
rest). His wife heard the noise and came to the window to look out,
where she was killed by a shot. [Trans.]

[2] Cambini was one of Savonarola's most ardent followers.

[3] Now Via Cavour. [Trans.]

time; and they brought three stone-throwing machines into the Via Larga and the Via del Cocomero, by which some people were wounded and killed. It was said that 15 or 20 persons were killed here and there, and about 100 wounded.

At about 6 in the night (2 a.m.) they set fire to the doors of the church and the cloister of *San Marco*, and penetrating into the church began to fight. Finally, whilst the *Frate* was in the chancel singing the office, two *Frati* came out and said: "We will agree to give up the *Frate* to you, if you will take him to the *Palagio* in safety," and this was promised; so at 7 (3 a.m.) the *Frate* himself and Fra Domenico and Fra Silvestro were given up to them, and they led them off to the *Palagio* with many insults on the way. It is said that they kicked him, saying: *Va là, tristo!* (Go along with you, bad man!); his hands and feet were put in irons, and they confined him closely like a great malefactor, heaping abuse and outrages upon him.

9th April. The same sort of thing went on; weapons were laid aside, but tongues continued to wag, and hell seemed open; people never tired of saying *ladro e traditore* (Wretch and traitor). And no one dared to say a word for the *Frate*, or they would have been killed; the citizens were jeered at as *Piagnoni* and hypocrites.

10th April. At 9 in the evening (5 p.m.) the *Frate* was carried to the *Bargello* by two men on their crossed hands, because his feet and hands were in irons, and Fra Domenico also; and they seized them and put Fra Girolamo to the rack three times and Fra Domenico four times; and Fra Girolamo said: "Take me down, and I will write you my whole life." You may imagine that it was not without tears that right-minded men who had faith in him, heard that he had been tortured; he who had taught this prayer, *Fac bene bonis et rectis corde*. No, it was not without tears and grief, and urgent prayers to God.

13th April. We heard that the King of France was dead,[1] having died on the 7th instant, during a thunderstorm and rough weather, amidst driving rain and disturbance of the elements. I happen to remember it, as I

---

[1] The Pisans wrote to Venice: "The death of the King of France seemed to us good news when we first heard it; now it seems to us excellent, since this *Signoria* rejoices at it for the reasons that you understand."

got soaked through when I went to see the trial by fire, because it was on that day, about 20 in the evening (4 p.m.). The same day we heard that the emperor had had his thigh broken by his horse falling upon him. Also that the Turks had come to Otranto. Also that two gentlemen who had wanted to poison the Duke of Milan had been beheaded.

15th April (Easter Day). Several refectories were burnt down in the convent of the *Murate*,[1] and much damage was done, chiefly to property belonging to citizens. It was not known how the fire had broken out.

17th April. We heard that the Duke of Orleans had been made King of France.

19th April. The protocol of Fra Girolamo, written by his own hand, was read in Council, in the Great Hall; he whom we had held to be a prophet, confessed that he was no prophet, and had not received from God the things which he preached; and he confessed that many things which had occurred during the course of his preaching were contrary to what he had given us to understand. I was present when this protocol was read, and I marvelled, feeling utterly dumbfounded with surprise. My heart was grieved to see such an edifice fall to the ground on account of having been founded on a lie. Florence had been expecting a new Jerusalem, from which would issue just laws and splendour and an example of righteous life, and to see the renovation of the Church, the conversion of unbelievers, and the consolation of the righteous; and I felt that everything was exactly contrary, and had to resign myself with the thought: *In voluntate tua Domine omnia sunt posita.*

21st April. Plague was discovered in many houses, in about four houses again in the Via della Scala, and four other houses here round San Pancrazio,[2] as far as the

---

[1] The *Murate* (the walled-up nuns) was a Benedictine order. In the beginning (1390) one nun shut herself up in a small house on the Ponte Rubiconte, where after six years another joined her; and by the year 1424 they numbered thirteen. In this year they moved to a convent in the Via Ghibellina, purchased for them by their benefactors, and the convent became so popular that the Pope had to limit the number to 150. Their sanctity was held in great repute; they also made beautiful gold and silver embroideries, for which they were reproved by Savonarola. [Trans.]

[2] The church of *San Pancrazio*, which in early times gave its name to one of the quarters of Florence, still stands in the Piazza of the same name, but has long been closed, and is at present used as part

Croce al Trebbio. There were several deaths in two days, because the moon was waxing. The people near were rather alarmed.

22nd April. There was a "Pardon" in *Santa Maria del Fiore*, on occasion of the Jubilee that the Pope had conceded to us; and penitences were granted which could absolve from each and every sin, especially from those excommunications that the *Frate* had caused us to incur by his sermons; the people, on account of their great faith in him, having gone to listen to him when he was excommunicated.

23rd April. The *Frate* was tortured; and certain citizens were detained, Domenico Mazzinghi and others.

24th April. We learnt that Pagoloantonio Soderini had gone to Lucca, out of fear (of being implicated in the business) of the *Frate*.[1]

26th April. A papal messenger arrived with a Brief giving permission for the *Frate* to be treated as might seem good to the envoy whom the Pope would send.

27th April. All the citizens arrested for this cause were scourged, so that from 15 in the morning (11 a.m.) till the evening there were unceasing cries at the *Bargello*.

28th April. A Court was held to try the *Frate* and those citizens whom he had named; and it sat till 7 at night (3 a.m.), without coming to any conclusion; and it was strictly forbidden to lay hands on any of the citizens.

30th April. The Council met again, and appointed the *Gonfalonieri*, and voted the restitution of their rights to certain prisoners in the *Stinche*, and some other provisions; they also voted that those citizens who had been guilty of any error in the Government should pay a fine; but no allusion was made to the *Frate*. About 23 citizens were condemned to pay fines, and to be deprived of their rights; one had to pay a hundred, another two hundred, another a thousand, making a sum of 12 thousand florins.

---

of the tobacco factory which was set up in the suppressed convent. There are two recumbent stone lions in front of the portal. Most of the works of art were removed; but a large fresco, the chief work of Neri di Bicci, remained on the walls of the convent, and is now almost completely obliterated by damp and smoke. [Trans.]

[1] Paolo Somenzi, chancellor of the Duke of Milan, wrote to the latter: "Paolo Antonio Soderini was very fortunate in not being found yesterday, or he would have been killed like Francesco Valori."

1st May. All the citizens were sent back home; and only the three poor *Frati* remained.

2nd May. The tabernacle which had been placed on the High Altar in *Santa Maria del Fiore* to contain the Host was taken away again, and the crucifix replaced there as before.

5th May. The price of corn was 35 *soldi*, and the commune gave it for the same sum.

7th May. We heard that the Pisans had made a raid towards Pescia. It was said that there was a plot by a Frenchman, which did not succeed.[1]

8th May. We heard that Frate Girolamo had written a commentary on the *Miserere mei* in the *Palagio*, in the *Alberghetto*.[2]

9th May. It was voted by the "Eighty" that the Jews might lend on interest. The Lord knows if this was lawful; and it was not carried through in the Great Council.

12th May. The officers of the plague went into the hospitals and drove out the unfortunate sufferers; and wherever they found them in the city they sent them out of Florence. They were actually so cruel as to place a hempen rope with a pulley outside the *Arte de' Corazzai* (Armourers' Guild), to torture those who tried to return. It was a brutal thing and a harsh remedy.

13th May. We heard that the Pope was sending us an envoy and the General of San Marco to try Fra Girolamo; and that he had given permission to the Florentines to impose a tax of three *Decime* on the priests and monks. Some friends of the *Frate* interpreted this as follows: "*This Frate has been sold for 30 pieces of money like the Saviour, because three times ten make thirty.*" Observe that many priests rejoiced at the misfortunes of the *Frate*, and now they had to suffer.

14th May. Two great bells were drawn up into the *Campanile* over the door of San Lorenzo in Florence, without any religious ceremony.

18th May. The second row of windows in Filippo Strozzi's house was finished.

[1] The Pisan letters do not speak of this raid, but speak instead of the storming of the castle of Buti, a profitless enterprise of the Florentines, and of the rout which they suffered a few days later in the neighbourhood of Maremma; all of which things our writer does not mention (*Lettere*, cit., 1499, May 4, c. 4., and 1499, May 19, c. 15 t.).

[2] The name of a prison in the Palazzo della Signoria.

19th May. The Pope's envoy and the General of San Marco arrived in Florence, in order to examine Fra Girolamo.[1]

20th May (Sunday). This envoy had him put to the rack, and before he was drawn up he asked him whether the things that he had confessed were true; and the *Frate* replied that they were not, and that he was sent by God. And then they put him on the rack, and he confessed that he was a sinner, the same as he had said before.

22nd May. It was decided that he should be put to death, and that he should be burnt alive. In the evening a scaffold was made, which covered the whole *ringhiera* of the *Palagio de' Signori*, and then a scaffolding which began at the *ringhiera* next to the "lion" and reached into the middle of the Piazza, towards the *Tetto de' Pisani*; and here was erected a solid piece of wood many *braccia* high, and round this a large circular platform. On the aforesaid piece of wood was placed a horizontal one in the shape of a cross; but people noticing it, said: "They are going to crucify him"; and when these murmurs were heard, orders were given to saw off part of the wood, so that it should not look like a cross.

22nd May (Wednesday morning). The sacrifice of the three *Frati* was made. They took them out of the *Palagio* and brought them on to the *ringhiera*, where were assembled the "Eight" and the *Collegi*, the papal envoy, the General of the Dominicans, and many canons, priests and monks of divers Orders, and the Bishop of the *Pagagliotti* who was deputed to degrade the three *Frati*; and here on the *ringhiera* the said ceremony was to be performed. They were robed in all their vestments, which were taken off one by one, with the appropriate words for the degradation, it being constantly affirmed that Fra Girolamo was a heretic and schismatic, and on this account condemned to be burnt; then their faces and hands were shaved, as is customary in this ceremony.

When this was completed, they left the *Frati* in the hands of the "Eight," who immediately made the decision that they should be hung and burnt; and they were led straight on to the platform at the foot of the cross. The first to be

---

[1] The former was Francesco Romolino, Bishop of Ilerda and afterwards Cardinal, and the latter Fra Girolamo Turriano of Venice, General of the Dominican Order.

executed was Fra Silvestro, who was hung to the post and one arm of the cross, and there not being much drop, he suffered for some time, repeating "Jesu" many times whilst he was hanging, for the rope did not draw tight nor run well. The second was Fra Domenico of Pescia, who also kept saying "Jesu"; and the third was the *Frate* called a heretic, who did not speak aloud, but to himself, and so he was hung. This all happened without a word from one of them, which was considered extraordinary, especially by good and thoughtful people, who were much disappointed, as everyone had been expecting some signs, and desired the glory of God, the beginning of righteous life, the renovation of the Church, and the conversion of unbelievers; hence they were not without bitterness and not one of them made an excuse. Many, in fact, fell from their faith. When all three were hung, Fra Girolamo being in the middle, facing the *Palagio*, the scaffold was separated from the *ringhiera*, and a fire was made on the circular platform round the cross, upon which gunpowder was put and set alight, so that the said fire burst out with a noise of rockets and cracking. In a few hours they were burnt, their legs and arms gradually dropping off; part of their bodies remaining hanging to the chains, a quantity of stones were thrown to make them fall, as there was a fear of the people getting hold of them; and then the hangman and those whose business it was, hacked down the post and burnt it on the ground, bringing a lot of brushwood, and stirring the fire up over the dead bodies, so that the very least piece was consumed. Then they fetched carts, and accompanied by the mace-bearers, carried the last bit of dust to the Arno, by the Ponte Vecchio, in order that no remains should be found. Nevertheless, a few good men had so much faith that they gathered some of the floating ashes together, in fear and secrecy, because it was as much as one's life was worth to say a word, so anxious were the authorities to destroy every relic.

26th May. Certain women were found kneeling in the Piazza on the spot where the *Frati* had been burnt, out of veneration.

27th May. The papal envoy gave notice that anyone who had writings of the *Frate* was to bring them to him in San Piero Scheraggio, to be burnt, on pain of

excommunication, and also the red crosses. Many were
brought to him; and afterwards everyone mocked about
it, because no heresy was found in anything of his. The
Signori who had to pass judgment upon these three
Frati were: Piero son of Niccolò Popoleschi, *Gonfaloniere*;
Chimenti Ciarpelloni, Filippo Cappegli, Alessandro Alessandri, Lionardo son of Giuliano Gondi, Antonio Berlinghieri, Lanfredino Lanfredini; and the "Eight" who
pronounced the sentence were: Piero Parenti, Antonio
son of Domenico Giugni, Francesco Pucci, Domenico
Fagiuoli, Doffo son of Agnolo Spini, Ruberto son of Giovanni Corsini, Francesco son of Cino, and Gabbriello
Becchi.

29th May. The papal envoy left.

1st June. A *Capitano della Guerra* was appointed, whose
name was Pagolo Vitegli, and he was given the bâton.

4th June. A large and sparkling flame of fire was seen
to shoot through the air, very low down, and its trace
remained for some time.

5th June. The new *Capitano* went to Pisa. And in these
days the Pisans made a raid as far as San Miniato al
Tedesco, and took a quantity of booty and many prisoners,
burning an inn below San Miniato on the road to Stibbio.

7th June. The Pisans set up their camp at Ponte di
Sacco, but the next day they fled, because our troops were
approaching and were increasing in numbers.[1]

10th June. On the meadow of the *Servi* and of the
Tiratoio [2] certain caterpillars appeared, which devoured
everything, so that the sloe-bushes became white and
peeled; and within the space of four days these caterpillars turned the colour of gold. The boys caught them,
saying: *These are Fra Girolamo's caterpillars!* and some
looked like gold and some like silver. They were as follows:
they had a human face, with eyes and nose, seeming

---

[1] "This morning we have letters from Cascina, telling us that
when our troops were ready to take the field at Ponte di Sacco and
have a combat, it was heard that Paolo Vitelli had arrived at Montopoli with 200 crossbowmen well mounted and well armed, and that
Vitellozzo with all their men-at-arms was not very far off; therefore
matters are at a standstill, and the idea of making another attack
almost abandoned" (*Lettere*, quoted, 7th June, 1499, Pisan style).

[2] *Tiratoi* were the large open buildings for drying and stretching
cloth; there were several next to the river in the piazza which is
now called Piazza Mentana, and others in the Via de' Servi, with
meadows beyond them.

to have a crown on their head, and round their face a diadem (a halo) as used to be made, whilst between the crown and the head was a little cross; their bodies were golden, and they had a small and slender black tail (*sic!*) with which they ate these sloe-bushes. It seemed miraculous that they were never seen again, and as if it must signify something; and some thought it signified that the life of the *Frate* had been golden, and that after him ill weeds must be rooted out; and thus the sloe, appearing to be the most useless and disagreeable, was to be consumed by the tail, that is to say, by those who came after.

19th June. The "Eight" declared 28 citizens incapable of bearing office, all on account of the matter of the *Frate*.[1]

On the same day the *Signoria* appointed 50 men who had to lend 1 thousand florins each, at 12 per cent. on consignment.

24th June (San Giovanni). A *girandola*[2] was made, on which they placed a pig and giants and dogs and one dead giant. It was said that this was done in contempt of the *Frate*, and that the dead giant was Francesco Valori, and the like foolery. They dragged about the giant, who continually fell down, and they kept on saying: *Quel porco del Frate!* (That pig of a Frate), and other senseless things.

24th June. A citizen who was an exile from Siena was murdered by a man who wanted the reward of 1000 florins, in the middle of the *Mercato Vecchio, in su la terza* (third canonical hour, about dawn), opposite the apothecary's shop with the sign of the *Re* (king).[3] And several young men had also been wounded the night before. The cause of all this was that everyone had been indulging in a vicious life, and at night-time one saw halberds or naked swords all over the city, and men gambling by candlelight in the *Mercato Nuovo* and everywhere without shame. Hell seemed open; and woe to him who should try to reprove vice!

27th June. The man who murdered the other yesterday

---

[1] *Parenti*, who was one of the *Otto di Guardia e Balia* at this time, gives in his History the reasons of this deprivation, as follows: "As it appeared that the *Frate's* party was reviving, means were taken to suppress it; some of the inferior men were flogged, and many citizens who had entered the Council in the time of Francesco Valori were deprived of their rights."

[2] See note to 5th July, 1478.

[3] The man murdered was Ludovico Luti, the enemy of Pandolfo Petrucci; and the assassin was Tiberto son of Francescone Masotti da Brisighella.

in the *Mercato Vecchio* was hung, in the very place where he committed the crime, after having been taken all through the city and tortured on the hangman's cart. He was punished justly and speedily.

28th June. A muster was made by a son of the *Madonna* (Lady) of Imola, called Ottaviano,[1] who came as a Florentine leader with 100 men-at-arms and 50 crossbowmen, in fine array.

30th June. The bell was taken away from San Marco, and was sent to the *Osservanza* at San Miniato.[2]

4th July. San Marco was opened.

7th July. The price of corn was 26 *soldi*.

18th July. We heard that Montepulciano had driven out the foreign soldiers and cried *Marzocco*.

26th July. It was voted in the *Palagio*, in the Great Council, that there should be an election for all the offices from 600 *lire* downwards, in the following manner: All those who had a heritage from their father, or their grandfather, or great-grandfather, from 50 years and upwards should have three tickets put in the election bags, those from 40 to 50 two tickets, those from 30 to 40 one ticket, and from that downwards till 25, also one.

27th July. We heard that our *Capitano* had taken 150 cavalry with all the baggage and stores that were going to Cascina; and many soldiers had been killed, and a brother of the Governor of Pisa had also been killed, who was a gentleman of Venice.[3] It was said that the *Capitano* had done this in a wily manner, having sent some of his

---

[1] Ottaviano Riario, son of Caterina Sforza.

[2] Villari has published the debates of the *Signoria* of the 29th June, in which it is decided to consign this bell first to the church of San Lorenzo, and then to that of the *Frati di San Francesco* outside the *Porta a San Miniato*.

[3] The *Anziani di Pisa* wrote: "You will have heard of the assault made upon us by the enemy and the death of Mag. Messer Johanni Diedo, whose body having been given up to us the same evening at 2 (10 p.m.) by the enemy, we ordered that it should be brought here to Pisa, where yesterday at 20 in the evening (4 p.m.), with all the monastic Orders, the Chapter, and the Confraternity, we took him from San Martino where he had been placed on arriving from Cascina, and deposited him in the *Campo Santo*. Four of us went to the funeral, and almost all our citizens. The shops were closed during the ceremony, and there was a sermon preached in the *Duomo* in his praise, as much honour being shown to his memory as possible. May God save his soul! He is extremely lamented by the whole town" (*Lettere*, quoted, 1499, 28th July, s.p. (that is, *Pisan style*)).

men to pillage, in order to draw out those of Cascina, and so it happened that when he himself came up, he divided them, and fell upon them from several sides; and not one of those who had come out from Cascina escaped.

This year there was an abundance of fruit, the most that I remember.

6th August. Two ambassadors were sent to Venice, Messer Guidantonio Vespucci and Bernardo Rucellai.[1]

21st August. We heard that our troops had taken Buti by assault, the place having surrendered at discretion, and they cut off the hands of five bombardiers. All this time new spingards were being made and sent there. And one man was hung, and 33 people who were in the *Castello* were taken prisoner, some children among them. They came to Florence in bonds.[2]

31st August. We heard that our troops had captured the bastion of Vico, killing all who were in it; we had many killed and wounded also.[3]

3rd September. Vico Pisano was being bombarded, and the noise reached us so plainly on the bridges that I counted 150 reports.[4]

5th September. We heard that our troops had taken Vico, guaranteeing the lives and property of the inhabitants.

10th September. We heard that our troops had defeated the Pisans, and taken 200 horses and killed hundreds of

---

[1] They were sent to treat of an arrangement of the Pisan affairs, but their mission was not successful, the Doge declaring that he wished to continue to help the Pisans, though the others would have abandoned them.

[2] "Yesterday our enemies took the *Cartello* of Buti by force, employing their usual inhuman cruelty, taking prisoner and tormenting with divers tortures the men of the place, ejecting the women and violating some; and cutting all the bombardiers' hands off with such inhumanity that the barbarians and Turks could hardly use more" (*Lettere*, quoted, 1499, 22nd August, s.p.).

[3] From the Pisan documents it results instead that the bastion of Vico was bombarded on the 30th, and being old could not hold out; and that it was captured on the 31st because already ruined by the artillery, and abandoned by the defenders, "who were frightened, we believe, by the cruelties of the enemy at Buti." So what the chronicler says as to those killed in the bastion hardly seems true.

[4] So great was the terror of the Pisan *Signoria* at this time, that they abandoned Vico on the 31st August, and after Vico, the rest: "We see our total ruin before us without being able to do anything to stop it" (*Lett.*, cit., 31st August, 1499, s.p.).

men; there were also dead on our side. This was at Pietra Dolorosa, one of our bastions near Verrucola, which they were attacking, and our *Capitano* having information of it, rode across the plain, and rounding the hills towards Pisa, closed them in.

11th September. We heard that Siena was in arms, and that the followers of Petrucci had taken the Palagio and the Piazza, and were on our side; we sent Rinucci, one of our leaders, there, and he captured one of the gates, and helped Petrucci's party.

On the same day we heard that the Count of Urbino was coming with some soldiers to the aid of the opposing party in Siena; but the Baglioni came out from Perugia and assaulted him, blocking his way, so that he could not pass.[1]

We heard also that the Venetians had been routed by our troops in the Val di Lamona, and many men-at-arms had been taken: these various tidings reached us within the course of twenty-four hours.

Also twelve Pisan prisoners arrived in Florence, and all said that they were constables.[2]

13th September. An agreement was made with the Sienese.[3]

23rd September. The alarm was sounded through all the valley of Dicomano, because Venetian soldiers had taken the Borgo di Marradi. Giuliano de' Medici was with them. Those of Faenza, who had left us and sided with the Venetians, had let them pass through; they set up their camp at Castiglione, and it was feared that they would enter the Mugello.

24th September (Monday). Signore Rinuccio lodged at

[1] In August the Venetians had gone against Forlì, the city of Contessa Caterina Sforza, with the double object of annoying the Duke of Milan, whose sister she was, and of making a diversion in the Pisan war to the injury of the Florentines by holding the road in the direction of Siena. Florence was solicitous to send troops in aid of the Contessa, so that she should not recall her son who had gone to the camp before Pisa. Guidobaldo della Rovere, Duke of Urbino, had been taken into the pay of the Venetians together with Bartolomeo d'Alviano, Astorre Baglioni, the lords of Camerino, of Rimini, of Faenza, and one of the Orsini.

[2] A captain and four constables are also mentioned by the *Lettere* already quoted (10th September, 1499, s.p.).

[3] A truce was made for five years, obliging the Florentines to dismantle the bastion of Ponte a Valiano, and making other concessions to the Sienese.

Dicomano, with eight squadrons of cavalry and many mounted archers; and the next day he went to the Mugello. And during these days large bodies of infantry were hired at Florence, and four or five thousand men were sent to the Mugello and Romagna. It was also said that Piero de' Medici had joined the Venetian camp. And this the Venetians were doing in order to draw us away from Pisa; it was always they who supported the Pisans, who could not have borne the costs if it had not been for the Venetians, whose manner of acting was utterly wrong; one does not know what cause they had to intervene.[1]

27th September. We heard that our troops had taken certain bastions at Librafatta. Think whether there was sufficient work, being forced to repair to several places at once. However, God has always aided us, because our wars are lawful; but not so are those of the ambitious and envious Venetians.

28th September. The Signore di Piombino passed through Florence with many squadrons of horse, and a number of foot-soldiers, at our pay, and went into the Mugello near the Uccellatoio; and it was said that Faenza was in a tumult, some being for Florence and some for Venice.

At this date the price of corn was 22 *soldi* a bushel.

30th September. The soldiers were being given their pay during these days; they came to receive it, and then went away again.

3rd October. The Venetians bombarded Marradi; but we got provisions into the place by an attack which was a fine feat of arms.

4th October. We heard that our troops had taken Librafatta, which capitulated at 22 in the evening (6 p.m.).

5th October. Marradi was still being heavily bombarded.

6th October. We heard that our army had gone into Cassaglia, near Marradi, and is well provisioned. It is thought that we shall seek an encounter shortly; and it is said that the enemy will move off if they can, but that we shall probably surround them. On this day a miracle happened: those besieged in the fort of Marradi being short of water, having been actually without it for several

---

[1] "A Venetian who had come with their galleys assured the Pisans that the Venetian *Signoria* had the cause of Pisa as much at heart as if it had been their own" (*Lettere*, cit., 10th September, 1499, s.p.).

days, and not being able to hold out thus, vowed to give a silver castle to the Virgin Mary if it rained; and no sooner was the vow made, and the money being collected, than it suddenly grew cloudy and rained so plentifully that they collected 50 barrels of water.

This year there was an abundant harvest of everything, fruit, wine, olives and grapes; and all prices were low. God does not forsake the poor.

11th October. Marradi held out steadily, no longer having any fear, after this miraculous gift of water.

12th October. According to the request of the *Capitano* at Pisa, we sent him all the stonemasons in Florence; but they turned back and did not go, after all.[1]

13th October. We heard that our *Capitano* had taken two of the gates of Pisa, and that there were cries of *Marzocco*.[2]

14th October. We heard that the *Capitano* had taken the tower of Foce, and given the castellan 2000 ducats, and a dwelling wherever he chose in our territory. Also that he was making an agreement with the Pisans which would soon be concluded, and that he had published a proclamation to the effect that all the Pisan peasants could come out and sow their fields in safety; and the Pisans made a show of wishing for an agreement, but merely for the sake of being able to sow.[3]

17th October. Certain men called *Ghingherli* came out from Pisa, and raided as far as Montetopoli, capturing 120 head of cattle and the ploughmen; but the country-people attacked them and recovered the booty, taking one of them prisoner.

21st October. The *Capitano*[4] came to Florence; not the *Capitano della Guerra*, but the *Capitano di Firenze*; and the *Bargello* gave up the post. For we had been for some time without a *Capitano*, and had made shift with the *Bargello*. He was a Roman and lived in the house of the *Capitano*.

---

[1] Perhaps because the camp had moved elsewhere, since many stonemasons were used by the Florentine army to destroy Santa Maria in Castello.

[2] There is no mention made of this in the Pisan documents, and other facts are recorded elsewhere which make this improbable.

[3] Up to the 8th November no sowings had been made in the Val di Serchio, to the great uneasiness of the Pisans, who drew their supplies for six months from this district.

[4] The *Capitano del Popolo*, who was a Messer Mario Salamoni, a Roman noble.

24th October. We heard that Piero de' Medici had passed the Pieve Santo Stefano, and was near Bibbiena; and then that he had taken it, with the help of the Venetian army at Marradi. And they fortified themselves at Bibbiena, and it was said that he had friends there.

27th October. These Venetian troops which were with Piero de' Medici at Bibbiena captured another small castle called Fronzoli. Everyone said that our troops could have surrounded them, if they had chosen, and they would not have been able to escape; the Signore di Piombino had already arrived with his horsemen, and all our leaders might have joined and have captured the whole force. Nevertheless, from whatever cause it arose, we were not victorious; and our soldiers were now sent into quarters.

5th November. Fracassa passed through here, on his way from San Benedetto, lodging at Dicomano, with 400 horse; and then he went to the Ponte a Sieve and along the valley of the Arno, to Arezzo.

6th November. Another count was quartered at Dicomano, with 300 horse, all belonging to the Duke of Milan, and he went in the same direction.

8th November. Count Rinuccio passed through Dicomano with 400 horse, and went into quarters in the Val di Sieve, not approaching the Casentino where the Signore di Piombino then was; and after this, the Signore di Piombino left Pratovecchio with his troops, and they lodged at San Lorino and at Caiano, and even at Londa, terrifying all the neighbourhood, who mistook them for the enemy; finally going into quarters at Dicomano.

24th November. The Arno was in flood, and did much harm; a bridge over the Mugnone between the *Porta al Prato* and the *Porticciuola* was destroyed, the Mugnone being also in flood and entering the Borgo Ognissanti, where it drowned a miller and his horse laden with flour, and a woman who was crossing the said bridge. And on this same day it happened that while some muleteers, with ten mules laden with gunpowder and artillery, were lodging at Ricorboli, some young men wanted to try a shot, and they set fire to the gunpowder, and destroyed the house and the mules; five of the muleteers were so badly hurt that they had to be taken to the hospital. I believe that some of them died.

25th November. Our *Capitano* lodged in the plains of

Poggio a Caiano, having left the Pisan territory, as they were sending him to the Casentino.

27th November. We heard that the enemy in the Casentino had taken a small castle, called Santerma, in which a quantity of corn and provisions had been stored; and they pillaged it and slaughtered all the garrison.

30th November. The enemy were encamped at Pratovecchio. And at this time there was such heavy rain that they had to go into permanent quarters everywhere as far as Vicchio, preying upon the whole neighbourhood. The prospect of an agreement looked doubtful; no money was voted, and great uneasiness prevailed. Some soldiers deserted, and others threatened it; mostly those who were in garrison in the castles, especially in the district of Pisa.

18th December. We heard that our troops had recaptured Marciano, taking 70 or 80 mounted men-at-arms and a number of foot-soldiers, and that they were also in possession of all the passes. Everyone in the neighbourhood cried: *Lasciate fare a noi, che non 'anno remedio!* (Let us go for them, as they have no way out!) We were in despair here at Florence, asking ourselves why the leaders did not choose to move, and what it meant; for the state of things was clear, and left no room for doubt. And yet they besieged Bibbiena, and again took numbers of men, both horse and foot, so that the enemy were continually routed, and began to consider how they could escape.

20th December. We heard that the enemy in the Casentino had been pillaging, and that our men in Camaldoli had recovered the booty and taken some of them prisoner. It had been raining for many days, and there was snow on the Alps. This was thought fortunate for us, as the snow prevented the enemy from passing. Intelligent people considered that they were at our mercy, and it really was so; but the evil lay in the fact that our leaders did not desire a great victory which would have put the Venetians to shame.

23rd December. It was said that our troops did not wish to interfere with the enemy's movements, and that they would not do what lay in their power, otherwise they would most surely have been victorious.

25th December (Christmas night). The following infamy was committed by God's people here in Florence, in Santa Maria del Fiore: At night, whilst the first midnight mass was being said, certain persons, I do not know whether to call them men or demons, brought in an old hack, and made him run about the church, with much shouting, making everything in a mess and behaving in a most disgraceful way. They slashed at him and wounded him with their weapons and poked at him with sticks, resorting to every kind of cruelty, till he fell bleeding to the ground, desecrating the temple of the Lord. And the said horse, ruined and tortured in this way, fell almost dead upon the steps of Santa Maria del Fiore, and there remained the whole day for everyone to see, torn to pieces and dying. Which thing caused good and wise men to tremble with fear for a judgment of God; remembering also what had been done a few years before, when the tombs outside Santa Maria Novella had been opened, in contempt of the resurrection, on the very night of the Resurrection; besides ink having been put in the holy-water basins at Santa Maria del Fiore; and, what was worse, the door of the church having been broken open by night, and persons having gone up into the pulpit and smeared it with dirt, violating it before the crucifix where the word of God is spoken; and many other iniquities, being without the fear of God. And it was said that the crown had been taken off Our Lady of San Marco, and given to a courtesan: I cannot vouch for the truth of this, but it was said by many. And on the night of the Nativity, there was put in the censers, in many churches, assafetida instead of incense, and goats were let loose in Santa Maria Novella.[1]

27th December. In these days our *Capitano* took by assault a castle called Fatucchio, about seven miles beyond La Verna, and many persons were killed who had taken refuge there. The best part of the enemy's forces, who had been on the pass and became hemmed in, had fled here, in order to return to their posts.

28th December. Our Pisan enemy took Montetopoli by assault, and pillaged it, taking prisoners, and burning down many houses.[2]

[1] *Giovanni Cambi*, in his *Storie*, also relates these facts, adding: "And they did this because the *Frate* being dead, it seemed as if they were at liberty to commit every kind of sin, he by his preaching having put a stop to all such things," etc.

[2] "Our soldiers" (wrote the *Anziani di Pisa* to their ambassador at Venice), "riding out the other night, that is, Thursday, assaulted Montetopori about daybreak, and took and sacked the castle,

11th January. Our *Capitano* was occupied all the time in closing the passes to the enemy beyond La Verna, and it was said that a fort was being made at Monte Lione.

14th January. We heard that the enemy in the Casentino had put into Bibbiena 1000 soldiers, who had come secretly, and who each brought a sack of flour on his back. It is said that this was managed by subterfuge.

19th January. We heard that our *Capitano* had taken about 70 mules laden with artillery and provisions which were coming to Bibbiena, and about 60 light horse and many foot-soldiers, including a Venetian commissary who was carrying a fair sum of money to Bibbiena. This was thought great news. The enemy were in any case vanquished, and yet victory did not follow. It was said to be the fault of our citizens. Whoever caused it was grievously to blame, since it would have been a great triumph for Florence to shame the Venetians, but it is not the first time that the Florentines have acted in a similar manner.[1]

21st January. We heard that the Pisans had made a raid into the Valdinievole and carried off a number of cattle. Thus we had both good and bad news; we were obliged to be on guard in two places at once.

26th January. We heard that our troops had captured about 200 light horse who were fleeing, near Montefatucchio in the Casentino. The soldiers fled from Montalone also, after having set fire to the castle; and some of them were captured and said that there were no more provisions of any kind in Bibbiena, and the garrison was in a sorry condition.

13th February. We heard that the Duke of Urbino and Giuliano de' Medici had been allowed to go away, with 40 horsemen; leaving perhaps 400 soldiers to guard the place.[2]

burning part of it. It is true that many of the enemy escaped, with what they could carry, and that they shut themselves up in the fortress; and this we did not attack, because already having pillaged the castle, we were sufficiently laden with booty. Some of our men were wounded, and they all returned to Pisa the following night" (*Lettere*, cit., 28th December, 1499, s.p.).

[1] The *Capitano* of the Venetians, the Conte di Pitigliano, was censured in like manner.

[2] The Duke of Urbino, being ill, had a safe-conduct from Vitelli, without the consent of the commissaries, and Giuliano de' Medici went away with the duke.

15th February. We heard that ambassadors were appointed to go to Venice: Pagoloantonio Soderini and Giovan Battista Ridolfi; and one to go to Rome: Messer Antonio Malegonnelle. It was thought that peace would be concluded.

17th February. The tabernacle of Our Lady of Impruneta was sent for, to enable us to decide whether it would be to our advantage to join the League, and leave the King of France.[1]

19th February. We heard that the Count of Pitigliano, sent by the Venetians, had made an incursion into Galeata and pillaged it, and was now stopping there. Here, meanwhile, we were merely looking on, and not besieging Bibbiena, which could not have held out an hour; so that everyone murmured, and it continued to be said that there were those who did not wish us to conquer. And it was bound to appear so to everyone, when certain victory did not ensue. Even the peasants of the neighbourhood began to say: *E' sono in prigione, lasciate fare a noi!* (They are in a trap, let us attack them!) But permission was never given here, so that everyone marvelled.

1499. 5th April. There were letters from the ambassadors at Venice, which were read in the Council informing us that the demands of the Venetians were unjust, and that the hope of an agreement seemed improbable. The King of France wrote that there were not many days left for us to decide whether we would make an alliance with him or not; and it was much discussed whether we should leave the king or the duke, many perils appearing on both sides.

8th April. A horseman arrived from Venice with the olive-branch to acquaint us with the terms of the agreement made with the Venetians and the Pisans, which were as follows: We were to give the Venetians 180 thousand florins within ten years, and the Pisans were to hold certain forts of Pisa, and to elect a *Podestà* of our jurisdiction in their own way. And this displeased the people greatly, because the Venetians should have given us money, seeing

[1] That is to say, so that they might be inspired to know whether they should join the League or remain the allies of the King of France. *Parenti*, differing from the *Piagnoni* (followers of Savonarola), attributes to them the fact of the tabernacle being sent for, with the hidden motive of causing their sect to be brought forward again and its influence felt.

that they were imprisoned in Bibbiena and worsted. And the ambassadors were much blamed.¹

12th April. We heard that a young man called Ottaviano,² who belonged to the *Signoria* of Faenza, had been murdered at San Benedetto. He had once been here in Florence, and I recollect that he squinted a little. It was said that Messer Giovanni Bentivogli had caused him to be put to death; but this may not be true.

14th April. A horseman came to us from Venice, bringing the ratification of the agreement. And we heard that there had been a tumult in Pisa, caused by some who did not approve of the agreement, so that the Venetian commissary was forced to go to Pisa and have five men put to death on account of this disturbance.³

17th April. We heard that the Pisans had hoisted the banner of the King of France, and that nothing would persuade them to consent to such an agreement, or ever to submit to the Florentines; and that they had decided to melt down the silver in their churches to help them to resist, and would lay down their lives sooner than yield.

23rd April. The "Eight" passed a decree of banishment against Simone Tornabuoni and *il Grasso* de' Medici; and some days ago they had also banished one Marcuccio Salviati, who was in the pay of the Venetians and had been intriguing with Piero de' Medici, and it was for this same fault that they banished the said Simone and *il Grasso*.⁴

¹ The Florentines and Venetians had appealed to the Duke of Ferrara, and on this day the notice came of the sentence that he had pronounced, as is testified also by *Cambi*, who adds, that it was pronounced "although our ambassadors were absent, not wishing to be present," which does not agree with the blame given them by Landucci.

² Ottaviano Manfredi (see note on 28th June, 1498), son of Carlo II., who was in the pay of the Florentines, was assaulted and killed on the Alpe di San Godenzo by his enemies of the Val di Lamona. See *Parenti*, above quoted.

³ According to the sentence given above, the Venetians were to withdraw the soldiers who had been helping the Pisans against the Florentines, before the 24th April; but the Pisans, being discontent with the sentence, no sooner was it known than they removed the Venetian soldiers who were guarding their gates and forts (*Guicciardini, Storia d'Italia*, libro iv.). This was the tumult spoken of here.

⁴ Under this date, in the *Libro di Partiti degli Otto di Guardia e Balìa*, we find the sentence pronounced against Tornabuoni and Andrea d'Alamanno de' Medici, nicknamed *il Grasso*; and fifteen days earlier we read there the other sentence on Marco di Bernardo di Marco di Forese Salviati, called *Marcuccio*.

24th April. We regained Bibbiena, in a state of ruin.

26th April. We heard that the Duke of Ferrara had judged and given sentence in favour of the Pisans, and that besides the stipulations above mentioned, they were to hold the towers of the gates and to collect the taxes. There was a final consultation in the Council of the "Eighty," who refused to accept the agreement on any account, and in this way nothing was done about it.[1]

3rd May. We heard that the two parties in Pistoia had had a quarrel, and about 16 men had been killed and more than 40 wounded by artillery and otherwise. They burnt down the gates to let in the peasants on their respective sides.[2] During these days the Florentines had the walls of Bibbiena destroyed. The price of corn was now 15 to 16 *soldi* a bushel.

15th May. We heard that the sultan was dead; and he had been dead four days before a new one was chosen. On the same day the shops of the Venetians here were looted.

19th May. We heard that the Duke of Milan had sent to order the Pisans to give the city back to us; but he wished to force us to furnish him with men-at-arms at our expense when he should need them. . . .[3]

2nd June. They sent for the *Capitano* from the Casentino to go to Pisa.[4]

3rd June. A worker in the brickfields at Settimo took two of his children, aged two and seven, and cut their throats with a knife, as if they had been kids.

5th June. The *Capitano* and Signor Rinuccio passed here, on their way into the Pisan district. And men were sent from these plains to lay waste the land round Pisa.

12th June. These men laid waste their corn-fields; and our camp was pitched between Cascina and Pisa. At this

---

[1] Nor would the Pisans accept this agreement, in spite of the duke having made the conditions more favourable to them; and it is to this fact that the words "nothing was done about it" must refer.

[2] These disorders between the ancient factions of the *Cancellieri* and the *Panciatichi* had begun even before this; and they are narrated at length by Salvi, *Historia di Pistoia*, t. iii.

[3] There is a blank in the MS. at this point; Guicciardini, however, gives the number of 300 men-at-arms and 2000 infantry.

[4] When the war came to an end in the Casentino, Vitelli had gone to Città di Castello, and Count Rinuccio into the district of Arezzo. Piero Corsini was sent to fetch Vitelli.

time a tax was voted, called the *Graziosa*, and they collected money.¹

During these days a multitude of hairy little caterpillars appeared in Florence; they came into the houses and bit people, and the bites became painful and swollen, which showed that they were poisonous.

17th June. Mortars were loaded to go to Pisa, and they were sent on skiffs along the Arno.

21st June. The mortars were placed at Cascina.

26th June. A horseman with the olive-branch came to inform us of the capture of Cascina. He arrived at 20 in the evening (4 p.m.), and it had been taken at 17 in the day (1 p.m.), surrendering at discretion to the *Signoria* and the *Capitano*. And many prisoners came here from Cascina, and they were put on the *ballatoio* ² of the *Palagio*.

2nd July. We heard that the Turks had landed and advanced as far as Zara, capturing 200 men and beasts, and had burnt and destroyed all the country. Also that the sultan himself had landed and was coming towards Raugia, and that his fleet was outside the straits in the archipelago. And letters from Venice showed that the Venetians were quite dismayed. We heard besides that the King of France was to pass this way, and that he had a large quantity of artillery at Turin, and was continuing to send more.

12th July. The artillery from the Casentino returned here, in order for it to be sent to Pisa.

13th July. Messer Ascanio,³ the cardinal, passed here without being known, and went to the Duke of Milan, who was beginning to believe that the king was coming against the Milanese.

18th July. Two *Collegi* ⁴ went to the camp at Pisa with 30,000 florins counted out.

19th July. We heard from Rome that the Duke of Milan

¹ "In order to make some provision of money, to put an end to the present war, and to hasten the business of the city of Pisa," a decree was passed on the 11th June, imposing a tax of *una quintina e mezzo* (a fifth and a half) on the Florentine citizens. From another decree, of the 21st January, 1500, we find that this tax was commonly called *el Piacente*, and it is probably the same which Landucci erroneously calls *la Graziosa*, the latter being the name of a tax imposed in 1443, favouring the poor, and particularly hard on the rich.

² The gallery behind the parapets. [Trans.]

³ Ascanio Sforza, brother of Ludovico il Moro.

⁴ See note to 25th March, 1478.

was setting up Piero de' Medici again, and giving him 10 thousand florins, so that he might oppose us and hinder us from having Pisa.

31st July. Our camp was pitched before Pisa at 15 at night (11 p.m.); it was in great force and excellent order.

1st August. They took a tower called Asciano, and cut off the hands of six men who were in it and would not yield.[1] They were waiting for the bombards.[2]

3rd August. We heard that they had broken down a piece of wall more than 40 *braccia* long with the bombards, and many soldiers had entered the breach, but were repulsed with some loss, for the war was now being carried on with desperation.

5th August. A peasant came from Pisa who declared that the Pisans had blinded him, and that they shot with poisoned arrows. I believe that he came at the instigation of the Pisans, in order to terrify anyone who thought of entering the city.

7th August. We heard that the *Capitano* had taken the *Porta a Mare* and the *Torre Stainpace*.

11th August. A Lucchese ambassador left here in haste, because it was understood that the Lucchesi had sent help to the Pisans; our *Capitano* having discovered a man who was carrying, concealed in a ball of wax, a letter in which the Lucchesi offered to send money to the Pisans.

15th August. We heard that the *Capitano* had taken the church of San Pagolo inside the walls.

19th August. A vote was passed by the *Signori* and *Collegi* that Pisa should be sacked; but this vote was not passed afterwards in the Council. And in these days many sick and wounded returned from camp, not so many soldiers as citizens who had gone to look on. A number of them died, especially nearly all the wounded, who had been wounded with poisoned weapons. And we had to send fresh commissaries.

24th August. The tabernacle of Our Lady of Santa Maria Impruneta was sent for to Florence, and many gifts were made.[3] And the following incident happened as it

[1] *Portaveneri*, with whom this Diary agrees admirably, also records this piece of cruelty; and adds that for this reason the Pisans cut off the hands of a Florentine who was their prisoner.

[2] These mortars or bombards were the first clumsy cannon, difficult to move and slow to load, far behind the French ordnance.

[3] On the 19th August the *Signoria* gave the order that the taber-

was passing under an olive-tree on the way here: a little branch of the olive-tree caught on to a star of Our Lady's mantle, and remained fastened to the star; and some of those who were carrying the tabernacle wished to knock the branch off with a stick, but although they tried several times, they could not detach it; hence it was considered to be a miracle (because at this very time a battle was going on with the Pisans, and there was a great question whether we should be victorious or not); and now those who observed this said: "It is a good sign that she should bring the olive-branch to Florence." And this fact was spread through the city. And when the tabernacle reached San Felice, they took the mantle off and detached the olive-branch, and fastened it on again in the same place where it had been before, that is: on the right shoulder, for everyone to see, coming and going. It was a little fork made by two small branches, about a span long.

27th August. We heard that the King of France had taken seven castles: Tortona, Razza, Nori, Valenza, Castelnuovo, Pontecorona and Bovera, and that he was on the way to Pavia.[2]

29th August. One of our commissaries came riding in hot haste from Pisa. There was a suspicion of treachery.

1st September. We heard that the King of France had taken Alessandria. In fact he took everything wherever he went.

2nd September. There passed through Florence a cardinal-legate, papal ambassador to the King of France.

3rd September. We heard that the Duke of Milan had gone away from Milan, and that there were cries in the city of *Trau*[3] and *Francia*. He left the citadel furnished with men and provisions for six years or more. And Cardinal Ascanio was carrying away the treasure towards Germany. We heard also that the Genoese had hoisted the French flag.

---

nacle should be brought into Florence on the 25th; but Vitelli having begged that it should come on the 24th, because he wished to attack the Pisans on that day, another consultation was held on the 21st, at which an order was given to anticipate the arrival by one day.

[2] *Razza* and *Bovera* are *Rocca d'Arazzo* and *Voghera*.

[3] Giovanniacopo Trivulzio, who had rebelled against the Duke of Milan, and was a commandant in the French army during this war. His name was badly mangled at that time: *Rinucci* in his *Ricordi* calls him *da Treuzo*, and *Portaveneri* writes *da Treussi*.

A Religious Procession of the XVth Century
From the painting by R. Belloni.

5th September. Our camp at Pisa was raised, and there was great murmuring throughout Florence: everyone marvelled.

On the same day the cross on the *Cupola* was straightened, having been twisted by a great storm years before.

12th September. We heard that the duke and his sons had been captured, and the treasure taken also; and that a league was being formed between the King, the Venetians, the Pope, and the Florentines. This was not true.

13th September. The *Capitano* wanted to send the bombards to Livorno on board some vessels, and two large ones fell into the sea, and a *dragonetto* [1] besides, which was a great loss.

17th September. We heard that the Pisans had fished up the *dragonetto* of ours which had fallen into the sea; and also that some French had entered Pisa.

19th September. We heard that the King of France had taken the citadel of Milan and was in possession of the whole duchy; the messenger bearing this news arrived here at 22 in the evening (6 p.m.), and immediately the joy-bells were rung, bonfires were lighted in the city, and *panegli* (illuminations on the towers)[2] were put on the *Palagio* and everywhere. All Florence rejoiced greatly.

21st September. Three ambassadors were sent to the King of France: Messer Francesco Gualterotti, Lorenzo Lenzi and Alamanno Salviati, to congratulate him.

26th September. We heard that the Turks had taken Corfu, and had made a treaty with the Christians: the first stipulation was that religious faith should not be interfered with, everyone being allowed to worship in his own fashion; also they only demanded half of the sum paid yearly by the Venetians, and there was to be an exemption for five years before the said sum would be demanded.

27th September. We heard that the King of Naples had sent to the Pope, informing him that if he did not hinder the King of France coming against the Kingdom of Naples, he would summon the Turks to Italy. And this would have succeeded if the King of France had wished to advance towards the south, threatening Naples; and it is credible because the Turks had now a way of conquering, without interfering with the Faith. But God did not will that such an evil should befall unfortunate Italy.

---

[1] A sort of small quick-firing cannon.
[2] See note to 25th February, 1494.

29th September. We heard that our *Capitano* had been arrested at Cascina as a traitor to his country. And the next day he was brought to Florence, arriving at a quarter to three (10.45 p.m.), with many torches. And it was the King of France who had advised the *Signoria* to arrest him for treachery. The *Signoria* was also warned by de Trau, who had captured a horseman of the duke's who revealed that our *Capitano* was in league with the duke, and received money from him when at Pisa. And we heard that one of our citizens being at Milan with the king, and telling him how our camp at Pisa had been raised, the king asked him the reason, and the Florentine replied: "Because we are deceived by our *Capitano*"; then the king said: "Have him arrested!" And when this news came here by *estafette*, everyone was eager to take his life.

1st October (Tuesday). The *Capitano*, that is to say, Pagolo Vitegli, was beheaded in the Palagio de' Signori, high up on the *ballatoio* (gallery behind the parapet), and it took place at a quarter to 24 (7.45 p.m.), the Piazza being full of people. It was expected that his head would be thrown down into the Piazza; it was not thrown down, however, but it was stuck on a spear and shown at the windows of the *ballatoio*, with a lighted torch beside it, so that it could be seen by everyone. Then the people dispersed, considering that justice had been done, to the great honour of the city. He had been put to the rack several times first, and had been declared a rebel two hours beforehand, the proclamation being published throughout the city.[1] And note that the *Gonfaloniere* was Giovacchino Guasconi, who had contrived to lay hands upon the *Capitano* secretly. He was much commended by the people as a wise and good man, of great spirit.

And all this time confessions were extorted from certain chancellors (secretaries) of the *Capitano*, so as to get at the truth.

[1] In Parenti we read the following terzain, published on this occasion:
" *Paolo sono che venni, vidi e finsi*
(I am Paul, who came, saw, and feigned)
Di dar Pisa a Marzocco et exaltarlo,
(To give Pisa to the Marzocco of Florence and exalt him,)
Ma quel di gloria e me di fama extinsi."
(But extinguished his glory and my fame.)

11th October. One Messer Cherubino of the *Borgo* was hung at the windows of the *Podestà*, who had been mixed up with the *Capitano* in the treason that the latter had intended to commit.[1]

19th October. We heard from Venice that the Turks had made an incursion to within 20 miles of Venice, and burnt about seventeen *ville* (estates in the country) and taken 8 thousand prisoners, and slaughtered as many; so that all the country-people fled to the parts nearest Venice. And because certain commissaries and military leaders of theirs did not do their duty in resisting the Turks, these commissaries were arrested and taken to Venice. They were one Messer Bartolomeo da Lutiano and one Carlo Orsini, who had been against us at Bibbiena. This incursion had happened on the day of San Girolamo.

22nd October. We received the articles of the league between us and the King of France, the Venetians, the Pope, and the Sienese. There were great rejoicings, with bonfires and illuminations.[2]

23rd October. The said league was published, promising much to the Florentines, and declaring that we should not be obliged to make any payments until we had received all which belonged to us. It stipulated that we should help with men-at-arms when the conquest of Naples was undertaken.

25th October. We heard that there were 20 thousand Turks at Velona (Vallona); and some said that they were in Puglia.

1st November. The Madonna (Lady) of Imola collected her property and had it sent here to Florence, and she also sent her daughters here, to be placed in the *Murate*,[3] because the Pope, with the authority of the King of France, wished to take her state from her and give it to a son of his.[4] On which account the Lady decided to stay there and defend herself.

---

[1] *Parenti* calls this Cherubino of Borgo a San Sepolcro, "head of a party and a constable of Vitelli"; and adds that Cerbone of Monte Santa Maria, one of his chancellors, Messer Antonio da Castello, his confederate, and his doctor, were arrested.
[2] The convention between the King of France and the Florentines was published by *Molini* in t. i. of the *Documenti di Storia Italiana*, p. 32.
[3] The convent of the *Murate*; see note to 15th April, 1498.
[4] Cesare Borgia, Duke Valentino (Valentinois).

10th November. We heard that the King of France had left Milan and returned to France; and, as the duke's heir, demanded from us 30 thousand florins, which the duke declared he had lent us. And, nevertheless, Pisa did not surrender to us.

27th November. We heard that the Pope's son had taken Imola, but had not yet taken the citadel; and he was bombarding it so heavily that even at my place at Dicomano I could hear the bombards, and those of the citadel were firing into the city and destroying all the houses. The Lady had gone away to Forlì, where she fortified herself; and it was said that she had left in the citadel one who had given her as hostages his wife and children, declaring that she might put them to death if he ever gave up the fortress.

29th November. A vote was passed in Council to liberate Ser Giovanni, who was imprisoned at Volterra.[1]

2nd December. A master-builder began to have the foundations of the *Campanile* of San Miniato dug out, in order to build it up straight.

10th December. We heard that the fortress of Imola had fallen,[2] and that many men had been slain.

13th December. We heard that the camp was at Forlì.

16th December. We heard that the Lady of Imola had come to an agreement with the Pope, by which she was to give him Forlì, and the Pope was to make one of her sons a cardinal, and also to give her money.

21st December. We heard that Forlì was lost, and nothing remained but the citadel, where the Lady was.

25th December (the Holy Nativity). The Jubilee began at Rome, and a number of northerners passed through Florence.

9th January. We heard that the Lady of Imola demanded her dowry from the Pope, and that the Queen of France wished her to have it.

---

[1] Permission was asked for this Giovanni di Ser Bartolomeo Guidi (mentioned already 10th November, 1494, and 3rd January, 1494) to leave the vault below the old citadel at Volterra, where he had been since the year 1494. In the petition he is said to be sixty-five years of age, and "in bad health, both on account of his sojourn in this place and on account of many bodily ailments from which he had suffered before he was sent to this prison." In the decree of the 6th January his sentence was transmuted into that of perpetual confinement within the *Vicariato* (government district) of Mugello.

[2] Into the hands of Valentino.

13th January. We heard that the Lady had lost the fortress of Forlì, and had been taken prisoner. And about 500 men were killed there, all those in the citadel being slain except her, and she was wounded.

14th January. Travellers were stopped on the road near Viterbo by certain *Côrsi* (Corsican brigands), and they robbed the host of an inn of the baggage-train belonging to a certain *signore* who had lodged with him, which consisted of at least 16 mules, going to the Pardon. And the host fleeing and crying out, the *Côrsi* were pursued and their booty taken from them; eight of them were captured, and when they reached Viterbo they were hung at once; but there continued to be robberies on the road.

16th January. We heard that the Lady of Imola had been sent to the Pope, but was taken from him by the French. And the French now found out that the Pope had made a league with the Venetians and the duke, and was against the king; and they were not willing that the Pope's son should have the fortresses.

5th February. We heard that Messer Ascanio and the Cardinal of San Severino had entered Milan, and that the duke was behind them with many German troops. The people were said to be recalling him, and his forces took the city, though the citadel still held out for the French. They entered on the 3rd February, the day of San Biagio.

6th February. We heard that the Pope had taken refuge in the castle of Sant' Angelo, as Rome was in arms and the streets were blockaded.

9th February. We heard that the duke had entered Milan on the 5th February, at 16 in the morning (noon).

12th February. We heard that the French who were leaving Romagna, in passing Tortona, being assaulted for the sake of robbery, collected their forces and pillaged the place, slaying even the children, and committing great cruelties as usual.

15th February. We heard that the duke had left Milan, as the citadel was firing upon the city and doing great damage.

It was said also that the Turkish ambassador had come to Naples, and that the king had received him with great honours and jousting.

16th February. The Duchess of Milan came through

Florence, on her way to Naples, that is to say, the widow of the young duke who was poisoned. She was the daughter of the Duke of Calabria, and she was taking with her her two daughters; her son had been taken away from her by the French king and sent to France. She left here on the 19th, and we bore the costs for the whole time of her stay in our territory.[1]

During these days the plague had ceased, and was no longer spoken of.

25th February. We heard that the duke had conquered many places, Bergamo and others.

27th February. We heard that the Turkish ambassador had come to the Pope at Rome to demand a safe-conduct for the Turks to go to Milan against the King of France. But it was not granted.

11th March. We heard that the King of France had reached Lyons, and was advancing with a large force.

12th March. Two men of Bruscoli were hung, who had murdered the Commissary de' Canigiani, as already mentioned.[2] They were taken on the executioner's cart, and were tortured all through the city; and after being hung, one of them was quartered and the quarters stuck on the gallows.[3] They had been captured at Castellina, on their way to the Jubilee.

1500. 25th March. We heard that the King of France had sent on 1500 lancers, and was approaching in great strength.

26th March. We heard that the duke had taken Novara, and that there were great losses; but he had not taken the citadel.

3rd April. We heard that a league had been made between the King of Hungary, the King of Naples, the Pope, the Venetians, and Ferrara; and that we might join it if we would. We had no desire, however, to desert the King

---

[1] On the same day, the 16th, the *Priori* decided that they would lend their silver plate to Stefano Parenti, the steward of the *Camera dell' Armi*, to honour the duchess.

[2] See note to 8th August, 1496.

[3] Carlo di Piero di Carlo Canigiani was killed, as we read, on 8th August, 1496. His murderers, who were Ludovico di Santi di Vico, *alias* Vico da Bruscoli, Michele di Antonio del Chierico, and others, were not caught at the time; but three and a half years later these two fell into the hands of justice, and in execution of the sentence of the "Eight," pronounced on the 10th March, 1500, the former (Vico da Bruscoli) was quartered.

of France, who ought to recognise the great fidelity of the Florentines, who have become the enemies of all the rest of Italy, exposing themselves to the utmost peril.

12th April. We heard that the Duke of Milan had been captured by the King of France, at 4 o'clock at night (midnight). And it was said that the duke's own people had given him up, and that none of the duke's party chose to go on with the war, being assailed with fear; and it was said further that the soldiers were not paid.

14th April. We heard the truth about the duke's capture, and that 12 thousand men had been killed. Here a great *festa* was held: the shops were closed, there were *panegli* (illuminations), and many large bonfires; guns were fired, the *spalliere* (draperies) [1] were put on the *ringhiera*, and the crown on the Lion [2]; and at the door of the *Signori* was placed a beautiful figure of Christ, as though we wished to say: *Non abbiamo altro Re che Cristo* (We have no other King but Christ). I believe that this was by Divine permission, as Fra Girolamo had often said that Florence had no other King but Christ. And this evening, as a smith was going to place the *panegli* on the gates of the city, when he was on the top of the Porta a Pinti arranging the *panegli*, not noticing a certain *piombatoia*,[3] he fell through it to the ground, and was smashed to pieces, dying on the spot.

18th April. We heard from our ambassadors in France that the king had written that he placed his soldiers and his artillery at our disposal, to go to Pisa.

23rd April. A vote was passed to impose a *balzello* (special

[1] See note to 18th November, 1486.

[2] Regarding this custom of crowning the *Marzocco*, I think it opportune to give the following notice extracted from the *Diario d'Agostino Lapini*, of the sixteenth century: "1564, on the 5th March, a Monday morning, about half-past seven, the Lion was taken away from the Piazza at the corner of the *ringhiera* where the fountain now is, and where the said Lion had stood for many years. It was moved 20 *braccia* towards the gigantic David, and now stands there, and will perhaps stand there always. It used to be the custom, on the occasion of great festivities, to put a crown on the head of the said Lion; but this custom has now fallen into disuse. It was placed where it is at present on the 6th March, the very day of the Carnival." See also note to 23rd October, 1484.

[3] A hole in the pavement of the projecting battlements of fortifications, through which stones, boiling water, boiling oil, etc., was let down on the enemy; arrows could also be shot through them. [Trans.]

tax) on those who had not been (in office)[1]; which was regarded as a piece of tyranny.

25th April. A messenger arrived in Florence from the King of France, who came to go to Siena and cause Montepulciano to be given up to us; and to Pisa in order to force it to capitulate; and to Lucca to notify that we were to have back what belonged to us; but although he went everywhere, it led to nothing.[2]

26th April. We caused Our Lady of Santa Maria Impruneta to be brought into Florence, and made a great procession in her honour, in the hopes that she would lend us her aid.[3]

9th May. We heard that the Turks had landed many soldiers in Puglia, and that the Venetians, out of fear and thinking to gratify them, sent them Messer Ascanio and many other Milanese citizens who had fled to Venice. In spite of having given them a safe-conduct, the Venetians were guilty of this want of faith, for which they were much blamed by those who heard of it.

10th May. We heard that our ambassadors in France had made an arrangement with the king that he should cause Pisa, Pietrasanta, Serezzana, and Montepulciano, to be surrendered to us; and should receive in return 30 thousand florins.

19th May. We heard from Rome that a procession had come from Naples with a tabernacle which they said had done many miracles on the way, making the blind to see, curing the palsy and other infirmities. It was brought with great veneration, those accompanying it being much chastened, and having their backs all bleeding from the penance which they had inflicted upon themselves.

23rd May. We heard that Lucca had risen in arms, the people being against the chief citizens, because the latter

[1] That is, those who were not eligible for office. In the *Registro di Provvisioni, ad an.*, we find, under this date, a decree which imposes "on everyone described or comprised in the assessments of the Florentine citizens or on those who have matriculated, or who exercises any of the 21 *Arti* (belongs to any of the 21 Guilds) in the city or in the suburbs of the city of Florence, a loan or tax which will bring in at least the sum of 40,000 large florins."

[2] From the order of the *Signoria* to send an escort to meet this messenger as usual, we see that he arrived on the 24th.

[3] This image was brought to Florence in the hope of recovering Pisa, together with all the rest which had been lost on the coming of Charles VIII. The decree of the *Signoria* referring to it is of the 20th.

were for giving us back our possessions, in obedience to the king, who threatened them; but the popular party did not choose to obey his ambassadors; and as far as we were concerned, he was never obeyed. I believe that he was really desirous to let us have our rights, but was not able to send troops, being occupied with other matters.

24th May. We apothecaries of Florence assembled, about 40 *maestri* (master-apothecaries), in San Gilio,[1] to resuscitate a *Compania* (Guild) of ours, which had been begun in 1477, but abandoned later; and we appointed certain men who would do what was necessary.

6th June. We heard that in the Mugello at Collina a peasant had murdered four children, from eight years old downwards, who were his nephews; and had wounded an old man to death. The *Podestà* there had him arrested.

8th June. We heard that the Pisans had surrendered to the King of France, and had hoisted his flag; and on this day came a messenger of the king and asked them whether they really meant to yield; and they declared that they were willing to yield to the king, but did not choose to be under the Florentines. He replied that this commission had not been given him, and they must yield unconditionally; and they agreed, but nevertheless nothing came of it.

10th June. We sent ambassadors towards Librafatta to meet the French, who were beginning to arrive, one of these ambassadors being Luca degli Albizzi.[2] And we heard that Pietrasanta had hoisted the French flag, and that there were cries of *Marzocco*; and these French were coming with the object of causing Pisa and Pietrasanta [3] and Serezzano to be returned to us. And we heard that the Pisans still wished to defend themselves and stood firm, so it seemed as if we were being befooled.

At this time we heard that five thunderbolts had fallen in one day at Bologna, one in San Michele, and one in the Servi, one at Crociati, and two in the city, and had caused great damage.

[1] The present Via Sant' Egidio was then called *San Gilio*, and extended from Via Pinti to the Piazzetta of San Michele Visdomini. The church is connected with the hospital of Santa Maria Nuova. [Trans.]

[2] The second was Giovan Battista Ridolfi (*Ammirato*).

[3] Beaumont, the French commander, caused the Lucchesi to surrender Pietrasanta to him, but he kept it for the king and did not hand it over to the Florentines (*Ammirato*).

20th June. We heard that there were cries of *Marzocco* at Montepulciano also.

21st June. We heard that the French had gone with our troops to encamp before Pisa, and the Pisans had fired upon the French and killed several of them. The French leader came here, and it was said that the French went in and out of Pisa as they chose. Treachery was suspected, and this suspicion was justified.

At this time the plague appeared in several houses, and many people were suffering from French boils.

2nd July. We heard that there had been a hailstorm at Rome, in which the hailstones lay two *braccia* deep, with such a violent wind and tempest that the Pope's palace was ruined, and part of a room where the Pope was sitting fell on the top of him; but as it pleased the Lord, he remained under a beam, one end of which was supported against the wall and thus kept from falling, so that he was not killed. His head was slightly injured, and his cheek and one hand; but twelve or thirteen persons who were with him in the room were killed. This was on St. Peter's Day, at about 20 in the evening (4 p.m.). And the Pope caused himself to be bled a little. It was considered a great sign and a good augury for the Pope.[1]

At this time we were sending to the camp at Pisa as much bread as could be made in Florence, all the beasts that came into Florence being taken and laden with bread. And we sent them a sum of 8 thousand gold florins. We now had good hopes of Pisa.

On this day certain women came out of Pisa clothed only in their chemises; but our troops took them, suspecting that they carried messages, and decided to search them. The soldiers were so shameless as to search them to their skins, and they found letters to the Pope's son. Think what wars bring about, the innumerable cases that happen, and the sin of those who cause it all.

15 houses with plague had now been discovered in Florence.

8th July. We heard that some Gascons had come to our camp at Pisa with the French, and that they had begun to pillage the provisions in the camp; and their commander giving them leave, they went into the Val de Nievole and

---

[1] *Tomasi*, in the *Vita del Duca Valentino*, gives particulars of this event which happened on the 29th June.

pillaged some houses in the neighbourhood; which caused a great scandal here, it appearing as if we were being made fools of by this French commander.

9th July. We heard that Luca degli Albizzi, our commissary in the camp, had been arrested by the French commander, after we had sent him there with 700 soldiers; so that we wrote immediately to the king, informing him how these brutal and crazy Frenchmen were behaving, and requesting that they should return to their country, as they appeared to have served us ill.[1]

12th July. Our camp was raised, and our troops went into the territory of Lucca, sacking some castles belonging to the Lucchesi.[2]

The King of France wrote to the French in Italy that Pisa must be made to surrender at all costs, and therefore they must return there. And our ambassadors in France wrote that the king had been displeased that the camp was raised at Pisa, and that he wished the place to be forced to capitulate without fail, and his troops must go back there at once,[3] on pain of being declared rebels. And in this fashion things lingered on day after day without a change.

At this time we heard that there had been a tumult at Perugia, and that the Baglioni had been expelled, 100 men having been killed. Also that the Sienese were in arms, and that the father-in-law of Petruccio had been killed.[4]

During these days the builders began to place the brackets of the great cornice of the *Palagio degli Strozzi* that is to say, on the half of it towards the *Mercato Vecchio*.

The price of corn was now less than 20 *soldi* a bushel.

9th August. We made no conquests, being without money, and not well provided with prudence. Everyone marvelled that our ambassadors, who were always near the king, could never discover whether he wished honestly to help us or not.

---

[1] Albizzi was arrested by the Swiss who were in the camp, and was obliged to pay 1300 *scudi* as ransom. It is true, however, that he had opposed Beaumont with regard to raising the camp (*Ammirato*).

[2] *Portaveneri* writes under this date: "The French passed into the territory of Lucca, and the Lucchesi gave them provisions, and bore great insults out of fear."

[3] That they should return, that is, to the siege of Pisa.

[4] Niccolò Borghesi.

11th August. Pistoia rose in arms, on account of internal disputes.

During these days all the people here were discontented, chiefly because of the *barzello*, which had been very hard upon them, and also because they could see that no conquests were made, and there would be large costs to pay.[1] The Pisans had sacked Altopascio and taken Librafatta.

17th August. We heard that the Pistolese were still fighting amongst themselves, and that 150 men had been killed, and houses burnt down; and the church of San Domenico was burnt down. The people from all the country round, and from the mountains, rushed to the town; and it was said besides that Messer Giovanni Bentivogli had sent men on foot and horseback.

19th August. We heard that the Pisans had taken the bastion, and killed everyone in it, and that they were encamped at Rosignano; and our leaders did not send to relieve any place, it almost seeming as if they were stunned. We were without soldiers, in fact, or to speak more correctly, with but few; their number not sufficing to go to the succour of a place when needed, so that we were between the devil and the deep sea. It was a very distressing and perilous time, so much so that on the 20th August, the day of San Bernardo, the bells of the *Palagio* were not allowed to be rung, on account of the dangers within and without [2]; but God has always helped this city.

30th August. Soldiers were hired and sent to Pistoia and to Livorno and to garrison the castles.

1st September. Many people passed through here on their way to the Jubilee.

5th September. We heard that the Turks had taken Corfu and Modone, and had killed everyone, and razed

---

[1] *Rinuccini*, in the *Ricordi* already quoted, writes on this point: "These *Signori* conducted themselves very badly in this their magistracy, because they only thought of getting money, unjustly forcing the citizens to lend money to the commune, and forcing them to pay many taxes before the time, so that when their two months' term of office expired at the end of August, they had acquired the hatred of all the people, and little or no reputation."

[2] The chapel in the *Palazzo della Signoria* was dedicated to St. Bernard, and on this day every year a tribute of wax was offered by the monks of the Florentine *Badìa* and by the *Spedale degli Innocenti*, and a most splendid *festa* was held. It was also the custom to ring the bells of the *Palazzo* all day, a custom which lasted till the grand-ducal days.

Modone to the ground. And it was said besides that the Turks had defeated the Venetian fleet and captured it; and that 30 thousand persons had been killed, on board the vessels and in the cities together.

15th September. The great cornice of the *Palagio degli Strozzi* was finished, on the side towards the *Mercato*.

18th September. We heard that the Pistolese were again in tumult, and that many people had been killed, the *Panciatichi* being the victors.

19th September. It rained so heavily and continuously that the Arno was in flood, and caused much damage to these plains; but the heaviest rain was at Dicomano; and in the Mugello the Sieve rose higher than ever before, but the Dicomano and the Moscia were worse, the Moscia breaking down the bridge of Londa and all the buildings near the river. And in Turicchi the ditches brought down masses of stones to the bank of the Sieve, and caused the villages to be ruined and the fields riddled through all this part of the country as far as the cliff. And I can speak of it, for it affected me, spoiling many of my fields, among others one called *Chiassaia* because a certain *chiasso* (alley) went across it leading to the cliff; it meant a loss of 25 ducats.

8th October. We heard that Valentino was leaving Rome with a large body of soldiers and artillery, and was going in the direction of Faenza or Pesaro.

13th October. We heard that Valentino was advancing towards the *Borgo* (San Sepolcro) with his troops, having Vitellozzo with him, and it was feared lest he might attack us.

15th October. We heard that Rimini had surrendered to Valentino, and that the people had given 10 thousand ducats to their *Signore* that he might go away.

16th October. We heard that Pesaro had done likewise, and that the *Signore* was coming here.

29th October. We had letters from Murano at the head of which was drawn a bull that had been found underground, being made of copper, which was as follows: It had a city on its head, in its right paw it held a man's head, and in its left paw a banner with the cross; and on its flank were three bells upside-down; in the middle of its body was a man, and under the hinder-parts a chalice with a wafer; on the left side of its body was a very strange crucifix, with several inscriptions upon it, one of them down on the body saying: *quarto luce*. It was interpreted in many ways, but because there were the arms of the Pope upon it, it was given to him: the Lord knows the meaning of it. It is true that the world is too heavily laden with sins. I have noted this down because I saw the letter with the drawing at the top.

9th November. Valentino had taken Berzighella, and he and his troops were in the territory of Forlì.

16th November. The lanterns were placed on the *Palazzo degli Strozzi*; there were four of them, one at each corner, which cost, for making alone, 100 gold florins each.

21st November (Saturday), 22nd November (Sunday), 23rd (Monday), 24th (Tuesday), and 25th (Wednesday), it snowed continuously in Florence, and froze, so that the snow lay till the following Sunday, without the roofs dripping. There had never been seen in Florence a greater quantity of snow, or a fall that lasted so long. The boys made many snow-lions, etc., in the streets.

29th November. We apothecaries reconstituted our *Compagnia*, which had been founded in 1477, but was almost forgotten; we drew up fresh articles, and elected *Capitani* and did all that was needful.

15th December. A Franciscan monk was detained here who belonged to the *Osservanza* and was vicar[1] of the province; he had preached at Pisa during this time of war, and had encouraged them to stand firm, assuring them that God would liberate them; and he was detained in order to discover whether he had done wrong or had any secret information. Nothing more was heard of it, and they let him go.

29th December. Two men of Castiglione Aretino were beheaded; they were party leaders who had disobeyed the *Signoria*.[2]

[1] The *Vicario* was an official of the Republic sent to govern part of the territory; for the places subject to Florence there were 17 *Capitani*, 12 *Vicari*, and minor officials called *Podestà*. also *Castellani* for the fortresses. [Trans.]

[2] On the 28th December the *Signori, juxtis ut dixerunt causis moti et pro conservatione eorum regiminis*, decided to write to the *Otto di Guardia e Balìa* a *Bullettino* which requested that, omitting all the ceremonies of the law and statutes, they should immediately condemn to be beheaded Dino di Tonio di Giovanni dell' Agnello, and Mariotto, *alias* Totto di Matteo di Francesco, both of Castiglione Fiorentino, *tam quam omicidas et homines male conditionis*. Castiglione Aretino became Castiglione Fiorentino after the acquisition of Arezzo in the year 1384.

30th December. About 11 o'clock in the evening the inn of the Bertucce fell down; the lower vault fell in first, and then another vault above, and lastly the roof, burying many people who were there drinking; about 16 in all. Three of them were found dead, and many dangerously injured, the latter being dragged out from corners where part of the vaulting had been held up. All the wine and the casks were lost. The ruin was complete; and it was thought a marvel that only three of the 16 died.

2nd January. A Jubilee (= a Pardon) was proclaimed here, sent by the Pope for those who could not go to Rome; and it was to be granted as follows: The churches of Santa Maria del Fiore, Santo Spirito, Santa Croce, and Santa Maria Novella were to be visited, with the *penitenzieri* [1] (confessors), who had the same authority as at Rome, in every case; and it was generally said that whoever was able to do so, should give in alms as much as he was in the habit of spending in a week; and besides there were dispensations for vows,[2] there being a collecting-box for each confessor.

6th January. We heard that the Pisans had raided as far as Ponte ad Era (Pontedera) and captured about 27 men; and five threw themselves into the Arno and were drowned; they also carried off a number of cattle.

14th January. Certain of the chief young men in the city armed themselves and went about the streets at night; and meeting the *Cavaliere* of the *Podestà*,[3] wounded two *birri* (sergeants) so that they died; several of our party were wounded also; and they went as far as the *Palagio del Podestà* to let out the prisoners. It was considered a reprehensible and arrogant act.

16th January. We heard that the men of Faenza had defeated Valentino.

[1] *Penitenzieri* are confessors who have the power to absolve in special cases. They exist only in basilicas or the more important churches, and stand at the altar-rails holding a long wand over the penitents' heads. [Trans.]

[2] Penitents make vows, promising certain gifts to the Madonna or other saints or to the church, and writing these vows on pieces of paper, they put them in the collecting-box of their special *penitenziere* (confessor). [Trans.]

[3] The office of the *Cavallieri* was to go round with the sergeants, and, as a rule, an arrest could not be effected without the presence of a *Cavaliere*. The *Podestà* had three under him, and the *Capitano* (*del Popolo*) had two. [Trans.]

7th February. We heard that the Pistolese had had an encounter outside the city, and that 200 men had been killed. The *Cancellieri* had 1600 men and the *Panciatichi* 800, but nevertheless the *Panciatichi* lost fewer than the *Cancellieri*. The *Panciatichi* were said to be the conquerors.

24th February. A Sienese physician, of the house of Belanti of Siena, was murdered by three men, sent (it was said) by Pandolfo Petrucci, who fell upon him from the butcher's shop which is at the corner of the Via Ghibellina next to the *Stinche*. One was caught by the people at the time, and another was caught in the evening, being found in the neighbourhood of Sant' Ambrogio; the third fled and escaped, having acted, it was said, with great cunning, for after he had struck the first blow, he exclaimed to the others: "Strike him!" and took to his heels and left them, so that the people noticed them only and let him go. It was said that he had betrayed them.[1]

26th February. They were hung at the *Canto delle Stinche* (Corner of the Prison of the Stinche), where they had committed the crime. They went on the executioner's cart, being tortured most cruelly with red-hot pincers all through the city; and here at Tornaquinci the brazier for heating the pincers broke. There not being much fire left, and it not sparkling properly, the *Cavaliere*[2] shouted at the executioner, and made him stop the cart, and the executioner got out and went for charcoal to the charcoal-burner, and for fire to Malcinto the baker, and took a kettle for a brazier, making a great fire. The *Cavaliere* kept crying all the time: "Make it red-hot!" and all the people were desirous that they should be tortured without pity. The very boys were ready to assassinate the executioner if he did not do his work well, hence they (the condemned men) shrieked in the most terrible way. And all this I saw here at Tornaquinci.

2nd January.[3] We heard that the Pisans had thrown

---
[1] The murdered man was Luzio Bellanti, "a man of letters and worthy of esteem" (as *Parenti* calls him); and the murderers, as is shown by the sentence pronounced by the *Otto* on the 25th February, were Guasparri di Battista da Modena, Giampietro di Conte d'Astolfo, called Bagoni da Carpi, and a certain Giorgio, also da Carpi. This latter escaped by flight.

[2] See note to 14th January, 1500.

[3] The confused chronology, and the fact that we find this circumstance recorded in the *Storie* of *Giovanni Cambi* and in those of *Pietro Parenti* as having happened at Pistoia in February, induce us to believe that the author of this Diary is in error.

Florence: The Old Bridge and Covered Way

from the windows of the *Signori* two men who were the servants of a military leader called Bianchini, because they had gone to complain to him of certain acts of injustice to which they had been subjected. They (the Pisans) were always cruel men. And for this reason Bianchini left Pisa and came into our territory, although many did not trust him.

5th March. We heard that certain Pistolese, of the *Cancellieri* party, followed three of the *Panciatichi* who were leaving Pistoia to come here, and when they reached San Piero a Ponte, the said *Cancellieri* assaulted them, and they fled into a house; and their enemies broke open the door and seized them, and leading them about a mile away, slew them. Such is the force of party passions in a city! I myself am without party or political passion, and desire nothing but that the will of God should be done.

At this time the plague increased. It was in more than ten houses in Florence.

9th March. The plague was increasing rapidly, in this waning of the moon, and was discovered in many houses in several parts; chiefly in the Via della Scala, where it was discovered in four houses on the same day, there being one house where three people died in one night, so that no one remained alive, and the door had to be broken open from outside to take away the dead bodies.

10th March. We heard that the Pistolese were burning down each other's houses throughout the district, and that they had an encounter on the 12th instant, and slew numbers on both sides; many more of the *Cancellieri*, according to what was said.

24th March. The Pistolese killed the head of a party, called Zavaglia.[1]

1501. 2nd April. The Pistolese had a skirmish in which sixty-four men were killed; and in this fashion they destroyed each other, and did no good to their respective causes. No remedy could be found, but everyone regretted it.

13th April. We heard that Valentino had thrown down the walls of Faenza. It was thought that he would certainly take it.

15th April. There came to Florence ten citizens of Pistoia, belonging to the chief families in the city, to explain to us their sad case. One of our commissaries was

[1] *Salvi*, quoted above, says that his name was de' Gheradini.

N

sent from here, and he went to Pistoia and hung certain rioters; but nevertheless others continued fighting and would not submit.[1]

21st April. We heard that the men of Faenza had killed many of the French, about 400, and that Valentino had entered the city, but had been repulsed and expelled with ignominy.

23rd April. We heard that the King of France had sent our ambassadors away, and we feared that he had become inimical to us.

26th April. We heard that Valentino had been about to sack Faenza; but the city ransomed itself, paying him 40 thousand florins not to be sacked.

27th April. Matters at Pistoia remained unchanged. The plague was in a number of houses; and the price of corn was 40 *soldi* a bushel. Here no one was working, especially among the silk-workers; and the poorer classes were in need and discontented.

29th April. We heard that Messer Giovanni Bentivoglio had fled from Bologna for fear of Valentino; and later that he had come to an agreement with Valentino, which was so.

2nd May. We heard that Valentino was encamped at Firenzuola, so that the inhabitants were deserting the district and fleeing to the gates of Florence; and here we were in fear of a tumult in the city.

3rd May. We sent 20 thousand florins to the King of France, and Lorenzo, son of Pierfrancesco, went to France with the money.

6th May. We heard that Valentino was asking for a safe-conduct, and the Pope sent a messenger here, and we granted it him.

8th May. The artillery which was in Empoli was fetched here, and 90 pair of oxen were required to draw it.

9th May. Piero Soderini and Benedetto de' Nerli were sent as ambassadors to Valentino. And during these days all these plains were deserted, and one saw the scanty possessions of the wretched peasants heaped on to carts and beasts of burden all along the roads.

12th May. We heard that Valentino had reached Barberino di Mugello, and was doing all sorts of damage,

[1] The commissary sent by the *Signoria* was Niccolò di Tommaso Antinori.

burning and robbing, and cutting the corn. And watch was kept in Florence all these nights, lights being placed in the windows.¹

13th May. Valentino's troops reached Carmignano, and made an incursion as far as Peretola and Sesto. This morning, at about dinner-time, the *Signori* published a proclamation that when they made certain signals: that is to say, when the guns fired twice and the bell tolled six times, twice over, everyone capable of bearing arms was to join his *Gonfalone*; and that no one was to bear arms apart from the *Gonfaloni*, on pain of being declared a rebel.² Therefore everyone closed their shops and cleared out the goods, taking them to their houses, being convinced that there was great peril; and everyone outside did his utmost to get into Florence.

On the said day, the papal troops were quartered at Campi and round about there, doing a great deal of damage. Some peasants seized several of them who were on horseback, and brought them to Florence. And on this day ambassadors went to Valentino at Campi, the Bishop de' Pazzi and Francesco de' Nerli; and when they returned, said, in passing, that matters would be arranged. And everyone marvelled, and said to himself: "What have we to do with Valentino? We are not at war with him." And everyone was desirous to go and attack him, as it was not only for the peasants to avenge themselves, it being no small thing and entirely wrong to let him ruin our land and behave so abominably; and we ought to feel ashamed, as Florentines, of making a compromise about our property with one who is not worth a farthing. He was actually so presumptuous as to wish for Campi, and allowed us till 18 this afternoon (2 p.m.) to surrender, or else he would sack it; therefore it was agreed to give him 300 men-at-arms, and not hinder him from taking Piombino.

15th May.³ An agreement was made that we should

---

¹ By a proclamation of the *Signoria* everyone was ordered to keep a light burning in the windows all night.
² The guns were to be fired from the *ballatoio* of the Palazzo; and the armed men of the *Gonfaloni*, at this signal, were to "*ire*," as says the decree, "*contra inimicos Reipublice Florentine et ad tuendam civitatem ab hostibus eam opprimere volentibus.*"
³ On this day the *Signoria* gave leave to their musicians to go and play in honour of the Duke Valentino, who was then near Florence (*Delib., ad an.*).

give him 36 thousand florins a year for three years, and that he should be our *Capitano*, beginning from this 1st May, 1501, and that we should give him immediately 9 thousand florins. He also wished us to overlook anything that had been done against our state from the day when he left Imola till now; and this was on account of its being said by many that there were some citizens who had proposed his coming. It may have been true that some had made this error.[1] Several things happened on this day: one of Valentino's men, wanting to enter Florence by force, through the Porta di Faenza, with his naked sword in his hand, the guards who were placed at the gate stuck a lance right through him, and he died on the spot. And many others, hanging about the gates and the camp, robbed them and took away their horses, sometimes one and sometimes four, so that they could not go about singly; and they on their side were as bad, pillaging and doing all kinds of damage.

16th May. The *Signoria* sent two mace-bearers and two *comandatori*[2] (messengers) to order them to leave, and to arrange that they should have the oxen that they had demanded, namely 80 pair; and they were so presumptuous as to rob them and take away their maces, and even to wound one of them very severely, saying that they did not choose to leave without money.

17th May. Valentino's troops moved their camp and went to Signa, taking up their quarters beyond the Arno towards Ugnano and the place of the Pandolfini, and raiding as far as Montelupo, robbing and committing every sort of cruelty. Some they beat on the head, others they hung up in various cruel ways, whenever they could, in order to extract from them where things were hidden, because they found many houses empty. And here meanwhile they were spoken of quite differently. We gave them the oxen which they required, that is to say, lent them; and a proclamation was published besides that no one must despoil them, and that anyone who had done so, must return what had been taken, on pain of

---

[1] Historians agree in declaring that there were some in Florence who had a secret understanding with Valentino, and in blaming the pusillanimous conduct of the magistrates, which *Nardi* calls "asinine patience."

[2] At that time the *comandatori* were the servitors of the magistrates who were sent to communicate their orders to people. [Trans.]

death. The "Eight" also went in person this morning ceremoniously all over these plains, and arrested those (of our people) who were loitering about the roads.

17th May. We had letters from the King of France, saying that he did not wish this Valentino to injure us and impose payments, and we must send him away; and if he would not leave, the king had given orders to Milan [1] that help should be brought us; so that we thought of not keeping our promises to Valentino.

18th May. The whole morning we heard of nothing but the iniquities of Valentino's troops; among other things they sacked Carmignano, and carried off all the girls that they found there, who were gathered in a church from all the country round. And it was said besides, that there were some, worse than the devil in hell, who, finding a woman with her brother of about seventeen years old—— (I do not know if I can record this villainy, which made me tremble with the fear of God on hearing it. Such a sin calls down the destruction of a city; and one reads in the Old Testament that a city was in fact destroyed, to the very foundations, for this same sin. Woe to those who have been the cause of it, and also to those who could have punished such a crime and did not do so; for we could destroy Valentino, having three times the number of men that he has. However, it is not news to me what our citizens are capable of; they do not care to put themselves out even for a great evil. And this has been seen several times, when they might have conquered and won much honour, but did not choose to act, on account of discords amongst themselves). Some others, finding a young husband and wife, bound the husband to a pillar, and in his presence dishonoured the woman shamefully and beat her. And thus, at each moment, we kept hearing of outrageous things. When the King of France was here, we did not hear of the smallest case to do with women; and the French were in our houses together with gentlewomen, but there was never an idea of their behaving badly.

On this day we heard that the Pisans had taken Ponte di Sacco, and were raiding on all sides; and it was continually said that 4 thousand Gascons were coming behind this serpent (Valentino). And there was a tumult three times on this same day in the *Piazza de' Signori*. The first time the

[1] That is, to his soldiers who were in Lombardy.

Cavalliere wanted to arrest a man who had been banished, and in laying hands upon him, certain ruffians came to the man's help, and a servant of the "Eight" was wounded; and the banished man, being also wounded, fled and passed by here at the Tornaquinci, with his face covered with blood. People began to shut their shops everywhere. A second time it was because one of the de' Baroncelli struck one of the de' Campi on the head with a dagger, cutting off one of his ears and a piece of his head; it was on account of this de' Campi having been one of the "Eight" when a son of this de' Baroncelli had been put to death, who was, it seems, a ruffian, and went about the countryside[1] committing excesses; this quarrel caused the shops to be closed a second time. The third time there was no reason for the tumult, but the city was excited.

On this day Valentino demanded our artillery which was at Empoli in loan; and also money. He received the answer that neither the one nor the other would be given him; that with regard to the money, we need not pay it to him till the end of August, and we would keep to the articles fixed, and he must leave.

19th May. Valentino left Signa and went between Montelupo and Empoli, continually pillaging and doing iniquitous things; and this evening Piero Soderini was sent to him as an ambassador.

20th May. The poor peasants with their families and possessions began to go outside the walls, but towards evening there was a rumour from near Malmantele that Valentino was turning back, and this rumour reached Florence, so that those peasants who had gone outside returned to the city in much disquiet and with great lamentations. And this fear of his returning grew to such a degree, that the people fled into Florence from all the country round; their numbers increasing when it became known that Vitellozzo had sent our oxen to Pisa for the artillery, and did not want to return them. It was thought that he did not wish to pitch his camp at Empoli. People seemed bewildered when they saw that the *Signoria* took no sort of action. Valentino's troops behaved like the Turks, putting all the villages to fire and flame, and carrying off the girls and women; and someone saw on the road to

---

[1] *Parenti* also relates this case of Piero Cambi and Giovanni Baroncelli, who was declared a rebel.

Rome the loads of girls that they were sending there, to present them as gifts, or perhaps to sell them as the Turks do the Christians. And I do not marvel at it, for this army was led by two cruel men, Valentino and Vitellozzo. The latter takes after his father, who was too cruel for words: once, seeing a boy of the opposite party before him, who had been sent by his mother and who went on his knees to beg for pardon and mercy, he seized a knife from his side and slew him with his own hand. And he burnt down towers full of women and children and many people who had fled there with their possessions, and amid terrible shrieks and cries, left not one alive.[1] This son of Vitellozzo took after his father, neither of them fearing God, having beggared hundreds of peasants to avenge their passions; thus avenging themselves upon those who had done them no harm whatever, like cowardly men who do not fear the hand of the Lord, nor know how great it is, and how near them.

22nd May. Valentino's troops were quartered round Empoli, and made incursions all through Valdelsa and the villages, robbing and pillaging. One heard of nothing but cruelty. And here the city was always more and more crowded with unfortunate peasants with their poor possessions and their families, grown-up people and children, in great bitterness of spirit.

23rd May. Valentino left Empoli and went towards Castello Fiorentino with the artillery; but it was still said that he would turn back, and this fear was born of the understanding that was known to exist. And in case of its being true, everyone took care to provide himself with sufficient bread, so that in the evening there was no bread left at the bakers'; and the price of corn rose to 53 *soldi* a bushel.[2] Florence was filled with melancholy, and seemed frightened at a trifle.

24th May. Valentino sent to let us know that he would not go away unless he were given at least 8 thousand florins. Every day one was hearing of the cruel doings of his troops: they first sacked Castel Fiorentino and then Barbialla, where they slew more than 60 men and six

[1] *Litta* also records this cruelty. The boy was of the family Fucci of Gittà di Gastello which Niccollò Vitelli, the father of Vitellozzi, wished to exterminate.

[2] The *Signoria* made special arrangements for providing bread, and for tranquillising the people, who were rioting on account of this shortage of bread.

women, and robbed everything. Unheard-of things were said of them, and yet provisions were sent them from here, and all our commissaries were continually ordering us not to offend them in any way, and to give back anything that had been taken from them, making every Florentine subject despair. He who was robbed and killed had no remedy.[1]

26th May. We heard that the King of France was sending 30 thousand men to go against Naples, half of them being in the neighbourhood of Pontremoli, and half of them coming from Romagna; and this evening they were at Castrocaro with Signore Begnì.

27th May. Valentino went away towards Colle, and the men of Colle resisted him and slew a whole brigade of his; and the next day they went towards Casoli di Volterra, destroying the whole country. Wherever they went, half the harvest was spoilt, as they cut the corn for their horses; and to obtain reparation, we waited from day to day for the French to arrive from the south and the north.

2nd June. We heard that our troops at Pisa, the archers of the prefect,[2] had captured three Pisans.

3rd June. One Messer Gambacorti and other Pisan citizens were brought to Florence.[3]

4th June. We heard that certain of our peasants from Ronta had killed a Frenchman on the Ronta road, who was a relative of Signore Begnì; this was considered bad news, because he was coming past here with the French army, and was a priest. He was buried at the *Servi*, and given a grand funeral, in order that the Signore Begnì should not think it such a crime on our part, and great excuses

[1] These are not exaggerations of the author, but the actual truth, as is shown by the proclamations published at the time, and by the disdainful words with which all contemporary Florentine writers stigmatise this vile procedure of the Government.

[2] The Pisans were so bold as to raid in the neighbourhood of Cascina, imagining that it was unguarded, but the soldiers of Giovanni della Rovere, who was a prefect of Rome, lord of Sinigaglia, and one of the Florentine leaders, had returned there.

[3] The capture of Gambacorti was thought very important, as the Florentines were anxious to have him in their hands so as to be able to examine him and find out many secrets about Pisa. The *Signoria* wrote of it on the 2nd June to the commissary Vespucci with satisfaction, ordering him to send this prisoner to Florence with a sure escort. Valentino, in a letter of the 3rd, wrote to the *Signoria* begging them to treat him *graciously*, as he might be useful as an intermediary for making peace with Vitellozzo, who was very friendly with him.

were made to him.¹ It is always some foolish person who puts a city in peril. But, according to the opinion of many people, he (Aubigny) was a wise, good and noble man, who did not condemn us as having done this thing out of hate.

6th June. The French foot-soldiers, with Signore Begnì, reached Dicomano; they behaved very well. And at the same time there passed beyond Empoli and through the Valdelsa a much greater number, it being said that there were 30 thousand altogether, and that more were coming.

10th June. 4 thousand horse reached Dicomano, who behaved quite differently from the foot-soldiers. They did every sort of damage: cutting down the corn for the horses, wherever they passed, sacking the cellars, beating the peasants, and paying no regard to the commissaries or anyone. And in the hills, when they wanted to take some fowls from certain peasants and the latter turned upon them, not allowing it, they slew them. And some other peasants resisting them, there was a skirmish, in which twenty men perished.²

11th June. The French came into Valdisieve as far as Ponte a Sieve, and then went on along the valley of the Arno.

14th June. We heard that they had entered Siena and taken possession of it; and that the *Signori* were sent home, and Pandolfo Petrucci had hidden himself.

18th June. We heard that they were near Rome,³ and that others had come by sea, disembarking at Livorno to go on by land. And that the Cardinal di Roanna (Archbishop of Rouen) was coming to Florence from Milan, the King of France having an idea of making him Pope; at least such was the opinion. We heard besides that the Pope had left Rome and gone to Orvieto.

¹ The magistrate of the *Otto* wrote at once to the *Vicario* of the *Scarperia* and to the *Capitano* of Marradi to seek diligently for the culprits. On the 11th the Republic ordered Tosinghi, their commissary with the French army, to explain the innocence of the Florentines with regard to these assassinations, which were not at all uncommon on the frontiers; and to point out that "a stately funeral, at the public expense, had been given to this prelate, who was said to be a nephew of Monsignore d'Ubigny"; another document calls him the *Protonotario di Scozia*. And finally the Republic wrote a letter of condolence to Aubigny.

² For this fact also the *Signoria* wrote to the commissary that he was to make excuses, and ordered him to arrange that the French should have as large a quantity of provisions as possible, so that they need not seek them, and added that he was to do his best to get them to leave the Florentine territory promptly.

³ It is always the French army that is meant.

19th June. We heard that Federigo, King of Naples, had caused an immense and most pious procession to be made on the day of the *Corpus Domini*, in which he had walked barefoot; and when they reached the church, he made an oration to the people, saying that he believed in Christ and in the Sacrament, and it was his will that all should do so; he testified to the people that he was not summoning the Turks to Italy to go against the Christian faith, but in order to help them; and said that if the people did not wish to have him for their *Signore*, he would resign, but if they were ready to support him they were to say so. And all the people with one voice cried that they would support him; and it was said that consequently he was on the way to Rome.

22nd June. We heard that there had been a great earthquake at Modona, many houses having fallen, and a number of people being killed; amongst other things a church had been ruined.

On this same day, here in Florence, whilst putting up the awnings round San Giovanni, the ropes became entangled, and caught on to the cross on the column of San Giovanni, that represents the miracle of San-Zanobi, and pulled it to the ground; and besides, the ropes being still in disorder, caused some tiles to fall from a roof, by which a man was killed and a boy had his leg broken. These were thought bad omens.

24th June. We heard that Signor Begnì with his troops had entered Rome; and every day these Romans were up in arms: think what a state Rome was in!

3rd July. The French passed Rome, and met Don Federigo's army, 5 thousand men being slain.

4th July. The Pistolese had another battle (between their parties) and 200 men were killed, nearly all of whom were foreign soldiers. And the next day there was another skirmish in which 100 were killed. A dozen men's heads were stuck on lances and carried about this poor unfortunate city; and they played *palla* (tennis)[1] with these heads both within and without Pistoia.[2]

[1] *Palla* is supposed to have been played in open spaces, with small, hard balls and a wooden bat; *pallone* seems to have been a kind of rackets, played against the walls of the houses. It would appear more likely that the Pistolese played *calcio* (football) with the skulls, or ordinary "ball." Landucci might well have used the word *palla* for any game played with a ball. [Trans.]

[2] Parenti gives these details also, that is to say, that the heads of the *Panciatichi* killed in the combats which had taken place in the district were carried about Pistoia on lances.

7th July. We heard that the French had found certain casks of wine concealed underground and poisoned, and that they had drunk out of them.

At this time the price of corn was 36 *soldi*; and there were hardly any cases of plague.

13th July. We heard that 60 Turkish vessels had arrived at Piombino.[1]

14th July. We heard that the French had had something of a defeat, but none the less had passed Capova (Capua), and were advancing.

21st July. One Rinaldo, a Florentine and a gambler,[2] was arrested, who, because he had lost at play, threw some horse-dung on the statue of the *Vergine Maria*, at the *Canto de' Ricci*, in a little alley next to this church, which is in a small piazza behind the houses; and he struck the image on the diadem. A boy who saw it told of there having been a man who had done this, and he was followed and watched, and was arrested at the *Osservanza di San Miniato*; when the serving-men of the "Eight" approached him, he stabbed himself in the left breast, but they took him, and led him before the *Podestà*, where he confessed that he had thrown at the Virgin out of rage at having lost. During the night he was hung from the windows of the *Podestà*, and the next morning being the day of Santa Maria-Maddalena, there was a double *festa*.[3] All Florence

[1] This Turkish fleet was commanded by Captain Camallo, and came to stop the French and Spanish armies which were marching against the King of Naples.

[2] Here the author has confused the Christian and the surname: the perpetrator of the crime here narrated was called Antonio di Giovanni Rinaldeschi, as is shown by the sentence of the *Signori Otto* pronounced the same day, the 21st.

[3] In order to understand the meaning of the words *fu una festa doppia* (there was a double *festa*), it must be mentioned that the chapel of the *Palazzo del Podestà* was dedicated to Santa Maria-Maddalena penitent, and that the magistracy bore the expense of both the religious and the lay fêtes which were held on this day. Then, when the magistracy of the *Podestà* was substituted by the tribunal of the *Rota*, which was soon transferred to the Palazzo dei Castellani, formerly called Altafronte, the *festa* was held in the chapel of the new residence of these judges, but the bells of the ancient *Palazzo* continued to be rung on this day, and a *palio* was run from the Office of Works of the Duomo to the Arno. The memory of the other so-called *festa*, namely, the execution of Rinaldeschi, has been preserved till our day, an ancient picture representing the fact being exhibited under the *loggia* (portico) of the church of the Madonna de' Ricci every year on this anniversary.

came to see this figure of the Virgin, and when the bishop had removed the dirt, there was not an evening on which pounds of wax-tapers were not fastened before it, the veneration perpetually increasing. And in a few days innumerable images have been brought as votive offerings, as may be seen.

22nd July. The cross on the column of San Giovanni, which had been pulled down by the ropes, was set up again.

24th July. We heard that the French had been defeated near Naples; however, they continued to advance intrepidly.

25th July. The Lady of Imola came here to Castello, having left Rome, as Monsignore Begnì had demanded her release from the Pope; and she came to stop here.[1]

28th July. We heard that the French had taken Capua, and sacked it, and put everyone to the sword. This was on the 24th, the eve of San Jacopo.

On the same day we heard that the Pistolese had had an encounter, in which the *Panciatichi* had had the worst of it, several of their party being hung at the windows in Pistoia; and that they had made a priest hang them, and then wanted him to hang himself. About seven *Panciatichi* were hung.

2nd August. We heard that the French had taken Naples at the first assault.

4th August. A vote was passed in Council that the Great Council should return, and that 600 men would be a sufficient number for it.[2]

6th August. We heard that it was true that the King of Naples had lost his kingdom, and been taken prisoner by the King of France. And there was a great *festa* here on this day, the bells being pealed, and there being many illuminations and bonfires in the city, and also much firing of guns. The French entered Naples this very day; and the King don Federigo, and whoever else wished to leave, were to be allowed to take their property with them, being given two days' time.

21st August. A Frenchman, with a number of horse-

[1] Caterina Sforza (liberated according to others through the intercedence of Monsignore d'Allegri), being left a widow by the death of Girolamo Riario, now married Giovanni di Pier Francesco de' Medici, to whom the villa of Castello belonged.

[2] This decree was made because this Council, on account of the difficulty of collecting such a large number of citizens, delayed all the business.

men, came to Florence, on his way to Naples, where he was to be lieutenant (viceroy) of the King of France.

29th August. We heard that the Pistolese had made peace, and elected a *Signoria*, four of one party and four of the other; and for the *Gonfaloniere* they had put into the ballot-boxes two names of each party, to be drawn by lot. Thus they were at peace after so much slaughter. If this were but the end of it!

During these days the Pisans captured some of our soldiers.¹

5th September. Two or three men were slain at Pistoia.

7th September. One of the *Cancellieri* was slain by the Pistolese here at the Porta al Prato in Florence. A fine kind of peace they have made!

8th September. We heard that Piombino was freed from Valentino's soldiers, and that he himself was ill in Rome.²

9th September. We heard that the emperor was on Lago Maggiore, and had captured Navarra and other castles with great cruelties.

11th September. A number of Germans passed here of those who had been with the King of Naples, as the emperor had published a proclamation commanding all the Germans who were in the pay of other countries to return to him, on pain of being declared rebels.

17th September. There passed Florence about a thousand foot-soldiers and about 600 horse who came from Naples and were going into Lombardy, for the King of France.

18th September. We heard that Piombino had given itself freely to the Pope.

During these days there was no physical sickness, but the city was sick and impoverished; the city funds paid no interest, and nothing for dowries or accidents; everyone suffered. The price of corn was 33 *soldi* a bushel, wine a ducat a *soma* (2 barrels), and oil 16 *lire* a barrel; and not much work was done.

9th October. We apothecaries decided, in the Apothecaries' Guild, that we could no longer make candles at two *denari*.³

---

¹ They captured those who had gone to raid at Limone.

² The Lord of Piombino having fled some time before, the citizens had yielded to Valentino's men on the 3rd September.

³ The florin in the year 1501 = about 7 *lire*, and a *denaro* was the 240th part of a florin. [Trans.]

10th October. There was very rough weather, rain, thunder and lightning, many buildings being struck, amongst others the *Campanile* of the church of the *Allegri*[1]; it happened in the morning, when the people were in church, as it was Sunday, and just when the priest was robed to go up to the altar, and it caused part of the *campanile* to fall on the church, killing five people and severely injuring more than 40.

14th October. There was an earthquake in Florence at 2 in the night (10 p.m.); but it did not ruin anything.

25th October. A vote was passed in the *Palagio* that all trading must be done with gold florins and *lire*.[2]

2nd[3] October. There was a proclamation of peace in Pistoia, with the guarantee that whoever broke it would be heavily punished.

3rd November. Our troops before Pisa took prisoner 57 of the Pisan horse, who were raiding towards Volterra; our men managed to intercept them.

14th December. The Cardinal of Ferrara came to Florence with a large troop of horsemen, on his way to Rome to fetch the Pope's daughter, and take her to marry his brother at Ferrara; and he had 150 baggage-mules. He was received with great honour, many Florentine young men going to meet him. He lodged in his own house at the *Canto de' Pazzi*,[4] and his horses were put in the Pope's stables. On the 15th he left again.

27th December. The tabernacle of Our Lady of Santa

---

[1] A church no longer in existence, called so after the family of the Allegri, whose houses were in the neighbourhood of Santa Maria Novella. [Trans.]

[2] 1501, 14th October. The decree says that "The *Priori*, etc., understanding how much disorder has been caused and continues to be caused in the city by the variety of money, and by its being clipped and of bad alloy, and desiring to remedy this matter, order that all trading, of whatever bank, exchange, contract or obligation of whatever kind or quality it may be (except the contracts for dowries), shall in future be done with large gold florins, of good quality and of the same weight as coined by the Mint of the Commune of Florence, or with *lire* of Florentine money, either silver or copper, and not otherwise." See note to 22nd October, 1471.

[3] This date of the 2nd October is evidently wrong, perhaps through an error of the scribe of the MS. of the Marucelliana. *Salvi* asserts that the articles of the peace were published on the 21st of the month.

[4] The Duke of Ferrara's house was that which had belonged to Messer Piero de' Pazzi.

Maria Impruneta came to Florence, and a solemn procession was made and great veneration paid to it; this was said to be on account of the King of France having demanded unjust concessions, wishing exiles to be recalled and the ruling magistrates to be nominated according to his pleasure.

1st January. The *Signoria* sent ambassadors [1] to present the Pope's daughter,[2] who had now reached her husband at Ferrara, with costly gifts. She had not come through Florence on her way from Rome to Ferrara.

11th February. The ambassador of the emperor came to Florence, and lodged in the house of the Portinari. He went to the *Signoria*.[3]

23rd February. We heard that the Pistolese had come to blows, the *Cancellieri* having driven out all the *Panciatichi* and burnt their houses, with the death of many men. One can say now that there is no help for this business of Pistoia; it is of no use guaranteeing the peace or trying any other remedy. Florence may be excused, for she cannot do good to those who do not choose: we must let them smash each other's heads: they are fond of blood.

10th March. We heard that the Turks were in the Gulf with a great fleet, and that the Venetians had had an encounter with them, with losses on both sides.

15th March. Our commissaries went to Pistoia and hung a band of the chief rebels.

23rd March. We heard that the Pisans had taken the town of Vico Pisano, and later that they had taken the fort also, it having been given up to them by our commissary who was one of the de' Pucci, the castellan, a de' Ceffi, and a certain constable of Piedmont.

1502. 4th April. The said commissary and the castellan of Vico were declared rebels, and their goods confiscated. And this evening a certain Francesco di Monna Tarsia was arrested, who had been in the fort of Vico.

23rd April. A vote was passed to lay waste the Pisan

---

[1] Tommaso Soderini was sent with this embassy, and carried a gift of cloth of gold and cloth of silver to the value of 800 ducats (*Bonaccorsi, Diario*).

[2] Lucrezia Borgia, who was marrying, as her fourth husband, Alfonzo d'Este, Duke of Ferrara, he having consented out of political reasons and being tempted by her great riches. [Trans.]

[3] Two ambassadors were sent by the emperor: the Marchese Ermes Sforza and Giovanni Graismer.

territory; and the price of corn at this time was 25 *soldi* a bushel.

30th April. A quantity of artillery and bombards were sent to Pisa, and more soldiers were continually being hired to go there, Antonio Giacomini [1] being made commissary.

10th May. Our troops began to lay waste the Pisan territory, corn, vines, fruit, and whatever there was; and we settled that those Pisan peasants who joined us were to be exempt, their land being left unharmed.

15th May. A stone fell from the house of the Woolmercers' Guild, at the corner of that little alley which is opposite Orto San Michele, having loosened itself because it was cracked, and it fell on the head of an unfortunate man, who was killed by it.[2]

16th May. There were messengers here from the King of France, who were going to the Pope and to all the powers, to declare that no one was to molest the Florentines, under pain of his displeasure, and he manifested great love and friendship for us.

17th May. We heard that the Pisans had captured certain peasant-*marraiuoli* [3] (who were laying waste), and had hung, drawn, and quartered them.

18th May. Certain Pisan prisoners came to Florence, having been sent by Giovacchino Guasconi from Volterra as they were carrying letters to Rome.

19th May. We heard that our troops were sending us a band of Pisan prisoners, amongst whom was the head of one of the leading families, who was wounded so that he could not walk; and the soldiers in garrison at Vico Pisano laid waste our territory and that of Bientina: so in this fashion all was going ill.

---

[1] This man is thus described by Giovanni *Cambi*: "A popular man of mark; not bearing a high reputation amongst the higher classes, but one in whom the people have great faith and, to no one else would they entrust such an undertaking as this laying waste (of the Pisan territory)."

[2] When the *Archivio dei contratti* was instituted in 1569, and the space above the *loggia* of Or San Michele destined for its offices, this little alley was occupied by the fresh staircase made to reach these offices; and in 1571 it was entirely closed by the construction of a shop opposite the *loggia*.

[3] The *marraiuoli*, in these old times, were some of those who laid waste the enemy's land, the word coming from *marra* = pickaxe. [Trans.]

20th May. We heard that the men of Barga had captured Fracassa, with many companions, who were going to Pisa.

22nd May. We heard that our troops had captured 28 Pisan soldiers, and had hung them all.[1]

26th May. We heard that our troops had taken as booty 100 mules laden with goods and 130 Pisans with their horses.

29th May. We heard (definitely) that Fracassa was captured, with a number of soldiers, and that the son of Count Jacopo[2] had been captured at the same time. Antonio Giacomini also came on this day to see the *Signoria*.

And we had the news that Vico Pisano and the citadel had already capitulated to our troops, on certain conditions, early this morning.

2nd June. One Lorenzo Lorenzo, a physician, who was a lecturer at the *Studio* (University), and greatly esteemed, was prompted by the devil to throw himself into a well, and was drowned.

5th June. We heard that Arezzo had rebelled.[3]

6th June. We heard that the citadel (of Arezzo) had not been lost, and that there were in all only 12 or 14 houses which had risen in arms; and our troops raised their camp at Vico and went to Arezzo, passing here this day.

8th June. Antonio Giacomini left here, having been made commandant of the camp, and went to Arezzo.

9th June. We heard that Guglielmo de' Pazzi[4] had been

---

[1] *Portoveneri* gives the number as twenty-four, who belonged to Vico Pisano, and had come out to raid between Pontedera and Cascina.

[2] The *Signoria* on this same day deputed Piero Popoleschi and Luca di Maso degli Albizzi to examine Fracassa and the other prisoners brought by the men of Barga, and to acquaint them with the result of the examination. On the 4th June they ordered the release of Alessandro, a chamberlain of the above, and also of the barber and two servants; the *Capitano* himself was released (provided that he did not leave the city) on the 1st July, and on the 4th was liberated altogether on his oath not to fight against the Republic for two years. The son of Count Jacopo, Niccolò Piccinino, was detained in the *Palagio* till 7th June (*Deliberazioni, ad an.*).

[3] According to Jacopo *Pitti* in his *Storia Fiorentina*, the news of this rebellion reached Florence on the night of the 4th, at one o'clock in the morning. For details see the *Racconto* of Arcangelo Visdomini, published in 1755, as well as the *Relazione* of Giovanni Rondinelli, *sopra lo stato antico e moderno della città di Arezzo*; the *Diario* of Francesco Pezzati, edited in the *Archivio Storico Italiano*, t. i., and the *Vita del Giacomini* written by *I. Pitti*, and published in the *Archivio* above quoted, t. iv. parte ii.

[4] Commissary-general at Arezzo.

captured, and that Vitellozzo was approaching Arezzo; and that the peasants were waiting in suspense to see how things went, and whether there were any grounds for the report. We also heard that Rassina had rebelled.

We heard that Vitellozzo had entered Arezzo with a large body of foot-soldiers and a quantity of artillery; and that Valentino was on his way with many troops, being beyond Siena. Consequently the people here were much dismayed, fearing lest there should be good grounds for the report; and things seemed to promise ill, as harvest-time was approaching.

During these days the Pisans raided, and looted, and slaughtered, as if the field were clear for them; and thus there was a conflagration all round, and it appeared to the most intelligent people to have been a folly to raise the camp (at Pisa) so hastily. On this day a vote was passed to impose several taxes (*decime*) and the manner was settled in which they were to be paid.[1]

11th June. We heard that it was not true that Vitellozzo had entered Arezzo, nor about Valentino; that these reports had only been circulated in order to get taxes voted.

12th June. We heard that the Pisans were encamped at Bientina, although they had been repulsed by our troops.

13th June. We heard that Vittellozzo had taken a certain hill fort, and that our troops had not been able to succour the citadel.

15th June. We heard that the men of Castiglione Aretino had captured 40 mules laden with flour, which were going to Arezzo; and that the mills of Arezzo had been destroyed by our troops.

16th June. Piero Soderini went to Milan to seek help from the French forces there.

18th June. We heard that the citizens of Arezzo had taken the citadel, and beheaded the Bishop [2] de' Pazzi and certain other officials who were in the city; it was not

---

[1] The preface of this day's decree, by which the taxes here spoken of were imposed, declares the reason of them: to provide money for the needs of the city, and "for the imminent and sudden perils which are seen to be arising"; and the word *condizioni* signifies the various modes of assessing them and the arrangements made for their payment.

[2] Cosimo de' Pazzi, son of the commissary. After his father was captured by the Aretini, he retired into the citadel and bravely directed its defence.

true, however, that they had beheaded them, but they had sent them prisoner to Città di Castello, Guglielmo de' Pazzi, the bishop, and several others; and the lives and property of the remaining citizens were to be spared.

19th June. We heard that our camp was going back to Montevarchi.

20th June. We heard that Piero de' Medici had entered Arezzo; and that there were cries of *Marzocco!* and *Palle!*

On this day, here in Florence, 50 men were called up for their *Gonfalone*, which was stationed here at Tornaquinci, and a *Gonfaloniere*, to guard the city; so that fear got hold of us, and everyone began clearing away their goods on all sides, making a most terrible commotion.[1]

21st June. The young *Signore* of Faenza was then at Rome with Valentino, and we heard that Valentino had caused him to be murdered, with three others besides. He had them strangled and thrown into the Tiber, and it happened when he was playing at *palla* (tennis) with some other lads like himself, for he was still a boy.[2] I believe that this deed was done because Valentino perceived that the people were too devoted to the lad, and he, being a diabolical man, was jealous for the supremacy.

22nd June. We heard that the King of France had sent a messenger to protest, declaring that all those who proceeded against the Florentines would find him their enemy.

23rd June. We heard that Valentino had taken Urbino, and then Città di Castello; and that the French who were

---

[1] Landucci had his apothecary's shop at the Canto de' Tornaquinci. With regard to these provisions *Parenti* writes: "The guards were redoubled in Florence, the locks on the doors were changed, and 50 foreign soldiers were set in each quarter under the orders of the *Gonfaloniere* of the companies of the people. It is supposed that this was done so as not to arm the people, in case they should turn against the upper classes, it being thought that they would behave in a disorderly way in the endeavour to change the government and withdraw it from the hands of the *universale*."

[2] The death of Astorre III. Manfredi, of Giovanni Evangelista his natural brother, and of others their adherents, is related by the historians with divers particulars; our author adds the moment in which they were strangled. Antonio Giustinian, the Venetian ambassador at Rome, wrote to the *Doge* on the 6th of this month: "It is said that, the other night, there were thrown into the Tiber and drowned the two young Lords of Faenza, together with their steward" (*Dispacci di A. Giustinian*, published by Professor Pasquale Villari (Firenze, 1876), t. i., p. 18.

coming to our aid[1] had reached the Mugello; it was said besides that Valentino had taken Cortona. So many things were going on all round.

24th June. No *palio* was run (for San Giovanni), so as to avoid a gathering of the people, for fear of what might ensue.

26th June. We heard that Valentino had sent to say that he wished to make an alliance with us, or else he would come and attack us; and he gave us four days in which to decide.[2]

27th June. Five gates of Florence were closed, which were: *San Giorgio, San Miniato, la Giustizia, Pinti*, and the *Porticciuola al Prato* of the mills; this being done for fear of people and letters being brought in. And the order was given that the houses along the Arno should not place ladders in the river for anyone.

2nd July. We heard that Borgo[3] had rebelled, and Anghiari had capitulated on certain conditions, and La Pieve[4] was in a sorry state. Thus it seemed as though the Florentines were wounded to death; everyone was mocking them.

This same day the French arrived here and were quartered from Sesto up to the gates of San Gallo and of Faenza.[5]

3rd July. We heard that Cortona was ours again.

[1] The aid that had been begged for by Piero Soderini. The captain of these forces was Monsignore d'Imbault.

[2] With regard to this, it is interesting to know that four days beforehand, on the 22nd, the *Signoria* had decreed severe penalties against those citizens who, being present at the meeting, should reveal anything concerning the letters of Duke Valentino. Also on the 25th secrecy was imposed as to the letters which had arrived in the night.

[3] Borgo a San Sepolcro.

[4] Castel della Pieve.

[5] In order to have an idea how quarters were provided at that time for passing troops, I will mention how the *Signoria* on the 29th June ordered a bailiff to go outside the *Porta a Faenza* with Bernardo Portinari, a commissary deputed to prepare the provisions for the French who were about to arrive. And on the 1st July they ordered many citizens, who had removed their household effects from their villas outside the *Porta a San Gallo* and the *Porta a Faenza*, for fear of looting, to replace these effects, so that the said French could sleep and eat there. On the 3rd, leave was given to the musicians to go and play in honour of the French captain, and the next day a bugler was ordered to go with them for the captain's use in the camp (*Deliberazioni, ad. an.*).

4th July. There was a muster of the soldiers that had been levied here during the last few days, 200 of them. And all this week processions and sermons were held every morning in each quarter of the city.

On this day, during the night (at 3 o'clock in the morning) the French soldiers went away towards Ancisa, there being 100 (mounted) men-at-arms and a number of foot-soldiers. This same night, there were painted on the houses of the *Gonfaloniere*, of Piero Soderini, and Madonna Strozzi, pictures of gallows, and other impertinent things, by men who do not fear God, and who do not know that they must uphold their reputation, or else they are lost. God preserve us from such wickedness![1]

5th July. We heard that the enemy was encamped at Poppi and Chiusi: it seemed as if we were to be preyed upon.

6th July. We heard that the King of France had sworn upon his crown to avenge all the insults to the Florentines and to do everything for our advantage; and also that he was coming into Italy, being already at the frontier.

7th July. We heard that the enemy's camp at Poppi was raised, and they had retired; and that our troops had come to Ponte a Sieve on their way to the Casentino, and the French were impatient to attack the enemy.

During these days the Pistolese were raiding all over these plains as far as Campi.

11th July. The Florentines who had been prisoners at Arezzo returned here, being exchanged for those of Arezzo that we had held, the bargain having taken place at Siena. Amongst those on our side were Guglielmo de' Pazzi and his son the bishop, whilst we sent back to Arezzo a son-in-law of Bernandino d'Arezzo.[2]

---

[1] *Parenti* puts the reason of these insults down to the distrust between the party which inclined to an agreement with Valentino, consisting of the majority of the chief citizens, and the popular party, which relied on being the most numerous, on trusting in God, and on being in the right. The latter, he writes, "threatened the former secretly, not being able to do so openly, and at night painted gallows and halters at the doors of Piero Soderini and de' Salviati, though the same was done at the house of Francesco d'Antonio di Taddeo, *Gonfaloniere* of justice, who supported the popular party admirably."

[2] The *Signoria* decided on the 4th to consign all the prisoners from Arezzo to the Bishop of Arezzo and Guglielmo de' Pazzi, to the end that they might exchange them for the Florentines who were at Arezzo (*Deliberazioni, ad. an.*).

14th July. We heard that the King of France had taken into his pay all the "Signori" (lords of towns) in Italy, the exiles of Romagna, and also the Marchese of Mantua and Messer Giovanni.¹ And it was said that Valentino had broken his hip, a horse having fallen upon him.

15th July. A *bargello* (police captain) was appointed here for Pistoia, and another for Valdinievole, with many mounted archers. And this night there was an earthquake in Florence, at 3 o'clock at night (11 p.m.), but it was not anything much.

16th July. The Captain of the French troops came to Florence with a few horsemen; and the men-at-arms, who were also with him, went to the Mugello and Dicomano. The Captain lodged in the house of the Pazzi, and went the same day, after having dined, to visit the *Signoria*.²

We heard that Vitellozzo had fled.

17th July. These French troops reached our other camp at Ponte a Sieve (where there were already many French).

18th July. The French captain left here, and we loaded the artillery and sent it up to the camp in Valdarno.

21st July. We heard that the captain had gone to Arezzo and had a parley with them (the rebels).

25th July. We heard that the French captain had arranged for us to have back all that belonged to us there except Arezzo itself. This did not seem very good news to the people, but on the contrary out of all reason.

28th July. We heard that the King of France had cited three men to appear: Vitellozzo, Valentino and Pandolfo Petrucci of Siena.

29th July. 150 Pistolese, men, women and children, were slain by each other. Nothing was ever of the least use with them.

30th July. We heard that Vitellozzo had sacked Arezzo.³

31st July. We heard that Valentino was against Vitellozzo.

7th August. A boy, one of the Vettori, hung himself in his father's house.

¹ Bentivogli.
² This same day, in order to do him honour, the *Signori* ordered their steward to lend the Pazzi whatever silver-plate they might wish for (*Deliberazioni*, cit.).
³ *Parenti*, on the contrary, states that Vitellozzo carried off with him the bells of the citadel and part of the property of the *Monte di Pietà*, to pay himself for what the citizens were owing him.

9th August. Commissaries were sent to Arezzo to fetch our property which had been scattered about.[1]

11th August. A proclamation was made that 50 Pistolese of each side must appear here within four days, on pain of being declared rebels and having their property confiscated.[2]

12th August. The French who were at Arezzo, and at the other cities round there, made great exactions. In Arezzo they took the arms away from the citizens and forbade them to leave the city without their permission, demanding 200 florins from anyone who left. There was a certain man who paid them this sum, and then having loaded nine beasts of burden, started off, but when he reached the gate they took eight loads for themselves, and sent him away with only one. Their tricks are a fine example to others!

15th August. 100 Pistolese appeared here, and we sent our soldiers there, these Pistolese not being allowed to leave Florence. The price of corn at this time was 40 *soldi*.

22nd August. A French envoy came from the King of France, to cause our property to be given back to us; and on the 24th went away together with our commissaries.[3]

26th August. We heard that they had retaken Arezzo, and that the chief citizens had gone away to Siena and elsewhere.

On the same day a vote was passed in the Great Council that a *Doge* should be elected in the Venetian manner.[4]

27th August. The Pistolese came to an agreement, and their excise-duties were taken off; they gained by their follies.

2nd September. An evergreen oak in my *villa* (country-place), only 50 paces from the house, was struck by lightning; and it was seared and dried up to the very roots, never recovering.

---

[1] Piero Soderini and Luca degli Albizzi.

[2] This proclamation, containing the names of those cited to appear, may be read in the usual book of the *Deliberazioni dei Signori e Collegi, ad an.*

[3] On the 23rd the *Signori* promised to pay a thousand francs to Monsignor di Melun, if he were able to recover for the Republic the artillery, munitions, bells, etc., which Vitelli, Baglioni, Orsini and Piero de' Medici had taken away from Arezzo, Cortona and Borgo San Sepolcro (*Deliberazioni*, quoted).

[4] That is, *Gonfaloniere* for life, in order to avoid the many inconveniences caused by the frequent change of magistrates.

8th September. The French left Arezzo and went along the Valdelsa, doing great damage.

20th September. In these days the French were still at San Miniato al Tedesco, and were destroying the country wherever they passed; it seemed as if they did not choose to leave our territory.[1]

21st September. The tabernacle of Our Lady of Santa Maria Impruneta was sent for to Florence, to the end that God should concede to us a good and wise *Doge*.

22nd September. The Council assembled, and elected a *Gonfaloniere* for life, who was Piero di Messer Tommaso Soderini; there were 150 candidates, but only three were voted for, namely, Messer Antonio Malegonnelle, Giovacchino Guasconi, and the said Piero; and in the final drawing Piero Soderini was the successful one, thank God; and they immediately sent for him from Arezzo, where he had been all through the war. It was he who had gone to Milan to fetch the French troops, and had brought them here like a good and valiant man. How well he discharged this dignity, and how well he presided over the Great Council! Truly it was a work of God.

7th October. Piero Soderini came back to Florence, having been at Arezzo, as was said above.

12th October. At this time we heard that at Rome the Pope was at variance with the Orsini [2] and those houses, so that he had taken refuge in Castel Sant' Agnolo; and at Bologna soldiers were levied for fear of the Pope, and the Venetians levied them also at Ravenna.

16th October. We heard that many castles of Romagna

---

[1] The *Dieci* (Ten) wrote on the 11th September to the Florentine commissaries in Arezzo: "His Majesty the King is pleased that Monsignore di Lancre with his company, together with those of Melun and Fois, should remain here at our service for 15 days or three weeks." This matter being kept strictly secret, it is natural that Landucci, not being aware of it, should have thought ill of the French for their delay. See *Scritti inediti di Niccolò Macchiavelli risguardanti la storia e la milizia, illustrati da G. Ganestrini*. Firenze, 1857.

[2] Historians speak of the alliance made between these and other lords, in the Diet held at the *Magione*, in the Perugian territory; but the Florentines abstained from taking part in it. The *Magione* was the *Badìa* or *Castello* of the Knights of Malta, a great quadrangular building still existing, with corner towers and a fine interior court. The dispossessed lords of Umbria and the *Marche* assembled there in 1502 to make this alliance against Valentino, who took a tremendous vengeance at Senegallia. [Trans.]

had rebelled against Valentino, namely, Camerino and others.

31st October. The Cardinal of San Severino entered Florence with many horsemen; he was met with great honour.

1st November (Tuesday). Piero Soderini, the *Gonfaloniere* for life, entered the *Palagio* with the new *Signoria*. All Florence was in the Piazza, as this was a new thing never done before in our city. Everyone seemed to have hopes of living in comfort.

13th December. In the night the roof and the stalls of the butchers in the *Mercato Vecchio* were burnt down, but no harm was done to the shops near.¹

29th December. Certain godly laws against the unmentionable vice and against swearing were reformed; and other good laws were made. Also it was decreed that when they (those accused) were not sentenced and punished by the "Eight" or *Conservatori*, they were in such case to go before the *Signori e Collegi* and the "Twelve." ²

3rd January. We heard that Vitellozzo had been murdered in Città di Castello, and that Valentino had taken Senegallia; and also that there had been warnings of certain plots here.

5th January. We heard that Valentino had taken Città di Castello, and had slain Vitellozzo and a brother of his who was a priest and notary, as well as others who were friends and relatives of Vitellozzo. Behold how divine justice sometimes brings about punishment! You now see the extermination of this house: Pagolo was beheaded here, and the death of the rest of the brothers follows. I am not surprised: I remember that when their father Niccolò was at the head of a city, and had conquered all his adversaries, there remained of the opposite party only an unfortunate mother and her boy, and she said to the boy: "I want you to go and throw yourself on your knees before Messer Niccolò and ask pardon and mercy," thinking that he would pity the child's innocence; but he was so cruel and villainous as to seize a knife from his side and slay

---

¹ The stalls were under an open roof, apart from the shops. [Trans.]
² A decree of this date fixed the mode of carefully judging those who should be impeached, accused, or examined by the magistracy of the "Eight" or the Conservators of the Laws; and established, amongst other things, that a third *Monte di Pietà* should be opened.

him with his own hand. It was said besides that his enemies having fled into certain fortresses, he burnt them down when they were full of women and children and many other people, not letting one escape.[1] Woe to him who is cruel and does not fear God!

We heard that a plot had been discovered at Siena, and that Pandolfo had had two citizens beheaded, one of them a de' Tagliacci, and had arrested one of the Scipioni. Such is the manner in which detestable parties cause men to act, without the fear of God, imagining that they are to live for ever, and that it is they who have to inherit the world: it shows the greatest ignorance possible, to think, in spite of experience, that there is no need of faith; but perhaps some men actually exist in Italy who are of this opinion!

We heard that the Pope had arrested Cardinal Orsini and the Bishop of Florence, who is also an Orsini.[2]

11th January. Ambassadors came from Siena to the *Signoria* asking for aid, as Valentino was threatening them; and they received the reply that we could not move against the King of France, and were in the same case as they were.

15th January. We heard that Pandolfo and his sons had left Siena.

22nd January. We heard that Valentino was in the Sienese territory, near Buonconvento.

30th January. There was the proclamation of a procession that was to be made out of veneration for the *cappa* (cloak) of San Francesco, which we had obtained from the castle of Monte Acuto when that fortress was taken and destroyed by the Florentines because it was against us in the struggle with Arezzo. Therefore, coming into the hands of the *Frati Osservanti* of San Miniato, a procession through Florence was ordered before the said *cappa*, which was very old and worn. It took place with great veneration, all Florence following, and then it was carried to the *Osservanza* di San Miniato, to remain there.[3]

---

[1] These are the same facts that we have already read on page 183.

[2] Rinaldo di Jacopo Orsini.

[3] Count Alberto, lord of the castle (a fortress near Florence), had received this garment from the saint's own hands in the thirteenth century; and his descendants had preserved it religiously till this year, when the Florentines destroyed Monte Acuto, because Count Francesco had helped the rebels of Arezzo. This relic is now preserved in the church of Ognissanti at Florence, where it was brought in 1571 (*Compendio delle divozioni e meraviglie del Sacro Monte della Verna.* Firenze, 1756).

We heard that Pandolfo Petrucci had gone to Lucca, and that Valentino was resolved upon the assault of Siena, although there were difficulties in provisioning his troops.

2nd February. 400 infantry who had formed part of Valentino's troops passed here; they were Germans, and had been paid off by him. We also heard that he had come to an agreement with the Sienese, by which their exiles were allowed to return; and he was now going in the direction of Rome.

3rd February. The *cappa* of San Francesco was taken in procession, and great veneration was paid to it. It was placed in the Piazza de' Mozzi, and a sort of stage was made for it, with tall pillars, like at San Felice when Our Lady of Santa Maria Impruneta comes there. And the procession went to meet it there, and accompanied it to the *Osservanza* where it will be kept.

8th February. The roofing over the butchers' stalls in the *Mercato Vecchio* was rebuilt, and the stalls made as before.

19th February. The *Gonfaloniere's* wife, Madonna Argentina,[1] went to the *Palagio de' Signori* to live, for the first time. It seemed a very new thing to see women inhabit the *Palagio*.

1st March. All the papers of the *Cinque del Contado*[2] were burnt, causing much injury and loss. The price of corn was 35 *soldi* a bushel. At this time there was heavy rain, lasting four months.

7th March. We heard that an alliance had been made between the King of France, the King of Spain, the Emperor, and the Pope; and there were rejoicings.[3]

11th March. We heard that Valentino had taken a small castle[4] belonging to the Orsini, and that some *Signori* had been slain by his artillery which destroyed a house and buried them beneath the ruins.

1503. 1st May. Soldiers were levied for Pisa.

7th May. We heard that the Spaniards had reconquered

---

[1] Argentina daughter of Gabbriello Malaspina.
[2] Officials for the *Contado* (district just outside the walls).
[3] It is certainly a mistake of the transcriber to have written the notice of the alliance under this date; which is probably that of 1501. See *Muratori, Annali, ad an.*
[4] In those times the name of *castello* was frequently given to a group of houses with fortifications round it. [Trans.]

the whole of the Kingdom of Naples, with the exception of Naples itself.

13th May. Many soldiers were levied for Pisa; and this morning Giampagolo Baglione had a muster in the Piazza of 40 mounted men-at-arms, and then went to Pisa. And all this time foot-soldiers were being sent, mustered by several constables, and many men were despatched besides to lay waste the enemy's land. The price of corn rose to 3 *lire*.

24th May. We heard that the *Badìa* at San Savino had fallen in on the top of about 60 spoilers, and it was said that the Pisans had propped it up with the express purpose of crushing these men.

29th May. The executioner was murdered by the people, being stoned to death on the place of justice. It had happened that a certain young ensign, who had slain another on account of some jealousy, was to be beheaded this morning, and the executioner did not succeed in cutting off his head either at the first, or the second, or even the third blow of the axe; the *Cavaliere*, who stood next to him, struck him twice with his stick; and because the condemned man was a youth of only twenty years of age, the people felt such compassion for him that there was a tumult, and they shouted: *a sassi, a sassi!* (stone him, stone him!), so that the *Battuti*[1] also received a good many blows. And the *Cavaliere* and the others present escaped with difficulty, throwing themselves down from the wall,[2] such was the rage of the people, who slew the executioner; and afterwards the boys dragged the body as far as Santa Croce. Some men believed that this had happened because of his having hung the three *Frati*.[3]

30th May. A vote was passed in the *Palagio* that salt should be sold at seven silver *quattrini* a pound, which was very hard upon the poor people: they are patient, however, because there are fewer taxes.

1st June. We heard that the Bishop de' Soderini[4] had been made a cardinal, and there was a great *festa* with bonfires and illuminations. The Pope appointed about nine cardinals.

[1] A band of penitents who went about dressed like monks, and beat themselves as a penance. [Trans.]
[2] The place of execution was close to the city wall. [Trans.]
[3] In the *Vita del Savonarola* written by *Burlamacchi* and published by Baluzio in vol. i. of his *Miscellanea*, p. 576, this fact is recorded.
[4] Francesco, Bishop of Volterra, the brother of the *Gonfaloniere*.

3rd June. There passed here from Campi 100 men-at-arms belonging to the Marchese di Mantua, led by us, to go to Pisa.

4th June. We heard that the French had arrived at Pisa to support us, so that matters looked bad for the Pisans. The price of corn was 15 *soldi* a bushel, and they (the Pisans) had not been able to harvest any, as their land was laid waste.

14th June. We heard that Vico had capitulated on certain conditions.

15th June. We heard that our troops had taken la Verrucola.

25th June. Whilst the *palio* of Santo Lò [1] was being run a storm of rain came on, and much hail in Florence, especially on the further side of the Arno; and it broke the ropes and tore down the awnings round San Giovanni: it did a great deal of damage.

1st July. We defeated the Pisans, who had made a raid, and we recovered all the booty. Matters looked ill for them, poor things!

15th July. The hat for the Cardinal de' Soderini was taken to the *Badìa* of Fiesole by a large troop of horsemen and young men; and on the 16th the cardinal entered Florence, and said mass in Santa Maria del Fiore, which was splendidly decorated and the service was very devout.[2]

19th July. Silver *quattrini* (a *quattrino* = $\frac{1}{60}$ of a *lira*) and *grossoni* of 20 *quattrini* were begun to be coined.[3]

---

[1] On the 26th June is celebrated the *festa* of Sant' Eligio, bishop, in Florence, commonly called San Lò, patron of the goldsmiths, the coppersmiths, and the blacksmiths, who placed his statue in a niche outside Or San Michele. On this day there was a horse-race, and the reward of the victor was the *palio* offered by the city of Arezzo on the day of San Giovanni Battista. A decree of the Republic ordered the Merchants' Guild to assign it to the *Camera del Comune* (Chamber of the Commune), "notwithstanding the protests made by the Guild on account of the loss incurred by the *Oratorio* (Chapel) of San Giovanni, of which they were the administrators, and to the profit of which went all the *palii* brought as offerings."

[2] He returned from France, where he had been ambassador, and repaired to the *Badìa*, in order to proceed thence with pomp towards the city and make a splendid entrance, which is minutely described by *Cambi*.

[3] For these new kinds of money see *Orsini, Storia delle monete della Repubblica fiorentina*, p. 279, where one reads the decree of the 22nd June, 1503, which orders that, in order to remedy the inconvenience that has arisen for some time from using "divers kinds of money of adulterated and clipped silver, and *quattrini* of such a bad quality that 12 *lire* or more of them were required to make a large gold florin, this new money should be coined."

28th July. We heard that at Rome the Cardinal of San Severino and the ambassador of the King of France had been assaulted by about 40 men disguised with masks, and that a squire of the cardinal had been killed and the cardinal's mule wounded.[1]

30th July. Our troops were taken away from the Pisan territory and sent into that of Arezzo, because it was said that Valentino was coming on that side. They were always too hasty in moving the camp.

4th August. The French arrived in the district of Pescia, and then here at San Donnino, the force being composed of Frenchmen, and men of Mantua and Ferrara, sent by the king in aid of the Kingdom of Naples.

13th August. There arrived at Dicomano 4 thousand French horse, on their way down to Naples: they were quartered at the country-houses, and I had some at my place; there and at the Moro together were 24 troopers, all at my cost. I sent Benedetto, and he did them honour as best he could, bearing with them at the peril of his life: they nearly slew him several times.[2]

14th August. They left, and were quartered at Ponte a Sieve. They hastened away, because they were needed in the south.

19th August. We heard that the Pope had died at 23 in the evening (7 p.m.); and on the 20th the bells were tolled for his death.

21st August. We heard that Valentino was dead, and also four cardinals. This was not true; only one cardinal was dead. It was said that Valentino had poisoned a flask of wine and that this cardinal died in consequence; and it was said besides that the Pope had also drunk of it by mistake. If so, for the sake of poisoning the cardinals, he had poisoned his father. God only knows if it were true or not; anyway, the Pope lay dying for a day or two. See what a situation Valentino is in now, with so many enemies besetting him!

26th August. Several cardinals passed here, who were

[1] Federigo Sanseverino, cardinal with the title of San Teodoro. According to *Nardi's* tale, some French gentlemen coming out of the cardinal's house were assaulted.

[2] Landucci had land in the manor of Dicomano, in the parish of San Martino a Poggio. Part of this property he had bought from a family of this place called *Dal Moro*. Benedetto was one of Landucci's own sons.

going down to Rome, riding in haste. One of them had his horse fall on the top of him and his leg broken at Montebuoni and remained here in Florence to have it set.

29th August. There arrived here 4 thousand Swiss soldiers, and they were quartered outside the gates; they were sent by the King of France in aid of Naples; and every day others passed on the same errand.

31st August. We heard that the *Signore* di Piombino[1] had recaptured Piombino.

1st September. The *Signore* di Mantua [2] came here, and lodged in the house of Tovaglia, being in the pay of the King of France. Two days later he left, and went towards Naples. The king was making great efforts, despatching troops every day.

4th September. The Cardinal di San Giorgio passed here, but did not stop in Florence, hastening on.[3]

5th September. Monsignore della Tramoia arrived here; lodging in the house of the Salviati. He also hastened on to Naples, being sent by the king.

7th September. There arrived here three cardinals: those of Ascanio, Roano and Aragona. They lodged in the house of Giovanni Tornabuoni, and having dined, rode away.[4]

12th September. In less than half an hour six or seven thunderbolts fell in Florence: amongst the rest, there was one which fell on the gate of San Piero Gattolino (Romana), and another on San Giovanni, which caused the cross to fall to the ground; and another in Via Gora, and others in several parts of the city. And outside there were yet more. At Peretola one Bartolomeo Nelli was riding along the road, when the lightning struck him, killing him and his

---

[1] Jacopo IV. Appiani; recalled by the people.
[2] Gianfrancesco Gonzaga.
[3] Giovanni Antonio Sangiorgio, a Milanese, Bishop of Alessandria, and a cardinal with the title of dei SS. Nereo ed Achilleo.
[4] These three cardinals were: the Sforza already mentioned, Georges d'Amboise, Archbishop of Rouen, Cardinal of San Sisto, papal legate in France, who came to Rome in great hopes of being chosen Pope; and the last, Luigi d'Aragona, of the royal house of Sicily, Cardinal-deacon of Santa Maria in Cosmedin. Francesco Pepi was first sent to meet them; and on the 6th the *Signoria* ordered several citizens to ride out the following morning "ad honorandum R^{mos} *Cardinales Florentiam proxime venturos*," on pain of anyone who should fail to do so being restricted within the city for a month; but no one did fail.

horse; and another horse which was a little way behind was terrified and went lame. Two other deaths were spoken of, one at Poggio a Caiano, and one at Calenzano; whilst in a house in the Mugello a man, woman and child were killed.

16th September. The cardinals entered into conclave; and first a mass of the Spirito Santo was said by a cardinal before the tomb of San Piero; and after a fine sermon had been preached, they shut themselves up. There were 38 of them.

23rd September. The Cardinal of Siena[1] was made Pope. He was elected on the 21st at 14 in the morning (10 a.m.), and called Pope Clemente; later he took the name of Pope Pius III.

1st October. We heard that the French had already passed Rome, and that Valentino had given them 200 men-at-arms, keeping the same number for himself. The Spanish set out to oppose them, and were approaching. We expected each day to hear of some great defeat.

6th October. Valentino came to Rome with the remainder of his troops, being ill and carried in a litter.[2]

At this time the price of corn was 36 *soldi* a bushel, and wine outside the city cost 15 *soldi* a barrel.

15th October. We heard that the Orsini had wanted to slay Valentino at Rome, and that they took one Raffaellino de' Pazzi, a Florentine, who was with him, armed and on horseback, and binding him on the horse, threw him into the Tiber. Valentino was warned, and put into Castello Sant' Agnolo.[3] It was said that all the Roman Orsini were for the Spaniards, and that the Marchese di Mantua had turned back to Rome from the south; it was also said that

---

[1] Francesco Todeschini Piccolomini, a Sienese.

[2] Valentino was anxious to withdraw to Rome, out of fear of Alviano, who was doing everything possible to get hold of him, and he reached the city on the evening of the 3rd October. The Pope consented to his return, perhaps out of pity (as Giustinian writes), but more in the hope that, being ill, he would die, and thus it might be possible "to lay hands on the money and property that he had carried away from Rome."

[3] The duke endeavouring to flee from the city, the Orsini prepared to follow him; but being abandoned by most of his party almost as soon as he had left his house, he was obliged to take refuge in the Vatican, from where he was taken to the Castel Sant' Angelo. The tale of Pazzi's death was not true: in June 1504 he was at Naples (*Giustinian*, tom. ii., p. 244, and tom. iii., p. 521).

the French were dying of hunger, some fleeing one way and some another, and their forces being weakened, the Spaniards took heart. What a position for the French to be in!

20th October. We heard that Pope Pio was dead, having died on the 19th, at 18 in the afternoon (2 p.m.); and the bells were tolled the same day. He had lived less than a month after being elected Pope.

24th October. My son Antonio went to the *Studio* (University) at Bologna to study for his degree of medical doctor.

30th October. The cardinals entered into conclave to choose a new Pope.

2nd November. We heard that the Pope was elected, and he was (Cardinal of) San Piero in Vincola, a Genoese.[1] The news reached here at 18 in the afternoon (2 p.m.), and the bells were rung at the *Ave Maria*; he was elected yesterday, at 3 in the morning (11 a.m.), and was called Pope Giulio II. There were great celebrations.

14th November. We heard that the Venetians had taken the whole of Val di Lamona, and were in possession of one of the forts of Faenza.

17th November. We heard that the French had had an encounter with the Spaniards, and that there had been great losses, mostly on the French side.

21st November. We heard that the Venetians had captured Faenza, and had made the following agreement: the city was to be exempt (from taxation) for 10 years, and the country for 20 years.

28th November. We heard that Valentino had been captured at Ostia, and had been beheaded. It was said that he had wanted to give Romagna to the Venetians, and to pass through here with his troops, realising that he was lost beyond help, having made everyone his enemy. It was not true, however, that he was dead.[2]

---

[1] Giuliano della Rovere, of Albizzola near Savona, Archbishop and Legate of Avignon, and Cardinal of San Pietro in Vincoli.

[2] The Borgia not choosing to consign the conveyance of the fortresses of Cesena and Forlì, as the Pope had requested, the latter gave orders to the commander of the vessels at Ostia to detain him as a prisoner. Other writers besides Landucci record this report of his death, which was current at the time (Villari, *N. Macchiavelli e i suoi tempi*, tom. i., p. 465.)

29th November. We heard that Don Michele, leader of Valentino's troops, had been captured here in the neighbourhood of Città di Castello and Borgo, and all his men-at-arms had been plundered.[1]

5th December. Don Michele was brought prisoner into Florence. See if Valentino is not completely ruined! and if he has not been paid in full for his cruelties!

We also heard that the Venetians had captured Imola, and thus taken from him all that he had in Romagna. He has enjoyed it a shorter time than Count Girolamo. Those unfortunate cities of the Church, in Romagna, have these sorts of revolutions every day, and cannot rest.

9th December. The Marchese di Mantua came to Florence from the Kingdom of Naples: he had left the French, because he foresaw great danger of famine and sharp warfare; and he went back to Mantua the next day. It was said that the King of France and the Spaniards had agreed to a truce.

18th December. The Cardinal di Roano [2] (Rouen) came to Florence, with a nephew of his lately made a knight: they lodged in the house of Giovanni Tornabuoni; and they were going on to France. And the Cardinal of Ferrara was returning to Ferrara.[3]

28th December. Our ambassadors left here who were going to Rome to the new Pope; they were: the Bishop de' Pazzi, the *Maggiore* of the Altopascio, Matteo Strozzi,

---

[1] Don Michele Corriglia, a Spanish infantry-leader in Valentino's service, and "a most trusty instrument in all his actions whatever they might be." Thus *Nardi* describes him. Macchiavelli, writing from Rome on the 18th November, warns (the Florentines) that the troops under Don Michele were about to pass through Tuscany, and advises that they should be plundered.

[2] In order to show their friendship for the King of France, and to invest this cardinal with the grade of papal legate, the Florentines did him special honour. First they sent Giovanni Tornabuoni to meet him at San Casciano with a steward of the *Signoria*; then the workmen of Santa Maria del Fiore were ordered to adorn this church with large banners and other things, as was the custom on the coming of papal legates, and there were successively elected, to pay him their respects on his way through the territory of the Republic, Francesco Manelli, Girolamo Bettini and Giovanni Gondi, all accompanied either by a steward or by a bailiff of the *Rotolino*. They did not fail to place the silver-plate of the *Signoria* at his disposition (*Deliberazioni dei Signori e Collegi, ad an*).

[3] Ippolito d'Este, of the family of the Dukes of Ferrara, cardinal with the title of San Lucia in Selci, called also Cardinal d'Este.

Tommaso Soderini, one de' Girolami, and Messer Antonio Malegonnelle.[1]

And the same day we heard from Rome that two men had been quartered for having poisoned that cardinal above-spoken of. Also two cardinals had fled, one of them being that legate who was sent here to superintend the death and burning of the three friars. Valentino had been tortured at Rome; and Don Michele was still detained here.[2]

5th January. We heard that the French had been defeated, with great numbers slain, and had lost Gaeta, which they had taken by storm.

The same day, Piero de' Medici was drowned,[3] together with many French barons, in fleeing from Gaeta, where he had been; and all the French fared ill.

7th January. There came to Florence 50 horsemen, sent by the Pope to fetch Don Michele: and on the 9th they took him away to Rome. It was said, besides, that the cardinal called Niccoletto (Romolino) was arrested; he it was who came here before he was made a cardinal, being sent by Pope Alessandro to try the three *Frati* of San Marco, of the Order of San Domenico (that is: Fra Girolamo of Ferrara, Fra Domenico of Pescia, and another called Fra Salvestro), and who caused them to be burnt. It was said

---

[1] These ambassadors were elected on the 4th or 6th November by the Council of the "Eighty," and on the 29th were given their instructions by the *Signoria*. The Maggiore dell' Altopascio was Guglielmo Capponi, and the one called de' Girolami was Francesco di Zanobi.

[2] The papers of the Venetian and Florentine ambassadors at Rome enlighten us on this point. From these we see that on the night between the 11th and 12th April, Giovanni Michiel, a Venetian cardinal with the title of Santa Maria in Septifolio, Bishop of the Port, commonly called Cardinal of Sant' Angelo, was poisoned. The Pope procured his death for the sake of becoming master of his riches. In December, the poisoner, Asquino da Colloredo in Friule, the cardinal's secretary, was imprisoned and tried: two of his companions, the cook and the chamberlain, saved themselves by flight. On the night of the 19th of the said month, Romolino, a Catalonian, and cardinal with the title of SS. Giovanni e Paolo, and Archbishop of Sorrento; and Ludovico, also called Pierluigi, Borgia, nephew of Pope Alessandro, *arripuerunt fugam*, as *Giustinian* writes, and it was believed that this was in consequence of the revelations of Asquino, who mentioned some cardinals as being cognisant of this crime.

[3] Piero de' Medici is known to have been drowned in the River Garigliano, after the famous battle fought on its banks; and the Florentines are known to have rejoiced at his death.

that the Pope had made him a cardinal in return for this beneficial action, but that may not be true.

10th January. We heard that the Pisans had captured a brigade of soldiers, some of those at Livorno; there being amongst them a Florentine called Borgo Rinaldi, he had incited them to make a sortie, and when they were retiring the Pisans cut them off and took them all prisoner.

During this cold weather, many French, where it was possible, had fled from the Kingdom of Naples, robbed and denuded; in the neighbourhood of Rome there were many thousands dying of hunger and cold in the ditches, finding no one to come to their aid, on account of the cruelty they had been guilty of, in putting cities to the sword and sacking everything. And now, by divine permission, they were dying round Rome on the dung-heaps—being almost naked they threw themselves on the dung-heaps for warmth —and if the Pope had not had three or four hundred jerkins made for them, and given them money, and put them on board galleys to cross over into France, they would all have died. As it was, we heard that more than 500 died of cold. They were found in the morning lying naked and dead on the dung-heaps. In Rome they entered the houses whenever they found a door open, and could not be driven out; men went at them with sticks, but yet they could not be driven out. "Slay us, if you wish!" they said. There never was such an extermination. Nevertheless, the King of France did not send them any succour, but seemed to have forgotten them, this being God's justice, because they had robbed and slain others, and they are all blasphemers, with every sort of vice, and without faith and the fear of God.[1]

4th February. The news that the Venetians had taken Forlì was confirmed beyond contradiction.

7th February. The Arno froze, the cold being very severe.

---

[1] The despatches of *Giustinian* for the 6th and 8th January confirm Landucci's narration both with regard to the charity of the Pope, who "in this defeat showed himself entirely on their side," and with regard to the molestation that they received from the population of the city and of the country round, who did not forget the damage caused by these soldiers when they entered the Kingdom of Naples; and he also mentions that they finally took refuge in the dung-heaps, on account of the great cold from which they suffered, reaching Rome robbed of everything and almost naked.

12th February. There came to Florence a cardinal, who was a nephew of the Pope, who had just received his hat; and he lodged in the house of Guglielmo de' Pazzi.[1]

1st March. We heard that the alliance between the King of France and the King of Naples was broken.

14th March. A girl was executed who was the serving-maid of a miniature-painter; she had borne an infant, and killed it, and thrown it into the cesspool. And a man called Bardoccio, when he came to empty the cesspool, found this female child, and took it to the "Eight," who immediately had the girl arrested; and the man who had seduced her fled. The girl was taken on the executioner's cart and beheaded.[2]

1504. 31st March. It was voted that the goods which came from the district of Lucca should pay 20 per cent.[3]

21st April. The church of San Francesco next to San Miniato was consecrated, being completely finished.[4]

28th April. Ambassadors from the King of England passed here, on their way to the Pope.

3rd May. There arrived here a large body of Roman horse whom we had hired; and numbers of soldiers were levied for Pisa.

11th May. Gianpagolo Baglione mustered 100 men-at-arms and many mounted archers (in the Piazza), with a great show of banners! It was a fine company; and it went away to Pisa.

14th May. The marble giant [5] was taken out of the

[1] Galeotto della Rovere, Cardinal of San Pietro in Vincoli, raised to this dignity by Julius II. on the 29th November, 1503.

[2] The sentence of the *Otto di Guardia e Balìa* of the 13th March gives us the names of this unfortunate girl and of her seducer. She was called Ginevra di Nardo di Piero del Prete of Piacentina, and he was Luigi di Mariotto Biffoli, a miniature-painter, as is shown by some documents seen by the Cavaliere Gaetano Milanesi.

[3] From the general increase of this excise-duty, which was to come into force two months later, only salt and iron goods were excepted.

[4] On the 27th leaf of the *Libro di Deliberazioni e Partiti* of the Merchants' Guild, which superintended the building of this church and convent we read: *Nota qualiter hac presenti suprascripta die ecclesia Sancti Salvatoris de Osservantia fratrum Minorum Sancti Francisci, sita prope januam sancti Miniatus ad Montem, cum massima solempnitate et devotione et per epischopum de Pagangnottis, fuit consecrata ; et similiter altare maius de novo hedificatum in dicta ecclesia fuit consecratum, et cappa seracifi Sancti Francisci fuit missa in dicto altari.*

[5] This means the "David" of Michelangelo, at which he worked in one of the rooms of the Opera di Santa Maria del Fiore.

Opera (Office of Works of the Duomo); it was brought out at 24 in the evening (8 p.m.), and they had to break down the wall above the door so that it could come through. During the night stones were thrown at the giant to injure it, therefore it was necessary to keep watch over it. It went very slowly, being bound in an erect position, and suspended so that it did not touch the ground with its feet. There were immensely strong beams, constructed with great skill; and it took four days to reach the Piazza, arriving there on the 18th at 12 in the morning (8 a.m.). It was moved along by more than 40 men. Beneath it there were 14 greased beams, which were changed from hand to hand; and they laboured till the 8th July, 1504, to place it on the *ringhiera*, where the "Judith" had been, which was now removed and placed inside the *Palagio* in the court. The said giant had been made by Michelangelo Buonarroti.

23rd May. There began in Florence an influenza with a cold and cough; about 90 per cent. within and without the city suffering from this cough and fever; few died of it, however. It lasted several months, and no cure could be found for it—nothing but time.[1]

30th May. We heard that Librafatta had capitulated on condition that their persons and property were to be spared, and the Pisans who were in it remained our prisoners, on the understanding that we were to exchange them for those of ours who were in Pisa.

1st June. An iron was placed on the column of the *Mercato Vecchio* to which the prisoners could be fastened when they were condemned to the *gogna*[2]; there had not been one there before.

16th June. The Palazzo degli Strozzi was finished, that is to say, this half of it; and Lorenzo son of Filippo Strozzi took his wife there, the marriage being celebrated with great pomp.[3]

[1] *Cambi* tells us that this influenza with a cough began in Rome, and spread all through Italy and beyond it.
[2] See note to 22nd December, 1494.
[3] That is, the part on the Piazza degli Strozzi, the only part finished, the great top cornice being wanting on the other side. That the marriage of Lorenzo with Lucrezia daughter of Bernardo Rucellai was most magnificent is shown by the fact that on this occasion the musicians and the silver-plate of the *Signoria* were placed by the *Priori* at his disposition. *Luigi Passerini*, frequently inexact, in his *Genealogia e storia della famiglia Rucellai* erroneously places this marriage in the year 1508.

29th June. We heard that our troops before Pisa had attacked 35 horsemen who had come out from Pisa, and captured them, one of their leaders being Berzighella; and Rinieri della Sassetta and others were wounded.[1]

1st July. Our troops before Pisa made a great raid into the district of Lucca and slew many Lucchesi; and they took from them the provisions which they were carrying to the Pisans. They also raided the stores of the Lucchesi at Viareggio, and pillaged and burnt them all, taking booty to the worth of 25 thousand florins.[2]

3rd July. There came to Florence five Pisan prisoners; and one of them called Berzighella gave us information as to how things stood in Pisa.

On the same day three galleys reached Livorno, which came from France for our benefit.[3]

7th July. The Duke of Ferrara came to Florence, and lodged in his own house.[4] He came to the Nunziata, and did not wish for any presents; and on the 8th he left.

19th July. We heard that our galleys at Livorno had fought with the Genoese ships which were carrying corn to Pisa, and defeated them in such a manner that none reached there except a brigantine which carried rotten biscuit. The poor things were badly off, for here the price of corn was 48 *soldi* a bushel, and with them it was 4 *lire*.

28th July. We heard that the Pisans had sent their cattle to graze a little way outside the city, and that our troops had seized them. The citizens were reduced to hard straits, and being unable to go outside the city for any purpose, they could not harvest their corn, but nevertheless they were more obstinate than ever.

29th July. A thing happened hardly worth writing about, yet as it was much spoken of by many people and one kept hearing details for a long time, I will mention it, namely: Various persons are supposed to have seen a

[1] Rinieri della Sassetta was a captain in the service of the Pisans.
[2] The Lucchesi at that time gave great help to the Pisans, and the Florentine commissary, Antonio Giacomini, made various raids into their territory to punish them.
[3] We know from *Nardi* that these were "three slender galleys, which had been in Provence, belonging to Federigo, former King of Naples, their captain being a most trustworthy man and excellent seaman called Don Dimas Richasene, who brought them to Livorno on the 2nd July, 1504."
[4] This house was in the Borgo degli Albizzi, at the beginning, and next to the Palazzo Pazzi. See note to 14th December, 1501.

number of men-at-arms appear in a meadow near Bologna; and Messer Giovanni sending to know what they wanted, one man went to speak to them, whilst the others watched. He was seen to be slain as soon as he reached them; but a short time afterwards he came back, saying he had seen nothing. And someone saw a bugler come out of a wood, followed by soldiers on foot, and then by mounted men-at-arms; and when they reached the meadows they came to blows and many were killed; and then many carts came out of the wood and picked up the dead and carried them away. This was seen by many people from a little distance, but when they went near they saw nothing: and this happened several times. It was said to signify a great slaughter by the sword.

22nd August. The work of turning the Arno to Livorno was set in hand, but it was not continued.[1]

8th September. The giant in the Piazza was finished, and completely uncovered.

28th September. The price of corn was 3 *lire* a bushel.

19th October. There was a good sowing; the price of corn went down again to 50 *soldi*.

21st October. We heard that our troops were being taken away from Pisa, and the Pisans were attending to their defences.

1st November. There was such a big earthquake at Bibbiena that several houses were ruined, and two men were killed and many injured; and it was said, by some who were there, that eggs and pots and pans in the market-place were broken.

1505. 12th October. We heard that our men at Barga had defeated the Pisans, and taken many horses from them and made many prisoners.

20th November. A saint with a wheel on her head was placed above the gate which is half-way up the staircase in the *Palagio del Podestà*, leading up into the *Palagio* from the court, to signify the order to be held in judging the cases in this *Palagio* by the four doctors, who are called the *Ruota* (Roll); and this order began to-day.

---

[1] The *Gonfaloniere* and Macchiavelli took into their heads to turn aside the Arno near Pisa, throwing it into a marsh near Livorno, so as to leave Pisa dry, and to deprive it of all communication with the sea. This undertaking, which had been opposed by competent persons, did not succeed.

20th December. I gave a memorandum and a drawing to Simone del Pollaiuolo, as he was an architect, and it seemed to me that he was fit to carry out my idea; which was, that in that place where now stands San Giovanni Evangelista [1] in Florence, a fine temple with a fine cupola ought to be built, in honour of San Giovanni Vangiolista, and to the glory of God and of our city; giving him this design, according to which all the houses and shops in the Piazza di San Lorenzo, a square of about 100 *braccia* each way, should be taken down to make room for this temple, which would be opposite San Lorenzo and facing the street; and we should have as an advocate in heaven with San Giovanni Battista, one who was the beloved of Christ and his brother, according to the flesh, and not less so in eternal life. I made him understand all my ideas about it, which pleased him very much, and he told me several times that he had never seen a finer invention, and explained how he thought he could lay it before those in authority; he was most impatient.

9th January. A column fell from the *Campanile* of Santa Maria del Fiore, from one of the lowest windows towards the cupola, and almost struck a citizen; it was said to have touched his clothes.

14th January. The Arno froze so hard that the young men played *palla* [2] upon it.

24th January. A young man was hung; and the doctors and scholars of the *Studio* (University), where there were a great number of doctors and worthy men, requested the "Eight" to allow them to have the body to dissect, and it was granted them. And they did this work in some of their rooms at Santa Croce, and it lasted till the first of February, 1505, their meetings taking place twice a day. The physicians were there, and my son Messer Antonio also, every day, to look on.[3]

This same 24th January, the *gravezza* (tax) was published.

[1] Now called San Giovannino degli Scolopi (in the Via dei Martelli); and the convent is now used for a large day-school. [Trans.]
[2] See note to 3rd July, 1501.
[3] By the decree of this day the *Otto di guardia e balia consesserunt Medicis et Artium et Medicine doctoribus corpus et seu cadaver Bernardonis Belledonne, qui pro fure fuit laqueo suspensus, quod de eo possint facere notomiam, cum hoc quod dici faceant et celebrari, pro ipsius Bernardonis anima, missam et alia divina officia et consueta in predictis, eorum sumptibus.*

15th February. There was a muster in the Piazza of 400 recruits whom the *Gonfaloniere* had assembled, Florentine peasants, and he gave them each a white waistcoat, a pair of stockings half red and half white, a white cap, shoes, and an iron breastplate, and lances, and to some of them muskets. These were called battalions; and they were given a constable who would lead them, and teach them how to use their arms. They were soldiers, but stopped at their own houses, being obliged to appear when needed; and it was ordered that many thousand should be made in this way all through the country, so that we should not need to have any foreigners. This was thought the finest thing that had ever been arranged for Florence.[1]

At this time stone seats were made all round the *Mercato Vecchio*; although many people did not like them. The price of corn went down to 28 *soldi* a bushel.

17th March. The "Eight" published a proclamation to the effect that anyone who had been guilty of a certain villainy, and there were several, should lose their heads, if they did not appear; they had dared to threaten a father if he did not give them his son. The young men of Sodom were no worse than this when they asked Lot for the angels. And these deserve the same punishment that befell those. It is unwillingly that I have recorded this, because it is the unspeakable sin. May God forgive me.[2]

18th March. A "Pardon" was proclaimed in Santa Maria del Fiore, confirmed by Pope Giulio II.; it was like the first, in 1481, *Perdone di colpa e pena* (a pardon of sins and remission of punishment.)[3]

1506. 1st April. We took into our pay Don Michele, who

[1] This was the militia arranged by Macchiavelli. Each company was to consist of at least 300 men, under one captain and flag, all living in the same *Vicariato*; they were armed with pikes or other sharp weapons and a few muskets. They were exercised on feast days; and a constable, who was over several companies, held a review twice a year. [Trans.]

[2] In the *Libro di Partiti* of this magistracy, under this date, we find that there was a public proclamation of the decree passed on the day preceding, by which were condemned to death Piero di Felice, a second-hand dealer, Andrea di Ludovico Martini, Girolamo di Lorenzo d'Angelo Biliotti, and Giovanni di Guglielmo di Paolo, *alias* the dwarf Altoviti, whom historians describe as a wicked, terrible, and most crafty man. The first three, having appeared, were absolved from the condemnation, and perhaps the last may have also been absolved later.

[3] See note to 18th April, 1481.

had been one of Valentino's leaders, and had been imprisoned here.

10th April. The Jubilee of the *Servi* at the Nunziata: it began this day, Holy Friday (Good Friday), and lasts till vespers on Holy Saturday (Easter Eve).

11th April. The Jubilee began at Santa Croce also, on Holy Saturday, and lasts three days, till Monday at sunset; this was given likewise by Pope Giulio.[1]

19th April. Don Michele made a muster of 100 foot-soldiers and 50 horsemen, archers and *stradiotti*.

1st May. He was sent into the Casentino where he burnt down houses; and then he was sent to Dicomano, on account of certain disorders, and burnt down more houses, and ruined all belonging to the Dalla Nave.[2]

2nd May. The price of corn was 20 *soldi*.

18th May. Luzio Savelli made a muster here of 50 men-at-arms and some light horse, to go to Pisa and lay waste.

4th June. A muster was made of the men of Dicomano

[1] On the 26th March the *Signoria* ordered that one of their criers should proclaim in the public places of the city this Jubilee conceded by the Pope to the church of Santa Maria de' Servi. By other decrees of the 8th and 10th April they gave leave that two of their mace-bearers and two of their stewards should go to the aforesaid church and to that of Santa Croce, *ad standum et indulgentiis*, on the 10th, 11th, and 12th of this month.

[2] On the 15th April the Republic gave to Don Michele the commission in writing to ride as soon as possible with his company through all the provinces to correct those subjects who failed in obedience to the governors and to force them to obey; and also to purge them of thieves and of those who were condemned to the gallows, to the block, or as rebels. He was informed that the places which were most in need of this work of his were *part of the Mugello, that is, mountain places, and chiefly the manor of Dicomano and the mountain of San Godenzo, where every day armed disputes and homicides occurred;* he was also to visit the *mostre delle bandiere*, that is, the companies of the *Milizie*. Don Michele, who had had practice with Cesare Borgia, was not slow in carrying out their commands, and his hand was heavy; so that on the 5th May the *Signori* wrote to him: " We understand that you have detained one Nofri di Domenico dalla Nave, of Dicomano, who has let us know, through his friends, that he is innocent ; if he really is so, you must not do him any harm. In the case of his being guilty, which you must inquire into carefully, you will punish him according to his crime and as justice requires." And on the 7th, with another letter, he was commanded to send the said Nofri to the "Eight," with a suitable escort and with the papers appertaining to the trial; they expressed their surprise at the same time that he should have condemned as rebels five more of the Dalla Nave, when he only had authority "*to punish those who had already been declared rebels*," etc.

and of Ponte a Sieve, which were 800 in number; and those of Dicomano went to Pisa.

On this day, at my place at Vegna,[1] the lightning struck quite near the house, touching a very large oak, which no one remarked, there not being a scratch upon it; nothing whatever to be seen. But in a few days the top branches, which were full of acorns, began to wither, and every day it went on withering lower down, till in less than a month it was dried up to the very roots, and has never shot up again.

10th May. They finished setting up the "Judith" in the *Loggia de' Signori*, under the first arch towards the Vacchereccia.[2]

22nd June. The awnings of San Giovanni were torn by a gale of wind, and broke a roof at the corner of the Cialdoni.

24th June (San Giovanni). One of the wheels of the *carro del palio* (car of San Giovanni) broke when it was on its way to the starting-point; and in the morning, whilst the *palio* was taken to be offered in the Piazza, the little cross fell from the hand of the figure of San Giovanni which stands above the cross-bar of the banner. Many thought these bad omens.[3]

At this time we heard from Genoa that the people had slain many of the chief citizens, and many had fled.

1st August. The price of corn was 17 *soldi* a bushel.

5th August. We heard that the Pisans were defeated and many of them taken prisoner, and also 40 horses; and many of these Pisans were brought as prisoners to Florence.

4th September. We heard that the Pope had reached Perugia, with many cardinals and men-at-arms; and he sent a legate of his here to request assistance.[4]

---

[1] *Vegna* is the name of one of Landucci's farms, as is shown by the books of the *Decime*.

[2] Taken off the *ringhiera* in 1504 in order for the "David" to be placed there in its stead, and put up inside the court, it was now placed here; and later again moved to make way for Gianbologna's "Rape of the Sabines," and put under the arch of the Loggia which faces the Via della Ninna. (Now, in 1927, after many vicissitudes, it stands on the steps of the Palazzo Vecchio, between the Marzocco and the copy of the "David.")

[3] This year the *palio* was run by horses ridden by *fantini* (boys), as is mentioned in a decree of the *Priori* of the 10th of this same month.

[4] Pope Julius, desirous of revindicating his right to the towns belonging to the Holy See, and now in the possession of small lords or of the Venetians, began with Perugia, and on the 13th September

6th September. The Cardinal of Roana (Archbishop of Rouen) left here, who came from France to go to the Pope; he lodged in the house of Giovanni Tornabuoni.

8th September. A man killed himself by cutting his throat, on account of having lost 18 ducats.

11th September. Our ambassadors left here, and went to Piombino to visit the King of Naples, who was going to take possession of his kingdom.[1]

On the same day they finished repaving[2] the church of the Nunziata de' Servi, and putting the tombs on each side in order, and in the middle they had raised it a little with certain triangular supports placed along the centre.

At this time the large cornice round the roof of the church of Santa Maria del Fiore was made, on the side towards the *Campanile*, high up by the eaves of the roof.

20th September. We heard that the Pope had reached entered there, accompanied by twenty-four cardinals and 400 men-at-arms, after an agreement made with the Baglioni, who had gone to meet him, recognising the impossibility of resisting him. The Florentines, who were requested to lend their aid, took their time, and on the 25th gave the commission to Macchiavelli to go to the pontifical court; and later they elected four representatives to go to the Pope in Perugia, these being: Francesco Pepi, Antonio Strozzi, Guglielmo de' Pazzi, and Alessandro Acciaioli; but as the Pope was on the point of leaving the district of Perugia, this embassy was revoked on the 28th of the same month.

[1] The ambassadors sent to visit and pay honour to King Ferdinando of Aragona on this occasion of his passing through Tuscany were Giovanvettorio Soderini, Giovanbattista Ridolfi, Niccolò del Nero, and Alamanno Salviati. The Florentines had founded great hopes upon this king, especially for the matter of Pisa, and on this account flattered him much and sent him, "besides confections of all sorts and various delicacies, a large provision of calves and sheep and game, and many casks of both white and red wine of different kinds, many *moggia* (a *moggio* = about 8 bushels) of white bread, 120 pounds of white wax, and many *cantari* (a measure of many pounds) of biscuit for the crews, and other things according to occasion" (*Nardi*, before quoted). The commissary for the above provisions was Bartolomeo Bartolini.

[2] As far back as 2nd November, 1501, the *Frati* made an agreement with Tommaso and Valente del Chiaro, who undertook, on certain conditions, to furnish 700 or 800 *sesangoli d'alberese* (a whitish kind of stone) for this pavement (*Ricordanze del Convento*, p. 98); and when this work was finished, a certain Frate Angelo of Florence wrote in 1506 a most careful *Ricordo di tutte le sepolture che sono nella Chiesa*, making notes of the inscriptions, the coats of arms, and the figures, when the tombs were adorned with these latter (*Ricordanze*, already mentioned).

Urbino, and that the King of Naples had reached Naples.¹

24th September. A vote was passed in the *Palagio* that the tax of the *Dogana* (the excise-duty) and that for Contracts should be increased.²

1st October. We heard that the Pope had reached Cesena, and that he had declared war against the Venetians.³

29th October. We heard that Messer Giovanni Bentivogli had been driven away from Bologna, and had gone to Mantua, and was taken prisoner by the French under a promise of safe-conduct; at least so it was said.

3rd November. We heard that the Pope had entered Bologna by agreement. It was not true, however.

4th November. The monastery of Santa Caterina ⁴ was struck by lightning, and one nun killed and two others seriously injured; also a citizen who was at the door, that is to say, at the grating, was frightened out of his wits; and later one of the injured nuns, who was a daughter of Niccolò Michellozzi died; and the other (who died) was a daughter of Bartolomeo Ricciardi; it was whilst they were at prayers in the chapel.

11th November. There was an earthquake in Florence at 9 in the morning (5 a.m.). It was not much.

On the same day, the day of San Martino, the Pope entered Bologna by agreement.

12th November. There were two more earthquakes at 9 and 10 in the morning (5 and 6 a.m.).

13th November. In the evening, at about 24 in the evening (8 p.m.), at San Michele Berteldi, it began to be said that an image of Our Lady, which is over a door, had

---

¹ With the letters that Machiavelli wrote to the *Dieci di Libertà* we can establish the Pope's itinerary, which was as follows: On the 21st September he reached Fratta; the 22nd, Gubbio; 2nd October, Cesena; 9th, Forlì; 19th, Palazzolo, and 20th, Imola.

² These increases of the taxes were imposed by the decree of the 18th of this month, in order to ensure being able to pay the soldiers and the creditors of the commune.

³ See above, note 1.

⁴ Convent of *Santa Caterina di Siena* (*Via Larga*, now Via Cavour). Founded in 1500, at the expense of Santa Lucia (*beata*), the former wife of Ridolfo Rucellai, who had become a monk through Savonarola's preaching. It was suppressed in 1808, and was associated with the Accademia di Belle Arti. At present it is occupied by schools and laboratories. [Trans.]

miraculously closed its eyes; the one opposite the door of the *Stufa* (Baths).[1] It seemed as if she did not wish to see the sins that are committed there. Before a day had passed, numbers of candles were lighted, and great veneration was paid to it, so that a wall was built in front of it like a church, and if it had not been unfitting for women to go to this place near the *Stufa*, many women would have gone there; and, in spite of this, many waxen images were brought to it and many votive-offerings.

27th November. Two Pisans were hung here at the windows of the *Bargello*, one of them being a certain leader, degli Orlandi, who had been a prisoner here for many months; and because the Pisans had taken one of our leaders from Volterra, and had slain him and dragged him through the streets, these two were hung.

31st December. We heard that the *fuorusciti* (exiles) of Genoa had entered the city and slain many men of the people; so goes the world.

1st January. The newly-coined copper coins were issued, and it was decreed that no foreign money could be used except silver coins of a (just) weight.[2]

15th February (the day of the Carnival). In the Piazza Madonna, whilst erecting the pole for one of the Carnival huts, two lads fell and were killed on the spot.

17th February. Five Pisans who had been captured at sea in a brig off Livorno were brought to Florence; they belonged to the families of the chief citizens.

22nd February. The Cardinal de' Soderini came to Florence from the Pope's court at Bologna. And at this time the Pope left Bologna and went through Romagna to visit the other towns of the Church.

25th February. The Cardinal of San Giorgio came to Florence from Bologna; he lodged in the convent of the

[1] This *stufa* was called the *Stufa di Piazza Padella*, or also the *Stufa degli Obizzi*, from the family to whom it belonged, and it was incorporated in the year 1592 in the convent of the *Teatini* which was then built. Some of the unseemly things committed in the *stufe*, or baths, are gaily represented in *Cecchi's* comedy called *Lo Stufauolo*.

[2] *Orsini's* book already quoted does not give us any information about this newly coined money; but it is to the matters here recorded that the decree of the *Priori* on the 30th of this same month probably refers, when it places a bailiff of the *rotellino* at the disposition of the *Signori della Zecca* (Mint) for the month of February, *solum pro inveniendis pecuniis prohibitis*.

Cestello. And the next day two more cardinals came from Bologna, that is, Santa Pressedia and Sanmalò.¹

1st March. The picture of the Nunziata de' Servi was uncovered and shown to these four cardinals, at 24 in the evening (8 p.m.), with great reverence and cries of *misericordia* (mercy), for the church was full of people, although great secrecy had been observed, because if it had been known throughout the city, there would have been immense crowds.

22nd March. Two Pisan prisoners were brought to Florence; and many other prisoners had been taken, and a number of cattle. More were taken every day.

1507. 29th April. We heard that the King of France had taken Genoa by assault, with the help of the *fuorusciti* (exiles).

The Pope now left Viterbo and went back to Rome.

We also heard that our troops had made a raid on the Pisans, and taken a number of cattle, so that the poor creatures were faring badly.

And the news reached us that the King of France had left Genoa and gone to Milan, and that he had demanded from the Genoese a payment of 300 thousand florins, stipulating that they must make a wall from the *Castelletto* to the *marina* (harbour), and that he would send a governor whom they must pay, and that they must pay 200 hired soldiers regularly; however, he let them off 100 thousand ducats and only demanded 200 thousand.

18th May. A cardinal passed here who was carrying three hats to the King of France, for him to give to his friends.²

23rd May. The King of France entered Milan, and there were jousts and feasts; and a thousand young men completely armed, except for helmets on their heads, went to meet him mounted on fine horses.

¹ Antonio Pallavicini, a Genoese, cardinal with the title of San Prassede, and Guillaume Briçonnet, Lord of Touraine and Bishop of San Malò.
² On the 4th January, in Bologna, to please the Cardinal Georges d'Amboise, the Pope promoted three of his nephews to the dignity of cardinal, namely: Jean, Viscount de Thourat de la Trémouille, Archbishop of Auch, son of that Louis de la Trémouille who had commanded the French army in Italy, and of Marguerite d'Amboise; René or Réginald de Prie, Bishop of Bayeux, son of Antoine Baron de Busançais and of Madeleine d'Amboise; and Louis son of Charles d'Amboise, Bishop of Albi, Governor of Bordeaux and of Guienne. The promulgation, however, took place in Rome on the 17th May.

INTERIOR OF THE CHURCH OF SANTA CROCE

They now began to pave the *Piazza de' Signori*, or rather, to repave it.¹

We also received the articles of the agreement with the Pisans, if anything will really come of it.

15th July. The King of France went to Savona, and there met the King of Naples, and they came to an understanding; and it was said that the emperor was about to come here, and that the Venetians were levying men and felt great distrust.

We also heard that the emperor had held a Diet and Council of many lords, and that it was decided that he would not fail to come and assume the crown, and that these lords were levying 160 thousand combatants, and 22 thousand horse, and that the Venetians and the Pope had an understanding with him, and the Venetians were continuing to levy many men.

25th July. The *palio delle navi* (boat-race) could not be held, because there was hardly any water in the Arno. There had not been any rain for several months, and no mills could work; the corn harvest was scanty, and many springs in the district had run dry.²

2nd August. As it pleased God, the house in which I lived, next to the shop (the shop being in the middle of a house), was burnt down, and I lost my rooms, in which were all my things, worth more than 250 gold ducats. I had to buy all my household goods, clothes and furniture afresh, three rooms completely stocked; my son Maestro Antonio alone losing more than 50 or 60 ducats' worth: a red-cloth³ cloak, a purple tunic, both new, and all his other clothes and silk waistcoats, with all his books which

¹ We find in the *Storie* of *Cambi* the following record of this work: "In the year 1507 the workmen of Santa Maria del Fiore, at the instance of our *magnifici* (gracious) *Signori*, began to repave the piazza of the *Palazzo* of the gracious *Signori*, and began at the door of the *Palazzo* towards the *Loggia* of the gracious *Signori*, and made each year two *quadri*,* because the Office of Works of Santa Maria del Fiore, which was legally obliged to keep it in order, found the means with difficulty."

² Till the end of the eighteenth century the custom of having a boat-race on the Arno on the day of San Jacopo was continued, and other spectacles sometimes took place besides.

³ *Panno rosato* is a cloth of a special red dye, still made in Florence. [Trans.]

* This appears to mean that they did half one year, and half the next.

were worth more than 25 ducats. I and my three other sons had nothing left but our shirts; and what was worse, Battista's bed had caught fire whilst he was asleep, and he escaped perfectly naked, and went to borrow a shirt in the neighbourhood. Nothing was saved except what the women had with them in the country, and Messer Antonio who was with them; so that they were not here to see the grief we suffered. But I accept adversity like prosperity, and thus give thanks to the Lord for the one as for the other; and I pray Him to pardon my sins and to send me all which tends to His glory. May God always be praised by all His creatures; every infirmity and pain can be comforted by such a thought, and we may learn from the saintly Job, who said: "The same Lord who gave them me has taken them away, praise be to God!"

18th August. The Cardinal of Santa Croce came to Florence [1]; he was a legate, and was now going to the emperor. We received him with great honour.

24th August. 20 Pisan prisoners were brought to Florence, and were put into the *Stinche*, and some were sent to work at the Poggio Imperiale.[2]

28th August. 40 more Pisan prisoners were brought to Florence, and were sent bound as far as the Poggio, to work there.

13th October. The Porta al Prato was struck by lightning, and a stone on which the Cross was carved was detached from the arch of the gate, and the gate caught fire, but it was put out.

14th October. A small house near Santa Trinità fell in

[1] This was Bernardino Carvajal, a Spaniard, Cardinal of Santa Croce at Jerusalem. Hardly had the news reached Florence of this ambassador's journey than Niccolò Macchiavelli was sent to Siena, where he was passing, to find out with what sort of train and following he was travelling, and perhaps also to endeavour to discover something of the gist of his embassy.

[2] These and many other Pisan prisoners came to Florence from Cascina, on this day and on those preceding and following; and by a decree of the "Ten" they were first imprisoned in the *Stinche*, and afterwards sent to the Poggio Imperiale, that is to say, to Poggibonsi and elsewhere, to work at the fortifications. Some of these were persuaded (to escape) by their relatives and friends, and others ran away of their own accord. Out of a score sent to Arezzo on the 25th August, "to work at that wall," at the foot of the order of the "Ten" relating to it we read: "All fled the ... day of December, 1508." See in the *Archivio di Stato di Firenze* the book of *Deliberazioni dei Dieci di Balìa*, from 1506 to 1511, c. 32, *et seq*.

and crushed three persons, one of them being a carpenter, son of Cortopasso, who had his shop there.

1st November. The marble cornice on the roof of Santa Maria del Fiore towards the *Campanile* was finished.

20th February. We heard that the emperor had taken a town belonging to the Venetians, and sacked it and put the inhabitants to the sword, with every sort of cruelty.

1508. 31st March. The *Signoria* had letters saying that in the mountains of Lucca and Pistoia fires had been seen in the evening, and it appeared as if horses and men-at-arms came out of these fires. I give no credence to these things.[1]

1st April. A great Jubilee was proclaimed here, which was to begin on the 9th.[2]

2nd April. There were many preachers, who for the most part announced great tribulations, and the renovation of the Church, and much was spoken about the emperor.

7th April. We heard that the Venetians had been defeated by the emperor, and 50 (mounted) men-at-arms and 300 foot-soldiers were slain.

9th April. The Pope sent us a Jubilee or Plenary Indulgence, and it began this day. An altar was made in the Piazza de' Signori at the foot of the steps of the Loggia, and another in Santa Maria del Fiore, offerings being presented at both of them; and there was a great procession to visit the said altars. And this indulgence had such authority that it covered everything, including matters of restitution and to do with churches, applying to those who had them by simony, etc.; also if anyone made an offering for the dead, it counted as a votive-offering.

22nd April. A leader, one of the Colonna,[3] passed here with men-at-arms on his way to Pisa.

5th May. We began to send men of the battalion (i.e. the militia) over there to lay waste.

[1] We have sought in vain for these letters, but that does not prove that this notice is false, seeing that the papers remaining to us of the *Signoria* just at this time are very few in number.

[2] On the 9th, this *festa* with which the Jubilee began in Florence is again spoken of. It is true that by order of the *Signoria* there was a proclamation of this Jubilee or Plenary Indulgence, conceded by the Pope *confessis et contritis visitantibus ecclesiam Sanctae Mariae Floris et Sancti Salvatoris extra portam Sancti Miniatus, et eis ecclesiis offerentibus pro constructione Sancti Petri de Rona*, from the 8th to the 26th of the month. See *Deliberazioni dei Signori e Collegi, ad an.*

[3] Marcantonio.

4th June. A cardinal legate came here on his way to Bologna.¹

At this time the *Podestà* of Florence was divested of power and his office taken from him, on acount of certain faults that he had committed.²

5th June. This cardinal legate had the Nunziata of the Servi uncovered, and there was such a concourse of people that many swooned, and one woman, who was carried out of the crowd with great difficulty, bore her child in San Bastiano.

11th June. The *Palagio de' Signori* caught fire on the night of the *Spirito Santo*. Some damage was done, and a fireman was killed.

12th June. We heard that the battalions which had been laying waste had returned.

1st July. We heard that there had been a tumult at Bologna, because the cardinal legate had had several men put to death.

6th July. We heard that our archbishop, was who in Rome, had renounced the bishopric and given it to the Bishop de' Pazzi, who for his part renounced the Bishopric of Arezzo and gave it . . .³; and there were great rejoicings.

13th July. We heard that there had been great earthquakes in Candia, destroying many houses; and that in

¹ Francesco Alidosi, Cardinal and Bishop of Pavia. He came for the matter of Pisa, and to obtain aid in men-at-arms for the Pope. The Florentines tried to put him off with words, as appears from the papers of the "Ten" in their letters to Roberto Acciaioli, their representative in Rome; paying him at the same time extraordinary honour. The cash-book of the *Massaio della Camera dell' Armi, ad an.*, in the archives already quoted, has many pages full of the expenses incurred for him in the two days (4th and 5th) that he stopped in Florence, and also afterwards in accompanying him through the territory of the Republic.

² He was a Messer Piero Lodovico Saraceno of Fano, one of the five judges of the Council of Justice, and at this time, in his turn, *Podestà*, and was deprived of his dignity by a decree of the *Signori e Collegi* on the 30th May, after they had first taken the opinion of many learned doctors and worthy citizens, among whom was Francesco Guicciardini. The accusations were as to evil and dishonest practices and bad administration of justice (*Deliberazioni*, quoted, *ad an.*).

³ At this point there is a blank in the MS. From Rinaldo Orsini, a Roman, the Archbishopric of Florence passed to Cosimo de' Pazzi, who was succeeded in the Bishopric of Arezzo by Raffaele Riario.

one place, of which I do not know the name, the ground had been hollowed out and a large lake formed.

At this time the foundations of the Nunziata de' Ricci were begun; this church is also called Santa Maria Alberighi, and the veneration first began when dirt was thrown in the face of the image by the man who was hung for it.[1]

22nd August. They began to break through the wall in the Palagio de' Signori, in order to make the door going into the Great Hall of the *Dogana* (Customs).

24th August. During the night following San Bartolomeo, the Arno was so high that many people were drowned down at Brozzi, and at San Donnino four men and some mules. Amongst other things it carried away a stock of flax and wood, for it came suddenly when it was unexpected, there having been no rain here, but the Sieve and the Arno met with a rush, which caused the flood.

At this time a girl threw herself from a window, on purpose, and was killed on the spot.

27th September. The new Archbishop of Florence entered the city and took possession; he was the son of Guglielmo de' Pazzi, and had been Bishop of Arezzo first. He was escorted into the city with great pomp; and by privilege, a saddle was sent to Alfonso Strozzi, with buglers preceding it.[2]

In these days a chapel was built in Santa Maria Novella, next to the *cappella maggiore* (chapel behind the altar), on the left hand; that is to say, it was embellished with marbles and other things.

12th November. We heard that our troops before Pisa had gone against the Lucchesi and pillaged Viareggio and burnt all that remained there; which gave them a booty of 10,000 florins, because it is the port of Lucca. And then they made a raid close to Lucca, so that the men of Lucca

[1] This was the image that had been desecrated by Rinaldeschi, as is mentioned on 21st July, 1501. It represented the Annunciation, and in 1508 an oratory was built round it, which was afterwards enlarged and made into a parish church, which is still called the Madonna de' Ricci at the present day.

[2] The saddle was not sent to Alfonso Strozzi, but he himself and his brother Lorenzo, in virtue of an old privilege of their house, demanded and obtained it, together with the bridle, from the archbishop himself, when he had dismounted in the Piazza of San Piero Maggiore; as we find from a public deed drawn up on this same day, the 27th September, and published by Ughelli, *Italia Sacra*, tom. iii., p. 182.

came out; and the latter were defeated and about 40 of them killed, besides great damage being done. These poor creatures have gone about seeking trouble, always taking the part of the Pisans and helping them; they should have reflected that *Marzocco* was able to do them harm: they deceived themselves.

8th December. There was talk of the King of Portugal's acquisition of an island[1] discovered by his ships at 34 degrees beyond the equinox, opposite Alexandria.

14th December. The Cardinal of Santa Croce, the papal legate, passed through, on his return to the Emperor to make an agreement; and it was said here that the Emperor, the King of France, the King of Spain, the Pope, and the Florentines, and all their adherents, had made a league and agreement.

The said cardinal wished to say mass himself in Santa Maria del Fiore on Christmas morning, and he gave an indulgence to all those who heard his mass in the said church. There was a crowd of people.

6th January. Our archbishop said mass in Santa Maria del Fiore, and gave an indulgence for the whole day from sunrise to sunset, by an authority which had been[2] conceded to him.

20th January. A league was proclaimed between us and the Lucchesi for . . . years, with the stipulation that they were not to give aid to the Pisans either openly or secretly.[3]

20th February. We heard that the Pisans had captured about 87 of our musketeers.

2nd March. Two commissaries were appointed for the camp before Pisa: namely, Alamanno Salviati and Jacopo his brother.[4]

---

[1] According to the maps of those times, this "island" may have been anywhere, perhaps near India, about which there were very vague notions in Italy, although traders came now and then.

[2] Of these two solemn masses of the cardinal and the archbishop and of the indulgences conceded by them, we have confirmation in the notices published by the *Signoria*, who were present at the first of them with all the magistrates.

[3] The league was made for three years, and the deed, of which a copy is preserved in the *Archivio Diplomatico Florentino*, is of the 12th January.

[4] In the Council of the "Eighty" there were really elected, on the 2nd March, as general commissaries, *in agro pisanis*, Alamanno d'Averardo and Jacopo di Giovanni Salviati. But since a law on prohibitions, of the year 1444, forbade two of the same family to

10th March. The said ambassadors went to Pisa, and they ordered us to send there all the battalions from here. At this time we put in the stocks all the (Pisan) prisoners that we had in the *Stinche*, because we had heard that the Pisans had done the same to ours.

21st March. We heard that the arsenal at Venice had been burnt down, and many lives lost there; which was a great misfortune for them, especially as they were not in the League. Ruin seemed to threaten them.

1509. 5th April. We heard that our troops before Pisa had captured about 60 horses, and slain or captured many men who were carrying corn to Pisa: it was said that they had obtained it secretly from Lucca. 54 of those captured arrived here on this day, all bound to a rope; and they were put in the Palagio del Podestà; it was said that about 60 had been slain. These prisoners were paraded through the city, so that everyone could see them.

9th April. We heard that there was a certain Alfonso del Mutolo, who sent to tell our commissaries that he would let them enter by one of the gates, and as soon as there were a sufficient number of our men within, he let down the portcullis and they were trapped; then the Pisans immediately fired off a quantity of cannon against those who remained outside the gate, slaying many.

21st April. We heard that the Pope had pitched his camp before Faenza, and the King of France had pitched his before Cremona, and the King of Spain had pitched his before the cities of the Venetians in Puglia, and the Grand Master of Rhodes had pitched his in Cyprus. Unfortunate Venetians, how will you fare? You have to send armies in four different directions! I do not believe that you will mock any longer at the tribulations of the Florentines, or think any more of supporting the Pisans, as you have done up till now: the money will have to be employed elsewhere. Did you not understand that you were acting unconscientiously to attack those who had never injured you, and to take away cities from the Holy Father! You ought to be

serve together in the same office, Alamanno, who had obtained a lesser number of votes, was replaced on the same day by Antonio da Filicaia. Then, on the 6th March, Jacopo Salviati having alleged certain impediments, Alamanno was put in his place; so that on the 10th March, just as Landucci writes, he left with Filicaia to fulfil his commission. See in the *Archivio di Stato Fiorentino* the register of the *Legazioni e Commissarie, Elez. Istruz. e Lettere, ad an.*

content with having held Ravenna so long; but this is the
consequence of sin, and of acting against one's conscience,
and of not fearing God. You have been the cause of all that
the Pisans have suffered, for they would have returned to
us at once, if you had not persuaded them to resist; and the
same in the Casentino, and at Bibbiena, it was your doing
in every case: and it has all been folly, because if it had not
been for the discords of the Florentines, you would have
been entirely defeated. In any case you are bound to come
out of it ingloriously.

6th May. The tabernacle of Our Lady of Santa Maria
Impruneta was sent for here, on account of there not having
been any rain for some time: and the next day it rained,
by God's mercy, who is always gracious to us through the
prayers of the Blessed Virgin.[1]

8th May. The papal soldiers sacked Berzighella and slew
many and took many prisoners, even women.

During this time Pisa was very closely besieged, and the
inhabitants fared badly. Every day, however, one heard
things which showed their obstinacy—amongst others this:
A woman of Pisa came out of the city with her two children
and went before the commissary, saying that she was
dying of hunger, and had left her mother in Pisa who was
almost famished; and the commissary ordered that bread
should be given her for herself and her mother and children.
Going back into Pisa with the bread, she told her mother,
who was ill from want of food, and on seeing the white
bread, the old woman said: *Che pane e questo?* (What
bread is this?); and when her daughter told her that she
had had it outside, from the Florentines, the old woman
cried: *Portate via el pane de' maladetti Fiorentini; voglio
prima morire!* (Take away the bread of the accursed
Florentines; I had rather die!); and she would not touch
it. Think what hate the poor people bore to this city,
finding their lot so hard, without fault of theirs. Oh, what
grievous sin it is to command that there should be a
war! Woe to him who is the cause of it! I pray God to
forgive us; although this enterprise of ours is undertaken

[1] In the *Priorista* of Jacopo de' Rossi we read a longer relation of
the coming of this tabernacle, which had been decreed because
there had been five months without rain; and here also we read of
the desired grace having been obtained immediately (Casotti,
Memorie istoriche della miracolosa immagine di S.M.V. dell' Impruneta, Firenze, 1714, p. 141).

legitimately: think what is the sin of those who go to war without a legitimate cause!

16th May. We heard that the Venetians had been defeated by the King of France, on the 14th, near Carafaggio in the plain of the Alberello; and that 12 thousand men were slain there—this figure of 12 thousand being confirmed several times. Here there were great rejoicings, with bonfires, etc. Ah, you Venetians! Of your four armies, one has been speedily laid low.

25th May. Eight Pisan ambassadors came to Florence[1]; and on the 26th had an audience, and on the 28th two returned to Pisa to sign the articles.

During these days we heard that the King of France had sent to tell the Venetians that they were to elect a prince over them, of whom he should approve; and he went on conquering the cities of Lombardy. See whether pride has had its punishment, for them to be told to submit to be imposed upon!

Up till now, the Pope had conquered Ravenna, Faenza, and other places which belonged to the Church, without difficulty.

The King of Spain with his army was doing his part against the cities of the Venetians in Puglia.

28th May. We heard that a great army had been set on foot by the Turks; and the Pope had processions made, to induce people to undertake a crusade.

At this time the Venetians were as if dismayed and bewildered, finding all the powers against them.

The Marchese di Ferrara had gone to win back the Pulesine (Polesine), and took it immediately. The unfortunate Venetians could no longer go in aid of anyone; nothing remained to them; they were left as helpless as children, and their money was almost at an end.

2nd June. The Pisans ratified the agreement at 2 in the

[1] *Cambi* also records the arrival of these ambassadors, who were accompanied by Alamanno Salviati. He adds that the *Signoria* "ordered that no one should speak to them without permission, and that they should not go outside the town, although not a very strict watch was kept; so that one of the Pisan ambassadors, with regard to the *contado* (country round), said to our gracious *Gonfaloniere*: 'After this transaction is concluded, I will show you letters from more than forty citizens, who encourage me to break the agreement, and not to fear anything, but I wish to be faithful.'" In vol. iii. of the *Opere* of Macchiavelli (Firenze, 1876) are found some letters of Salviati relating to this fact.

morning (10 a.m.); and as if by a miracle, just at 2 a dove entered the *Palagio* by the door, and flew all round the court, and then flew over the heads of part of the "Ten" who were under the arcade of the *Palagio*, and dashing against the wall, fell at the feet of the "Ten," so that their *Proposto* (foreman), who was Piovacchino Guasconi, picked it up, but could not hold it, only some feathers remaining in his hand. This was thought a good omen, especially as it was at this hour that the Pisans had ratified the agreement—a sign that it was reality, and that an end had been put to so much evil, and there would be peace at last; although many said that there was nothing supernatural about it. Nevertheless it was a great thing that the dove should have gone to the "Ten" who had just made the agreement, and still more, into the hand of the foreman; and no one had ever seen one enter the *Palagio* in this manner before. Religious men say that it came from God; and it is true that God has permitted the Venetians to be deprived of their strength; so that the Pisans, having seen the Venetians thus laid low, immediately came to an agreement with us; and one can easily see that it was the Venetians who made them hold out so obstinately, and imperil their lives for so many years.

6th June. The *Signori* sent the bell to San Marco which had been taken away at the time of Fra Girolamo's arrest, because those in power had a great hatred of San Marco, and would willingly have destroyed this church out of this hatred of theirs for Fra Girolamo; therefore it had seemed to some of them that this bell ought to be banished from Florence, and they sent it to be kept within the limits of the *Osservanza*, where it remained till to-day, and now they have sent it back.[1]

7th June (the day of *Corpus Christi*). The surrender of Pisa was expected, and a horseman arriving at about 21

---

[1] Not only was the single bell taken away from San Marco, as was said on 30th June, 1498, but it was exiled from the city for 50 years, under pain of any one who should bring it back being declared a rebel. The decree has been published by my valued friend Alessandro Gherardi on page 205 of the *Nuovi documenti e studi intorno a Girolamo Savonarola* (Firenze, 1878), together with a record of the chronicler of the convent, and a letter of Fra Stefano di Castrocaro; from which documents it results that the chief credit for this restitution belongs to the *Gonfaloniere* Soderini, and that the occasion of it was the joy at the re-acquisition of Pisa.

in the evening (5 a.m.), and it being believed that he brought the good news, there was such a commotion in all the churches where vespers was being said, that people left vespers and went into the Piazza; and those who were in the *Stinche* endeavoured violently to break out, and before one in the evening (9 p.m.) they all succeeded; although some of them had formerly held good positions, like that *Podestà* of Florence who was imprisoned there for errors of which he had been guilty; he was from Fano, and he was so disgraced that he never returned home; he was a corrupt man, according to all accounts.[1]

8th June (Friday). At about 18 in the afternoon (2 p.m.), the horseman bearing the olive-branch arrived with the surrender of Pisa; and there was a great *festa*, the shops being shut, and bonfires made, and illuminations placed on all the towers and on the *Palagio*.[2]

On the same day the emperor's ambassador came to us, and on the 10th he had an audience and requested 100 thousand florins; and it was said that he came rather to prevent us from having Pisa back, as the Pisans had had recourse to Rome, when they saw that the Venetians could no longer help them. By God's mercy, he did not arrive in time, as the surrender had been made that very day.

Up till this day, the 8th June, the Pope had taken four cities: Faenza, Rimini, Cervia and Ravenna.

The King of France had taken, up to this same day, about nine, being Crissale, Trevigi, Carafaggio, Cremona, Crema, Brescia, Bergamo, Peschiera and Estri.

The emperor had taken eight, up till the 9th June: Gorizia, Trieste, Fiume, Piacenza, Verona, Udine, Civitale and Padova.

The King of Spain had taken seven, up till the 8th June, being Otranto, Cuttone, Brindizio, Trani, Napoli, Fulignano and Nola.

And the Marchese di Ferrara had taken three: Rovico, il Pulesine and la Saliera.

See in what a state the Venetians are! having lost all these cities which belonged to them. Their pride must be somewhat lowered.

[1] The same man mentioned on 1st June, 1508.
[2] All classes of citizens really celebrated this event; in a book of the convent of SS. Annunziata we read that "great *feste* were held," and that this convent spent on that day 3 *lire* 10 *soldi* "for gunpowder to make rockets."

20th June. We heard that the emperor had sold all the cities which he had conquered in Lombardy to the Venetians, and that they were to give him 500 thousand florins a year for twenty years. This is said; if it is true, they will need a gold-mine. They do all their business with money.

4th July. I, Luca, gave a plan that I had invented, to Giovanni, one of the fife-players of the *Palagio*[1]; I had given it some time before to Simone del Pollaiuolo, who afterwards died, and now I have given it to the said Giovanni, so that he may lay it before those who can put it into practice, if so please God. It is a design for making a temple to San Giovanni Vangiolista, in that place where the present church stands, opposite San Lorenzo; that is, to take the square piece of ground contained in the Piazza San Lorenzo, which is about 100 *braccia* each way, as I have explained in writing.

22nd July. We heard that Padua had risen in arms, one party adhering to the Venetians, and the other favouring the emperor; so that the Venetians attacked it and succeeded in entering it, with the loss of many men; and many of the partisans of the emperor were also slain by the Venetians, who it was said had an army 40 thousand strong.

18th August. We heard that the Moors of Barbary had retaken the city of Oran, which the Spaniards had won when they conquered Granada.

24th August. The emperor was approaching Padua with his army and with the French troops.

4th September. We heard that the emperor had retired, because it appeared to him that he had not a sufficiently large force.

10th September. 500 Spaniards passed here, who were going to the aid of the emperor, sent from Naples by the King of Spain. And it was said, besides, that thousands more were being sent, and it was this that made the emperor retire in order to await them. The same day two French cardinals passed here, on their way to Rome, one of whom was going to fetch his hat.

15th September. We heard that the emperor had attacked the enemy at Padua, and that there had been great losses on both sides, and that reinforcements were continually arriving for the emperor. Also that the Pope

[1] Giovanni Cellini, father of Benvenuto the sculptor, a man not without knowledge of the art of designing.

had ordered the bishops of France and Germany to come to the aid of the emperor, on pain of having their benefices taken from them and of being excommunicated. It was said besides that he had forbidden the Venetians the rite of baptism. And all the time many Spaniards were passing to join the emperor; more than 2 thousand altogether.

24th September. We heard that the emperor's army had greatly increased, and that he had taken the River Brenta from the Paduans, and his forces were making incursions into all the villages round, so that the villagers fled to Venice with their property and their wives and children.

15th October. The emperor raised his camp at Padua and retired. Think how these villages rejoiced.

28th October. We heard that there had been such tremendous earthquakes in Constantinople that 4 thousand houses were destroyed and seven thousand people killed, and an enormous number injured; one of our Florentines, Antonio, was killed, and several others were injured. This earthquake happened on the 10th September, 1509, at 4 at night (midnight), and it also destroyed a city in Candia and formed a lake; like a few years ago, when another earthquake in these same countries round Greece and at Adrianople, and other cities, caused great damage and ruin; and this time, besides the houses, a large part of the walls of Constantinople were destroyed. The Turks left there and went away into Bursia: which was an unheard-of thing, and, according to religious people, was a sign to the Christians and to the Holy Father that they ought to make a move and reconquer all the Levant. But the enemy of mankind had commanded them, and prepared a different lot for Italy, on account of our sins, and of the fullness of time not having yet come; because the wickedness of bad Christians must first be purged away, the wickedness of so many unbelieving Christians, blasphemers, adulterers, those who are engulfed in the unmentionable vice, homicides, without any fear of the omnipotent God, who take no heed of injuring his creatures, nor ever think that they themselves are created by Him. Oh, immense ignorance! it is terrible that so many still exist who have no scruple in slaying men, and pillaging the property and persons of the poor, those who live their humble lives without doing harm to anyone! no scruple in slaying, robbing, burning down houses, carrying off young girls to resorts of ill-fame, cutting down vines, ruining the luxuriant fruits given to man by God, destroying grain and corn and everything that God sends for our wants. Oh, what a miracle, that so many are found of such a perverse nature that they imagine that they are serving God! Lord, I pray that Thou wilt pardon them, because they are in the profound night of ignorance and have never considered what great marvels God can work; pardon me also, who have more need of it than anyone, have mercy upon me.

12th November. The ornaments on the doorway of the *Palagio* leading into the *Dogana* (Customs), going up into the larger hall, were finished.

15th November. There was a certain Spaniard who mounted a table like a juggler, to sell his prayers, saying: "In order that you may believe that they are composed by a saint who works miracles, and that what I tell you is true, come and take me to a hot furnace, and I will enter it with these prayers in my hand." In the end, he was taken to a furnace near Santa Trinità, with a crowd following him, among whom were many of the chief citizens, who came on from the *Mercato Nuovo* where he had been holding forth. When they reached the baker's, he said: "Give me an unbaked loaf"; and he threw it into the furnace to show that it was hot, and then he stripped to his shirt and pushed his hose down below his knees, and so entered right into the furnace, and remained there a little while, taking the loaf in his hand and turning it about. Note that the furnace was hot, the bread having only just been taken out, and yet he was not injured in the least. When he had come out of the furnace, he made them give him a torch, and lighted it, and put it lighted into his mouth and held it there till it went out. And often on the platform, day after day, he took a handful of *moccoli* (burnt-out ends of little tapers) and held them on his hand for some time, and then put them in his mouth and kept them there till they went out. He was seen to do many other things with fire—to wash his hands in a frying-pan of oil which was boiling over the fire, etc. All the people saw him do this again and again. Therefore he found a sale for as many of his prayers as he could write; and I can tell you that of all the things that I have ever seen, I never saw a greater miracle, if miracle it was.

1st December. The rule came into force that no other money but Florentine coins should be taken.[1]

20th December. We heard that the Ferrarese had had a great victory over the Venetian galleys in the Po.

24th February. We heard that the Pope had taken the interdict off the Venetians, and it was said that the Emperor and the Kings of France and Spain were not pleased at this, for their ambassadors at Rome would not meet the Pope.

1510. 1st May. We heard that the King of France had taken a castle in Lombardy, called Lignaco, by assault, and that about a thousand French had been killed there, and they sacked the castle and slew everyone, even the children. And it was said, besides, that some people had fled on to a strong hill, and not being able to ascend it or take it, the French had made a hole in the hillside and put in a good quantity of gunpowder, setting fire to this and destroying part of the hill.

11th June. A thunderbolt fell at San Donnino, killing a father and son, and two other children of his were frightened out of their wits and had fallen ill.

At this time a girl was found drowned in a well, and it was never discovered who she was, no one seeming to know her; and there seemed no one in all the country round who had lost anyone.

15th June. The houses in the Via de' Servi belonging to the *Arte delle Lana* (Wool-merchants' Guild) were begun to be built—that is, those that were built where the *tiratoio* [2] used to be, and the *tiratoio* was taken down by degrees, as they made the houses. The first one was begun towards the Servi.[3]

---

[1] Under this date we read in *Cambi*: "The new copper *quattrini*, which had been freshly coined, began to be used, and 7 *lire* of them were given for a gold *scudo* (crown), and they were said to contain half an ounce of silver to the pound; and the other copper *quattrini* were put at the price of 2 *danari* each; and *grossoni* were also coined which were worth 7 *soldi* of copper *quattrini* each, that is, 20 *grossi* for a gold crown; and all the clipped silver coins of other cities were done away with, and the weight of the silver coins fixed, and how much they were worth; all the clipped coins being cut up."

[2] See note to 10th June, 1498.

[3] The commerce of woollen cloth having notably diminished in Florence, some of the *tiratoi* could be taken down. One of these was called the *Tiratoio dell' aquila*, in Via de' Servi, and here new houses

18th June. They began to clear out the vaults under the *Loggia de' Signori*; these had been made when it was first built, but had been forgotten, and were only discovered when it was needed to lay a foundation on which to set the bronze "Judith"; when the *Gonfaloniere* was told of them, he was glad, as he thought it would be a useful place in which to keep artillery.

19th June. The *festaiuoli* of San Giovanni (directors of the festivities) published a proclamation that no shops were to be opened from the 20th June till San Giovanni was over, without their permission, on pain of a fine of 25 *lire*; and those who received permission had to pay, some two *grossi* and some three or four. This was very hard upon the poor, because the proclamation said that it was not meant for the wool mercers, nor the silk mercers, nor the bankers; therefore it was considered an injustice and a mean and infamous thing to force the artisans to be idle.

At this time there was an epidemic of influenza, with a cough and fever, in Florence and all through Italy. Almost everyone suffered from it; the fever lasted four or five days, and was called in Florence the *male del tiro* (shooting complaint). The reason of this was that amongst all sorts of celebrations on the day of San Giovanni, the first consisted in jousting in the Piazza, that is to say, a number of men-at-arms, fully armed with lances as if they were on a field of battle, were made to perform feats of arms; then a man walked on a tight-rope; and lastly they hunted a bull. It was extremely hot that day, and then it poured with rain, which soaked everyone who was out of doors. A great number of raised seats had been made, and the whole of Florence was there, and many foreigners besides; and people having got wet when they were so heated is supposed to have caused the influenza.

7th August. There were two earthquakes at 6 in the morning (2 a.m.), and at 7 (3 a.m.) came a third; and the next night there were two more at the same hour of the night.

We heard that in the country round Bologna there had

---

were made for the embellishment of the street. The arms of the Guild, in stone, are still to be seen on the houses numbers 12 and 28, and point out the boundaries of the old *tiratoio*. The original form of these "well-arranged houses," all of "the same style," as Cinelli wrote, is still kept externally by that of number 22.

VIEW OF FLORENCE AND THE ARNO

been such a severe storm of wind that it destroyed many houses. Think of the consequences to the fruit!

At this time the foundations and pavement of the Ponte a Rubiconte were renewed.[1]

24th September. The Pope reached Bologna.

26th September. Two cardinals came to Florence—no, three cardinals—who were going to Bologna to the Pope. They lodged at Santa Croce.

30th September. Two more cardinals came, on their way to Bologna. They lodged at the Servi.[2]

17th October. They left here, and went in the direction of Pisa and Lucca, to cross into France and not to go to the Pope, being French and somewhat in fear of the Pope, besides not wishing to insult the king.

During these days it was said that the King of France was coming to Bologna with two armies, to besiege the Pope, so that the Pope was supposed to have misgivings. It was also said that he thought of living in Florence.

And then the King of France came, and advanced as far as Bologna, escorted by the sons of Messer Giovanni (Bentivogli), who believed that the people would rise at their instigation; but there was not a movement, so that if the Pope had wished, he might have defeated the king when he first began to retire, before he withdrew to a considerable distance. Thus the Holy Father had no longer any misgivings, and expected to have Ferrara without delay.

2nd November. The following accident occurred at the Ponte a Rubiconte: They were rebuilding the wall between the *Porticciuola* [3] and the bridge, and as there was plenty

---

[1] The decree by which the officials of the *Torre* were ordered to repair this bridge, which was in such a state as to be in danger of falling in, is dated 26th April, 1509. See the *Registro di Provvisioni, ad an.*

[2] The date of the arrival and departure of these five cardinals agrees exactly with the documents. See the *Deliberazioni dei Signori e Collegi* and the *Copielettere dei Dieci, ad an.* First came San Malò, Bayeux and Sanseverino; then Santa Croce and Cosenza; and they all left together, in the direction of Pisa. There are some curious details of their prolonged stay in Florence in this *Copielettere de' Dieci*, at chap. 96, *et seq.*

[3] This was another *Porticciuola* (not the one by the *Borgo Ognissanti*); it also led to mills, of which there were several near the Ponte Rubiconte (now Ponte alle Grazie). [Trans.]

of water, about 12 *braccia*, the gravel and lime were brought by river in certain little boats. On these boats they had made a platform, and whilst some 25 men were carrying the gravel on to the little platform by the side of the wall, and were approaching it, the said boats filled with water, from the great weight, and drew down the platform and the men, so that three or four men were drowned. They afterwards used a large vessel with a platform, which sufficed for the weight without any danger. I saw some of the men drawn out of the water.

4th December. The apothecary's shop at the Canto de' Tornaquinci, kept by the sons of Giampiero, apothecary at San Felice, was burnt down; the site belonged to Cardinal Rucellai. It was completely destroyed, nothing being left except a few copper utensils, which were found under the ashes quite spoilt; the walls were razed to the ground.

22nd December. A plot was discovered against the *Gonfaloniere*, a certain man called Prinzivalle having intended to murder him. He was the son of Luigi della Stufa, of Bologna, and it was said that he had proposed three ways of killing Soderini; first, to murder him in the Council-chamber; secondly, in his own room; and thirdly, when he went out. A woman discovered this, and it was imparted to Filippo Strozzi, who as soon as he heard of it, went immediately to warn the *Signoria*; and they sent for Luigi della Stufa, the man's father, and detained him in the *Palagio*.[1]

30th December. He was confined within certain boundaries in the district of Empoli for five years, on pain of being declared a rebel if he broke these boundaries; and the son escaped.

3rd January. The "Eight" published a proclamation that any Florentine who was in the house of the Cardinal de' Medici, or of his brother, or of any of his family, should be declared rebels, unless they left such houses within three days; and all those who went to speak to them, or to stop in their houses for any reason, would be declared

[1] In the Life of Filippo Strozzi, written by Lorenzo his brother, this plot of Prinzivalle della Stufa is spoken of at length, but there is not a word about a woman having discovered it: it is mentioned, however, that Filippo discussed it angrily with his mother-in-law, Alfonsina Orsini de' Medici.

rebels, unless it were notified to the *Signoria* here within so many days.[1]

At this time there was a cardinal [2] so bereft of the fear of the Lord, that he contrived to corrupt, by means of bribes, a Florentine girl, the daughter of a worthy man, a good citizen, and of an ancient house, and who was married to another worthy man, whose names I will not mention, so as to spare their honour. He caused her to be secretly led away to him at Bologna, where he was with the Pope, to the great sorrow of her father and mother and relatives: and the thing was hateful to everyone. Finally she was brought back after a few days, amidst much murmuring about the disgrace to the city, because all the people were aware of it. For although it was a private case, it was regarded as one concerning the whole of Florence.

13th January. It began to snow in Florence and all through the district, and it snowed four days running without stopping, so that it was half a *braccio* deep all over Florence; and it froze, so that it lasted in the city till the 22nd, when it snowed again on the top of this, becoming a *braccio* deep in many places. A number of most beautiful snow-lions were made in Florence by good masters; amongst others there was a very large and fine one next to the *campanile* of Santa Maria del Fiore, and one in front of Santa Trinità; and many nude figures were made also by good masters at the Canto de' Pazzi; and in Borgo San Lorenzo a city with fortresses was made, and many galleys; and so on, all over Florence.

23rd January. The snow began to melt and soften, so that such a mess was made in all the streets, that one could not get along or go about to do one's business; for one or two days there was no means of crossing the streets without making gangways; and therefore I record it.

[1] As far back as 21st January, 1497, a decree had been made ordering the citizens, peasants, and those of the district who were "in the service and company of rebels and enemies," that is, of the Medici, to return home within a month: on the 30th December, 1510, the Republic re-enforced this law, commanding the *Otto di Guardia e Balìa* to cause it to be publicly proclaimed during the first three days of their office. This order was carried into effect by this magistracy with the decree of the 2nd January (*Libro de' Partiti, ad an.*)

[2] This cardinal was Francesco Alidosi, formerly Bishop of Pavia, and for that reason commonly called the Cardinal of Pavia. See the note on p. 245.

On this day we heard that Mirandola had surrendered to the Pope, on condition that the persons and property of the inhabitants should be spared.

15th March. We heard that the Pope had had something of a defeat before Ferrara.

This day we heard that whilst a certain *festa* was being celebrated at Cortona, platforms in the hall where the *festa* was held broke down, about 20 persons being killed and more than 100 injured; there were some Florentines there.

1511. 5th April. A marble figure which was over the door of San Giovanni towards the *Opera* (Office of Works) was taken down, in order to place the new bronze figures there in its stead.

11th April. A vote was passed in Council that the dowries of girls could not be formed of the State funds, nor a larger dowry be given than 1600 florins.[1]

[1] Sixteen hundred "sealed" florins was in fact the sum to which were reduced and limited the amount of the dowries of every "daughter of a Florentine citizen," but it was not said that the State funds must have nothing to do with them; on the contrary, the 1600 florins had to be made up as follows: 800 "large" florins, invested in State funds in the name of the girl, which when reduced to "sealed" florins, made 960; and all the rest in cash and gifts, the latter not to exceed the estimate of 150 florins. Only in the case when the girl "has not anything in the said State funds, or not as much as 800 'large' florins, the value of the said 800 'large' florins, or of those wanting, might be given in cash," etc. (See the *riformagioni* of the Great Council of the 11th April in the *Registro* 202 of the *Provvisioni*, c. 12.) The reasons which caused the Republican Government to make these decrees are worth mentioning, and are summed up in the following preface to the decree: "The most exalted and magnificent *Signori* considering what disorder is caused in our city, and what inconvenience and injury to individual citizens and to their unmarried daughters, by the reprehensible habit, introduced here not long since, of giving large and excessive dowries, from which it has resulted that many citizens of old and noble families, not being able to give such dowries, have been forced to make alliances with persons of a rank and condition very dissimilar to their own; and also, on the other hand, that many worthy young men, through their desire of a large dowry, have taken the daughters of men who are wealthy but of a class and rank far inferior to their own; and desiring to return to the wise and good custom of the citizens of former days, and to enable girls to marry more easily; having held a long and careful colloquy on this subject, and taken the opinion of their honourable *Collegi* and of a number of other wise and prudent citizens, deem it to be well to make the following decree."

Campi also records this decree and the reasons which led to it: amongst other things he narrates that dowries had even reached the sum of 3000 florins in cash alone, and that there were more than

17th May. We heard that the army of the King of France had had an encounter with that of the Pope, and had approached within two miles of Bologna.

21st May. A newly made cardinal came to Florence, who was a Florentine, called Messer Piero Accolti.[1]

22nd May. The tabernacle of Our Lady of Santa Maria Impruneta was fetched to Florence so that it should cease raining; for at this time there had been too much wet. Many gifts were made, exceeding any ever made before. There were eight very rich mantles, and many chasubles and cloaks, and silken draperies to the number of 24, and tapers of white wax and yellow wax, upto 90, and a beautiful cross.[2]

23rd May. We heard that the French troops had entered Bologna, and that the papal troops were defeated, and had gone with the Pope to Ravenna. And the Cardinal of Pavia[3] fled from Bologna, he who was papal legate, and governor of Bologna, and went to Ravenna where the Pope was. The Prefect of Ravenna, who was the Lord of Urbino and Captain of the Church, went to meet him, saying: "Thou traitor! Thou hast disgraced the Holy Church!" and he thrust his sword into his breast, piercing him right through, so that he died in a few hours. See the justice of God! for it was this cardinal who had carried off the Florentine girl, and think what he could do in Bologna, where he was governor. According to all accounts, he had done many similar things, and even worse.

20th June. We heard that the Pope had reached Rome, having left Ravenna; and no sooner had he reached Rome, than he excommunicated Bologna, and all those who should aid or favour that city, with such a powerful excommunication that the King of France and his whole army were excommunicated, and all those who should aid or abet them.

21st June. The three bronze figures over the door of San Giovanni towards the *Opera* (Office of Works), where 3000 girls in the city between eighteen and thirty years of age who were not able to marry.

[1] He had been made Cardinal with the title of Sant' Eusebio by Julius II. at Ravenna, on the 10th March of that year.

[2] In the *Registro* of the *Deliberazioni de' Signori e Collegi, ad an.*, there is a decree of the preceding day which establishes and enumerates the places, besides the usual ones, where the tabernacle is to be taken in procession. And in a cash-book of the steward of the *Camera dell' Arme* of this year, c. 75, we find a note of part of the expenses incurred by this celebration.

[3] Francesco Maria della Rovere.

the old marble ones had been before, were uncovered, being completely finished.¹

13th June. At about 20 in the afternoon (4 p.m.) there were torrents of rain in Florence and everywhere as far as into the Mugello; and in Florence there were several thunderbolts in less than an hour; one at San Giorgio killed a boy; one on the *Ponte Vecchio* on the tower of the *Parte Guelfa*, and it terrified some people who were sitting on the stone bench below, amongst others one of the Ridolfi, who was carried home; he did not die, however. Another fell at Sitorno and killed a woman; and another at Bellosguardo, outside Florence, killed the wife of one of the Tosinghi, who was there in her villa, and one of her servingmaids was killed also, on an upper floor. Another fell at Montebuoni, on the *campanile* of the church, and killed a mule; and yet another at San Benedetto, outside the *Porta a Pinti*, and it fell on the *Cappella Maggiore*, passing through the roof, and then piercing the altar in two places, finally burying itself in the ground between two pavingstones. I saw all this; and there was such a quantity of rain that the whole of the Mugello and Valdisieve was flooded, and also here at San Salvi, and in all these plains; masses of wood were carried away.

16th July. They took our artillery out of Santa Maria Novella, where it had been in the Pope's stables, and put it under the *Loggia de' Signori*, where they had cleared and arranged the vaults; and there was difficulty about getting in the first gun, as the rope broke, and it ran down the slope into the vault, and nearly killed the oxen and the men.

17th July. We heard that the papal troops had captured one of Messer Giovanni Bentivogli's sons, and that the French troops had pursued them and recaptured him; also that cries of *Papa* had been raised in Bologna, and that several citizens who wished to reinstate the sons of Messer Giovanni, with the support of the king, had been beheaded.

26th July. The first melons were sold in Florence; and nothing ripened this year, on account of it having been so

¹ These three bronze figures were the work of Giovanni Francesco Rustici, who had been commissioned to make them by the *Arte de' Mercacanti* (Merchants' Guild), as far back as the 30th December, 1506. See the documents relating to this, published by Cav. Gaetano Milanesi, in the *Giornale Storico degli Archivi Toscani*, iv. 63, *et seq*.

cool all the spring, and having rained up till now; which is the reason that I record the fact.

3rd August. News came that we had taken possession of Montepulciano.

4th August. Three men who emptied cesspools were drowned in a certain black well, near the *Porta San Piero Gattolino*, next to the convent of the Nuns of San Giovanni.

7th August. Ambassadors came here from Montepulciano, and signed the articles between us and them: and on the 9th the bells rang a peal, and there were great rejoicings and bonfires. It was an improvised *festa*, mostly celebrated by the people.[1]

3rd September. We heard that the Pope had put Pisa under an interdict, because it detained the cardinals who wished to hold a council there.[2]

4th September. We heard that there had been a terrible hailstorm at Crema in Lombardy, with meteoric stones of the weight of 150 pounds each, the larger ones; and some of the hailstones weighed 30 pounds each, so that roofs were broken and many men and beasts were killed.

At this same time great fires were also seen in the air, in the evening, at the castle of Carpi, and then the fire was seen to divide in three parts with loud thunder-claps; this being suddenly followed by hail and wind that carried away roofs and ruined belfries, doing immense damage.

23rd September. The Pope placed Florence under an interdict, for the same reason, that he imagined that we supported the Council.

23rd October. This interdict was taken off till the middle of the following month of November.

At this time the roof of the church of the Vergine Maria of *Por San Piero* was finished; that is, the part over the body of the church.[3]

4th November. On the night following this date, two

[1] The articles of the submission of Montepulciano to the Republic were stipulated in Florence on the 10th August, and an original copy of them is preserved in the *Archivio delle Riformagioni*, derived from the *Atti pubblici*, with the original ratification of the Commune of Montepulciano at the end.

[2] Julius II., upon his election, had promised to assemble the Council within two years, but never did so. This that they wished to hold at Pisa was against him, and promoted by the King of France and the emperor.

[3] By this is meant the church of Santa Maria degli Alberighi or de' Ricci.

thunderbolts fell in Florence in the middle of the night. One struck the *Palagio de' Signori* just above the dial, and coming down into the court, twisted a certain bronze band which was at the base of the "David" in this court[1]; and it also displaced a pilaster of the door which is at the foot of the staircase, and broke certain marble steps higher up by the *Sala*, and the same again above. Outside it came down by the door, and stained and spoilt three lilies above it, which was considered a bad omen for the King of France. And another struck the cupola (of the *Duomo*), displacing about three niches,[2] although they did not fall; and this meant some trouble for the Church.

12th November. The cardinals who wanted to hold a Council left Pisa.[3]

1st December.[4] We were allowed by the Pope to have masses said again, after having been deprived of them for so many months.

15th December. We were again deprived of the mass, the interdict returning.

We heard that the Pope's troops were in Romagna, in the direction of Bologna and Ferrara.

During the next days the papal camp was pitched before the bastion of Ferrara, which was shortly gained for the Pope.[5]

In a few days, however, the Ferraresi recovered the bastion, the papal troops losing it in January; and after that we heard that they had withdrawn, and that the King of France had sent 400 lancers to Bologna. Florence remained under the interdict all January.

[1] *Cambi* also records the fall of these thunderbolts, and how the statue mentioned on 9th December, 1495, was struck: that is, "a bronze David, by Donatello, on a column which rests on a base with four pieces of sculptured foliage, in the centre of the court of the Palace, and one of these pieces of foliage was broken in three places."

[2] Probably the little buttresses against the lantern. [Trans.]

[3] Because, after having held three sessions at Pisa, they decided to hold the fourth at Milan. (*Villari, Niccolò Machiavelli e i suoi tempi*, tom. ii., p. 153.)

[4] The MS. of the *Maruccelliana* has *October*, but December must be meant. *Cambi* makes us sure of it when he writes: "On the 1st December, the day of Sant' Andrea, the first Sunday in Advent, Pope Julius sent a suspension of the interdict for fifteen days."

[5] The papal troops had won two of the forts, but the Duke of Ferrara himself returned, and not only won them back, but forced the enemy to withdraw. [Trans.]

15th February. We heard that Brescia had rebelled against the king, and gone over to the Venetians, although the fortress held out for the French; and that the king was obliged to take the greater part of his troops away from Bologna and send them to Brescia. The papal camp stopped there, although it was said that Cardinal de' Medici had entered Bologna. It was not true.

19th February. 300 mounted bowmen and musketeers were levied here, all from our district. They were mustered in the Piazza.

On this day it was said that the Venetians had been defeated by the Pope near Parma.

23rd February. We heard that the king had retaken Brescia, and slain almost everyone; some said 18 thousand men, but later the number was reduced to 4 thousand or 5 thousand. Francesco Pandolfini, who was ambassador there, afterwards wrote that 9 thousand had been buried. Here we had rejoicings and bonfires for the king's victory.[1]

2nd March. It snowed and was intensely cold; and on the 10th there was another heavy snowstorm. The night was bitterly cold. Think how our men must have felt it out in the camp at Bologna.

We now heard that the Council at Bologna had ordered that no one should obey the Pope, and that masses should be said. It was expected that another Pope would be elected in a few days.[2]

11th March. We heard that a monster had been born at Ravenna, of which a drawing was sent here; it had a horn on its head, straight up like a sword, and instead of arms it had two wings like a bat's, and at the height of the breasts it had a *fio*[3] on one side and a cross on the other, and lower down at the waist, two serpents, and it was

---

[1] In the book *ad an.* of the steward of the *Camera* already quoted, we see that the expenses for this *festa* amounted to 69 *lire* 9.4 for 420 *panegli* (or *padelle* = little lights) for the *ballatoi* (galleries) of the Palazzo, 40 bundles of brushwood to be burnt on the Piazza de' Signori, 65 rockets to be let off from the said *ballatoi*, and 25 at the house of the French ambassador, and other things.

[2] This was only the consequence of the decree made at Milan during the fifth session, held on the 11th February, that is, to nominate the Cardinal of San Severino, the Legate at Bologna (Dumesnil, *Histoire de Jules II.*, etc. (Paris, 1873), p. 197).

[3] *Fio* is the name of one of the signs of the *Crocesanta* (Holy Cross), made like a Greek *v*. In old days it used to be put before the names or parts of a book that were wished to be specially pointed out.

hermaphrodite, and on the right knee it had an eye, and on the left foot an eagle. I saw it painted, and anyone who wished could see this painting in Florence.

17th March. We heard that the French who were in the fort at Brescia had again sacked all the monasteries in the city, and killed many monks and nuns, and stolen everything that remained.

18th March. The French ambassador left here; and the *Signoria* made him a present of about 2000 ducats, of a piece of brocade, and many other silk materials. There was a secret fear that the king was inimical to us, as the report went about that he intended to sack Florence and Siena. This ambassador was given besides a very rich altarpicture of Our Lady which had been in San Marco.[1]

21st March. The Pope allowed us to have masses said till the octave of Easter, and then a representative came from him to liberate us completely from the interdiction.[2]

1512. 29th March. We heard that the papal and Spanish troops, and also the French, had levelled a piece of ground for about four miles, to fight on. And during these days they took Ravenna and sacked it, being guilty of many cruelties; but they had not taken the fort. It was evident what evil the monster had meant for them! It seems as if some great misfortune always befalls the city where such things are born; the same thing happened at Volterra, which was sacked a short time after a similar monster had been born there.

3rd April. A *pardone di colpa e pena* (plenary indulgence) was proclaimed at the *Murate*, for three days: Friday, Holy Saturday and Easter Sunday.

12th April. We heard that the papal and Spanish armies were defeated by the French, and 10 thousand men slain,

---

[1] In the documents this ambassador is called *Monsignore Dotton* or *Di Uthon*, that is, d'Autun. The Republic wrote on the 18th to Roberto Acciaioli, its representative at the court of the Most Christian King, that he should express its thanks for a man of such merit having been allowed to remain so long at Florence (from the 25th June, 1511).

[2] Giovanantonio Gozzadini of Bologna, a cleric of the *Camera Apostolica*, who arrived on the 23rd of that month, and was lodged at Ognissanti. The *Signoria* spent 92 *lire* 15.8 on the presents which they sent him; that is, sweetmeats, tarts, marchpane, red wine, *trebbiano* (sweet white wine), large tench and eels from Perugia and Bientina, torches and wax tapers, etc. (*Libro del Massaio*, already quoted).

two-thirds Spanish and one-third French. About 22 French lords were killed, and amongst them a nephew of the king,[1] who many said had been our enemy: but perhaps it was not so. And it was said that if the French had not used so much artillery, which destroyed many hundreds of men-at-arms and cavalry, they would have been worsted. This was on the 11th April, the day of the *Pasqua di Resurresso* (Easter Day), near Ravenna, where the level had been made; and they had shattered one another in such a way, that although the French were victorious, nevertheless both armies were dispersed, and could do no harm to Florence, and the Spaniards might be thankful that they could go away without being plundered. Those who went through Romagna were plundered and even slain; but none of those who came through our territories had a hair of their head touched. They all went down to Rome, and the French went in the direction of Milan.

Every day came stories of more cruelties of the French and Spaniards, of how they reviled, and slew, and even sold monks and nuns and every sort of people; of how they stole the silver vessels containing the Host, and relics, without any fear of God or any reverence. So far I have said nothing of the young girls; but, amongst other cases, there was a father who, wishing to conceal his five grown-up daughters, in his dread, made a certain cavern and put them in it, with food for several days, intending to return and bring more food; but unfortunately he was killed, and as no one else knew about it, and the girls were unable to get out, they died there. Later the cavern was discovered, and the girls all dead, having bitten each other's arms. It is impossible to describe the horrors that one was continually hearing. It was said that a certain captain of the King of France, upon entering Brescia, took the beautiful daughter of a gentleman of the city, keeping her for many days, and when her father continually sent to demand that he should give her back, he refused. Finally, he told the father that if he wanted the girl back, he must give him a thousand ducats; and the said citizen collected the sum and brought it to him; and this captain took it, and then said that he wished to keep the girl one more night. The unfortunate father, overcome by despair, said:

[1] Gaston de Foix, nephew of Louis XII. (the model of whose delicate face is still to be seen in the museum at Ravenna).

"Signore! Since you will not give her back to me, take my life also!" and the Frenchman, being without fear of God, seized his sword from his side, and slew him. If this sin deserves punishment from the omnipotent God, who will not say that this man is bound to go to hell? May God keep us, and pardon them their great sins.

At this time the *Campanile* of San Spirito was built, behind the sacristy of the church.

22nd May. There died at Siena a certain Pandolfo Petrucci, who in his day was a great force in the city, lording it over everyone, chasing away his adversaries, and even taking the lives of some of them; now at last he dies. Oh, how much wiser it is to be humble, than to wish to be above others! It is far less perilous for body and soul. If men who are rich and great were wise, they would avoid desiring to rule that which ought to be common to everyone, because in that way they bring too much hatred upon themselves; let them be satisfied with their riches, and be content with the common good, becoming great in commerce, leading honest Christian lives, giving abundant alms to God's poor, and loving their country with an upright heart.

5th June. We heard that the Swiss had retaken Brescia and Peschiera and other cities of Lombardy, and that the French were fleeing from the country.

At this time the articles of the agreement with the King of France were confirmed, namely: that we were obliged to give him, when he should have need of them, 400 horse, paid by us, and that he was obliged to give us, when we should have need of them, 600 horse, paid by him; and he would do even more for us, if need should arise. His promises seemed straightforward.

13th June. We heard that the Cardinal de' Medici had escaped from the French king who held him prisoner and was sending him to France; and now he came to Bologna.[1]

16th June. We heard that Milan had rebelled against the king, and several other towns also; so that it was said that the French were in serious straits; they were restricted to the suburbs of Milan, and in great fear of running short of provisions, having difficulty in obtaining them.

[1] He had been taken prisoner by the French on the 11th April, in the battle of Pavia.

20th June. We heard that the French had left Milan, and avoiding the Swiss army, had gone to Pavia, always in great difficulties as to provisions. The Pope, meanwhile, had seized Bologna, and the Bentivogli had left, making it uncertain whether the French would not lose everything. Genoa also had turned, and was fighting the forts held by the French; whilst at Milan the forts held out for the king, but were not molested.

1st July. Some of the Pope's troops passed Dicomano, as he was sending about 1 thousand cavalry to Bologna; and it was said that the French had left Italy—those, that is, that had been able to escape, and had not been slain or captured on the passes, for many of them fared badly. And our troops, who were with those of the king, had a safe-conduct from the Swiss to return here, but it was not regarded, and they were all plundered, saving their lives with difficulty.

11th July. There was a letter from the Pope commanding the people of Florence to deprive the *Gonfaloniere* of his power and send him back home, which seemed very strange and overbearing, causing everyone to think that he wished to change the government, and to reinstate the Medici in Florence.[1]

On the same day an ambassador of his arrived, who was a Florentine, called Lorenzo Pucci, with a fine body of horsemen: it was imagined with the same object.[2]

---

[1] We read in *Cambi*: "The Pope sent for our ambassador, and told him to write to the Florentines at Florence that the permanent *Gonfaloniere della Giustizia*, that is, Piero Soderini, should resign his office, and in the case of this not being done, the Pope threatened the city. On the 10th July, 1512, these letters were read in the Council of the 'Eighty'; but nothing was decided that evening, as it appeared absurdly presumptuous of the Pope to think himself already so triumphant as to command the Florentines; as if he did not know, that a little while before, King Charles had passed there in person with 14,000 cavalry, and they had had no fear, so how could they fear the Pope now, he having less cause than the aforesaid King Charles to do injury to the Florentines, who had always been favourable to him and never gone against him? And this was the stronghold of the Florentines, the hope that they had in God, who would liberate them from such injustice on the part of their Pastor."

[2] "This Lorenzo d'Antonio Pucci was chancellor of the Pope; and when he reached San Gaggio he stopped, like one who reflects that he has to expound an unwelcome message to the city." These and other particulars respecting his arrival and his discussions with the *Signoria* are related at length by *Cambi*, quoted above.

14th July. At about 21 in the evening (5 p.m.), the *Campanile* of Santa Croce was struck by lightning, or rather, by a storm of wind or some mischance, and it fell upon the church, breaking seven of the rafters, so that the whole choir was uncovered and completely ruined; and the beams in many places pierced the pavement of the church, injuring many tombs; and they broke part of the steps of the high altar, which were shattered in such a way that it seemed almost incredible: a loss of more than 20 thousand florins. It was considered a bad omen, signifying that these princes and lords, instead of reconciling the Church of Christ and amplifying it, ruin it by their ambitions. Where there ought to be the union of all Christians against the unbelievers, and the will to die for the faith of Christ, at present they only think of shedding the blood of Christ, showing no pity for the poor, afflicted and lacerated people of unhappy Italy. Glory and praise be unto God for ever!

26th July. We heard that the King of France was again levying a large number of troops, and that he had imposed a tax of 2 millions of florins on his subjects, including the religious orders. He was making a great effort.

28th July. We heard that the Spaniards had come to blows with the papal soldiers, and that the viceroy had fled, and that they had burnt his tent. It seemed as if the Lord were aiding Florence, for all those who had it in their minds to do us harm were deprived of their strength; as has been seen several times. The Spaniards felt very downhearted.

21st August. We heard that the troops of the Church and of Spain were coming against Florence; and as the fear grew, people began to flee from the districts of Barberino and the Val di Marina, coming to the gates of Florence; all Sunday there was such a throng of carts, and mules, and cattle, that a vote of 50 thousand florins was passed in the *Palagio* for our defence. But so far our territory had not been touched.

23rd August. The *Signoria* published a proclamation that anyone who slew a certain Ramazzotto da Bruscoli would receive a reward of 2 thousand ducats, and anyone who delivered him alive into their hands would receive 3 thousand; and that if the capturer were under a sentence, the sentence should be remitted, and he could also free two others; and likewise he who slew him could free two others, of his choosing, except prisoners of state.[1]

During these few days the whole of the plain of Prato was deserted, so that the gates of San Gallo, Faenza, the Prato and San Friano were blocked to such a degree that there was a row of carts more than a mile long waiting to be able to enter, and it was necessary to let almost everything pass through without paying duty, unless there were some loads of corn, and wine, and oil. Carts of flax and locked chests passed through, and nothing was looked at, and nothing was stopped. The poor women and children were laden with their scanty possessions; anyone who saw them could not help feeling moved and forced to weep. It was voted that flour should not be taxed.

24th August. The incursion had not yet reached Barberino, but we heard that the enemy were doing all kinds of damage.

At this time we heard that there had been such a terrible hailstorm in Rome, on the day of Our Lady in the middle of August (the Assumption), that it became as dark as night, and many animals were killed; and it also struck on to a statue of Our Lady, but did not leave any traces, although other statues were spoilt. The hailstones were as large as eggs.

25th August. It was decreed that Our Lady of Santa Maria Impruneta should be brought here.[2]

During these days men-at-arms and foot-soldiers, as many as presented themselves, were levied in great numbers, and we prepared for everything; more care being taken for Prato than elsewhere, no men at all being sent into the

[1] See, with regard to this proclamation, *Il Sacco di Prato e il Ritorno de' Medici in Firenze, in MDXII.*, published by *Cesare Guasti*, Bologna, Romagnoli, 1880, in two volumes. The second of these volumes consists entirely of documents, and by comparing them with the records of Landucci, we can establish the correctness of the latter.

[2] It was not brought, however, till the 26th September, because, on the 30th August, the *Signori* wrote to Andrea Bondelmonte, parish priest of Santa Maria Impruneta: "On account of the turbulence caused by these sinister times, we do not wish you to let or allow the venerated *Nostra Donna* to be moved, until you hear further from the most exalted *Signoria*. We wish her to come at a quieter and more tranquil time, in order that we may be able to honour her more splendidly. Act in accordance with our instructions." This whole letter is published in the *Sacco di Prato*, already quoted, tom. ii., p. 131.

Mugello; and the enemy took the Scarperia and the Borgo,[1] and did not do much harm in the Mugello, but demanded provisions.

26th August. Ambassadors came here from the viceroy, who requested three things of the *Signoria*: first, that we should enter the League; secondly, that we should let the Medici return to Florence; thirdly, that the *Gonfaloniere* should resign his office and return to his house.

27th August. Six Spanish prisoners were brought into Florence, who had been captured by our soldiers in the Mugello. And all this time the country round was being deserted in every direction, but the fear of the peasants was not so great when they saw how the citizens were making preparations, and the poor creatures took heart, for in reality it seemed to intelligent people as if there were no such need for fear; on the contrary, it was rather for the enemy to fear, because if they came down into these plains, they would fare badly. This was the opinion of every intelligent person. We had levied so many battalions of militia, and all the men-at-arms were eager to encounter the enemy, for the sake of gain, and had a mind to slay everyone. Our troops now numbered 17 thousand men, counting the militia and the men-at-arms together.

That day the enemy came down and took Campi without resistance, and having entered it, they slew a band of men and stole everything that they could carry, burning flax and many things and taking away many prisoners, although they lost four men and had some wounded. And the reason that they gained the place so quickly was that some of the inhabitants had opened one of the gates in order to go away, but did not succeed, all being captured, and then the enemy entered, and having taken everything that they wanted, left again and went off in the direction of Prato.

29th August (the day of *San Giovanni Battista*[2]). At about 18 in the afternoon (2 p.m.), the Spaniards took Prato by bombardment and assault. That they should have taken such a strongly fortified place in one day was marvellous, because there were 4 thousand soldiers in it, and so many peasants of the district who had taken refuge there with their property and their wives and children, having come

---
[1] A castle in the Mugello.
[2] Meaning the day of the beheading of St. John the Baptist.

from all the country round, that there was a great collection of wealth; and yet they all became as timid as mice, and could not hold out for a single day. There were two reasons that those outside were so fierce; one was that they had been nearly starving for two days; and the second that they knew there was a store of wealth in the place; and a still more powerful reason for their success was that we did not send from here the help which we might have done. I do not know whose negligence it was, but I saw the soldiers standing about at the gates, and no one attempted to send them away, although we heard the report of the cannon all the time, which made many marvel at this delay. Therefore these cruel miscreants and infidels entered the place and slew everyone whom they encountered; not content with having such a large booty, they spared hardly anyone's life, and the few that remained they took and placed a ransom upon them, on rich and poor alike, and anyone who was unable to pay they tortured in the most disgraceful and abominable ways. They sacked the monasteries, and they slaughtered women and children with every sort of cruelty and infamy. It was said that 5 thousand persons were killed. It seemed as if it were by divine permission that our chief citizens were so dilatory; having 18 thousand soldiers, a number which exceeded theirs, we had already hindered them from obtaining provisions, so that they could not have held out more than two or three days without dying of hunger, and they would all have been slain or else taken prisoner in endeavouring to flee. It had not been at all prudent of them sending such a quantity of men and munitions to Prato; it was making almost impossible haste, to have taken Campi on the 27th and Prato on the 29th. It happened, however, on account of our sins. And now the traitors are so well-furnished with provisions that they can stay there as long as they wish, and have all become rich with so much booty; and we, meanwhile, have lost all hope of conquering the Pistolese in any way.

30th August. The Pistolese took the keys of the city to the Spanish camp, and made an agreement with them; and Pescia did likewise; so that the *Signoria* sent two of our citizens to the viceroy to make an agreement, and after going backwards and forwards for some time, the following terms were stated: first, we were to join the League, and pay 60 thousand florins; secondly, the

Gonfaloniere, who had been appointed for life, was to go back to his house; thirdly, we were to reinstate the Medici.

31st August. The ambassadors returned, having consented to everything; and on arriving here, they went to the *Palagio* at about 18 in the afternoon (2 p.m.), and dismissed the said *Gonfaloniere*, Piero Soderini, pacifically and with his own consent, as he said that he did not wish to be a hindrance to the people, and was contented with whatever was the will of God.

Therefore, we remained without a *Gonfaloniere*; and later he left the city. And many other citizens left likewise, some going to Siena, some here and some there, for greater security.

1st September. Giuliano de' Medici entered Florence, and the new *Signoria* entered the *Palagio* without a *Gonfaloniere*; all the citizens who considered themselves friends of the Medici, assembled at the door of the *Palagio* and in the Piazza, all fully armed, and barred every way into the Piazza. The viceroy, after all, was not satisfied with the first agreement, and there were many disputes, he now demanding 120 thousand florins in three payments: and still he did not go away, but insisted on demanding besides the ransoms of the unfortunate Pratesi whom they held captive and treated most cruelly and infamously. It was not enough that they had killed the greater number of them, and robbed them of everything; they also demanded ransom for those who remained alive.

3rd September. A thunderbolt fell on the Palazzo degli Strozzi here, and killed a master-builder, who had built this palace, and now he had come to give a look at something, and was so unfortunate, after having been in danger so often whilst building it, to die in this way when the danger seemed over; but so it pleased God. He was a good man.[1]

During these days certain Spaniards came from Prato

---

[1] A friend wrote from Florence on the same day to Alfonso and Lorenzo the sons of Filippo Strozzi, who were at Lucca: "This morning a thunderbolt fell on your house, at the corner towards the Piazza, and killed Mariotto da Balatro, the builder, who was working on the roof, and then it went down a chimney, and into the ground at the base, leaving many traces. I am sorry for the death of that poor man; and also for the omen; may God be gracious and spare the rest." This letter is published in the before-mentioned *Sacco di Prato*, tom. ii., p. 176.

to sell their booty; and amongst others one had a cartload of clothes; when he had almost reached the Piazza de' Signori, the populace seized all the clothes, and it was with difficulty that he escaped with his life. In several places they were taken and killed; one instance of this occurred at the *Servi*, when a priest recognised a Spaniard who had just appeared there as the man who had slain his father at Prato, and caused him to be murdered near the church; another had his hand cut off near the *Croce al Trebbio*, the people wanting to murder three of them who were together; and they only managed to escape by getting through the houses.

4th September. One was murdered in the Piazza di Madonna, and then dragged past Santa Maria Novella and along the Via de' Fossi and finally thrown into the Arno. It became necessary to publish proclamations threatening with the gallows all those who should do the Spaniards any injury or annoy and impede them in any way. Certain ignorant persons are always the cause of our foes becoming enraged and exasperated, to our misfortune; for when those at Prato heard of it, they tortured the wretched prisoners who were in their hands, and they did not choose to leave, but strove to do all the harm possible to the unfortunate country round Prato; wherever they went, they carried away what they could, and set fire to the rest.[1]

At this time nearly all our battalions left Florence; and a new *Gonfaloniere* had not yet been elected; according to what was said, the citizens were not quite agreed as to the manner of government. But the most important thing was to collect the money which had been promised, as the Spaniards would not leave Prato without it, and the cardinal did not come here. Amongst other cruelties committed by these miscreants, was their placing impossible ransoms

[1] The Florentine representatives with the viceroy wrote from Prato on the 1st September to the *Signoria*, on the request of the *Maestri del campo* (Commissariat-officers), "that it would be well that they should give a safe-conduct to anyone who wished to come to Florence or to other places to sell their booty within the term of four to six days, because if this were denied them and they were forced when the camp was raised to leave their possessions behind, they would burn everything and probably the town also." Therefore, on the 4th the "Ten" themselves, displeased at the unfitting things that had happened, gave repeated orders to their commissaries encamped outside the *Porta al Prato* at Florence to remedy this. See the quoted volume of the *Sacco di Prato*, etc., p. 158 and p. 177.

upon those prisoners whom they had not killed, and continually torturing them. This was far worse than slaying them in hot blood; to go on sacking the place all the time they stayed there, and to take more prisoners and ask ransoms from those whom they had already robbed of everything. But I think that the viceroy and all those who had the power to hinder this, will meet with their deserts; and it ought to have been put in the agreement that the sacking should cease, and chiefly that such treatment of the prisoners should not go on.

6th September. A decree was passed by the *Signori* and *Collegi*, and by the "Eighty," that the Great Council should be limited.[1]

7th September. This decree was passed in the Great Council.

8th September. The Council passed a decree that a *Gonfaloniere* should be elected for 14 months; who was Giovan Battista Ridolfi.[2]

11th September. A Spaniard was killed in the Piazza of Santa Maria Novella, and was dragged to the Arno, and they were continually being pursued; some stole their horses, and others their money. Proclamations were of no use, and these things brought more evil upon us.

12th September. The money was taken to the Spaniards. On this day there passed perhaps 20 of them on their way to Rome; and, in their fear, they asked the *Signori* for the escort of a trumpeter; it was of no avail, however, for they were assaulted beyond San Casciano in the direction of Rome, and killed and plundered. It was said that they had several thousand florins and also letters of exchange for Spain representing money that they were sending there, and it was said that those who assaulted them wore masks

[1] This decree established the method of election the pay, and the duties of the *Gonfaloniere della Giustizia*, as well of the *Arroti* (members of the "Eighty") in the Council of the *Ottanta* as also of the *Signori* and their notary, and of the *Dieci della Libertà e Pace*, etc. In the *Protocollo* (in the *Archivio di Stato di Firenze*), we read at the end of this decree: *Dicta provisio non venit in usum quo ad multa, et Vexillifer factus intra breve tempus renuntiavit propter parlamentum factum de mense septembris* 1512 *propter familiam de Medicis revocatam*.

[2] According to the above-quoted decree the *Gonfaloniere* was to remain in office for one year; only the first to be elected was to continue in office till the end of October 1513. This is the reason that it is here said that he was elected for fourteen months.

and were not recognised. During this time the Spaniards at Prato and everywhere continued their depredations, taking prisoners and not observing any agreement or league; selling everything that they had stolen from Prato and Campi — all the corn and cereals and household goods, and whatever else they could — and saying that they would burn whatever they could not take away with them.

16th September (Thursday). At about 19 in the afternoon (3 p.m.), Giuliano de' Medici and all his men went into the *Palagio* fully armed, and took possession of it, since there was no resistance. The *parlamento* (assembly in the Piazza) had to be summoned, and at about 21 in the evening (5 p.m.) the bell tolled and the *Signoria* came down on to the *ringhiera*, and read the articles, which were as follows: that 12 men were elected for each quarter who had the power to act for the city of Florence for one year, and might form and dissolve every office in the city. They made a proclamation that anyone who wished to come into the Piazza must do so unarmed; but nevertheless the Piazza was full of armed men, and all the streets and outlets from it were barred with men-at-arms, crying perpetually, *Palle*. The *Palagio* itself was also filled with armed men, even up to the bell-loft; but some of the people who had entered the Piazza voted that they were content with the *parlamento* and the new government. God be praised! Everyone ought to be content with what Divine Providence permits, because all states and jurisdictions are of the Lord, and if in these changes of government the people suffer some hardship, loss, costs, or discomfort, we must consider that it is on account of our sins and with the object of some greater good.

18th September. They began to dissolve the "Eight" who were at present in office, and to elect the *Capitani di Parte*, and elected others for the "Eight."[1] On this day the viceroy came to Florence with perhaps 50 horsemen, and went about to see the city and the churches, and he wished to go up in the cupola of Santa Maria del Fiore, to

[1] The *Capitani di Parte Guelfa* were then five, and only four of these new "Eight" were chosen for this office: Maniardo Cavalcanti, Giovan Francesco de' Nobili, Niccolò degli Albizzi, and Niccolò del Troscia: the first elected, Gherardo Paganelli, was not a member of the "Eight."

see it, and several citizens went with him, my son Benedetto among them. He left again the same day, returning to Prato, and gave orders for the army to set out.

19th September. The Spaniards left, and went to Calenzano, taking with them those prisoners who had not been able to ransom themselves; therefore our peasants who had taken refuge in Florence began to return home, although with some distrust. And the cardinal left here and went to visit the viceroy on his departure.

20th September. These men, more cruel than the devil, left Calenzano and Campi and everywhere else, and returned by the way they had come; they were quartered at Barberino, and many of the peasants now returned home with their scanty possessions.

21st September. They left Barberino, having burnt down houses and done every sort of damage, and we gave them several pieces of artillery.

22nd September. The first trestle of the roof of Santa Croce was drawn up, and being drawn up entire, a multitude of men had to be employed, as it was difficult and dangerous work.

24th September. The second trestle was drawn up.

26th September. The image of Our Lady of Santa Maria Impruneta came here, to celebrate the grace that had been granted us of our city not having been sacked; for we had been in great danger, with 18 thousand persons within the city, and as many without it, everything being in uncertainty all the time.[1]

On this day they added to the 48 *di balia* 12 more men. And to these 60 *di balia* they then added 50 men for each quarter of the town, making 260 citizens, who had full powers; and the proclamations were published in the joint names of the *Signori* and of the members of the *balia*.

2nd October. The Medici had their coats of arms repainted on their palace, at the Nunziata, and in many

[1] The letter written on the 24th of this month to the parish priest of the Impruneta by the *Signoria* begins as follows: "The Spanish army having left, by the grace of the omnipotent God and of His glorious Mother the Virgin Mary, and our city daily becoming better ordered, we give you notice that the *Signoria* together with their honourable *Collegi* have decreed, that early next Sunday morning, which will be the 26th day of the present month, the revered Tabernacle should be brought to the city," etc. (*Sacco di Prato*, vol. already quoted, p. 208).

places; and they caused the image of the *Gonfaloniere* to be removed from the Nunziata de' Servi.¹

5th October. A proclamation was made that whoever had property of the house of Medici was to notify it, on pain of the gallows; and many things were recovered.

13th October. The "Eight" sentenced Piero Soderini, former *Gonfaloniere*, elected for life, and now deposed, to be banished for five years to Raugia (Ragusa), with the provision that if he left this place he would be declared a rebel; they also banished his brothers for three years, one to Rome, one to Naples, and one to Milan, with the same penalty of being declared rebels if they should cross the boundaries set.

More members were added to the *balia*, making their number up to 500, for the decisions.

22nd October. There were lodged in the house of Giovanni Tornabuoni about six ambassadors, who were going to the Pope, from the Emperor, the King of Spain and the Venetians, and also from the dispossessed Duke of Milan, called *Il Moro*; one of them was a German bishop, who was going to Rome to be made cardinal.²

1st November. The new *Signoria* entered into office, and Filippo Buondelmonte was elected *Gonfaloniere* by the *balia*.

6th November. The Cardinal de' Medici left here and went to Bologna.

¹ It used to be the custom for the most illustrious persons of Florence, and also for foreigners, such as popes, cardinals, princes, military leaders, etc., to show their devotion by presenting to this temple their own portraits in wax, life-size, and clothed in costume. These stood on certain platforms made expressly for the purpose, but there being no longer sufficient room for all of them, the practice was begun, in 1448, of hanging them up with ropes from the ceiling of the church. When one of these images fell down, it portended misfortune to that person or some of his family. Out of political passion, the images of those hostile to the ruling party were taken away; and this instance of Soderini is one of these not uncommon cases.

² Matthias Lang, Bishop of Gurk, ambassador of the Emperor Maximilian. The Pope, who gave him a most gracious reception, sent his legate, the Cardinal de' Medici, to meet him, and receive him at Caffaggiolo. Upon leaving Florence, he lodged at Uliveto, the villa of the Chancellor Lorenzo Pucci, who paid him extraordinary honour; it is enough to say that his room was entirely hung with gold brocade. With him, besides the ambassadors mentioned, were also those of Siena and Lucca; and they were all treated magnificently. *Cambi*, who has left us the description of it, says that Pucci "for two meals" spent the sum of 1000 florins.

At this time it was said that the troops of the Pope and of the Venetians were pitching their camp before Ferrara; of the French nothing was said, nor did they come to succour Milan, although the forts were holding out for them.

4th November. Two of our citizens left as ambassadors to the Pope.[1]

On this day the roof of Santa Croce was finished, not completely as to the tiles, but with respect to the woodwork.

11th December. The above-mentioned bishop came to Florence, on his return from Rome. And it was said that he had been made cardinal, although he did not wear the hat. He lodged in the house of the Pucci; it was not yet true, however.[2]

12th December. He left, and had 30 thousand florins from us, for the League, and for peace with the Swiss.

At this time it was the pleasure of the new Government to spoil the hall of the Great Council, that is, the woodwork and all the beautiful things which had been made at a great cost, and so many beautiful hangings; and they built certain little rooms for the soldiers, making an entrance from the hall; which was a grief to the whole of Florence, not the change of the government, but the loss of this

---

[1] Jacopo do Giovanni Salviati and Matteo di Lorenzo Strozzi.

[2] It is the Bishop of Gurk (Matthias Lang) who is here spoken of, whose first visit to Florence was recorded above, on the 22nd October. Cardelli, in his *Vita dei Cardinali* (tom. iii., p. 359), and Coronelli, in his *Cronologia Universale* (p. 177), place the promotion of this bishop to the cardinalate under the date of 18th December, 1511. But against this there exists, in the first place, a letter of Antonio Strozzi, the Florentine representative in Rome, to the *Dieci di libertà*, on the 9th November, 1512 (*Archivio di Stato di Firenze, Lettere a' Dieci*, series 112, c. 225), in which he says that: "the Pope will give the hat to the Gurgense, but not to anyone else for the moment, and a friend has told me that only one hat has been arranged for"; and in the second place, a letter written by Lang himself, from Rome, to the *Signoria*, on the 26th November (same, c. 296), is signed *Mattheus, D.G.E.* (that is, *Dei gratia episcopus*), *Gurcensis, imperialis in Italia locums tenens generalis*. Finally, the *Diario* of Mons. di Paride de' Grassi, master of ceremonies at the pontifical court, states that the *creatio novi cardinalis Gurcensis, ac. publicatio et datio tituli*, only took place on the 24th November, 1512; adding that the Gurgense accepted this dignity, but did not wish to assume the insignia of it, in order that it might not seem as if he had intrigued for the sake of obtaining honours for himself, whilst he was the legate of the emperor, and his only interest was to represent him. All this, if I am not mistaken, shows that even in this quibble Landucci, as usual, is correct.

beautiful woodwork of such value. It was of great reputation, and it was an honour to the city to have such a beautiful residence. When an embassy came to visit the *Signoria*, its members were lost in admiration at what they saw on their entrance into such a magnificent place and into the presence of such an impressive council of citizens. But may all be to the praise and glory of God, and done according to His will.[1]

20th December. The election began in the *Palagio*[2]; and I also sent in my name, as some of my friends wished it, although it was not much to my liking; but only to act in the manner of the *Signori*.

19th January. The Cardinal de' Medici came to Florence from Bologna.

24th January. The "Eight" sentenced Martino dello Scarfa to be banished for five years from Florence, and to be fined 3 thousand florins, the half to be paid at once.[3] They also banished one Piero, a mace-bearer, for five years,

[1] The workmen of Santa Maria del Fiore had orders from the *Priori*, on the 22nd November, to consign to Baccio d'Agnolo, architect and master-builder, all the wood needed *pro sala dicti Palatii reactanda, que vocabatur Sala Consilii maioris*. And on the 31st December they ordered the chamberlain of the *Camera dell' Armi* to pay the said workmen for all the deal received or still to be received from the office, *pro conficiendis mansionibus custodiae salae novae* (*Libro di Deliberazioni, ad an.*).

[2] As is known, the *balìa* had already appointed, on the 21st September, the *arroti* to manage this election for all the magistracies and offices, and by subsequent decrees they made various provisions always with the same object. Worthy of note is that of the 19th December, which begins: "The Magci and Exsi Sigri and the other worthy citizens of the present *balìa*, thinking continually of ways in which they can benefit the citizens and provide that the honours of the city should not be withheld from anyone reasonably deserving of them, through some sinister machination," etc. This decree increased the power given to the 20 *accoppiatori*, ordaining that in the next general election, they should have the right of putting in the names of those citizens who had not been voted for, if at least two-thirds of their own body approved of them. (The *accoppiatori* were the election-officers who put the names in the bags, the 80 *arroti* had to be in attendance, and to declare the votes.)

[3] Martino di Francesco dello Scarfa was condemned to stay in the manors of Montelupo and Empoli, and the fine was reduced to only 1500 florins, if he should pay them within eight days of the notification, which he did. That his fault was hostility to the Medici is proved by the "Eight" saying that they pronounce the sentence *pro conservatione presentis optimi pacifici status et regiminis Popoli fiorentini, et pluribus aliis justis et rationabilibus causis moti.*

to Livorno, having deprived him of his office first, and put him to the rack; because he was supposed to have spoken ill of the government, and that is possible, for he was a foolish man, and apt to chatter thoughtlessly, criticising the citizens without intending any harm.

18th February. The beginning of a plot was discovered, and immediately at midnight about 14 young citizens of the chief families were arrested, some of the Capponi, Strozzi, Nobili, Valori, Boscoli, and others.[1]

19th February. The "Eight" made a proclamation that everyone should declare what arms he had, before the evening of the 20th instant, under pain of a fine of 100 florins; and the declarations were made on the 20th. And on this latter day it was said that the Pope was dead.

22nd February. The Cardinal de' Medici went to Rome in great haste; and here the bells were tolled at the *nona* [2] for the Pope's death. He had died on Sunday, the 20th.

This night they beheaded two of those who had been arrested for plotting against the government, one being Agostino Capponi and the other a young de' Boscoli, in the *Palagio del Capitano*; and besides, they sentenced Niccolò Valori to be imprisoned at Volterra for two years, and then banished for life to Città di Castello.[3]

4th March. The cardinals entered into conclave to elect the Pope.

11th March. Two hours before dawn a rumour arose in Florence that the Cardinal de' Medici was Pope; and there was much bell-ringing, and bonfires were lighted in many

---

[1] Eighteen or twenty were indicted as conspirators against the house of Medici for having wished to liberate the city and assassinate Giuliano and Lorenzo and Messer Giulio. The conspiracy was discovered by a paper being picked up on which their names were written, and which had fallen from the pocket of Piero Antoni Boscoli, who together with Agostino Capponi was thought to be at the head of the plot. On the 4th April, 1513, the *balìa* by order of the Pope, besides releasing Soderini, Scarfa, and others from their penalties, also released those condemned for this conspiracy: that is, Niccolò Valori, Giovanni Folchi, Ubertino Bonciani, Francesco Serragli, Pandolfo Biliotti, Duccino Adimari, and Giovanni Bartolommeo. As to Capponi and Boscoli, who were already executed, it was declared on the 20th of the same April that their property was free from confiscation.

[2] The fifth canonical hour, a little before noon.

[3] Luca di Simone della Robbia wrote the *Narrazione del caso di Pietro Paolo Boscoli e di Agostino Capponi*, which was published in tom. i. of the *Archivio Storico Italiano*.

parts of the city, with such joy and commotion, and such persistent cries of *Palle!* that it made everyone get up, even the women, and go to the windows; it began at 8 in the morning (4 a.m.), by someone going about crying through the city that he had been elected; nevertheless no news had come, for on inquiring at the *Palagio de' Signori* and the palace of the Medici, we were told that there was no news yet. It was quite impossible, however, to do anything but cry *Palle!* the whole day, although nothing was known. It seemed as if the people guessed what had happened, in the most marvellous way; for it is a true proverb which says: *Vox popoli, vox Dei*; but to intelligent people it looked rather foolish to be ringing the bells and making bonfires before we knew the truth.

At 2 o'clock that Friday night (10 p.m.) the news came, and it was true that the Cardinal de' Medici had been elected Pope, with the name of Lione X. If there had been bonfires and rejoicings before, they were redoubled now, and in a different spirit; innumerable bundles of brushwood, great branches, baskets, barrels, and whatever each poor man chanced to have in his house; all the smallest streets of the city did their part, without stint and the people not yet being content, ran all over Florence to pull down the wooden roofs above the shops and everywhere, burning up everything. They put the whole city in great danger, and if the "Eight" had not made a proclamation that no more roofs were to be pulled down and that the *Piagnoni*[1] were no longer to be insulted, on pain of the gallows, even the tiled roofs would have been destroyed and the shops looted. And this nuisance lasted all Friday and Saturday, bonfires continuing, and illuminations on the *Palagio*, up on the cupola, on the gates, and everywhere, with so much firing of cannon and continual cries of *Palle! Papa Lione!* that it seemed as if the city were upside-down, and anyone who had seen it from overhead would have said: "Florence is burning down the whole city," for there was such a tumult of shouting, and fires, and smoke, and reports of the cannon, large and small; and on Sunday the same, and on Monday worse than ever. They placed up on the gallery behind the parapets of the *Palagio*, a gilt malmsey cask at each corner, full of firewood and other stuff to burn, and also on the *ringhiera* and in the Piazza many gilt casks

[1] See note to 5th July, 1498.

were burnt, accompanied by the continual sound of the spingards (small guns). It was really incredible what a number of fires there were in the city; every single person had one at his door. And in addition to this, they made several triumphal cars,[1] and every evening set light to one in front of the house of the Medici in their honour; one was of discord, war, and fear, whilst another was of peace, and this latter they did not burn, as if to express that there was an end of all passions, and peace remained triumphant.

18th March (Friday). Our Lady of Santa Maria Impruneta was brought into Florence, and a great procession was made in her honour; she received nine new mantles, seven of them being of gold brocade from the *Signoria* and the Medici; and many other gifts, more than any other time.[2]

21st March. A *volta* (vaulted cellar for a restaurant) that they were making in the *Mercato Vecchio* towards the Column was finished roofing in; it had been the work of some months to dig it out, as they had found some old foundations very difficult to remove. And during this work, through want of precaution, many persons fell in at night, some breaking their arm and some their thigh, and it was even said that some were killed. Those who were making it had not much consideration.

1513. 8th April. In the night our archbishop died, who was a son of Guglielmo de' Pazzi; and on the 12th there was a great funeral in Santa Maria del Fiore, and he is buried there in the centre of the church. May God be merciful to him![3]

During these days we received a copy of the 30 articles which the cardinals had drawn up when they were in conclave before they elected the Pope, and which the Pope who should be elected was obliged to observe, on his oath, confirming them before they were published: amongst other articles were the following:

1. That he should not be able to make more than two cardinals of his kindred when the number was less than 24,

[1] These triumphal cars had allegorical figures and other representations upon them. [Trans.]
[2] This time the tabernacle was carried in procession to render solemn thanks to God for a Florentine having been elected Pope (*Casotti*, already quoted, p. 146).
[3] *Cambi* says of him that "he was a great and good man."

a majority of two-thirds of the cardinals always being required.

2. That he should be obliged to call together an assembly of Christians to set the Holy Church in order, and to take thought how to proceed against the unbelievers, and to read these articles twice a year in the Assembly.

3. That he could not remove his court from Rome to another part of Italy without the consent of half the number of the cardinals, and could not remove it out of Italy without the consent of two-thirds of them.

It had not rained for months, but now it snowed, and for some time was as cold as January, many people dying: they died in a few days, and one did not know of what complaint.

. . . April. Pope Lione was crowned at Rome, with much ceremony and great magnificence and display.

17th April. We heard that Messer Giulio de' Medici was made Archbishop of Florence, and there were great rejoicings all through the city, so that the houses at the back of the archbishop's palace, towards San Giovanni, caught fire; some bundles of firewood which a baker kept in a shop under the arches having caught fire first.

This same day Giuliano de' Medici, brother of the Pope, went to Rome to visit him.

17th May. Some of our citizens went to Rome as ambassadors to the Pope; they went in fine array, they themselves and their horses being magnificently accoutred, accompanied by many young men in divers costumes, and with 50 baggage-mules in their train.

28th May. We heard that the King of France had taken Genoa by assault.

9th June. We heard that the King of France had been defeated by the Swiss on the way to Milan.

On this day we heard also that the Pope had made three cardinals: Messer Giulio, of his own house, whom he had first made Archbishop of Florence; secondly, Messer Lorenzo Pucci; and thirdly, a son of Franceschetto, a relative of his,[1] and a brother of Ser Piero of Bibbiena.[2] It was said besides that he had made four Florentine knights;

---

[1] Innocenzio Cibo, son of Maddalena, the Pope's sister.
[2] Bernardo of Bibbiena, a servant and protégé of the Medici, who had been secretary of this same Pope when he was a cardinal, and was afterwards his treasurer.

but it was only two, Filippo Buondelmonti and Luigi della Stufa.¹

24th June. The *festa* of San Giovanni was kept.

25th June. A wooden castle was made in the *Piazza de' Signori*, and a mock-fight was held there, with lances and divers weapons, and with unbaked bricks, all the combatants being without armour; there were 100 men inside it, and 300 outside; and they fought in such a brutal way that some of the assailants were so injured by these bricks that a number of them had to go to the hospital, where some of them died. And, moreover, a platform fell in, and two women and one man were killed, on the same occasion.²

26th June. A citizen threw himself into the Arno from the *Ponte a Rubiconte* and drowned himself, wishing to commit suicide. And the same day another man threw himself into a well, but he was seen, and was taken out before he drowned.

There was also a bull-hunt in the *Piazza de' Signori*, and the three bulls did much damage, wounding several men in such a way that they had to go to Santa Maria Nuova (Hospital). And two of these bulls got out of the enclosure, one running along the *Corso* as far as San Giovanni, and the other as far as the *Piazza del Grano*, but they did not injure anyone, although the streets were crowded with people; the men ran after them, and finished killing them.

29th June. Messer Luigi della Stufa, who had been

---

¹ The Pope, writes *Cambi*, "made two (of these Florentine ambassadors) knights. He would have made more, but on account of avarice the citizens refused; for at this time avarice was at its height; greater than it had ever been up till this day; so that in Florence there only remained one Knight of the Gold Spurs, Messer Piero di Francesco Alamanni, seventy years of age."

² *Cambi* calls it a *festa diabolica e tutta bestiale* (a diabolical and quite brutal fête). Inside the castle, which was more than 80 *braccia* in circumference, were "certain ruffians, men of bad character, and outside were 400 soldiers of our territory; and in fact, a number of those outside were injured, and hardly any of those inside." The soldiers who were in the great hall of the Council "made a platform, jutting out over the door of the *Bargello* (who still lived here, and not in the *Palazzo del Podestà* as Polidori says in his notes on the *Relazione* of Della Robbia already quoted)," so as to enable two courtesans to see, and a plank of this platform broke and fell in with the two women, coming on the top of two brothers who were underneath, looking at the spectacle, and all four were killed.

knighted by the Pope, came to Florence, and he was escorted into the city with due honour.

22nd July. Messer Filippo Buondelmonti, who had also been knighted by the Pope at Rome, came to Florence, and the *Signoria* and the *Parte Guelfa* gave him the banners, and likewise to Messer Luigi.[1]

26th July. A thunderbolt fell at Bellosguardo, and killed a serving-man of Francesco Girolami, who was following his master on horseback; and Francesco was half-stunned, but only the servant died.

10th August. Lorenzo son of Piero de' Medici returned to Florence.

14th August. The new archbishop, Messer Giulio, who was a cardinal, came to Florence.

15th August. He heard mass in Santa Maria del Fiore and gave a plenary indulgence to all who attended this mass.

18th September. Francesco del Pugliese was banished for 10 years, not being able to approach within two miles of Florence, for having used some disrespectful words about the house of Medici.[2]

27th September. The *Signoria* commanded that this day should be kept like a Sunday, and so it was done, not a shop being opened, out of reverence for San Cosimo and San Damiano, and a procession was made.[3] On this day an image of Pope Lione was placed in the Pastorem; there was an inscription upon it, saying: *"Pastorem ut me facisti—* give me grace that I may vanquish war with peace, and that I may convert the Turks to the Faith."

7th October. The *Signoria* made a decree that the hospital of Santa Maria Nuova should not be taxed.[4]

[1] *Cambi* describes in detail the ceremony of the entrance and the reception, etc., of these knights, carried out with all the forms of ancient custom.

[2] The sentence is dated the 3rd December, and had to be complied with within twenty days. The Medici are not mentioned in the document, but that it was given on their account can be easily seen when we read: *Actentis quibusdam erroribus et inconvenientibus factis et commissis in vilipendium et dedecus presentis pacifici Status*, etc.

[3] All this was decided *actentis et consideratis innumerabilibus et gratiis ab omnipotenti Deo huic inclite civitati Florentie et collatis et que cotidie conferuntur ; demum nova creatione quatuor Cardinalium florentinorum ab apostolica Sede creatorum*, etc. (*Registro di Deliberazioni dei Signori e Collegi, ad an.*)

[4] The decree is of the *Balia* (*Reg.* quoted, c. 159) and dated the 5th October. It was made having regard to the great services of this hospital to the city; so that we read in the preamble the following

12th October. The *Signoria* of Florence recovered the lordship of Pietrasanta and of Mutrone, and on this day took them over. God be praised!¹

In these days we heard that the Spaniards had defeated the Venetians, and were making incursions everywhere, taking much booty. They (the Venetians) must remember when they laughed at the Florentines, and when they encamped before Bibbiena, and lent a hand to take Pisa from us, always encouraging the Pisans to hold out against the Florentines; now it is the reverse: they must expect to be paid back in their own coin.

18th October. We heard that the King of Portugal had sent his submission to the Pope, and had presented him with the following things: a Pope made of sugar, with twelve cardinals all of sugar, life-size; 300 torches of sugar, each three *braccia* long; 100 chests of sugar; and many chests of delicate spices, cinnamon, cloves, and other things; and a white horse of surpassing beauty; he also sent him a Moor, one of those from Calicut (Calcutta), about four *braccia* high, with many jewels in his ears and all over his garments.

20th October. A Spaniard came to Florence, who had with him a boy of about thirteen, a kind of monstrosity, whom he went round showing everywhere, gaining much money. Instead of being only one boy, there were two, attached to one another in an extraordinary way. . . . The boys did not seem greatly troubled.

At this time, one of the girders in the great hall over the *Dogana* was broken, because they had built above it.

12th December. A *frate* died at Santa Croce in Florence, who had been preaching for several days in that church, predicting many tribulations for the city, and all the people flocked to his sermons, because he was renowned and was considered a saint. He was a very abject little man, wearing

words: "And wishing to confess the truth, one can absolutely affirm these to have been and to be (i.e. the hospitals of Santa Maria Nuova and of the Innocenti) two firm and solid pillars of preservation of this great Republic and its liberty." Therefore all those "privileges, benefices, emoluments, immunities, and exemptions" enjoyed by the hospital of the Innocenti were also conceded to the said hospital of Santa Maria Nuova.

¹ The Lucchesi restored these two places to the Florentines in consequence of a sentence of the Pope, in which both parties, who at first had taken up arms, came to a compromise in their disputes.

only a short gown reaching to his knees and in a pitiable state. Anyone who saw him marvelled that he could live like that through the cold weather. He was held in great veneration, and was buried in *Santa Croce*; but, after a few days, his relatives came from Montepulciano and carried his body away.[1]

15th January. We heard that the Queen of France was dead.

17th January. One of the Martegli, a man of 50 years of age, who was seriously ill, threw himself into a well, and was drowned. Probably it was in desperation at his sufferings.

On the same day a nun threw herself from a high roof, and was killed on the spot; this was in the convent of Sant' Orsola.[2]

In these days we heard that there was a peasant's daughter, in the district of Arezzo, who went to a well not far from her home, where it was said Our Lady appeared to her, not only once, but many times; so that the bishop went there with several others and she showed them a sign: pointing to a star in the sky at midday. I record this because it was much spoken of.

1514. 19th June. A joust was proclaimed for San Giovanni.

21st June. A fine display was made.[3]

22nd June. There was a great procession.

[1] Jacopo Pitti writes: "At this time, twelve *frati* (formerly in a monastery) joined one another to lead a life of extreme poverty together, going through Italy, each to the province assigned to him, preaching and predicting things to come. One of these, Fra Francesco of Montepulciano, who was quite young, appeared at Santa Croce in Florence; severely reprehending vice, and affirming that God would punish Italy, and especially Florence and Rome; his sermons being so terrible that the congregation burst into cries of *Misericordia* (Mercy), amidst floods of tears. He descended from the pulpit breathless and exhausted, and caught a complaint of the lungs which soon killed him."

[2] The convent of Sant' Orsola was founded 1307, and finished building 1309, by Benedictine nuns; but in 1435 Pope Eugenius IV. transferred them to the convent of Sant' Agata, and gave the church, convent and garden of Sant' Orsola to some Franciscan Sisters from Perugia. This convent was one of those suppressed in the end of the eighteenth century, and became first a tobacco factory, and later a salt factory. It was in the Via dell' Acqua. [Trans.]

[3] The customary display of the goldsmiths, silk-mercers, etc.

23rd June. Eight *'dfici*¹ were made (platforms on wheels with figures on them), and the same number in the evening, representing the triumph of Camillus, in several acts—how he had taken many prisoners — and the spoils — and the implements of battle—and rich garments and silver; and behind the triumph of Camillus came men singing, and behind them, again, four squadrons of men-at-arms, fully armed, with their lances in their hands; it was a magnificent thing!

24th June. The usual *festa* took place; the running of the *palio*, and then the *girandoles* in the evening (set pieces of fireworks), and after these *girandoles* had burnt out, the people burnt all the old tapers which had been offered for San Giovanni, so as to make a change and have a grander show.²

25th June. There was a hunt in the *Piazza de' Signori*: two lions, and bears, leopards, bulls, buffaloes, stags, and many other wild animals of various kinds, and horses; the lions were brought in after the rest, and chiefly the one that came first did nothing, on account of the great tumult of the crowd; except that certain big dogs approaching him, he seized one with his paw and dropped it dead on the ground, and a second the same, without taking any notice of the other wild beasts; when he was not molested, he stood quite still, and then went away further on. They had made a tortoise and a porcupine, inside of which were men who made them move along on wheels all over the Piazza, and kept thrusting at the animals with their lances. This hunt was thought so much of, that the number of wooden platforms and enclosures made in the Piazza was a thing never before seen, the cost of bringing the timber and of erecting these stands being very great; it seemed incredible that any city in the world could have such a mass of timber. One carpenter paid 40 gold florins

---

¹ See note to 5th July, 1478.
² The *palii* of the cities and towns, and the tapers decorated with painted paper, given by the castles of the Pisan country district and of the Valdiniele, were first presented in the *Piazza de' Signori*, and afterwards went to San Giovanni. *Cambi* writes that this year "these large and beautiful tapers, decorated with painted paper, were kept in the Piazza by the directors of the festivities instead of going to be offered at the church of San Giovanni, with the idea of burning them in the evening, but they were stolen by the children and the populace."

for the permission to put up a platform against one of these houses, and there were people who paid three or four *grossoni* (*grossone* = about ⅓ of a florin) for a place on the stands. All the stands and enclosures were crowded, as also the windows and the roofs, such a concourse of people never having been known, for numbers of strangers had come from many different parts. Four cardinals [1] had come from Rome disguised, and many Romans accompanied by a quantity of horsemen. At the end of the evening it was found that many men had been injured and about three killed in fighting with the wild beasts; one had been killed by a buffalo. They had made a beautiful large fountain in the middle of the Piazza, which threw the water up in four jets, and round this fountain was a wood of verdure, with certain dens very convenient for the animals to hide in, and low troughs full of water round the fountain, for them to be able to drink. Everything had been very well arranged, except that someone without the fear of God did an abominable thing in this Piazza, in the presence of 40 thousand women and girls, putting a mare into an enclosure together with the horses; which much displeased decent and well-behaved people, and I believe that it displeased even the ill-behaved people.[2] Finally the lions made no more attacks, becoming cowed by the immense tumult of the people. I remember another time when the same sort of hunt was made, more than 60 years ago, two lions also being brought in; and in the first attack one of them threw himself upon a horse, and caught hold of him in the soft part of his body, and the powerful horse, being terrified, dragged him from the *Mercatantia* [3] to the middle of the Piazza; the lion got nothing but the mouthful of skin that was torn off; and this fact caused such a tumult, that the said lion was frightened and went and sat in a corner, and neither he nor the second one would make

[1] The cardinals, who came in disguise, as Landucci says, to see this *festa*, were six, according to *Pitti* and *Cambi*. The latter names some of them, saying that the Pope's nephew (Cibo) was there, the Sienese Cardinal, a Venetian, and Il Bibbiena (Bernardo Dovizi); and "they all went out clothed in black, like Spaniards, with swords at their sides, and their faces concealed."

[2] *Cambi* also records the bad impression made by this spectacle.

[3] The residence of the Tribunal of the Merchants' Guild was in that palace in the *Piazza de' Signori* which is at the corner of the Via de' Gondi, on which are still to be seen the sculptured arms of the twenty-one guilds of Florence.

another attack. Which shows that there cannot be a display amidst the tumult of the people. That earlier hunt had been held on the occasion of the Duke of Milan coming to Florence.

26th June (Monday). There was a joust in the Piazza di Santa Croce, there being about sixteen jousters, all soldiers, and they tilted for two prizes, a *palio* of gold brocade and one of silver brocade.

27th June. The jousting was finished, and the prizes given. And one of the jousters had received such a blow that he died in three or four hours. Note that it was much more marvellous having made platforms in the Piazza di Santa Croce when those in the Piazza de' Signori were still standing. The two squares were furnished at the same time, making one feel astounded at the quantity of timber.

And because the lions had not made the display that was expected of them in the Piazza, it was decided to put a large bear among the lions, but they remained several days without doing him any harm; then suddenly one of the largest male lions seized the bear by the throat and would have finished him off, if an incredible thing had not happened, as we were told by those present; namely, a lioness, watching the quarrel, went to the help of the bear, and bit the lion so severely that he let go. And after this they remained for some time together, without attacking each other; until the bear grew so large that the lions were glad to keep their distance.

3rd July. At midday, there was such a tempest of wind at Dicomano that it exceeded everything ever heard of; it began in the Valdisieve near the Ruffina, passed over Capraia, and Vico, and the church of San Jacopo at Frascole, and my place at Vegna, and then over Dicomano and the Island. Upon reaching Vico and the said church, it uprooted many walnut-trees, olive-trees, and oaks, and took off nearly the whole roof of the church; and upon reaching my place, it uprooted four enormously large oaks, two very large chestnut-trees, and many other trees, twisting them like withies; it also uprooted a large walnut-tree, and a cherry-tree, and many plums and pears and other fruit-trees, taking off the roof of a dovecote, and breaking many branches of the oaks and elms, and like a miracle, passed on its way high above. In our alder-copse it had twisted the trees like withies, which it should not have been able to do, considering that it came from the Valdisieve. At Poggio Marino it did great damage.

...December. It was the pleasure of our citizens to allow the Jews to return to Florence and lend money as before. Many men disapproved of this.[1]

At this time the King of France took for his wife a sister of the King of England; and he had greatly consolidated his kingdom. Everyone considered that being so powerful he could take possession of Italy when he chose.

9th January. We heard that the King of France was dead. How short a time his happiness lasted! He had been wedded about a month. One sees what the happiness of this mortal life is worth, and how soon it is destroyed. Ah, you men of France, how many thoughts prove vain when one least expects it!

Giuliano de' Medici now went to fetch the wife whom he had chosen, a daughter of the Duke of Savoy.[2]

11th February. The vicar of the Archbishop of Florence having summoned a certain *frate* of San Felice in Piazza,[3] and examined him as to certain errors of which he had been guilty, sent him this day into the pulpit at Santa Maria del Fiore, and his accusation having been read, he was made to abjure his errors and ask pardon of God and the people. There was such a crowd, that he was in danger of being stoned; an uproar burst out several times, and it was necessary to send for the *Bargello* and a number of his men armed with swords, before it was possible to take him back to the episcopal palace.

15th March. It snowed in the night and was so cold that all the almonds, which were already of a good size, were

[1] In a series of minutes and copies of documents and records concerning the Jewish moneylenders in the Florentine dominion, which are preserved in the *Archivio di Stato di Firenze*, c. 179, we read the following record: "On the 25th September, 1514, the Jews here inscribed were brought in by the *Ufficiali del Monte* (Officials of the Exchequer), with the object of lending money in Florence, for 10 years, to begin from the 1st December, 1514, with a tax of 150 florins for each bank, and for three or more 300 florins: Agnolo d'Ambra of Fano, Heredi di Moise of Rieti, and Salomone of Montalcino their director, Heredi di Isac di Vitale of Pisa and Heredi di Vitale of Pisa." On the 13th October, others were brought in, also for 10 years, to lend money in the towns of Prato and Empoli.

[2] Filiberta.

[3] He was called Don Teodoro, if we may believe *Cambi*, who describes this function minutely and gives many details concerning the errors of this *frate*.

spoilt, becoming rotten inside. And note that during the whole winter it had never snowed or been cold until this day. Everyone had felt sure that the winter was over; and yet it was cold now till the middle of April, and snowed again, so that all the rest of the fruit was spoilt, and the vines greatly damaged.

1515. 17th April. It snowed again so heavily that it lay deep all over the plains, as far as Valdisieve, and all through the Mugello, and there was severe cold till the 24th of the month, with fresh snow on the mountains.

At this time solid iron bands were placed all round San Giovanni in Florence, outside, above the middle cornice, and these were joined by strong iron pins and bolts, as the walls showed signs of giving way.[1]

24th May. A vote was passed in the *Palagio* that Lorenzo de' Medici should be *Capitano* of the Florentines, and that he should have full powers of appointing and dismissing those under him.

4th June. Madonna Alfonsina, mother of the said Lorenzo de' Medici, came to Florence.

17th July. Giuliano de' Medici came to Florence.

12th August. The *Signoria* gave the (commander's) bâton to the said Lorenzo, and there was a muster of many men-at-arms and of our peasants' battalions (militia).

13th August. The Cardinal de' Medici, who was our archbishop and legate of the Church, came to Florence, and was received with great state.

14th August. Giuliano de' Medici's wife came to Florence.

16th August. The Cardinal de' Medici and Lorenzo left here and went to Bologna, with all the men-at-arms that were in Florence.

17th September. We heard that the King of France had had an encounter with the Milanese and Swiss troops, and that 20 thousand men had been slain.

22nd September. We heard that the King of France had entered Milan by an agreement.

[1] For the *festa* of San Giovanni, as has already been stated, the Piazza of San Giovanni was covered with canvas awnings, and the ropes which supported them were fastened to certain irons in the walls of the church; but as some cracks began to appear, caused by the weight of the awnings themselves, increased sometimes by the violence of the wind, the Merchants' Guild decided to have the building encircled by iron hoops, placed above the second cornice.

26th September. It was said that an agreement had been made, and that it would be published.

18th October. The bronze [1] "San Giovanni Vangiolista" was placed in Orto San Michele, and the marble one which had been there was taken away.

21st October. We heard that there was an agreement with the King of France, and the bells were pealed, with bonfires and great rejoicings.

At this time it was said that the King and the Pope were coming to Florence, so that all kinds of provisions and vegetables began to get dearer; a barrel of oil going up to 18 *lire*, corn to 30 *soldi*, and wine to half a ducat a barrel, and 4 *lire* the poorer kind.

30th October. The "Eight" sent round to mark the houses for the soldiers that were expected to come with the Pope and the King, and they took the houses of the chief citizens and of every sort.

26th November. The Pope stopped the night at Santa Maria Impruneta.

27th November. He stopped at Marignolle, at the place belonging to Jacopo son of Messer Bongianni.[2] You may think if Florence were not upside-down with all the arrangements.

30th November (the day of Sant' Andrea — a Friday). The Pope made his magnificent and triumphal entry [3] into Florence, everything having been prepared at an incredible cost. The grandeur of it was incredible; but I will try to give a few details.

All the chief citizens went in procession to meet him, and amongst others fifty young men, on foot, the richest and most important in the city, dressed in a costume of purple silk, with a collar of miniver, each carrying in his hand a sort of small silvered lance, very beautiful to see; and they were followed by a throng of citizens on horseback. With the Pope came numerous infantry, and amongst them the papal guard, consisting of many German soldiers, in a uniform with which they wore two-edged axes in the French fashion. Besides these, many mounted bowmen

---

[1] This was made by Baccio da Montelupo for the Silk-mercers' Guild (Passerini, *La Loggia di Or San Michele*).

[2] Gianfigliazzi.

[3] Of these magnificent arrangements made in Florence for the arrival of Pope Leo X. *Vasari* speaks in the Life of Andrea del Sarto. See *Vasari*, edizione Sansoni, tom. v., p. 21.

and musketeers, all belonging to his guard. And he was carried all through the city by the *Signoria* under a rich *baldacchino* (canopy), and was put down at Santa Maria del Fiore, where he walked along the platform as far as the High Altar, the church being adorned with large banners, and a canopy over the centre of the choir, up to which there were more steps than usual: and there were so many lighted torches, that they not only filled the choir, but the whole nave down to the doors and everywhere round; and the other aisles under the cupola were also filled with lighted torches; and the platform which went from the door to the choir was one mass of lights and torches. And you must know that the choir was built on beams above the real choir, with an altar beautifully decorated in the centre.

And then he came down towards Santa Maria Novella, giving the benediction all the time, preceded by many buglers and fife-players, amidst such a crowd of people that it made one's eyes ache to see them. Perhaps there had never been such a multitude assembled in Florence before. He caused money to be thrown to the people as he passed through the streets, *grossi* and silver coins. So far there was nothing extraordinary; but now we will speak of the things undertaken by the directors of the festivities, which were so huge that some of them remained unfinished for want of time. It is unimaginable that any other city or state in the world could have been capable of making such preparations; their magnitude can be realised when you consider that although several thousand men laboured for more than a month beforehand, work-days and holidays alike, it was not possible to bring the whole to perfection, some few being incomplete; even so, however, the beauty of the work could be seen, and its incalculable cost. To show that this is true, I will describe the sights in order, but my words will express very little, the actuality far exceeding any description.

The first was at the gate of *San Piero Gattolino*, where for the sake of splendour they broke down the wall of the outer gate, and laid the portcullis on the ground, orna-menting the outside of the gate with four enormous pillars, 16 *braccia* in height, all silvered over, with bases and capitals like those of Santo Spirito; besides these there were several pilasters with great architraves and cornices and friezes, as such pillars require, reaching up to certain tabernacles on the face of the gate, with a number of statues in the niches and under the arches, all by the hand of good masters, which could not have been made at another time for hundreds of florins, and all illustrating famous stories, which delighted one's eyes.[1]

The second was at *San Felice in Piazza*, at the entrance to Via Maggio, a most beautiful triumphal arch, which reached right across the street. It had eight round pillars, as large as those of Santo Spirito, with numerous pilasters, and the requisite capitals and cornices, all ornamented without stint. Here also there were many statues by the hand of the chief masters, placed between the arches and in niches, making people pause to consider their meaning and admire their beauty.[2]

The third was at the Ponte a Santa Trinità, and surpassed all the rest in beauty. At the entrance to the bridge, towards Via Maggio, there was a splendid triumphal arch, as wide as the bridge; this had six pillars as tall as those of the last arch and larger, placed with such exquisite symmetry that I considered that Florence had many architects of greater talent than any that can be found in the world. These pillars formed a kind of portico, ornamented with many statues and so beautiful in colour that one did not know how to come away; nothing else approached it.

The fourth was at the church of Santa Trinità; they took the whole Piazza di Santa Trinità, and made a circular building like a castle,[3] with 22 square pillars round it, and in the spaces between them were hangings of tapestry, and above the pillars there was a cornice all round, with certain inscriptions in the frieze. Then there were more pillars at the turning into Via Porta Rossa. There was so much work in this, that it was not quite finished; but it was done at a great cost, and evoked one's admiration.

The fifth was in the Piazza de' Signori, at the corner by

[1] Jacopo di Sandro and Baccio da Montelupo made these adornments on the gate of San Piero Gattolino.
[2] This arch was the work of Giuliano del Tasso.
[3] *Cambi* calls it "a crescent-shaped wall and a tower like a fortress." In a book of the *Condotte e stanziamenti* of the *Otto di Pratica*, in the *Archivio di Stato di Firenze*, a payment of cccxv large gold florins to Jacopo, called *Baia*, is registered "for the theatre made by the church of Santa Trinità."

the Lion,[1] where the design was so beautiful that one could not wish to better it. There was a sort of quadrangle, with four triumphal arches, under which one could pass crosswise in two directions, and at each corner there were two high and wide bases, on each of which stood a column, making eight columns, each more than 16 *braccia* high with its architrave, and the requisite cornices.[2] The whole looked like marble, more perfectly arranged than one can imagine. It would be difficult for any city to make even this one edifice; it was so pleasing to the eye, that it was a pity to see it taken down, with all those wonderful figures by good masters.

The sixth was at the Palagio del Podestà; and consisted of 24 columns, not so tall, but very graceful, being all gilt; they extended many *braccia* towards the Via del Palagio, with great cornices all round, facing in every direction. There was much graceful ornamentation, all gilt, and many figures, also good and very costly; the whole design in fact so harmonious that it gave great pleasure.[3]

The seventh was at the *Canto de' Bischeri*,[4] and one could not help admiring it; there were twenty-seven square pillars, covered with gold ornamentation, forming a kind of quadrangle, through which passed the street which leads to San Piero. All these pillars had a festoon of pomegranates and cones down the centre, as is usual, all gilt, making each seem richer than the last; and then there were so many fine statues that one spent hours looking at them. The great triumphal arches, in a cross, as the streets run, were as high as the tops of the houses.

The eighth was at *Santa Maria del Fiore*, which had twelve marble columns in the façade, as high as and larger than those of San Lorenzo, with magnificent triumphal arches at the doors, and several large cornices above the columns, as requisite for such a great façade, which reached nearly up to the first round windows of the church. The mass of compartments and ornamentation astounded

[1] That is the *Marzocco*, which was at the north-west corner of the *ringhiera*.
[2] This temple with eight faces was built by Antonio da San Gallo *il vecchio*.
[3] This decoration between the Badia and the Palazzo del Podestà was the work of Granacci and of Aristotile da San Gallo.
[4] This was the work of Giovambattista, called *il Rosso*, near the spot where the present Via Proconsole and Borgo degli Albizzi meet.

everyone; and it was said that it had been made as a model for the façade, because it pleased everyone, seeming so superb and noble; one regretted seeing it taken down again.[1] And inside the church a platform was made leading from the door up to the choir, with a low balustrade on each side; and the choir had been raised above the real choir, with an extra number of steps round it, and an altar in the middle decorated with large banners, and a canopy overhead. And note that all this timber was worked in the church, on holidays as well as working-days; so that for more than a month the churches were inconvenienced.

The ninth was at the Canto de' Carnesecchi,[2] and took up the whole breadth of the two streets, with a splendid triumphal arch over the main street going into the Piazza, which had in front of it four great round columns like those of San Lorenzo, and six pilasters with their cornices and ornaments; very beautiful work. The top was higher than the houses, and there were so many figures by good masters that everyone felt astounded, staring and wondering.

The tenth was at the entrance into the Via della Scala, a shrine in honour of the Vergine Maria, with an entablature as high as the houses. It filled the whole street, with two pillars on each side, as high as the altar, or even higher, with many decorations.

The eleventh was at the Pope's gate,[3] the whole street being taken up on both sides, leaving only a little space at the doors of the houses, and all the windows of the houses being closed. Here there were several triumphal arches, one at the entrance of the street, one at the end, and another leading towards the *Sala*. This gallery ran the length of several houses, being ... *braccia* long, and having eight

---

[1] The façade of Santa Maria del Fiore in wood, and with various subjects painted in chiaroscuro by Andrea del Sarto, was designed by Jacopo Sansovino, who made some bas-reliefs upon it, and also some figures in high relief.

[2] The *Canto de' Carnesecchi* was where the streets now called Cerretani, Banchi, Martelli, and Panzani meet. Bologna's famous group of "Hercules killing the Centaur" used to stand here, before it was removed to the farther end of the Ponte Vecchio, and finally to the Loggia dei Lanzi. [Trans.]

[3] The gate which gave access to the quarter called the *Sala del Papa*. In this spot and on some ground formerly belonging to the monks of Santa Maria Novella, Eleonora di Toledo, wife of Cosimo I., had a convent built and dedicated to the *SS. Concezione*.

tall round columns higher than the altar, twenty-six pilasters, and twelve small columns, with certain tabernacles among them. Here there were two façades opposite one another, full of so many figures and so much ornamentation that everyone who stopped to look, lost himself in the midst of such a number of different subjects by the hand of the chief masters. Here could be traced various ideas and similitudes — there were the nine beatitudes, *Beati Pacifici, Beati mundo corde*, etc., and many other series of stories, which astonished me by the beauty of their design and execution; for there was nothing rough or clumsy about them, all the figures being perfect, and suitably placed by men of ability.[1] And note that to make all these things of wood, it was necessary to work at Santa Maria del Fiore, Santa Maria Novella, in the church and the cloisters, Santo Spirito, in the church, the cloisters, and the refectories, Santa Felicità in Piazza, San Jacopo Soprarno, Santa Croce, the Palagio del Podestà, the Studio (University), San Michele Addomini,[2] San Michele Berteldi, and many other places. The said churches were so taken up, that the office had to be said elsewhere. Holidays and work-days, night and day alike, this noise and commotion went on, and it lasted, I repeat, more than a month, several thousand men being employed. There was not the most humble painter of any kind in Florence whose aid was not required in some way.

The twelfth was a great prancing horse without a bridle, in the act of starting off in a gallop, and treading a giant beneath his feet, all gilt; it was considered to be very well done, and was placed in the middle of the Piazza of Santa Maria Novella, on a brick pedestal freshly made, four *braccia* high.

The thirteenth was an obelisk, in style and size like that of Rome, also of wood, and covered with canvas painted to imitate that of Rome; it was erected near the Ponte di Trinità, on this side of the church, at the corner towards the Ponte della Carraia.

The fourteenth was a very tall column, also of wood, covered with canvas on which various subjects were painted; it was erected in the centre of the *Mercato Nuovo*. To many

---

[1] In the Sala del Papa and in the Via della Scala the series of stories had been designed for the most part by Baccio Bandinelli.
[2] *Bisdomini*.

people this did not seem suitable, but on the contrary tasteless.¹

The fifteenth was a giant in the *Loggia de' Signori*, which appeared to be of bronze, and it was placed under the first arch towards the *Palagio*; this was not much appreciated.²

And so that you may realise that money was not spared, I must tell you that at *Santa Maria Novella* they took down that very fine staircase leading to the *Sala del Papa*, and replaced it by another, up which a man could ride on horseback, as may be seen. And even this was not enough, for they also threw down the gates and walls of the court, displeasing many people, in order to make a number of rooms inside it at a great cost.

They also pulled down the projections of the houses and all the pent-roofs over the shops in the Via Porta Rossa and many other places where they wanted to widen the street. They spoilt the steps of the *Badia* and the roof over them; in fact they spared nothing, breaking up all without discretion.

And you must know that I have not written the tenth part of what might be said; when you think that we had more than 2 thousand men at work, as it was estimated, for more than a month, belonging to various trades: carpenters, stone-masons, painters, carters, porters, sawyers, etc., and a cost of 70 thousand florins or more was mentioned, all for things of no duration; when a splendid temple might have been built in honour of God and to the glory of the city. Certainly, however, the money that was scattered in this way added to the earnings of the poor workmen.

1st December (Saturday). The Pope left Santa Maria Novella, and went to the house of his family, the Palazzo de' Medici.

2nd December (Sunday). He went to mass at San Lorenzo.

3rd December (Monday). The Pope left in the direction of Bologna, accompanied for a good part of the way by many citizens and by the same young men as before, dressed in costume.

7th December. (Friday) The Pope entered Bologna.

¹ This was made in imitation of the storied one at Rome.
² This giant was also made by Bandinelli.

11th December. The King of France entered Bologna.

13th December. The king went to visit the Pope, and they discussed all the matters to be settled. And the Pope administered the Sacrament to the king with his own hands, with much solemnity, and in the hope of peace. Nevertheless one heard nothing of their compact.

15th December. The king left Bologna.

18th December. The Pope left Bologna.

22nd December (Saturday). The Pope reached Florence at 24 in the evening (8 p.m.).

23rd December. The Pope went to mass at San Lorenzo.

24th December. The Pope went to vespers at Santa Maria del Fiore.

25th December. The Pope went to Santa Maria del Fiore, and said the mass himself. The church was decorated with great banners and a splendid canopy, the whole surpassing anything ever done before; amongst other things, the innumerable lighted torches were arranged in the following way: the galleries above the aisles were filled with them, from end to end of the church, and all the galleries of the cupola, round and round, were lighted in the same fashion. The service was conducted with great pomp, in the presence of an enormous concourse of people.

[1] 8th January. The Arno overflowed, flooding the whole of the meadow of the Ognissanti, as far as the Borgo Ognissanti, and did great damage in these plains, drowning several persons lower down the stream.

17th January. The church of the Nunziata de' Servi in Florence was consecrated by the cardinal.[2]

In these days the stables made by the house of Medici behind the *Sapienza*,[3] to the right-hand side of San Marco, were finished roofing in.[4]

10th February. Several cardinals left here, that is, San

---

[1] In the original MSS. another hand begins to write at this point.

[2] Antonio del Monte, cardinal legate of Leo X., by whose order he made this consecration; and the memory of it is preserved in a marble epigraph in the larger cloister, published by the learned P. Pellegrino *Tonini* in his *Guida storico-illustrava* of this church.

[3] See note to 9th November, 1497.

[4] They appear to have been begun in July 1515, as we read in *Cambi* under this date: "The Magnificent Lorenzo de' Medici had two stables made, one next to the other, each 100 *braccia* long, with 400 *braccia* of mangers, behind the *Sapienza*, between the church of the Servi and the church of San Marco."

Giorgio and others, who were with the Pope's court, to return to Rome.

At this time the price of corn increased in a few days more than 10 *soldi* a bushel, going up to 40 *soldi*; little work was done, and everything was raised in value. Wine cost 5 *lire* a barrel, oil went up to 18 *lire* a barrel, pork to 2 *soldi* 4 *denari* a pound, and all meat and fish was dear. River fish was sold at 16 *soldi* a pound, and other kinds at a high price, and also wood. So that the poor suffered much. It was expected the Pope would cause foreign corn to be brought, but nothing was done. Everyone was amazed to see the quantity of food consumed by the strangers in the following of the papal court.

The price of corn went on increasing, and by the middle of February reached 47 *soldi* and even more, and if the *Signoria* had not made a proclamation against those who raised the price, it would have reached 3 *lire* a bushel; they stopped it at 45 *soldi*.

19th February (Tuesday). The Pope left Florence, for Santa Maria Impruneta, at 18 in the afternoon (2 p.m.). He did not leave willingly, but thought that it was best, on account of the harm caused to the citizens by the price of corn.

17th March. Giuliano son of Lorenzo de' Medici, and brother of Pope Lione, died the following night, at 6 in the morning (2 a.m.), in the *Badia* of the *Ponte alla Badia*.[1]

At this time the price of corn stood at 40 or 42 *soldi* a bushel.

19th March. They buried the above-said Giuliano de' Medici at San Lorenzo in Florence, with great pomp.

During these days the Germans arrived in Lombardy, near Milan.

✠[2]

1516. 26th May. Men-at-arms were sent to take the Duchy of Urbino, and by the 4th June almost the whole

---

[1] "He died at the *Badia* of Fiesole belonging to the *Monaci regolari*, where he had had himself taken for the long illness that he had had, having become emaciated and as thin as a rail, and he died with resignation, being regretted by the whole city, as he had been a merciful man during his life" (*Cambi*).

[2] The cross which is found at this point in the Sienese MS. was certainly placed there to indicate the death of Luca Landucci, who was buried on the 2nd June, 1516.

of it was taken, except Pesaro and Santo Leo; and soon after that the conquest was completed beyond dispute.¹

19th August. We heard that Pope Leo, with all the College of Cardinals, had crowned Signore Lorenzo de' Medici Duke of Urbino.

1517. 1st July. Pope Lione X. made 31 cardinals, of whom the names were as follows:

1. The Archbishop of Como, da Trauzi.
2. The Archbishop of Siena.
3. Signore Frangoto Orsini.
4. The Archbishop di Trani of Montefeltro.
5. The Bishop de' Pandolfini.
6. The Bishop della Valle, a Roman.
7. The Bishop Colona, a Roman.
8. The Bishop (of) Cavaglione, a Genoese.
9. The Castellan.
10. Jacobacco.
11. Ivrea, son of the General of Milan.
12. Feltrensis.
13. Como.
14. Messere Ferando Puccetti.
15. A Frenchman, J. Laudovensis.
16. Portoghetto, son of the King of Portugal.
17. A Fleming.
18. The Governor of the Camera Romana.
19. Cesarino, a Roman.
20. Messere Luigi de' Rossi.
21. Giovanni Salviati.
22. Messere Antonio Ridolfi.
23. The Count Ercole di Rangone.
24. The *Datario* (the chancellor of the Pope, at Rome).
25. The son of Messer Jacopo da Trauzi.
26. Messere Francesco Ermolino of Perugia.
27. Devichi, a Spaniard.
28. The General of San Domenico (of the Dominican Order).

¹ This enterprise had long been a dream of the Pope, who had adduced as reasons for it, the fact that he wished to punish the duke for having murdered the Cardinal of Pavia, for having refused his men-at-arms to the church from which he received a stipend, for having secret understandings with the enemy, etc.; however, he really aimed at acquiring this state for Lorenzo in order to raise him in name and fact to the dignity of a prince.

A SEA-FIGHT BETWEEN GALLEYS
From the original by D. Tintoretto.

1518]   A FLORENTINE DIARY   289

29. The General of Sant' Agostino (of the Augustinian Order).
30. The priest notary Pisano.
31. The General of Santo Francesco [1] (of the Franciscan Order).

22nd August. The "Eight" sentenced about a hundred citizens to be banished.

1518. 4th May. They began to ring the *Ave Maria* at the *nona* [2] (a little before noon), for the Crusade about to be undertaken, that God should be favourable to it; and there were many fasts and processions.

[1] It seems necessary to add this note referring to the cardinals, making use of the *Memorie Storiche* of *Cardella*, already quoted, vol. iv., pp. 14 *et seq.*:
1. Scaramuccia Trivulzio.
2. Giovanni Piccolomini.
3. Franciotto Orsini.
4. Giandomenico de Cupis, belonging to a family from Montefalco.
5. Niccolò Pandolfini, Bishop of Pistoia.
6. Andrea Della Valle, Bishop of Mileto.
7. Pompeo Colonna, Bishop of Rieti.
8. Giambattista Pallavicini, Bishop of Cavaillon.
9. Rafaello Petrucci, Prefect of Castel Sant' Angelo.
10. Domenico Jacovacci.
11. Bonifazio Ferreri, Bishop of Ivrea.
12. Lorenzo Campeggi, Bishop of Feltro.
13. Francesco Conti, Archbishop of Couza.
14. Ferdinando Ponzetti, a Neopolitan.
15. Lodovico di Borbone, Bishop of Laon.
16. Alfonzo, the sixth son of Emanuele King of Portugal.
17. Adriano Fiorenzi, of Utrecht, who afterwards succeeded Leo X. with the name of Hadrian VI.
18. Paolo Emilio Cesi, a Roman.
19. Alessandro Cesarini.
20. Luigi de' Rossi, a Florentine.
21. Giovanni Salviati.
22. Niccolò (and not Antonio) Ridolfi.
23. Ercole Rangoni.
24. Silvio Passerini of Cortona.
25. Agostino Trivulzio.
26. Francesco Armellino Medici, a Perugian.
27. Guglielmo Raimondo Vich of Valenza.
28. Tommasio de Vio of Gaeta, called Cardinal Gaetano.
29. Egidio Antonino of Viterbo.
30. Francesco Pisani, a Venetian.
31. Cristoforo Numai of Forlì.

[2] The *Ave Maria* of midday, which it is still the custom to ring, was ordered to be rung by Leo X. when he had the idea of persuading the Christians to go against the Turks.

U

7th September. The duchess came to her husband, Duke Lorenzo de' Medici, in Florence, and there were great festivities. She was French.[1]

1519. 4th May. The Duke Lorenzo de' Medici died, and his wife died seven days later.

19th May. The church of Santo Josefe was begun, and on this day the celebration of its foundation was kept with great reverence, opposite the Crucifix behind Santa Croce.[2]

1520 or 1521. On the last day of March, the Hospital for Incurables was begun.[3]

1521. On the first day of December, Pope Lione died.

9th January. A Flemish Pope was elected, who was called Pope Adriano.[4]

1522. 30th May. The emperor took Genoa by assault, 14 thousand men being slain, and the city was sacked.

2nd August. The bells were pealed, and bonfires were made, in honour of the canonisation of the Florentine Archbishop Antonino.[5]

---

[1] Madeleine de Boulogne of Picardy, of the house of Burgundy.

[2] A history of this church, which seems to have been founded on this day, was written by Padre Stefano Fioretti, and published in Florence in the year 1855.

[3] A very sad sight was presented in those days by many unfortunate persons suffering from *il male francese*, which was then considered incurable, and they were abandoned and allowed to linger away even in the streets of Florence. On the 23rd May, 1519, Don Calisto of Piacenza, Canon of Sant' Agostino belonging to the Badia of Fiesole, preaching in Santa Maria del Fiore, exhorted his hearers, with good results, to provide for these unfortunate sufferers (*Regulamenti dei Regi Spedali di S. Maria Nuova e di Bonifazio* Historical Preface, p. xlii. Firenze, 1789).

[4] Adriano Boyers, called Florent, of Utrecht in Holland, Cardinal-Bishop of Tortosa; Hadrian VI.

[5] I think that the following document, dated 8th February, 1516, respecting the canonisation of this illustrious Florentine, may be of interest: "The Magnificent and exalted Signori, the Sisnori Priori di Libertà, and the gonfaloniere di giustizia, of the Florentine People, make known and manifest to all and any of whatsoever rank, quality or condition they may be, that His Holiness our Signore Pope Leone, moved by the odour of the good life and repute, and by the miracles worked through the merits of the Beato Antonino, formerly Archbishop of Florence, and desiring for the aforesaid reasons to canonise him, have commissioned for the execution of this matter the Most Reverend Fathers Jacopo Simonecta and Guglielmo Cassadoro, Auditors of the *Ruota*, to receive information respecting the said matters, from each and every person; therefore the said Auditors are prepared, like obedient servants, benignly to

1527]   A FLORENTINE DIARY   291

3rd August. A peasant of Santa Maria Impruneta killed all the members of his household, that is, seven persons; his wife, their children, and a son-in-law; and then, having set fire to the house, disappeared.

In this year manna fell almost everywhere, and it was so hot that the grapes dried on the vines.

1523. 14th September. Pope Adriano died.

19th November. Pope Clemente was elected; and he died on the 25th September, 1534.

1524. 23rd February. The King of France was taken prisoner by the emperor, and about 8 thousand men were slain round Pavia, the king going as a prisoner to Spain.

The last day of February. The pavement round the choir of Santa Maria del Fiore, of white, black and red marble, was finished; they had been working at it for about four years.

1526. 21st September. We had news that the Turks had taken Hungary, and that the king was dead; he had been drowned in a river.

In the month of December, the Signore Giovanni de' Medici was killed by *Lanzi* (German soldiers) near Mantua. Embrasures for the guns were made on all the towers of the city walls at Florence; there had not been any before, and the towers were now reduced to a level with the walls.[1]

1527. 6th May. Rome was sacked, and the Pope fled into the *Castello* with twenty-two cardinals; and there they were all taken prisoner by the Germans and the Spaniards, as it pleased God.

16th May. The government was changed peacefully, by

receive all information, and to examine everything, as is usual, necessary and opportune in such matters; and it is notified to everyone that they are so sent. Furthermore, the Magnificent *Signori* and *Gonfaloniere* notify to each and all, who may know anything of the life, repute and miracles of the Beato Antonino, either personally or by hearsay, for the love, honour and glory of God and the Saints, to be pleased to advise and notify the said Auditors of such facts, in the house of the aforesaid M. Jacopo Simonecta, situated in the Via de' Pandolfini in Florence, where they will be benignantly received and granted audience at any hour of the day" (*Registro di Deliberazioni de' Signori e Collegi, ad an.*).

[1] The towers of the gates were almost all mutilated and reduced to embrasures for guns, as can still be seen in the gates of the Prato, San Gallo and della Croce, by order of Federico da Bozzolo and the Count Pietro Navarra, sent by Pope Clement VII. to fortify the city; which thing greatly displeased the Florentines.

an agreement, and Ippolito de' Medici and the Cardinal of Cortona went away together.

In December, the Pope, who had been in prison for about seven months, was liberated.

27th December. The inscriptions for the enrolment of citizen-soldiers (militia) of Florence, *gonfalone* by *gonfalone*, were finished.

1528. 26th, 27th and 28th January. Four orations were made, one in Santo Spirito, in the pulpit, one in Santa Maria Novella, one in San Lorenzo, and one in Santa Croce, by four young Florentines, in exhortation of the said militia. And on the 5th February, 16 green banners, with the arms of the *gonfalone*, were hung in the Piazza, having been made new for the above-said militia.

1529. 19th September. We had the news that Cortona had surrendered on conditions to the Prince of Orange, *Capitano* of the emperor. And Arezzo had rebelled likewise.

2nd October. The Virgine Maria came to Florence, and was taken into Santa Maria del Fiore into the chapel of San Zanobi, so that she should guard her city from this war with which it is threatened; and as soon as she was here, the whole city was freed from its dread and terror.[1]

10th October. The army of the Emperor and the Pope came to the walls of Florence, and gradually encircling the city completely, laid siege to it. And this siege lasted almost a year, and there was such a scarcity that the price of corn rose to 3 *lire* 15 *soldi*—the *Signoria* fixing it at that. (The prices of other things were as follows:)

	lire	soldi	denari
A pound of Cheese	2	18	0
A couple of Capons	49	0	0
A couple of Hens	21	0	0
A pound of Salt-meat	2	15	0
A Kid	25	0	0
A Lamb	18	0	0
A pound of Ass's flesh or Horse-flesh		10	0
A Lettuce		6	0
Two sour Plums			4
One ripe Plum		1	8
A Pomegranate		6	0

[1] *Varchi* narrates that in order to prevent this image falling into the hands of the Lutherans (that is, the assailants), the *Signoria* sent to fetch it secretly.

A FLORENTINE DIARY

	lire	soldi	denari
A quarter of a peck of soft Beans		2	0
A bunch of Radishes		1	8
A flask of Oil	7	0	0
A pound of Preserves	2	10	0
A pound of Bologna Sausages	2	18	0
An ounce of Pepper		16	0
A couple of Eggs		18	0
A pound of muscatel Pears		12	0
A pound of Cherries		8	0
A pound of Mutton	2	10	0
An Onion		4	0
A flask of Wine	2	2	0
A pound of Fish	2	2	0
A Kid's head	1	5	0
A Liver and Lights	1	5	0
A pound of wax Candles	1	16	0
A pound of Honey	1	0	0
A Lemon		7	0
An Orange		6	0
A pound of dried Grapes		12	0
A Herring		7	0
A pound of crushed Almonds	3	12	0
Two Walnuts . . 1 *quattrino*			
A little bunch of Beet		1	0
A little bunch of Cabbage		1	0
A bunch of fresh Leeks		1	0
A fresh Pumpkin	1	15	0
An Apricot		4	0
A Gander	14	0	0
A pound of Sausage	2	16	0

1530. 25th April. We regained Volterra, which the Spaniards had been holding, Ferruccio taking it by assault.

28th May. We lost Empoli.

3rd August. Ferruccio, in a fine action between San Marcello and Gavinana, slew the Prince of Orange, and also died himself, or rather, was killed.

8th September. The Spanish and German army left.

12th September. Malatesta left with our troops.

8th October. There was such a great flood at Rome that more damage was done than when the city was sacked.

1531. 5th July. Duke Alessandro de' Medici came to Florence on his return.

From the month of August, the ducat, which was formerly worth 7 *lire*, was put at 7 *lire* 10 *soldi*. And the *barile*,¹ which had been worth 12 *soldi* 6 *denari*, went up to 13 *soldi* 4 *denari*. And the *grossone*, which had been worth 7 *soldi*, went up to 7 *soldi* 6 *denari*, and the coins which had been worth 28 *soldi* went up to 30 *soldi*; and 3 silver *quattrini* were now worth 4 copper ones.

1532. 1st May. The new *Signoria* should have entered into office, but they did not do so.

3rd December. There arrived in Florence 100 relics, in forty-five vases, sent by Pope Clemente; they were put in San Lorenzo.

1533. 17th April. The duchess, wife of Duke Alessandro, came to Florence; and on the 26th of the same month went on to live at Naples. She was the illegitimate daughter of the emperor.²

In the year 1529 the custom of wearing hoods began to go out, and by 1532 not a single one was to be seen; caps or hats being worn instead. Also, at this time, men began to cut their hair short, everyone having formerly worn it long, on to their shoulders, without exception; and they now began to wear a beard, which formerly was only worn by two men in Florence, Corbizo and one of the Martigli.

At this time also hose³ were begun to be made in two pieces, which had formerly been made all in one, and without a seam; now they slashed them up everywhere, and put silk underneath, letting it project at all the slashes.

27th May. The foundations of the new citadel outside the *Porta a Faenza* were begun to be laid, and men worked at them on holidays and week-days alike, even on Easter Day.⁴

25th September. Pope Clemente died.

11th October. Pope Paolo III. was elected.

1535. 25th April. Coins of 40 *soldi* each were begun to

---

¹ The *barile* or *gabelotto* was a coin so called because it was the sum paid on a barrel of wine when it entered Florence.

² Margherita of Austria—then nine years old—whom Charles V. had promised to Alessandro de' Medici as far back as 1529.

³ Hose meaning the short *breeches*, which were then still called *hose*.

⁴ The foundations began to be laid outside the gate, but the latter was included in the new fortress, which was called San Giovanni Battista, and the tower, which still exists, served as nucleus to the keep of the fortress.

be stamped with the head of Duke Alessandro on one side, and on the other San Cosimo and Damiano.

20th July. We had the news that the emperor had taken Tunis in Barbary.[1]

5th December. Almost all the outer walls of the citadel were finished, and the mass and *Benedicite* were sung, and a guard placed in it.

19th December. The duke left to go to Naples and visit the emperor, who had returned from Tunis in Barbary.

11th March. Duke Alessandro returned from Naples.

1536. 28th April (Friday). At 21 in the evening (5 p.m.) the emperor entered Florence with 5 thousand foot-soldiers and 2 thousand horse, and first went to Santa Maria del Fiore, and then to the palace of the Medici; and on the 29th April he went to see the fortress, and then came out and went along the walls towards San Gallo, and returned by the duke's stables. And on the 1st May he went to hear mass in Santa Maria del Fiore, where a pavilion of rich silk had been prepared for him.

2nd May. He went to hear mass at the Nunziata, and the picture was uncovered for him.

This same day, the ambassador of the King of Tunis came to the emperor and brought him the tribute, that is, four horses and two camels and eight falcons; and the emperor let the duke have the two aforesaid dromedaries. And on the 3rd May the said tribute was taken to the palace where the emperor was, here in Florence.[2]

4th May. The emperor left Florence at 15 in the morning (11 a.m.), and went to Pistoia.

6th May. He went to Lucca.

15th June. The duchess[3] came to remain here with her husband, Duke Alessandro de' Medici.

6th January (Saturday). At about 6 in the morning (2 a.m.), on the night of the Epiphany, Duke Alessandro

---

[1] This expedition of Charles V. has been described by *Damiano Muoni* in *Cenni-Documenti, Registri*; Milan, 1876.

[2] The summary of the articles agreed upon between the emperor and Muley Hassan, the Moorish King of Tunis, is published by *Muoni*, p. 88; and amongst the conditions there is this one of giving the emperor six Barbary horses and twelve falcons as tribute every year.

[3] Now being old enough for marriage. She returned to Florence on the 31st May, and on the 13th June "attended the wedding-mass with Duke Alessandro her husband" (*Varchi*).

de' Medici was murdered by having his throat cut, and he was buried without being seen by anyone except those who carried him.

These are the words of the proclamation: "The Councillors of our most illustrious and most excellent Signore Duke Alessandro de' Medici," etc., etc.

9th January (Tuesday). The Signore Cosimo de' Medici was made *Signore* in place of the duke.

20th January. Three cardinals and a bishop came here, that is, Salviati, Ridolfi and Gadi, and the Bishop de' Soderini, to make an agreement with the people, but it came to nothing.[1]

1537. 1st August. The army of the Florentine exiles at Montemurlo was defeated, which was considered miraculous, but they had shut themselves up in a trap; many were slain, and many taken prisoner.

The prisoners were as follows, on the 3rd August, 1537:

> The son of the *Capitano* Galeotto da Barga, who was hung.
> The Sacchettino,[2] by surname; hung.
> Vico Rucellai[3]; beheaded.
> Bacciotto del Sevaiulo[4]; beheaded.

And on the 4th August:
> The *Capitano* Gerardino[5]; beheaded.
> Giovanbattista Giacomini; beheaded.
> Lionardo Ringnadori; beheaded.
> The *Capitano* Guera[6]; beheaded, and hung by one foot at the citadel of Justice.

And on the 20th August:
> Baccio Valori; beheaded.
> Filippo, his son; beheaded.
> Filippo Valori, son of Nicolò; beheaded.
> Anton Francesco degl' Albizzi; beheaded.
> Alessandro Rondinegli; beheaded.
> Cecchino del Tessatore; hung.

[1] When Alessandro's death was known, they had wished to restore liberty, but they arrived too late; and being unfavourable to Duke Cosimo, were made to leave the State after a few days.

[2] Bernardo, son of Giovanni Sacchettini.

[3] Lodovico, natural son of Guglielmo Rucellai.

[4] Bartolomeo, son of Antonio Tagi, called Bacciotto.

[5] Andrea, son of Ser Lorenzo Gherardini.

[6] This Guerra di Modigliana was the captain of the fortress of the *Porta alla Giustizia* near the Arno.

1538. 18th December.
Filippo Strozzi cut his own throat with a sword, in prison at the Citadel.
Pagol' Antonio Valori; imprisoned in the vault of a tower.
Fabaie del Benino, who had fled, was recaptured, and beheaded.
Bernardo Canigiani.
Boccacino Adimari.
Giovan Francesco Capponi.
Cecchino Tosinghi.
Nigi del Tarchia.
Gio. Francesco Giugni.
Sandro da Filicaia.
A son of Gian Filippo Bartoli.
Lepre de Rinieri.
Amerigo Antinori.
The *Capitano* Betto Rinuccini.
Vieri da Castiglione.
Neri Rinuccini.
And many more, whom I do not enter.

He (Cosimo) was made Duke of Florence by an ambassador of the emperor.[1]

. . . October. The duchess who was the widow of Duke Alessandro went to Rome, where she was remarried to the Pope's nephew.[2]

. . . November. The Vergine Maria de la 'Npruneta was brought to Florence, because there had been so much rain; and as soon as the decision to bring her had been made, the rain ceased and it became fine in the most marvellous way.

18th December. Filippo Strozzi, who had been imprisoned in the Citadel for 16 months and 18 days, cut his throat, or had his throat cut, a matter which causes serious reflection.

[1] I read in the *Diario* of Francesco Settimani, under the date of the day following: "By the Council of the *Quarantotto* (forty-eight), the Signor Cosimo de' Medici was declared the second Duke of Florence, by a mandate of the Emperor Charles V., given in the city of Monzone, on the last day of September, and brought by the Count of Sifonte, a Spaniard, his Majesty's ambassador, who was escorted into the town with great magnificence."

[2] The Duchess Margherita of Austria was now married to Ottavio Farnese.

1539. 29th June. The Duchess of Duke Cosimo de' Medici entered Florence, having come from Naples to Pisa by sea.[1]

. . . July. The price of the corn now harvested was 70 *soldi* a bushel.

15th October. The well was finished in the centre of the large cloister of Santa Maria Novella, where there used to be a pine-tree 237 years old; and the whole cloister, where there was only grass, has been planted with oranges, which are a pleasure to see.

1st September. The "Eight," who used to live in the *Palazzo de' Signori*, now went to live in the *Palagio del Podestà*.

And the *Bargello*, who used to live next to the *Dogana* at the side towards Santa Croce, also went there (to the *Palagio del Podestà*).

1540. 3rd April. Duke Cosimo's wife, Duchess Leonora, had a daughter.

15th May (the eve of the *Spirito Santo*). Duke Cosimo went to live in the *Palazzo de' Signori*.

27th February. Two lions were brought into the Piazza de' Signori, in two cages like hen-coops; and when they were taken out of the cages, a bull went up to them, and one lion suddenly jumped on to his back, but did not do him any harm, and then one animal went one way and the other another, and they took no more notice of each other. And they took no notice either of many large dogs that were there. They were sent back to their den by the way they had come, and they returned there without any trouble whatever. In 1514 another lion had been brought there, who did nothing but kill a greyhound with one blow of his paw.

1541. 25th March. Duke Cosimo's wife, Duchess Eleonora, had a son, and he was given the name of . . . (Francesco).

1st August. He was baptised with great rejoicings and great state in San Giovanni.

24th August. Duke Cosimo went to visit the emperor at Genoa, and returned again.

1542. . . . April. Two tigers were sent to Duke Cosimo by the Viceroy of Naples, his father-in-law, in two cages; and they were put into the building where the lions are kept.

12th June. There was an earthquake in Florence, the

[1] Eleonora, daughter of Don Pedro of Toledo, viceroy of Naples.

severest ever known here; it lasted the time of a *paternoster*, and several smaller shocks followed. No harm was done in Florence, although it was felt throughout the district; except that in the Mugello it destroyed the whole castle of the Scarperia; and in that neighbourhood it destroyed 1740 houses, 113 persons being killed and more than 289 wounded and shaken, and injured by the falling houses.

6th August. A thunderbolt fell on the cupola, but hardly did any damage.

18th September. A thunderbolt fell on the cupola, and did no damage, or very little.

Another fell on the Palazzo de' Signori, where Duke Cosimo now lives.

And many others fell in Florence.

14th October. A thunderbolt fell on the cupola, and one on the Palazzo, and many others in the city.

22nd December. A thunderbolt fell on the cupola, and struck the lantern, breaking and destroying so many pieces of marble that it was thought it would cost more than 12 thousand *scudi* (crowns) to repair it.

Another also fell on the Palazzo of the duke.

FINIS

INDEX

ABBONDANZA, 124, 128
Agravo, 30
Alberti (Piero degli), Gonfaloniere, 120
Alexander VI., 55, 170, 206
Alfonso, Duke of Ferrara; mediates between Florence and Pisa, 157; marries Lucrezia Borgia, 191; comes to Florence, 215
Alms collected, 74, 87
Ambassadors:
    from emperor, 81, 111, 235
    from England to Pope, 213
    to Ferrara, 36
    to France, 38, 60, 84, 100, 107
    from France, 26, 38, 56, 58, 78, 96, 99, 107, 250
    to Pisa and Milan, 74, 78
    from Pisa, 233
    to Pope, 10, 55, 210, 264, 269
    from Pope, 18, 37, 44
    from Turks, 37, 44
    to Venice, 57
    Venice to Rome, 43
Angioli (Convent of the), 95
Antinori (Tommaso), 110
Antonino, Archbishop of Florence, 2, 290
Apothecaries (Guild), 32, 169, 174, 189
Aragon (Federico di), 4
Archbishops (of Florence). *See* Antonino, Medici (Giulio de'), Neroni, Orsini, Pazzi, Riario
Arezzo, 80, 151, 193–95, 198–200, 228, 292
Arno, in flood, 4, 5, 26, 50, 57, 107, 151
    frozen, 129, 212, 217
    to be deflected, 216
Articles (subscribed by Pope), 268
Aubigny (Begnì), 15, 72, 115, 184–86, 188
Ave Maria (at noon), 289

Badìa (in Florence), 18, 123, 285
    (at San Domenico), 2, 18, 52, 205, 287
Balìa, 73, 262, 263
Balue (Jean, Cardinal), 39
Balzello, 4, 86, 167
Bandini (Bernardo), 15, 16, 28
Bargello, 62, 65, 70, 108, 138, 140, 150
Bartoli (Domenico) Gonfaloniere, 123
Bartolomeo (de' Lapacci Bishop), 2
Battles:
    Carafaggio, 223
    at Livorno, 113
    near Milan, 167
    Montemurlo, 296
    Nancy, 13
    Parmigiano, 91
    on the Po, 238
    near Ravenna, 250
    Salto della Cervia, 89
    Terracina, 82
    Vico Pisano, 95

Bears, 43, 276
Belandi (Antonio), 35
Bentivogli (Giov. di), 45, 172, 178, 222, 253
    (Alessandro), 126
Bernardino (Fra), 44
Bernardo (Antonio di), 62, 63, 75
Bibbiena, 151, 152, 154, 156, 157
Bologna, 222, 223, 228, 245, 246, 249, 353
Bongianni (Gianfigli), 5, 10, 26, 41
Borgia (Lucrezia), 190, 191
    (Cesare). *See* Valentino
Borgo (San Sepolcro), 173, 196
Bread (scarcity), 116, 117
Brescia, 235, 249–52
Bresse (Philippe de) (Bre), 70
Bridal outfit, 5–7
Brigands, 165
Brigliaino, 18
Bruscoli (da), 254
Bull-hunt, 270
Buondelmonte (Fil.) Gonfaloniere, 263, 270, 271
Burgundy (Duke of), 13

Calabria (*Alfonso*, Duke of), 27, 28, 35, 36, 38, 42, 43, 47, 57, 58
    (*Ferdinand*, Duke of), 76, 77
Calandra, 1, 3
Calixtus III., 2
Cambini (Andrea), 157
Campi, 179, 205, 256
Candia (Duke of), 123
Canigiani, 39, 110, 166
Cannon, 10, 22, 35, 80, 84, 105, 147, 161, 159, 178, 192, 198, 262
Canto de' Bischeri, 289
    de' Carneschi, 283
    della Macina, 61
    a Monteloro, 5
    de' Pazzi, 107
    de' Tornaquinci, 8, 49
    delle Stinche, 176
    di Vacchereccia, 31
Capitani Generali, 21, 23, 25, 27, 28, 33, 35, 41, 100, 144, 146, 147, 154, 161, 278
    del Popolo, 150
Capponi (Piero), 64, 78, 84, 113
    (Neri), 90
Capua, 187
Cardinals (disguised), 275
Careggi, 8, 53
Carmelite Friars, 11, 126
Carnival, 101, 130, 190
Casa del Capitano, 28, 32, 68, 150
Cascina, 94, 95, 109, 114, 119, 146, 157, 158
Cascine (the) outside Florence, 49
Castagno (Andreino), 4
Castellina, 21, 22, 32
Castelnuovo, 24

301

302 A FLORENTINE DIARY

Castiglione (Aretino), 174, 194
  (di Marradi), 9
Catasto, 9, 29
Caterpillars, 144, 145, 158
Causeway to *Palagio*, 51, 97
Cavalcante (Giov.), 60, 79
Cegino, 129
Cestello, 1, 49
Charles V. (Emperor), holds Diet, 225
  attacks Venetians, 227
  sells cities back to Venice, 236
  takes Genoa, 290
  takes King of France prisoner at Battle of Pavia, 291
  takes Tunis, 295
  passes through Naples and Florence, and leaves Italy, 295
Charles VIII., reaches Italy, 57
  meets Piero de' Medici, 58
  enters Florence, 66
  in Florence, 66-72
  at Rome, 79-81
  takes Naples and whole kingdom, 83-4
  returns north and meets Savonarola at Poggibonizi, 88
  defeated at Parmigiano and leaves Italy, 91
  dies, 138
Cinque del Contado, 203
Citadel (new), 294, 295, 297
Citizens, (100) banished, 289
  fined, 140
  (28) deprived of rights, 145
Città di Castello, 22, 35, 195, 201
City walls (embrasures), 291
Clement VII., 291, 292, 294
Coinage, 6, 10, 51, 110, 190, 205, 223, 239, 294, 295
Coiner beheaded, 4
Cola Montano, 33
Colle (di Valdelsa), 28, 31, 100, 184
Collegi, 73, 94, 158, 201, 260
Commissaries, 23, 41, 93, 98, 230, 263
Compagnacci, 131, 136, 137
Conclave of Cardinals, 193, 208, 266
Conspiracies:
  of dell' Antella, 86
  of Capponi (Agostino), etc., 266
  near Careggi, 8
  of Pazzi, 15
  of Prinzivalle, 242
  at Siena, 202
  of the Tornabuoni and del Nero, 125
  at Venice, 23
Corbizi (Gonfaloniere), 78
Corsini (Luca), 79
Cortona, 97, 244, 292
Count Carlo (Montone), 27, 29, 30
Croce di San Giovanni, 186, 188
  (al Trebbio), 140
Cruelties of troops, 22, 73, 76, 88, 89, 114, 115, 165, 181, 183, 185, 237, 239, 250, 251, 258, 259

Decime, 20, 30, 103, 141, 194
Decrees:
  against discussing politics, 100
  against unnatural sin, 77, 100, 201, 218
  (other decrees under Great Council, Elections, Hospitals, etc.)
Desiderio, 2

Dicomano, 50, 51, 56, 70, 71, 73, 151, 173, 185, 198, 206, 219, 220
Dieci (*del consiglio*), 73, 74, 86, 234
Dietisalvi (Nerone), 8
Dissection of corpse, 217
Dogana, 75, 92, 95
Domenicans (General of), 142
Domenico (Fra), 132-5, 318, 143
Donatello, 2
  his "David," 97, 248
  his "Judith," 99, 220
Dove in *Palagio*, 234
Dowries, 244
Duties, 14

Earthquakes:
  at Bibbiena, 216
  in Candia, 228
  in Constantinople, 237
  at Florence, 31, 190, 198, 222
  at Modona, 186
  in Rhodes, 34
Eclipse:
  of the moon, 37
  of the sun, 125
Edifici, 20, 274
"Eight" Priori (the):
  accompany Cardinal San Giorgio, 20
  deposed, 25
  send away preaching hermit, 26
  send away San Bernardino, 44, 45
  find hidden money in San Marco, 79
  take to gambling, etc., 120
  try Savonarola, 144
  arrest loiterers on roads, 181
  manner of their election changed, 261
  banish the Soderini, 263
  go to live in Palagio del Podestà, 298
  (and also under other headings)
"Eight" (di Balìa) abolished, 73
"Eighty"(the),81, 82, 84, 115, 141, 157, 260
Election, and rules for voting, 4, 44, 45, 74, 75, 79, 83, 97, 99, 105, 109, 120, 146, 265
Emperor. *See* Charles V. Maximilian
Empoli, 64, 88, 178, 182, 183, 185, 293
Epitaphs in Great Hall, 103
Ercole I., (Duke of Ferrara), Capitano Generale, 21, 23, 27, 28, 71, 129, et seq.
Ercole II., (Duke of Ferrara), 233, 235
Escape of prisoners, 17, 33
d'Este, (Ippolito Cardinal), 129
Eugenius IV., 8
Excommunications:
  of Bologna, 245
  of Florence, 20, 26, 29, 247
  of Savonarola, 123
Executioner lynched, 204
Executions:
  Bandini (Bernardo), 28
  Bernardo (Antonio), 75
  a coiner, 4
  a criminal, 11
  a criminal, hung twice over, 46
  exiles after Montemurlo, 296 ff.
  girl for infanticide, 213
  a murderer, 146
  a murderess, 4
  Pazzi (Jacopo de') and others, 17 ff.
  pillagers, 23
  Rinaldeschi, 187

INDEX

Executions (*continued*):
   a thief (on day of San Giovanni), 46
   Tornabuono (Lorenzo) and others, 125, 126
   traitors from Pistoia, 25
   traitors from Prato, 9
   a young ensign, 204
Exiles (their fate after Montemurlo), 206 ff.
   (For other exiles *see* under names)

Faenza (city), 149, 175–8, 209, 231, 233, 235
   (Lords of):
     Manfredi (Galeotto), 45
     (Astorre), 195
Fashions (change of), 284
Federigo, King of Naples, 186, 188, 221, 222, 225
Ferrara (city), 248, 264
   (Dukes of). *See* Alfonso, Ercole I. Ercole II.
   (Cardinal of), 190, 210
Ferravecchi (tra,), 52, 77
Feranto, King of Naples, 4
Ferdinand I., King of Naples, 21, 83, 85, 91
Ferdinand II., King of Naples, 97, 100, 106
Ferruccio, 293
Fever, 122, 125, 127
Ficheruola, 35
Firenzuola, 178
Fires:
   at Canto Tornaquinci, 242
   in Landucci's shop, 225
   in *Palagio*, 228
   in Por San Maria, 31
   at tallow-chandler's, 177
Fivizzano, 58
Fleet (French) captured, 91
   (Neapolitan) at Pisa, 49
   at Ancona, 38
   destroyed, 57
Floods in Rome, 98, 293
Foix (Gaston de), 251
Forli, 164, 165, 174, 212
Fracassa, 96, 151, 193
San Francesco's cloak (procession), 203
San Francesco (church), 213
Francesco (apothecary), 11
Francesco da Montepulciano, 272
Francese (Napoleone), 19
Francis I., enters Milan, 278; visits Pope at Bologna, 187; is defeated by Papal and Imperial forces at Pavia and taken prisoner, 291
Franciscan monk detained, 174
Franciscans, 34
Frascato, 120
French ships sunk, 78
French troops:
   (Expedition under Charles VIII.)
   1494–1495
     quartered in Florence, 60–72
     victorious campaign in Kingdom of Naples, 82–5
     return north, 88 ff.
     defeated at Parmigiano, and leave Italy, 91
   (*See also* under Charles VIII.)
   (Expeditions under Louis XII.)
   1499–1503
     fresh relays continually pass on way to Naples, 169–208

French troops (*continued*):
   (Expeditions under Louis XII.)
   1499–1503
     are severely defeated by Spaniards, 209
     numbers die of hunger and cold, 212
   1507–1512
     take Genoa, 224
     victorious campaign against Venetians, 231–53
     finally repulsed and leave Italy, 253
   (*See also* under Louis XII.)
   (Expedition under Francis I.) between 1515 and 1527)
     defeated by the Emperor, 290
     lose Battle of Pavia and leave Italy, 291
French viceroy at Naples, 189
Friar forced to recant, 277
Frozen rain (storm), 50

Gaeta, 83
Galleys (French), 215
Gambacorti (Messer), 184
Genoa, 41, 46, 57, 184, 220, 224, 269, 290;
   assaulted and sacked by Emperor, 290
Genoese exiles, 223
Gentile (Bishop), 39
Ghinazzano (Fra Mariano), 128, 132
Ghirlandaio, 50
Giganti, 20, 145
Giovanni (Ser) di Bartolomeo, 62, 63, 75, 79, 164
Girandoles, 29, 145, 274
Giraffe, etc., 43
Godi (Cardinal), 296
Gogna, 77, 214
Gondi (Guido) house, 48
Gonfaloni, 61, 64, 73, 77, 78, 87, 118, 137, 175, 195
Gonfaloniere, election to be annual, 260.
   See Alberti Bartoli, Buondelmonte, Corbizi, Guascone, Lenzi, Popoleschi, Niccolo Soderini, Piero Soderini
Gonfaloniere's wife, 293
Gostanzo (Signor di Pesaro), 33, 35
Graziosa (la), 158
Gravezza, 217
Great Council, 67, 81, 82, 85, 88, 93, 106, 109, 140, 141, 146, 188, 199, 200, 260
Great Hall (of Dogana), 92–4, 99, 100, 103, 118, 139, 229, 238, 264
Guascone (Gonfaloniere), 162
Guelfa (Capitani di Parte), 261
Guido (Antonio), 84, 90
Gurk (Bishop of), 263, 264

Hadrian, 290, 291
Hailstorms:
   at Crema, 205
   in Florence, 46, 104, 111, 247
   at Rome, 170, 255
Harvest (abundant), 147, 150
Heat (great), 291
Herald (from Naples), 21, 28
Hermit, preaches 23
   tortured, 31
Hidden money, 75, 79

A FLORENTINE DIARY

Homicides (decrees against), 14, 77
Hospitals:
  for Incurables, 290
  La Scala, 24, 25
  Porcellana, 25
  Santa Maria Nuova, 22, 46, 120, 122, 123, 271
  San Paolo, 24
Hot wind (storm), 42
House (falls down), 226
Houses (new), 239
Hunger in city, 117
Hunt in Piazza, 274

Illuminations and bonfires, etc., 161, 167, 188, 235, 267, 268
Images of celebrities in SS. Annunziata, 271
Imola, 45, 146, 163–5, 188, 210
Impruneta (Madonna dell'), 29, 37, 57, 87, 112, 155, 159, 168, 191, 200, 232, 245, 255, 262, 268, 292, 297
Indulgences (Plenary) and jubilees, 12, 32, 116, 140, 172, 175, 218, 219, 227, 250
Inn (collapses), 175
Innocent VIII., 40, 54
Insults to image of Madonna de' Ricci, 187
  to image of Madonna at Or San Michele, 55
  to chief citizens of Florence, 197
Interdict. *See* Excommunications
Island (discovered), 230

Jewess (baptised), 107
Jews, allowed to lend on interest, 141
  (exiled) allowed to return, 276
Joust in Piazza di Santa Croce, 273, 276
Jubilee. *See* Indulgences
Juggler (Spanish), 238
Julius II., 209, 220–4, 244, 245, 253, 255, 266

Kings:
  of France. *See* Charles VIII., Francis I., Louis XI., Louis XII.
  of Naples. *See* Federigo, Feranto, Ferdinand I., Ferdinand II.

Landucci (Antonio, son of Luca), 209, 217, 225
  (Benedetto, son of Luca), 56, 77, 206, 262
  (Gostanzo, brother of Luca), 26, 33, 42
  (Luca, the author), 1, 3, 4, 5, 7, 8, 118, 126, 217, 225, 236, 265. *See also* Dicomano
Laying waste, 192, 219, 228
League. *See* Treaty
Leccio, 31
Lenzi (Gonfaloniere), 99
Leo X. elected, great excitement of Florentines, 268; crowned, 269; entry into Florence, 279; in the city, 279–85; at Bologna, meets French king, 286; returns to Florence, and leaves, 287; makes 31 cardinals, 288, 289; dies, 290
Levies, 23, 80, 85, 109, 125, 128, 149, 203, 204, 218, 219, 249, 255
Librafatta, 85, 86, 149, 169, 172
Lille (Seigneur de), 95, 96
Lion (Marzocco), 41, 167

Lions, 44, 274, 276, 298
Loans, 80, 109, 145
Loggia de' Signori, 85, 97, 135–6, 220, 240, 246
Lorenzo (son of Leonardo), 3
Louis XI., 38
Louis XII., takes citadel of Milan, 161; takes the "Lords" and others into his pay, 198; takes Genoa and enters Milan, 224; meets King of Naples at Savona, 225; victorious campaign against the Venetians, 226–33; excommunicated, 245; has reverses and leaves Italy, 253; dies, 277
Lucca, 89, 90, 169–72, 203, 213, 215, 230
Lutozzi (Piero di), 29

Madeira sugar, 9
Malatesta, 293
  (Robert, il Magnifico), 36
Male del tiro, 240
Manfredi (Ottaviano), 146, 156
Manna falls, 291
Mantua (Marchese di), 91, 100, 125, 203, 207, 210
  (Cardinal of), 36
Marradi, 50, 148, 149, 151
Maximilian (Emperor) makes proclamation, 93
  sends ambassador, 111
  goes to Genoa and Pisa, 112
  is routed at Livorno, 113
  his ship sunk, 113
  leaves Italy, 114
Medici (de'):
  Alfonsina (wife of Piero), 95, 278
  Andrea (il Grasso), 156
  Averado, 95
  Alessandro (Duke), 293, 295, 296
  Clarice (Lorenzo il Magnifico's wife), 46
  Cosimo (the Elder), 2
  (Duke), 296, 297, 298, 299
  Giovanni (son of Lorenzo Magnifico), Cardinal, 47, 52, 62, 265, 266. *See also* Leo X.
  Giuliano (son of Piero), assassinated, 15, 16; funeral, 17
  Giuliano (son of Lorenzo Magnifico), at Bibbiena, 154; returns to Florence, and enters *Palagio*, 258, 261; goes to Rome, 269; dies, 287
  Giulio (son of Giuliano son of Piero), Archbishop, 269, 271, 278
  Lorenzo (il Magnifico), ambassador to Pope, 10; wounded in Pazzi Conspiracy, 15, 16; goes to Naples, 28, 29; marries his daughter to Salviati, 36; ambassador to Ferrara, 36; Pietrasanta surrenders to him, 41; wins *palio* at Siena, 42; meets Bentivoglio, 45; dies, 53, funeral, 54
  Lorenzo (son of Piero), temporarily exiled, 56; ambassador, 64, 84, 88; returns to Florence and is made Capitano Generale, 178; crowned Duke of Urbino, 288; he and his wife die, 290
  Lucrezia (Lorenzo Magnifico's mother), 34
  Piero (son of Cosimo the Elder), 8

INDEX 305

Medici (de') (*continued*):
Piero (son of Lorenzo Magnifico), ambassador to Pope, 55; meets Duke of Calabria, 57; goes to meet King of France, 58; revolts against Signoria, 61; flees, 62; at Bologna, 65; banished, 75; price on his head, 95, 96; his property sold, 91, 93; threatens Florence, but retires, 118; plots, 127; at Bibbiena with the Venetians, 149, 151; at Arezzo, 195; drowned, 211
Medici (Duchess de'),Filiberta of Savoy, 277 278; Margherita of Austria, 294, 295
Medici (family), arms removed from buildings, 120; proclamation against their adherents, 242; to be reinstated, 258; proclamation as to property, 263; leave Florence, 292
Mercato Nuovo, 27, 127, 145
Vecchio, 1, 3, 39, 69, 145, 146, 201, 202, 203, 214, 218, 238, 268
Michelangelo's "David," 213, 214
Michele (Don), 210, 211, 218, 219
Milan, 161 ff., 224, 252
(For Duke of Milan, *see* Sforza)
Militia, 218, 227, 228, 259, 278, 292
Minerbetti (Piero), 10
(Tommaso), 55
Miracles: miraculous crucifix, 11; miraculous image of Virgin at Bibbona, 35; fiery flames, 36; miracle-working Frate, 37; miraculous image of Virgin at Prato, 40; miraculous occurrences, 105; miracle at Marradi, 149; miraculous appearances, 216; image of Virgin at San Michele Berteldi, 222; miraculous fires, 227; visions, 273
Mirandola, 244
Mock fight in Piazza, 270
Monstrosities, 12, 47, 173, 249, 272
Monte (the), 5
Monte a Sansovino, 24, 25, 31, 213, 214
Monte della Pietà, 44, 110
Montedomenici, 32, 38
Montemurlo (Battle of), 295
Montepulciano, 99, 168, 170, 247
Montesecco (Count of), 18
Montetopoli, 24, 88, 89, 150, 153
Moors, 236
Mugello, 28, 45, 50, 97, 149, 169, 178, 190, 199, 256
Murate (Convent of), 163, 239, 250
Murder: of a Sienese exile, 145; of a Sienese physician, 176; of a Frenchman, 184; of a girl, 112

Nancy (Battle of), 13
Naples, 28, 29, 58, 83, 86, 106, 204. *See* King of Naples
Nerli (Benedetto de'), 178
(Jacopo de'), 62
(Tanai de'), 47, 60
Neroni (Archbishop of Florence), 11
Nicholas V., 8
Nori (Francesco), 14, 15
Notaries (laws concerning), 104
Novara, 166

Orsini family, 34, 42, 203, 208
(Archbishop of Florence), 228

Orto San Michele, 37, 62, 91, 93, 279, 281
Osservanza (di S. Miniato), 48, 146, 174, 202, 234
Ostia, 35, 116, 209
Otranto, 33, 139
Outrages in churches, 12, 152, 153

Padua, 236
Palagio Vecchio, 16, 18, 41, 47, 60, 61, 63, 66, 70, 77, 85, 97, 98, 99, 106, 142, 158, 162, 171, 201, 203, 228, 248, 258, 261, 267, 298, 299
Palagio del Podestà (Bargello), 5, 17, 18, 31, 62, 175, 187, 216, 223, 231, 282, 298
Palaia, 88, 94
Palazzo (Casa) de' Medici, 61, 65, 97, 99, 285
Palazzo Riccardi, 2
Palio: on Arno, 225; of San Giovanni, 20, 46, 186, 220; of San Barnabà, 122; of San Lo, 205; at Santa Liberata, 33, 42; at Siena, 42; at Sant' Anna, 42; at San Vittorio, 42
Palmieri (Matteo), 12
Pandolfini (Pierfilippo), 31, 55
Paolo (Messer), 2
Papal: ban, 131; brief, 140; envoy, 42, 43, 44; troops, 36, 179, 187, 253, 254, 292, 293
Parlamento, 8, 16, 61, 73, 93
Parmigiano (Battle of), 91
Paul II., 8, 10
Paul III., 294
Pavia (Battle of), 291
Pavia (Cardinal of), 228, 243, 245
Pazzi:
family: effects sold by auction, 18, 20; freed, but exiled, 34
Andrea, 15, 16, 18, 19
Conspiracy, 15 ff.
Cosimo (Bishop of Arezzo), 194, 195, 197; (Archbishop of Florence) 228, 229, 230, 268
Franceschino, 15
Guglielmo (Commissary), 15, 19, 195
Jacopo, 15, 16, 18, 19, 20
Niccolò, 15
Renato, 15, 19
Peace. *See* Treaty
Peaceful change of Government, 291
Perugia, 171, 220
Pesaro (town), 173
(Signor Gostanzo di), 33, 35, 38
Petrucci (Pandolfo), 148, 171, 185, 202, 203, 204, 252
Piagnoni, 136, 138
Piancandoli, 28, 32, 43, 45
Piazza del Grano, 5, 116, 118
Piazza de' Signori: full of armed men, 18; tumult in (against Piero de' Medici), 61, 62, 63; tumults, 67, 68; burning of "vanities," 130, 131; fire-test, 136, 137; Savonarola's execution, 143
Pietrasanta, 40, 41, 58, 100, 168, 169, 272, 290, 292
Piombino, 179, 189, 207, 221
Pisans: receive Charles VIII., 60; with his help, throw off the Florentine yoke, 65; war between them and Florence, 66, 69, 74-8, 81-6, 92-9, 127, 128, 141-6, 154-61, 169-81, 190-2, 215, 220-4, 229-34; agreement fails, 225; hard pressed, 232;

yield and sign peace, 235; Milan favourable to them, 107 ff.; Venetians send aid, 108 ff.
Pistoia, 157, 172–3, 176, 186–91, 197–9, 257, 295
Pitigliano (Count of), 27, 41, 91, 155
Pitti (Luca), 8
Pius III., 208, 209
Plague, 23–7, 29, 32–40, 96–103, 106, 109, 114, 122–5, 127, 139, 141, 166, 170, 177
Podestà, 74, 228, 235
Poggibonizi, 31, 88
Poggio Imperiale, 21, 27, 31
Poggio a Caino, 31, 49, 208
Pollaiuolo (Antonio and Piero), 3
(Simone), 217
Ponte alla Carraia, 70
Rubiconte (= alle Grazie), 19, 51, 241, 270
Santa Trinità, 121, 281
Vecchio, 246
Ponte ad Era (Pontedera), 93, 178
Ponte di Sacco (Pontesacco), 92, 181
Ponte a Sieve (Pontassieve), 72, 73, 151, 185, 197, 220
Popes. *See* Alexander VI., Calixtus III., Clement VII., Eugenius IV., Hadrian, Innocent VIII., Julius II., Nicholas V., Paul II., Paul III. Pius III., Sixtus IV.
Popoleschi (Gonfaloniere), 144
Porte:
Porta alla Croce, 16, 19, 23, 64
Porta di Faenza, 32, 49, 180, 255
Porta San Frediano, 64, 68, 70, 120, 225
Porta San Gallo, 49, 54, 137, 255, 295
Porta San Giorgio, 196
Porta alla Giustizia, 11, 14, 19, 105, 196
Porta San Miniato, 14
Porta San Niccolò, 23
Porta San Pietro Gattolino (Romana), 117, 118, 207, 247, 280
Porta a Pinti, 14, 40, 54, 167, 196, 246
Porta la Porticciuola (al Prato), 14, 151, 196
Porta al Prato, 54, 280
Poveri Vergognosi, 74, 75, 101
Pratica, 125
Prato (the), 5
Prato: taken by Spaniards, 257; sacked, 257–60
Price of corn, and other provisions, 39, 40, 41, 108, 110, 112–18, 120–4, 128, 141, 146, 149, 150, 157, 171, 183, 187, 189, 192, 199, 203–5, 215, 216, 218, 219, 220, 279, 287, 292, 293, 298
Prinzivalle (della Stufa), 242
Prisoners: escape, 17, 33, 235; political ones released at wish of Charles VIII., 67; list of those taken at Montemurlo, 296, 297
Procession, made by King of Naples, 186; with miraculous tabernacle, from Naples to Rome, 168 (and *see* San Giovanni, Savonarola, Impruneta, and San Francesco)
Pucci (Lorenzo), 253, 269
(sons of Bartolomeo), 208

Queen of France (Anne of Brittany), 164, 273

Radda, 22, 23
Ramazzotto (da Borsoli), 97, 254
Ravenna, 232, 235; sacked, 250
Refugees, 23, 38, 178, 182, 183, 254, 255, 256, 262
Relics, 43, 294
Remission of debts, 79
Rhodes, 30, 34
(Knights of), 34, 231
Riario (Girolamo) first husband of Caterina Sforza, 188
(Piero), Archbishop, 11
(Rafaello), Cardinal, 15, 16, 17, 18, 223
Ridolfi (Antonio), 29
(Cardinal), 296
(Giovanbattista), 57, 260
(Signor Roberto), 27, 30, 34, 35, 36
Rimini, 173, 235, 267
Ringhiera, 17, 44, 142
Rinuccio (Signor), 109, 125, 148, 151, 159
Roberto (Signor). *See* Ridolfi
Rome, 34, 42, 75; Charles VIII. enters, 79, 165, 185, 186, 206, 211; sack of, 291
Rossellino (il), 3
Rouen (Cardinal of), 185, 210, 221
Rovezzano, 23
Rucellai (Bernardo), 84, 88, 187
(Pandolo), 8, 60
Ruota, 216

Salviati (Cardinal), 296
Salviati (Jacopo), 15, 17
Sant' Agostino, 49
Sant' Angelo (Cardinal), 206
Santissima Annunziata (de' Servi), 13, 14, 20, 32, 123, 215, 219, 221, 224, 228, 286, 295
Santa Croce, 5, 32, 54, 74, 123, 134, 175, 219, 221, 224, 228, 286, 295
Santa Croce (Cardinal), 226, 230
Sant' Eusebio (Cardinal), 245
San Felice in Piazza, miracle-play, 65, 69, 87, 281
San Giorgio, Cardinal Riario di, 16, 207, 223, 287
San Giovanni (Baptistery): festa, 20; *palii* and tapers cleared out, 41; festa, thief hung, and great storm, 46; festa little kept, 108; no *palio*, 196; great storm, torn awnings, 205; thunderbolt, 207; storm, awnings torn, 220; orders of the *festaiuoli*, 240; bronze figures above door, 244, 245; festa kept, with grand joust and procession, 270, 273; iron bands put round, 278
San Jacopo in Campo Corbolini, 32
San Lorenzo: begun to be built, 2; funeral of Giulio de' Medici, 17; funeral of Lorenzo de' Medici, 54; Charles VIII. at mass, 66; bells, 141; Pope Leo X. at mass, 285
San Malo, Cardinal di, 82, 83, 224
San Marco, 54, 87, 100, 108, 124, 129, 130, 134, 137, 138, 146. (*See* Savonarola)
Santa Maria del Fiore (Cathedral): ball and cross put up, 9; bell rehung, 11; thief, 12; plenary indulgence, 14; Pazzi Conspiracy, 15; indulgence, 32, 34; relics, 43; stone falls, 49; struck by lightning, 52; King of France received, 66; King of France swears to observe the

treaty, 71; Savonarola preaches, 74–123, 129–31; alms for Poveri Vergognosi, 74, 87; stands put for singing-boys, 102; insults and disturbance, 117–19; stands removed, 119; calumniating Friar made to recant, 124, 125; crucifix on High Altar replaced by tabernacle, 129; crucifix replaced, 141; Fra Mariano Ughi preaches on Fire-test, 134; indulgences, 140, 218; jubilees, 175, 227; scandal of old horse, 153; cornice finished, 221, 227; archbishop's mass and indulgence, 230; struck by lightning, 248; magnificent decorations for entry of Leo X., 286; pavement finished, 291

Santa Maria delle Grazie, 51
Santa Maria Maggiore, 124
Santa Maria Novella, 24, 32, 50, 74, 122, 175, 280, 298
Santa Maria de' Ricci, 229, 247
San Miniato, 164
San Pancrazio, 139
San Piero Scheraggio, 135, 143
San Severino (Cardinal), 201
Santo Spirito, 2, 32, 34, 48, 74, 111, 122, 175, 252
Santa Trinità, 281
Savonarola (Fra Girolamo): preaches in Santa Maria del Fiore, orders collection of alms and procession, 74, 75; advises new form of government, 76, 96; goes to meet Charles VIII., 88; held in immense repute, 89; commanded not to preach, 98; people turn against him and attack San Marco, 100; his boys confiscate "vanities," 101, and burn them in Piazza, 131; processions of children at Carnival, and on Palm Sunday, 101, 105, 121; publishes an epistle, 120; Pope summons him, 121, and excommunicates him, 122; at Epiphany the Signoria go to kiss his hand, 129; preaches and makes processions in San Marco, 130, 138; councils discuss how to act, and request him not to preach, 132, 133; Fra Domenico challenges trial by fire, 133, 134; trial by fire prepared, but evaded, 136, 137; street disturbances, and mob at San Marco, Savonarola and two companions give themselves up, 137, 138; taken to Bargello and tortured, 138, 142; papal brief, papal envoy, and general of Dominicans arrive, 140, 142; three friars condemned and executed, 142, 143
Scala (tax), 33
Scarcity of food, 116–18, 292
Scarfa (Martino della), 265
Scarperia, 256, 299
Sentences on exiles remitted, 65
Serezzana, 46, 49, 58, 69, 90, 168, 169
Sesti, 20, 30, 33
Settanta, 73
Sforza:
    Ascanio (Cardinal), 158, 160, 165, 168
    Caterina (Lady of Imola), 63, 64, 65, 188
    Galeazzo (Duke of Milan), 13
    Giangaleazzo (Duke of Milan), 45, 47
    Ludovico il Moro (Duke of Milan), 85, 107, 133, 157, 160, 165, 167
Ships of corn, 39, 78, 110, 113, 118

Siege of Florence, 292
Sienese: at war with Florentines, on and off, 21–109; invade Florentine territory, 21; make peace, 37, 109, 148; tumults in the city, 36–7, 92, 148, 185; plot in city, 202; implore aid against Valentino, 202
Signoria: very severe, 39; forbids Piero de' Medici to enter Palagio with armed men, 61; forbids pillaging, 63; refuses Charles VIII. to grant Piero's return, 68; not to imprison without consent of Great Council, 85; elected by lot for the first time, 90; decree that no monks may preach without permission, 119; futility during the terror of Valentino, 184; make terms with Spaniards, 257
Silvestro (Fra), 138, 143
Sixtus IV., 10, 40
Snowstorms, 55, 56, 174, 243, 249, 277, 278
Soderini (Francesco Bishop): made Cardinal, 204, 205, 223
    (Niccolo, Gonfaloniere), 4
    (Pagolantonio), 23, 93, 140
    (Piero, Gonfaloneire): ambassador to King of France, 60; ambassador to Valentino, 178, 182; seeks help from French at Milan, 194; made Gonfaloniere for life, 200; dismissed from office, 257; banished, 265
Soiana, 115
Spalliere, 44
Spaniards, 52, 236, 237, 254, 261, 262, 272, 291, 293
Spanish vendors of booty, 258, 259, 260
Special holiday decreed, 271
Spiritegli, 20, 65
Stinche, 17, 19, 23, 25, 33, 39, 79, 106, 125, 140, 176, 231, 235
Strozzi (family):
    Filippo (the elder), 51
    Filippo (son of Filippo the elder), 242, 297
    Alfonso (son of Filippo the elder), 229
    Lorenzo (son of Filippo the elder), 214
Strozzi (Palace), 48, 49, 50, 51, 52, 92, 96, 141, 171, 173, 174, 214
Stufa (Luigi), 270
    (Baths), 223
Suicides, 26, 116, 193, 198, 221
Sultan, 28, 32, 157

Taxes: on wine, lowered, 4; Ventina, Catasto, 9; on wine, raised, 14; on the priests, 20, 97; Sesti and Decime, 20, 30, 33, 194; Agravo and Sgravo, 30; Scala, 33; Balzello or forced loan, 31, 80, 115, 168, 254; on Piero de' Medici's effects, 97; temporarily lowered, 61; on property, 82
Tempio (Oratory of), 22
Thunderbolts, 47, 52, 54, 127, 169, 190, 199, 207, 220, 222, 226, 239, 246, 247, 248, 254, 258, 271, 299
Tigers, 298
Tiratoi, 144, 239
Tornabuoni (Alessandro), 40
    (Giovanni), 8, 21, 34, 63, 263
    (Lorenzo), 125, 126
    (Luigi), 126
    (Piero), 41, 126
Tortures (in public), 176

Treaties:
  peace throughout Italy, 9
  peace with Naples, 29
  league with Sienese, 37, 109, 148
  peace between Venice and the Holy League,
  between Spain, the Pope, Venice, Milan, and the Emperor, 85
  treaty proposed by Venice, but refused by both Florence and Pisa, 155, 156
  league between France, Florence, Venice, Siena, and the Pope, 163
  league between the Pope, Venice and the Emperor, against France, 165
  league between the Pope, Venice, Ferrara, and Hungary, against France and Florence, 166
  agreement with Valentino, 180
  league between France, Spain, the Pope, and the Emperor, 203
  treaty between Florence and Lucca, 230
  league between France, Spain, the Pope, the Emperor and the Florentines, 230
  peace with Pisa (final), 233, 234, 235
  treaty with King of France, 252
  league with Naples and Spain, 257, 258
  agreement between Pope and Francis I. at Bologna, 286
Triumphal entry of Leo X. into Florence, magnificent preparations, 280–5
Trivulzio, 160, 162
Tunis taken by Emperor, 295
Twelve men appointed to full powers, the "Dodici," 32

Ughi (Fra Mariano), 134
Urbino (city), 195
  (Count Federigo of Montefeltro, Capitano Generale), 10, 11, 34, 36

Urbino (city) (*continued*):
  (Count of, son of above; Capitano Generale), 100, 184
  (Duchy of), 287
  (Duke of), Lorenzo de' Medici, son of Piero, 288

Valentino (Cesare Borgia): at Imola, 163, 164; at Faenza and Forlì, 173–8; in Tuscany, 178–84; demands subsidies, 184; cruelties of his troops, 179–84; at Rome, 189, 194; at Città di Castello, 195, 201; ill at Rome, 208; prisoner at Ostia, 209
Valori (Francesco), 55, 83, 93, 137
Venetians: hire soldiers for Florentines, 23; declare war upon Ferrara, 33; war between Venice and the League, 38–40; they help Pisa, 104, 128; refuse to make terms, 147; at war with Florence, 148–55; propose unacceptable agreement, 155–156; attacked by Turks, peace signed, 163; fleet defeated by Turks, 173, 191; at war with Pope, 209–49; and also with France, Spain and Ferrara, 233–49
Ventina (tax), 9, 116
Verrocchio (Andrea del), 37, 38
Vespucci (Messer Piero), 19, 25, 30
Vico, 94, 147, 149, 191, 193, 205
Vitelli (Paolo, Capitano Generale), 94, 144, 162
Vitellozzi or Vitelli (Messer Niccolò), 22, 35 (Vitellozzo, son of Niccolò), 183, 194, 198, 201
Vivioli (Ser Lorenzo), 130
Volterra, 10, 11, 18, 22, 164, 293

Wars. *See* Naples, Pisa, Siena, Kings of France and Emperors.

Zanobi (San), 186, 292
  (Ser), 79